"DEAR BART"

Recent Titles in
Contributions in Military History
SERIES EDITOR: THOMAS E. GRIESS

The Art of Leadership in War: The Royal Navy From the Age of Nelson
to the End of World War II
John Horsfield

A Wilderness of Miseries: War and Warriors in Early America
John E. Ferling

Iron Arm: The Mechanization of Mussolini's Army, 1920-1940
John Joseph Timothy Sweet

American Sea Power in the Old World: The United States
Navy in European and Near Eastern Waters, 1865-1917
William N. Still, Jr.

A Hollow Threat: Strategic Air Power and Containment Before Korea
Harry R. Borowski

The Quest for Victory: The History of the Principles of War
John I. Alger

Men Wanted for the U.S. Army: America's Experience with
an All-Volunteer Army Between the World Wars
Robert K. Griffith, Jr.

Bullets and Bureaucrats: The Machine Gun and the United States
Army, 1861-1916
David A. Armstrong

General John M. Palmer, Citizen Soldiers, and the Army
of a Democracy
I. B. Holley, Jr.

History of the Art of War: Within the Framework of Political
History, The Middle Ages
Hans Delbrück, translated by *Walter J. Renfroe, Jr.*

WASHINGTON VIEWS OF WORLD WAR II

Glen C. H. Perry

Foreword by EDMOND P. BARTNETT

CONTRIBUTIONS IN MILITARY HISTORY, NUMBER 31

Greenwood Press

WESTPORT, CONNECTICUT • LONDON, ENGLAND

Library of Congress Cataloging in Publication Data

Perry, Glen C. H.
    "Dear Bart" : Washington views of World War II.

    (Contributions in military history, ISSN 0084-9251 ;
no. 31)
    Bibliography: p.
    Includes index.
    1.   World War, 1939-1945—United States—Sources.
2.   United States—History—1933-1945—Sources.
3.   Perry, Glen C. H.   I.   Title.   II.   Series.
D769.P47   940.53'73   81-13418
ISBN 0-313-23265-2 (lib. bdg.)   AACR2

Library of Congress Catalog Card Number: 81-13418
ISBN: 0-313-23265-2
ISSN: 0084-9251

First published in 1982

Greenwood Press
A division of Congressional Information Service, Inc.
88 Post Road West
Westport, Connecticut 06881

Printed in the United States of America

10 9 8 7 6 5 4 3 2 1

Contents

1943

1944

1945

Dedication

This book is dedicated to four men who were, with my wife Sylvia, our son Christopher, and my father and mother, the most important people in my life over the period it covers—roughly from early 1941 to mid-1945.

Most especially to Phelps H. Adams, Bureau Chief in Washington for the New York *Sun*, one of the most respected and best-liked members of the press corps there for two decades, and a boss who never made me feel other than that we were equal partners in a team effort, as well as close friends. He wrote many of the memoranda in this book, including some of the best and most important, and today neither of us can tell for sure which of us wrote some of them.

To the late Keats Speed, one of the great newspapermen of his time, a Kentucky gentleman unfailingly courteous and understanding as Executive Editor of the *Sun*.

To Edmond P. Bartnett, the "Bart" on the cover, to whom I reported for my entire seventeen years on the *Sun*, a man of quiet competence and of a gentleness and consideration almost unheard of in a city editor. He is kind of old now, a little weak in the legs, but as bright in spirit and as sharp in mind as when I first went to work for him in the summer of 1927. We remain close friends to this day, 16 August 1981, which happens to be his ninetieth birthday.

To the late Cornelius H. Bull, close friend and associate, but for whom the Arlington County Commandos would never have existed to become The Surviving Veterans of the Battle of Virginia, and a fighter who was happiest when the odds against his side were long.

Foreword

In the life of an editor the most exciting news to cross his desk is often the news he cannot print.

The crowded columns of the daily newspaper carry the records of the moment—the triumphs and tragedies, the crimes and the accomplishments of nations and men. But for every story that meets the reader's eyes there are countless others that editors are anxious to record, but cannot because they are shackled by the hated prohibitions "off the record" and "for your information only."

Never is an editor's desire to give all the news more hampered than in war time, but it is a time when frustration is canceled out by the clear awareness that the fate of a fleet or an army, or even a nation, may be bound up in the duty of those in authority to keep information secret which, in the possession of an enemy, could be catastrophic. And so in time of war comes open censorship, and a security curtain descends.

But, while censorship bans the printing of information vital to the national security, it does not deter trained and inquisitive reporters from ferreting out the facts, and turning them over to their editors. Leaving aside the possibility that at some future time they can perhaps be printed, such information is in fact of great immediate value.

It is the clear duty of an editor to print the news in perspective and in balance. And the more background information an editor has, the better able he or she is to avoid overplaying or underplaying a story. In a war, especially, it becomes an overriding mission for reporters to give their editors a background against which to interpret and evaluate the news as it develops. If a reporter is to do this effectively, it follows that he or she must develop sources of authoritative information, usually secret. You do not arrive at such a position simply by appearing on the scene and asking questions. You have to earn the trust of your source as to your ability to absorb the information, understand not only what it is but why it is and how it is, the background against which to analyze it intelligently, and, finally, the ability to keep secret what must be kept secret.

In the early days of World War II rumors flooded in to all the media of public information, country-wide: rumors of staggering defeats, rumors of battleships lost, rumors of impending enemy air raids. From the windows of my office in the *Sun* Building at 280 Broadway, I can still see the crowds flocking into doorways, rushing into subways, because of a false report that German bombers were on their way to hit New York. Rumors are the poison cells in the arteries of public information, and in themselves they present a powerful argument for giving the media the information with which to combat them, either by refusing to give them circulation or by printing the facts. The same thing is true of leaks.

As an example of the importance of evaluation, assume you are an editor, and there comes to your desk an Associated Press flash about a naval action in the Pacific in which Jap ships are sunk. A victory, sure, but how significant, how important? Should it be on page one? If so, how large a headline? Is this an accidental encounter, reaction to an enemy thrust, or is it the start of something big? A well-briefed editor can often find he has the background to make a pretty good estimate of the situation. He also has his reporter, with his reliable sources that trust him, to make a spot check and report back. Thanks to this established routine, the public is not unduly elated or, alternatively, not elated enough by the way the story is handled.

Thus it happened that there came into being what became known as the "backgrounder." You will find in this book an account of how one such background source was developed by the chief and assistant chief of the *Sun*'s Washington Bureau. The story involves a small group of top correspondents who became known as the "Arlington County Commandos" and who spent a number of evenings with "The Thin Man," as they called Fleet Admiral Ernest J. King USN, in which they were exhaustively briefed on what was happening in the war. This and similar background sessions were of inestimable value to me throughout the war.

The *Sun* men involved were Phelps Adams, Bureau Chief, and Glen Perry, his number two man. Never, in my opinion, did a major newspaper have more competent and dedicated reporters than Adams and Perry. Both came to the *Sun* fresh from college, and trained under me with the usual routine assignments in New York City.

Their worth quickly became apparent and in due time first Adams and then Perry were assigned to the important tasks that only Washington provides. Even now I glow with pride in their accomplishments, for Adams ended up as a vice president of U.S. Steel in charge of public relations, and Perry as director of public relations for that other corporate giant, E. I. du Pont de Nemours & Company.

Taking into consideration that no notes could be taken at such sessions, it will be evident that both men possessed sponge-like memories, and the nature of the information confided to them and their fellow correspondents was evidence that they were worthy of complete trust.

It is also worth noting that in the whole history of the war, there was never a single leak of information given by Admiral King, General Marshall and the other public figures whose words are reported here.

EDMOND P. BARTNETT

Preface

Beginning early in 1941, when the United States was neutral in the conflict that was to become World War II, the Washington Bureau of the now defunct *New York Sun* began sending confidential memoranda to its editors in New York about the conflict as seen by civilian and military and naval leaders in the capital, with special emphasis on its relationship to this country. We continued to write them, on no set schedule but as useful information came to hand, to the end of the war in 1945. Most of them went directly to City Editor Edmond P. Bartnett, the "Dear Bart" in the following pages.

If a book can be said to have stars, the stars of this one are two of the greatest officers this country ever had available in time of great national peril—Fleet Admiral Ernest J. King, and General of the Army George C. Marshall. They were supported by a cast that included Admiral Thomas Hart, Admiral William Leahy, Winston Churchill, Wendell Willkie, Field Marshall Sir Archibald Wavell, General Henry Arnold, Secretary of War Henry Stimson, Secretary of the Navy Frank Knox, Secretary of the Navy (and later of Defense) James Forrestal, Harry Truman, Harry Hopkins, Donald Nelson, Major General Patrick Hurley, and many others.

Sources of information were varied: phone conversations, one-on-one interviews, and small group sessions with correspondents sitting around a room listening to and questioning the authority invited to join us. There were fairly frequent off-the-record press conferences, postluncheon and postprandial talks followed by question periods and general discussion.

Phelps Adams and I wrote more than a hundred of these memoranda, and this volume presents what seems to me to be the pick of the litter. They appear as originally written, with no attempt to make us look more omniscient than we actually were by revising on the basis of 20-20 hindsight. There were—and still are—a certain number of muffed pop flies and overlooked ground balls in interpreting what we were told, and sometimes it was our informants who were wrong.

Finally, it should be held in mind that Washington's view of the war was for the most part a top level view. These memoranda contain references to MacArthur, Montgomery, Alexander, Eisenhower—top figures. The men who led the actual fighting—the Bradleys, the Jake Devers, the Clarks, the Ridgways and many others—may have figured importantly in service conversations, but Washington really wasn't close to them.

You could make a good case for the argument that these men more than any others were the architects of victory. I do not dispute it. All I am saying is that they seldom appeared on the capital's viewing screen long enough and importantly enough to gain more than temporary visibility. General George Patton was mentioned infrequently in these memoranda, and every schoolboy knows what *he* contributed to victory. It is just that George Patton's war and Washington's war were not really the same.

It may surprise followers of contemporary personal journalism to learn that the words "confidential" and "off the record," as used in the United States during World War II, meant precisely what they said. There was a Censorship Code and a government group, headed by the late Byron Price, to enforce it. There was no real problem. During our entire period of participation in hostilities there was only the merest handful of violations, almost all of them inadvertent, and all but one trivial.

It was the protection afforded by the code to the leaders of the war effort, and its acceptance by the press, that allowed them to speak candidly to correspondents about the progress of the war. The great danger of censorship is loss of confidence in the government's handling of the news. Off-the-record sessions, those reported here and others, coupled to the right of appeal to the Censorship Board, virtually eliminated press complaints of unfair treatment. I believe that, due to an important degree to this method of handling news, no previous war had ever been covered by an American press as well informed and hence in as good a position to interpret and evaluate the news as in World War II.

It is a fair question, I believe, to ask what good was this material to the press when they could not print it? That question was faced in the foreword by Bart himself, who was as well placed as anyone could be to know the answer. This vast store of top-level background information enabled reporters to interpret and analyze the news we received—and disseminated—far more intelligently. It gave us an insider's view of history *as it was being made* afforded to only a fortunate few.

GLEN PERRY

Acknowledgments

My thanks and gratitude go to many who made this book a reality. To Phelps Adams, of course, for the numerous memoranda he contributed, and for his unceasing encouragement.

To Bart, for his helpful suggestions and his never-failing encouragement and interest in the progress of the work.

To Robert Wohlforth, fellow member of the Class of 1926 at Princeton, and presently treasurer of the publishing house of Farrar, Straus and Giroux. Phelps and I had fooled around with the idea of making a book out of the memoranda, and some years ago sent some selected ones to Houghton Mifflin. Nothing came of it and the memos gathered dust in the Perry attic, until one day in 1978 at a Class luncheon I sat next to Bob, and the subject came up as we chatted. He was interested, asked to see some of the memoranda and, having read them all, urged me to go ahead. He is the first of three "but fors" in this list. *But for* his interest it is quite likely the dust would have continued to gather.

To Commander Thomas B. Buell, USN Retired, who came to Darien from West Point, where he was an exchange faculty member for three years after commanding a destroyer. His purpose was to talk about Admiral King, whose biography he was writing, and to read the King memos. We became friends, and *but for* him I should never have met Colonel Griess, to whom he introduced me by letter.

To Colonel Thomas E. Griess USA, retiring head of the History Department at West Point; but for his enthusiasm Greenwood Press might never have seen or accepted the manuscript.

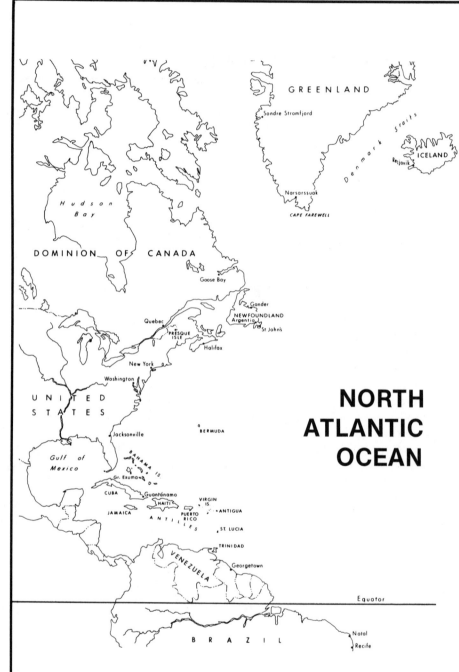

NORTH ATLANTIC OCEAN

GREENLAND

Sondre Stromfjord

Denmark Straits

ICELAND

Reijavik

Narsarssuak

CAPE FAREWELL

Hudson Bay

DOMINION OF CANADA

Goose Bay

Gander

NEWFOUNDLAND

Quebec

Argentia

St John's

PRESQUE ISLE

Halifax

New York

Washington

UNITED STATES

Jacksonville

BERMUDA

Gulf of Mexico

BAHAMA IS.

Gr. Exuma

CUBA

Guantánamo

HAITI

VIRGIN IS.

JAMAICA

PUERTO RICO

ANTIGUA

ANTILLES

ST. LUCIA

TRINIDAD

VENEZUELA

Georgetown

Equator

BRAZIL

Natal

Recife

FAEROE IS

Narvik

SWEDEN

FINLAND

NORWAY
Oslo
Stockholm
Leningrad

Scapa
Flow

North
Sea

Baltic Sea

U. S. S. R.

Londonderry
Prestwick
Moscow

ENGLAND
IRELAND
Liverpool
London
Bristol
Cherbourg
Rouen
Brest
Lorient
St. Nazaire
Bay of
Biscay
Bordeaux

Hamburg
Berlin
Bremen
GERMANY
Essen
Cologne
Mannheim

Warsaw

POLAND

Stalingrad

Paris

Vienna
AUSTRIA
HUNGARY

FRANCE

ITALY

YUGO-
SLAVIA

RUMANIA

Marseille

Med

Rome

BULGARIA

Black Sea

Yalta

CAUCASUS MTS.

ADRES

Madrid
SPAIN
Lisbon
Gibraltar

Ankara

TURKEY

Athens

SICILY

MALTA

CRETE

SYRIA

IRAQ

Algiers
Oran

Tunis

onean

Sea

PALESTINE

Casablanca
MOROCCO

Tripoli

El Alamein
Cairo

CANARY IS.

ALGERIA

LIBYA

EGYPT

SAUDI
ARABIA

RIO
DE
ORO

Red Sea

CAPE
VERDE IS.

Dakar

FRENCH   WEST   AFRICA

ANGLO - EGYPTIAN
SUDAN

Freetown

EUROPEAN THEATER
1941-45

ASCENSION
IS.

xvii

UNION OF SOVIET SOCIALIST REPUBLICS

SEA OF OKHOTSK

KAMCHATKA

SAKHALIN

KURILE IS.

OUTER MONGOLIA

MANCHURIA
(MANCHUKUO)

Vladivostok

SINKIANG

Peiping

SEA OF JAPAN

KOREA

Tokyo JAPAN

Yellow R.

YELLOW SEA

TIBET

CHINA

Shanghai

KYUSHU

Yangtze R.

Chungking

Changsha

EAST CHINA SEA

RYUKYU IS.

OKINAWA

BONIN ISLANDS

INDIA

BURMA

Canton

FORMOSA (TAIWAN)

VOLCANO ISLANDS

IWO JIMA

MARCUS

Calcutta

Mandalay

Hong Kong

MARIANA ISLANDS

Rangoon

BURMA

THAILAND

FRENCH INDOCHINA

LUZON

Manila

PHILIPPINE ISLANDS

ROTA

SAIPAN

GUAM

ENIWETOK

ANDAMAN IS.

Bangkok

CAMRANH BAY

LEYTE

ULITHI

YAP

CAROLINE ISLANDS

KRA ISTHMUS

SOUTH CHINA SEA

MINDANAO

PALAU IS.

TRUK

PONAPE

MALAYA

STRAIT OF MALACCA

Singapore BORNEO

BISMARCK ARCHIPELAGO

SUMATRA

JAVA SEA

CELEBES

VOGELKOP

Hollandia

Rabaul

SOLOMON ISLANDS

Batavia

NEW GUINEA

JAVA

TIMOR IS.

Port Moresby

GUADALCANAL

Darwin

CORAL SEA

INDIAN OCEAN

AUSTRALIA

Brisbane

Perth

Sydney

Melbourne

TASMANIA

Source: From *Master of Sea Power: A Biography of Fleet Admiral Ernest J. King* by Thomas B. Buell. © 1980 by Thomas B. Buell. By permission of Little, Brown and Company.

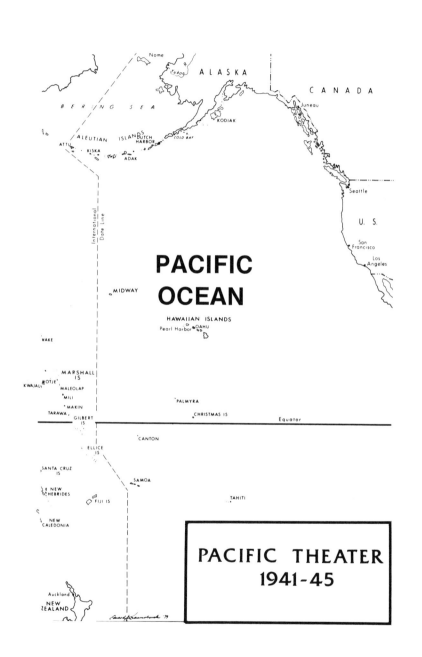

BERING SEA

ALASKA

CANADA

Nome

YUKON

KODIAK

Juneau

ALEUTIAN ISLANDS
DUTCH HARBOR
COLD BAY

ATTU

KISKA

ADAK

Seattle

U. S.

International Date Line

San Francisco

Los Angeles

PACIFIC
OCEAN

MIDWAY

HAWAIIAN ISLANDS
Pearl Harbor OAHU

WAKE

MARSHALL IS

WOTJE

KWAJALEIN

MALEOLAP

MILI

MAKIN

TARAWA

GILBERT IS

PALMYRA

CHRISTMAS IS

Equator

CANTON

ELLICE IS

SANTA CRUZ IS

SAMOA

NEW HEBRIDES

FIJI IS

TAHITI

NEW CALEDONIA

Auckland

NEW ZEALAND

PACIFIC THEATER
1941-45

1941

So far as my records show, the memorandum that opens this series of such reports, based on a dinner with Wendell Willkie (the unsuccessful Republican presidential candidate in 1940), was the first of its kind the *Sun*'s Washington Bureau sent to the New York headquarters. It was written by me nearly a year before the United States became an avowed participant in what *Time* christened World War II. But it would seem to me to be nitpicking to rule out pre-Pearl Harbor material on the ground that we were not "declared" combatants.

The fact is that we were, in 1941, actively and deeply involved in the war as the major supplier of munitions and other material to the Allies, especially Great Britain. While it was true that our far western states could hardly have been more indifferent to what was happening in Europe, they were seriously perturbed about Japan; it was also true that the Middle West wanted no part of hostilities anywhere; the eastern states watched with interest developments across the Atlantic, and were grateful that we were not in it.

The situation in Washington might be described as ambivalent. The Congress came within a very few votes of defeating the legislation that provided the United States with the manpower necessary to beef up the army and the navy to something approximating adequate defense levels. Members of the Senate and the House were in a most difficult position. The views of their constituents were coming in loud and clear: keep out of it! Anyone who had said publicly that this Congress would declare war on anyone would have been regarded as, at best, poorly informed, and at worst, fanatical to the point of psychosis.

It was different at the executive end of Pennsylvania Avenue. President Franklin D. Roosevelt had a difficult role to play. He had to speak and act in such a way that he did not alarm the country. At the same time he knew very well indeed what the stakes were in this war, and never doubted that we would be in it up to our necks before it was over.

It was clear to him that Britain would be sunk without massive American aid. Gradually the intellectual community came to agree with what he was doing, and Mr. Roosevelt gradually felt more free to act in ways that did not always match what he said publicly.

I recall having read that Prime Minister Churchill, at his first meeting with President Roosevelt, in Placentia Bay, Argentia, Newfoundland, on 9 August 1941, asked the president if there was danger of Japan entering the war soon. The reply was, "I think I can baby them along for another six months."

We had already sent a considerable number of four-piper destroyers to England for the use of the Royal Navy's fight against U-boats. We were patrolling Atlantic waters between Iceland and the North American mainland, and were actually escorting British convoys in those same waters, thus shortening considerably the distance the Royal Navy had to cover. These were, palpably, acts of war, very real even if undeclared, and there was no doubt in Washington that a victorious Germany would, sooner or later, call us to account for them.

All in all, it is to me a safe conclusion that these early memoranda reflect de facto involvement in the war long before 7 December 1941, and hence belong in this volume.

CONFIDENTIAL

Wednesday
12 February 1941

Dear Bart,

We had dinner with Willkie at the Carlton—sixteen of us who had been closely associated with him in the 1940 campaign—and he talked very freely about his experiences in England. Naturally I could make no notes, but I have a pretty clear recollection of what was said, and will report the highlights.

First, he made the statement that anyone who can penetrate the British defenses and establish a bridgehead in the British Isles will deserve it. He took Dover as an example, but when I asked him about it, he said the system of defenses described held good for the entire coastline, so far as he could see. On landing, the invading army would have to go through some yards of live fire from flamethrowers all along the shore. After that three or four rows of barbed wire—not the kind we put in fences, but wire as thick as your little finger, with barbs several inches long. Behind that, myriad machine gun nests. Behind them light field pieces and still further back the heavy artillery.

England has been divided into defense areas, functioning, or at least capable of functioning, independently, so that should the Germans through the use of paratroops, succeed in occupying a sector, the others around it would remain clear and would make it possible for the British forces to move in. Mr. Willkie said that every possible precaution and forethought had been taken to meet invasion, either by water or by air. Communication systems, such as telephone circuits, have been duplicated several times over, so that should the Germans get control of one and seek to send out false orders, it could be cut out and another circuit used.

He says it is apparently true that England has daytime control of the air. And while he was in London, for the first time they shot down a plane they couldn't even see (it was at night) through the use of a new device which I gather is the klystron described in the *Saturday Evening Post* last week.

It is his opinion that England cannot be successfully invaded. He thinks the great peril to the British is the German air-submarine threat against communications in the Atlantic.

As for personalities: Churchill he much admires. Thinks he is very intelligent and definitely the man for the moment. This is of course in line with the theory Willkie has expressed to me before, that the time produces the man. He believes, for instance, that had the country swung far to the right last summer, nothing could have stopped Taft, and had there been a Teapot Dome, Dewey would have been a shoo-in, whereas actually the conditions called for a man of Willkie's type. Similarly, he believes that while Churchill might not be right for peacetime, he is the ideal Prime Minister for the present situation. He made a most interesting observation, that Churchill is much impressed and influenced by literary people. It is interesting because precisely the same thing is true of Willkie himself. It's funny how we see ourselves in others.

The rest of the cabinet he thinks second-rate or dull. Bevin was mentioned. Willkie said Bevin was a combination of Bill Green and John L. Lewis, with something of Green's solid quality. He didn't seem to think much of him. But Churchill, he said, has got his eyes open, knows exactly what he is doing.

His experiences with royalty were amusing. There was attached to the Cowles-Thorne-Willkie party a fellow from the Foreign Office, getting them in touch with people they wanted to see. The King [George VI] wanted to see them, and a luncheon was arranged. But that morning Willkie decided he wanted to go to Manchester to see what things were like there, so he instructed the attaché to break the date. This was done, the date being set for the next day.

On that day Willkie decided he wanted to see De Valera. So he told his aide to put the King off until tea. The lad was disturbed, said they'd made dates with the King and Queen, and also Queen Wilhelmina of the Netherlands and King Haakon of Norway. Cowles, speaking for Willkie, said to tell King Haakon to meet them at the airport when they returned from Ireland and they would let him ride back to London in the car with them. We never found out if he did, or whether Willkie saw either Haakon or Wilhelmina. He did see George R.I.

He found him nervous and hard to talk to. He said he'd make a remark and it would fall, plunk. He made another, and it would drop. Finally the King asked if he would have tea or scotch and soda. "Where I come from there's no question about that," said Willkie. "I'll have scotch." The King himself mixed the highball while Willkie sat down to await the refreshment.

Then the King said they were going to allow news photographers in the palace for the first time, and did Willkie mind being photographed? Answer: no. Then he suggested to Willkie that the Queen would like to see him. So they walked up a couple of flights of stairs, and talked with her. Willkie got along better with her. Liked her, in fact. He finally told her, "You're doing better with me than you did with Joe Kennedy." "It's not because I didn't try," answered the Queen.

He told another amusing thing. When he was at Horta, a Rumanian commissioner called him up with a sad story about King Carol being incarcerated in Spain, and wanted Willkie to head an organization in America to effect his release. Willkie said he hadn't time, and closed the conversation with the following limerick:

> "Said the glamorous Madame Lupescu,
>   As she came to Rumania's rescue,
>   It's a mighty fine thing
>   To work under a king.
> Is democracy better? I esk you."

Here is something doubly confidential. Willkie told us that the President was enthusiastic about his suggestion that we send more destroyers to Britain, and said "It can be done." This was completely off the record, but I deduce that whatever Mr. Big or Secretary Knox says, we are in fact going to send more destroyers to England, and not so far in the future, either. It may be possible to say this on our own authority sometime, and we are looking for a good opportunity.

For all of his really deep and sincere feeling about national unity, Willkie doesn't like Roosevelt, didn't want to go to the White House. But he couldn't do much about it, although he did make Roosevelt shift it to last night instead of this morning. When Willkie left Washington he hadn't done a line of his Lincoln Day speech, according to Grace Grahn, his secretary.

Those at the meeting were Walker Buel, *Cleveland Plain Dealer*; Ray Henle, *Pittsburgh Post-Gazette*; Dick Wilson, *Des Moines Register*; Jim

Wright, *Buffalo News*; Marquis Childs, *St. Louis Post-Dispatch*; Harold Brayman, Timmons News Service; Bill Lawrence, U.P.; Bill Ardery and Ted Koop, A.P.; me; Leo Casey, Grace Grahn, Willkie. That't all I can remember. There may have been more.

Regards

UNITED STATES TO SEND
DESTROYERS TO GREAT BRITAIN

CONFIDENTIAL

Tuesday
18 February 1941

Dear Bart,

Willkie spoke off the record at the Press Club yesterday, and he filled in our information on the Irish phase of his trip to Europe. He said he talked for several hours with De Valera, and that the Irish leader had three points:

1) What Mr. Willkie regarded as a full and complete history of 750 years of fighting between England and Ireland.

2) A feeling of disappointment that Winston Churchill had declined to supply the Irish with arms with which to defend themselves, apparently suspicious that the arms might not be used against the Germans.

3) A desire to keep Ireland, a defenseless country, from being ruined by bombing and invasion.

Willkie answered as follows:

1) Neither he nor De Valera nor anyone else can rewrite a single page of the 750 years of fighting, and that this might be regarded as water over the dam.

2) Having listened to what De Valera had to say on Point One, he didn't blame Churchill for being suspicious, and added that he himself would not have given the arms in like position.

3) If Hitler decides that the best way to get at England is by taking over Ireland, that country's neutrality isn't worth a farthing.

4) Willkie added that Ireland is immensely popular in the United States, that there is an almost nostalgic feeling for Ireland, and that this is Ireland's strongest asset. He added that Ireland's course now is jeopardizing that asset, and he closed with the suggestion that Ireland stop fooling around and get in line.

Willkie told me he would like "like sin" to go to China, and that he thinks he could get permission, but that he has got to earn some money and that the chances are he will be practicing law within a few weeks.

As I said in yesterday's story, there is a growing feeling here that Germany won't chance an all-out attack on England. Too risky, for one thing. Modern was shows no instance of a successful attack by sea on strongly held land positions—to the best of my knowledge—except through treachery. England found out how tough it was at Gallipoli.

More than that, few people realize how close Germany came to winning the world war in 1917 through submarine attack, when she was restricted to two bases and had no air force helping. Today she has bases all along the Norwegian, Dutch and French coasts, and has a new technique.

This consists of sending small submarines out in schools, to lie inert so that engine noises cannot be picked up, while airplanes scout for victims. Communicating by radio, the planes flash information to submarines, which gather in large number in the path of a convoy, lie there until the convoy arrives, and then attack.

It is a deadly peril to Britain, the biggest threat she faces. That is why she is going to get forty more destroyers—I heard that from a Navy source over the weekend. As you know, forty-six destroyers of the 1,200 ton type are being refitted as fast transports and anti-aircraft ships, and the dope is that forty of them will be sent over. Technically it can be argued that destroyers are not being sent, since these vessels will have been converted into other classes. Thus saving Mr. Knox's face.

But make no mistake about it. England needs that type of vessel.

Regards

AMERICA, ALTHOUGH NOT AT WAR, AIDS GREAT BRITAIN

Since he is long dead, I feel free to say that the member of Congress who asked me to come to his office and gave me the information in the following memorandum was J. Parnell Thomas, Representative from New Jersey. Parnell came from Bloomfield, N.J., where I was born, and his family and mine knew one another slightly. So when I was assigned to the Washington Bureau, I called on him in the hope that in addition to becoming a friend he might also become a source of information. It worked out well for me both ways. He was a member of the House Military Affairs Committee as well as the Un-American Activities Committee, and he proved such a valuable source that

Representative Vito Marcantonio of New York once demanded on the floor of the House that I be investigated to find out where I got my information about what the Dies Committee was up to.

CONFIDENTIAL

Monday
10 March 1941

Dear Bart,

Since my last memo, I have been told some very interesting things about the appearance of Secretary of War Stimson and General Marshall at an executive session of the House Military Affairs Committee. The Congressmen present were sworn to secrecy, which is why this stuff is off the record.

Stimson didn't appear to take the committee very seriously. He said he was very busy and asked that questioning be made as brief as possible. He added that he would talk only in general terms. One Congressman spoke up and said that if that was the way the Secretary felt he didn't care to ask any questions.

One thing Stimson said that aroused interest came when he referred to "our new war." Marshall wrote him a note pointing out that he had used the words "our new war." Stimson read the note, laughed, and said, "Our peace-loving friend here (turning to General Marshall), calls attention to the fact that I said 'our new war.' " He did not withdraw the phrase, but continued with his testimony.

Marshall was much more informative. He said, first, that the airplanes we have sent to Britain, which are not our newest and best pursuit ships, have proved themselves better than anything Germany has, which indicates our new stuff is quite a bit superior.

He then told the committee that American diplomatic and military observers had been working closely with the British secret service, and there had emerged a significant thing: They know pretty well what is going on in Japan and Italy, have accurate pictures of their strength. But they are able to get practically no information at all from Germany. The secrecy there is apparently something marvelous. They don't know what Germany's plans are, except as logic indicates the form they will take, and they haven't the least idea what Germany's new military devices are, if any.

However, he said one thing that gives cause for alarm for when the all-out blitz comes. From time to time Germany has introduced new devices into the war. They have on occasion proved very successful. And then, after ten days, they have been withdrawn. As a specific case he cited a new aerial torpedo which had very good results. After a thorough test it was no longer used. The same with a system for attacking convoys.

The inference the British and American inner circles draw is that all of these things, as they prove their worth, are laid aside for the big show, all of them to be hurled at Britain at once.

He thinks the chances of an actual invasion attempt are about 50-50. From other military sources, I gather that invasion is not the greatest danger Britain faces. The risks of such an attack are so great, and the cost so heavy, that there is considerable doubt that Hitler will try it, particularly when he may be able to win in other ways. The real peril is the supply line between the United States and the British Isles. Shipping losses have been very heavy and the worst is yet to come. If England can be cut off, then she may have to give way without being invaded.

There are rumors that Roosevelt will take to the air in a couple of weeks to call for American convoys of goods going to England. If that is done, it is hardly believable that the Germans will refrain from attacking such convoys. And that would of course mean actual hostilities. Nobody here doubts that the start of such hostilities is pretty near at hand. And we are in the war in a very real sense already.

Germany of course does not want to fight us, else she would have opened hostilities long since. We have given her plenty of opportunities. Not that Germany is at loss to invent opportunities if she wants to start trouble.

Japan is a question mark. Indications here are that she is scared to death by the British and American attitudes. Our naval people hold the Japanese to be very inferior, and I gather they would like to knock them off any time—which would, of course, mean that we wouldn't need a two-ocean navy. Chances are she would not live up to her Axis commitment unless England appeared to be hopelessly beaten. Even then she'd hesitate a long while before coming to grips with the American fleet.

But this convoy thing is the road to war for us. And it wouldn't be surprising if we were in by May 1st. Undeclared war, of course. I am convinced that if Congress votes a declaration of war, it will be nothing more than an acknowledgement of something that has already happened.

Regards

CORNELIUS H. BULL

This seems an appropriate time to introduce Cornelius H. Bull, already mentioned in Mr. Bartnett's foreword, who is frequently referred to hereafter as the ''good friend'' who was my pipeline to Admiral King. He was an attorney who represented a small organization, the American Veterans Association (A.V.A.), on Capitol Hill. The A.V.A. wanted to prevent the two major veterans' organizations—the American Legion and the Veterans of

Foreign Wars—from draining the U.S. treasury with their excessive demands. These two groups contended that it should not be necessary to have a disability directly connected with military service in order to apply for a pension.

The A.V.A. took the position that mere military service, especially when of a noncombat nature, was no more than discharging one's responsibility to one's country, and did not entitle a man to a pension. On the other hand, it believed strongly that not enough was being done for veterans with service-connected disabilities. It was a David-Goliath battle.

The *Sun* also opposed opening the floodgates of the treasury, and one day I wrote a small piece for the paper making this clear. The president of A.V.A., based in New York, saw it and sent it down to Mr. Bull with the suggestion that he look up this possible ally. So he dropped into my office in the Munsey Building one day; that was the start of a beautiful friendship, and a joyous two-man war on the Legion and the V.F.W.

What kind of a man was Nelie Bull? He was the kind of man whose acceptance of a dinner invitation left the hostess relaxed in the sure knowledge that all present would have a wonderful time. He looked like a small edition of a veteran marine drill sergeant, had been an infantryman in the First World War, and was wounded and invalided home to become an attorney in Washington.

He played a delightful guitar and had a vast repertoire of songs, some good for general and others for restricted use. He was a good friend and author of short stories with Elliott White Spring, of "Springmaid" fame. He was a good friend of Stringfellow Barr, president of St. John's College, Annapolis, of Virginius Dabney of the Richmond papers, of Charles Kinsolving of *Newsweek*, and of a whole slew of naval officers. What drew us together was a mutual love of laughter and wit. It was he whose casual reference to H.M.S. *Ridiculous* spurred the creation of a whole new Royal Navy, such as H.M.S. *Impossible*, H.M.S. *Improvident*, H.M.S. *Spurious*, and so on down the line of battle. A common detestation of the New Deal was another point of contact. But I have yet to mention a most important thing about my friend: he was Admiral Ernest J. King's personal attorney, close friend, and confidant.

My friendship with Bull, and his friendship with King, turned out in 1942 to be two of the three legs of a triangle that some believe made a significant contribution to victory in the war at sea. The third leg was an effort by King's enemies, of whom he had more than most people could use, to get him fired from his post as Comminch [Commander in Chief of the United States Fleet]. We'll get to that in due course.

KING CRITICIZES BRITISH NAVY BLUNDERS

Admiral Ernest J. King, who figures largely in this book, had been dismayed at the tactics of the British Navy for some time. In the four memos which follow, he speaks disparagingly of the state of the Royal Navy, and reveals what the U.S. was doing to help it carry on. Obviously, his lack of enthusiasm neither declined nor even stood unchanged with the passage of time.

The story of the hard-luck British carrier *Illustrious*, including the mystery of its whereabouts, also unfolds herein—quite a saga.

CONFIDENTIAL

Thursday
15 May 1941

Dear Bart,

I intended to write this yesterday, but I got hung up on Capitol Hill and didn't find time.

First, about the British carrier *Illustrious. Editor and Publisher* ran a short piece about a month ago that the papers of an Eastern city were cooperating on keeping out news of a British aircraft carrier being repaired there. It added that the news services were cooperating. The United Press was not conscious of having cooperated in any such effort, and began to scout around to find out in what city its nobility had been thus demonstrated.

They figured it must be Philadelphia and queried their man there. He said, "Sure, the *Illustrious* is here." He had been practicing censorship at the source. I put this up to Captain Leighton Wood, U.S.N., at lunch one day, and he confirmed that the carrier was here, but said he understood it was at Norfolk. He conceded that most likely the Philadelphia angle was right.

A good friend of mine had a long talk with Admiral King the other day. King is commander of the Atlantic Fleet. He was disgusted with what he called the stupidity of the British Navy. He says he cannot understand how they continue to make mistake after mistake. For example, allowing an aircraft carrier to be caught unescorted off Norway and sunk by surface raiders. Carriers never go out without heavy protection in the U.S. Navy book. He said there is a long series of errors, and thinks the law of averages ought to make them right once in a while.

He raised another interesting point. Some of us down here who are interested in navy stuff are trying to figure out where the English Grand Fleet is. It is doubtful that it is in the north of Scotland. For one thing, it isn't of any use there, and wouldn't help in case of an invasion attempt, since smaller vessels will figure in that scrap. [Actually, when the time came to invade Europe across the English Channel, every kind of naval craft was used, the battleships included, and their big guns came in very handy. Our second-guessing rates no valid excuse except our insufficient background in amphibious operations.] Secondly, the Germans haven't made any claims of bombing the Grand Fleet since it left Scapa Flow. I think they would have if it was within reach, just on principle. On the other hand, they'd look foolish if they made such claims and had the British reply that the fleet wasn't even there.

Admiral King says he literally has no idea where the fleet can be based. Says he ought to know but doesn't. Add to this fact that there aren't many ports in the world where such a fleet can be based. If the answer doesn't put the big British battlewagons—with the exception of the Mediterranean squadron, of course—somewhere around Singapore, I'll be surprised.

The strategic implications are many. Japan can't afford to go south with her fleet, because the British fleet could handle her warships, and her islands would be left unguarded from action by the American fleet. On the other hand, she couldn't go out after the United States because that would lay Japan open to attack by the British. This thesis, if true, means Japan is not going to move anyplace, for a while anyway.

This paragraph is particularly confidential. King had two conferences with FDR, one here and one at Hyde Park. In them he discussed the Atlantic situation with the president, and made the point that he had desperately little stuff with which to do a job. The president said, "You're telling me?," and the Navy Department is now engrossed in figuring out how much destroyer and cruiser strength it can take from the Pacific for the Atlantic Fleet. The indication is plain that FDR has taken his decision to convoy. My friend asked King what Japan would do. He said he didn't know.

So much for that. Now, as to Representative Albert Engel: he swore me to secrecy on a document he showed me. It is a report by Truman Smith,

American Military Attaché at Berlin in 1937, on German air production. It tells how many planes Germany was manufacturing, where the factories were, the same data on engines, plus a resume in which Smith pointed out the profound implications of this program on Europe and the world, including the United States. This report, which if acted upon then could have saved us a hell of a lot of money today, was put in a file. Apparently they just didn't believe Smith.

Regards

Monday
26 May 1941

I am now in a position to give you pretty full information about *Illustrious*. I'm sorry to say we cannot print it.

In the first place, the *Illlustrious* is at Norfolk, and not Philadelphia. I've got that on such high authority that Lyle Wilson's story has got to be discarded. Her damage might be described as "plenty," and it'll be three or four months before she can go back on sea duty.

She was hit ten times by dive bombers in an attack that lasted five days. This is an extraordinarily low percentage of hits. And most of the damage was suffered when she was tied up to a dock at the base—either Malta or Alexandria [Egypt]—I think the latter. In any event, she ended up at Alexandria.

Maximum damage resulted from a mine dropped alongside, which crushed part of one side and threw the hull somewhat out of alignment. She suffered 138 casualties among her officers and crew. One bomb at least got down into the interior of the vessel before bursting. It is not true that 28 bodies are still out of reach of repairmen.

Despite the serious damage to *Illustrious* she was sailed from Alexandria to Norfolk at an average speed of 25 knots. Fortunately she had excellent weather all the way. Had she encountered gales, she might never have made it. She is commanded by a 30-year-old officer.

Her crew is allowed to go about Norfolk, but they wear civilian clothes and keep to themselves.

So much for her. Now, about the *Hood*. Navy people are pretty depressed about her, not because of her usefulness—she is an old type that [the battle of] Jutland proved not very useful—but because of the psychological effect, both on the Germans and the democracies. The feeling is that the British blundered in letting her get off by herself, since she is relatively lightly armored. She had hitting power, but couldn't take it. Battle cruisers can't fight in the same league with battleships. *Bismarck* is within two knots of being as fast as *Hood*, and if she surprised her the Britisher couldn't hope to escape.

Also, as I said in my story today, the British have always had trouble with their magazines. Jellico, on his bridge at Jutland, is said to have watched one battle cruiser after another blow up, and asked, "What's the matter with our bloody ships today?" The last word was the significant one. "Today" happened to be their first test in actual combat.

The truth is that the battle cruiser is a compromise type, sacrificing protection for speed. To an American naval officer, speed is merely a desirable attribute in a big ship. Hitting power and protection are the essential factors. And every battle in modern war has tended to prove they are right.

Admiral King told my informant on Friday that the record of the British Navy in this war has been one long series of errors of omission and commission, blunders and mistakes, with only a few brilliant episodes like the sinking of the *Graf Spee*.

For instance, they let an aircraft carrier get caught off Norway all alone a year or so ago. A surface raider sank her. It is fundamental that a carrier doesn't go out without covering forces, since she is not built for surface fighting. Again, *Gniesenau* and *Scharnhorst* were spotted at Brest three weeks before they were bombed. It didn't matter, as both have been put out of commission, but it might have made all the difference in the world. And these new British battleships have 14-inch guns when it was known the Germans and Japs have 15-inch and we have 16-inch. [The fact is that *Yamato* and *Musashi*, Japan's largest and most secret battleships, mounted 18-inch guns. Our intelligence surmised the existence of these two super-battleships, but had no details as to their armaments since so far as we knew, no one outside of Japan had ever seen these vessels.] The amount of metal they can throw is about the same, approximately, but the hitting power of the bigger shell is far greater. In any event, the loss of *Gniesenau* and *Scharnhorst* apparently was the motivating factor in causing the Germans to risk *Bismarck* on sea duty. I haven't been able to learn whether *Hood* was on her way here or not. There are reports she was.

Incidentally, Navy people have a good deal of interest in the Japanese situation. They feel we should have knocked off the little brown brothers years ago, and they still favor it as a step previous to entering the Battle of the Atlantic. In consequence, they are interested in this French business in Indo-China that is going on.

Regards

That Admiral King's lack of enthusiasm for the Royal Navy had neither declined nor even stood unchanged with the passage of time is clearly reflected in the opening paragraph of the following memorandum. It is pretty much concentrated on the messed-up situation in Washington in the period before the United States was attacked.

Looking back, the instant coalescence of all factions of American society into a unified nation intent on victory brought about by Pearl Harbor interposes itself between us and the pre-December 7 attitude, with Congress, like the general public, furiously debating, with no consensus in sight, political, economic, social and military problems.

This memorandum briefly reflected that situation. It is, I think, vitally important that all Americans understand, and never forget, that World War II was the last life and death struggle in which this country could count on allies giving it time to build and train a winning air-sea-land machine *after* hostilities broke out.

Friday
22 August 1941

Here is something that reaches me from one of the three highest ranking officers in the American Navy. He is absolutely appalled by the way in which the British maintain their ships. When one of them comes in for Lend-Lease repairs, the British estimate the cost, the American Navy automatically doubles the amount and generally finds that the repairs come to three, four or as much as eight times what the British figure.

Apparently the British never conceived of a war in which their vessels could not return at will to repair yards or drydock to fix up serious damage sustained at sea. American capital ships have very complete machine shops aboard, and can repair a great deal of damage without coming to port. That is one reason the British have to use our facilities so much. Another, of course, is that German bombing has made some British shipyards potential traps for ships requiring long periods of time for repairs.

This same officer, as I have told you before, has little use for the British Navy. He thinks it is inefficient, blundering and stupid.

Turning to that vote to extend the service of selectees, there was no one in Washington half as terrified as the Republicans when the balloting drew near the end and it became apparent that the bill might be licked. They'd been playing politics to beat hell. Many of them voted against it in the hope that it would pass and still put them on record against it. When it looked as if there were enough Democrats against it to lick it, they realized that the Republicans would be blamed (and rightly) for disrupting the entire military planning of the nation. Even after the vote was taken they were in a sweat lest somebody change his vote. Speaker [Sam] Rayburn may have been anxious to get the thing closed off without that happening, but he wasn't any more so than the Republicans.

Regards

Wednesday
29 October 1941

Here is some data on the Battle of Crete that I got hold of. It has extensive implications for the United States. We can unfortunately not use it, but it's interesting for background.

The British first sent the battleship *Queen Elizabeth* and a supporting screen of destroyers into the waters between Crete and the Greek mainland. Whether she was attacked or not I do not know, but she came out without damage.

Then the British sent in, as a group, three battleships, *Valiant*, *Barham* and *Warspite*, an aircraft carrier, eight cruisers and eighteen destroyers. German Stukas, with high-altitude bombers and fighter protection, attacked, and raised hell with the British fleet.

All three of the battleships were put out of action by bombing attacks. One dive bomber came so close to *Valiant* that it carried away her aerial with its wing. *Valiant* suffered three direct hits. At least one landed just off her bow and exploded, blowing a 27 foot hole in her. The other two landed aft and went clean through three decks before exploding and setting the ship on fire.

This performance was amazing, since it indicated the Germans had armor-piercing delayed-action bombs. The fire on *Valiant* came within fifteen feet of the after magazines before it was checked, and they were scared to death she was going to blow up. The fear was particularly great because one of the cruisers had done just that two hours before, so close to *Valiant* that men on her deck were blown off their feet.

Barham was so badly damaged that she has been out of port just two hours since she escaped from the fighting zone, and the British are afraid to fire her heavy guns as she was so badly strained.

All of the eight cruisers were also put out of action, and most of them—I don't have the exact figure—were sunk. Eleven of the eighteen destroyers were either sunk or put out of action.

The significant point is that this was done to British vessels without a German vessel anywhere around. Land-based aviation made the waters between Greece and Crete untenable. This helps to explain why the British don't want any part of an attempt to land an expeditionary force on the continent.

It is also making our military and naval men wonder what would happen should we send a naval force near enough to Japan for land-based planes to get at them. The prospect isn't too pleasing. I understand that the Army already has a copy of this report on the Crete show, and the Navy is getting one next week. The British are holding it very closely, naturally.

You can write it down that American naval units are not going to come within reach of land-based planes if Admiral King has anything to say about it.

Incidentally, here is the story of what happened to *Illustrious*: she had a flight of planes on her deck when some Italian planes showed up. The British planes took off and the Italians fled with the Britishers in hot pursuit. Six more planes were brought up, and when some more Italian planes showed up, they too took off in pursuit. But before any more planes could be brought up, a flock of German bombers appeared and wrecked the carrier and her deck.

To get back to the Crete situation, you will recall that the Royal Air Force has pulled out, leaving the navy to its fate. This has made for the most tremendous bitterness between the two services at Alexandria and Malta. I am told there is continual fighting between them, and that morale has suffered.

As for the submarine situation, I am told the Germans are using rather small subs, about 650 tons, with extremely strong and hard outer shells. American units have found they can't stop them with depth charges unless a direct hit is scored. The number of such craft owned by Germany is not known, but it is believed to be large. Some German airplane factories were converted to their manufacture last winter.

Incidentally, a naval officer just back from patrol was asked about Roosevelt's statement that the Navy believed it had sunk some subs, but that he didn't. The officer replied, "Then we've hit parts of them, because I've seen them come up to the surface." So it may be that our Navy is holding back, á la British, about its success with submarines.

The subs still hunt in schools. The battleship on which this officer was riding found six of them in two hours one day in the North Atlantic. The place is lousy with them.

By the way, people here are marveling at the stoutness of construction that allowed [United States] destroyer *Kearny* to get back to port after taking a direct torpedo hit. Such an explosion, on the starboard side about a third of the ship's length aft the bow, would have sunk any destroyer in the world but our new ones.

Regards

PEARL HARBOR—AMERICA JOINS THE WAR

On the day after Pearl Harbor I determined to keep a diary of events for the remainder of our war as seen from Washington, a sort of pre-New Year's Day resolution. It lasted just about as long as do most such resolutions— there just wasn't time—but it seems to me it gives a good enough play-by-play account of those first days to warrant inclusion here.

One of the untold events of the night of Pearl Harbor Sunday was an incident on the White House portico as the special meeting of Cabinet members broke up. It was very cold for early December, and few of us were dressed for standing around.

The last man to emerge from the White House front door was Harold Ickes, Secretary of the Interior. Like the rest of them, he growled a "No comment" as he swept by. George Dixon, gifted writer of humorous stories and columns for the *New York Daily News*, put a final question as Ickes grr-ed his way past, offering it with the greatest politeness: "Mr. Secretary, would you say the situation is serious?"

In 1979, as I read over this short-lived diary and the memos that follow, what impressed me most was the revelation of confusion and misinformation that permeated the capital. The announcement of the sinking of *Haruna* by a B-17 bomb dropped down its smokestack was probably put out to give a depressed America a shot in the arm. This was, of course, before high level bombing of moving targets, such as ships, was exposed as essentially useless.

The reason is not complicated. A factory or a railroad yard or a bridge is a fixed object. A bombsight in a plane hunting such objectives need concern itself only with such variables as plane speed and course, altitude, wind direction and force. The target is fixed. But to hit a ship steaming at full speed, the bombsight must make assumptions about its future course, and there is only one point at which the bomb must be released if it is to hit. So, using a bomb sight in reverse, a ship can tell when a plane has reached that point, alter course, and be somewhere else when the bomb reaches sea level.

Pearl Harbor came as a terrible shock to official Washington, not because it happened, but because of where it happened. The expectation in Washington was that the Japanese declaration of war would take the form of an attack on the Philippines at more or less the time it happened. Sumner Welles, Assistant Secretary of State, told the Overseas Press Club a week before Pearl Harbor that matters were no longer in the hands of the diplomats, a way of saying they were in the hands of the military.

As for the country as a whole, there was shock because it happened, and only secondarily because of where. Under such circumstances, and because accurate information about the disaster to our battle fleet was slow in becoming public knowledge, it is not surprising that the country, like Washington, was confused and subjected to wild rumors. If only one or two battleships had been put out of action, as Willkie was told by Mr. Roosevelt, then it was not foolish to suppose that the Navy was still ready to go out after an attacking fleet.

Let me hasten to add that holding back the full extent of our losses was essential at the time. There was strong evidence the Japanese did not know how effective their attack had been, and to give away the truth might have induced a second attack, this one on the Panama Canal or on Pacific Coast cities. It was, one could say, not until the Battle of Midway was won that American strategists could put the possibility of a major attack on such objectives on the back burner with the heat turned way down.

Sunday
7 December 1941

For some reason we didn't have our radio turned on all day. We drove to Alexandria for a social call, leaving Peabody Street about 3 o'clock. We arrived at the Shepard apartment in Belle Haven a little after 4, having been delayed somewhat when a quick stop on 13th Street brought someone banging into our rear end. As he opened the door, Mr. Shepard asked me excitedly what was new in the war.

"What war?" I asked. He told me Japanese planes were attacking Hawaii and that there was hell to pay. We crowded around the radio for a while, picking up the bulletins that were all over the dial, and heard Upton Close, said to be a Far Eastern expert, saying this might well be German submarines trying to provoke us into war, and that the Japanese government would probably disavow the attack even if its own Navy was responsible. Not five minutes later came word that Japan had declared war. Rarely has a commentator been shot down so quickly.

We were back in Washington about 5:45 P.M. and I took the car to a parking lot at 13th and E Streets, Sylvia and our son Christopher, aged about 3, went home by taxi. I went first to the office, hoping to be able to reach Phelps Adams, Bureau Chief, who had been in New York but was supposed to have returned. He wasn't there, but Ed Conroy, our telegrapher, who always spent Sunday afternoons in the office reading the *Washington Post* and the *Star*, was. I threw the news at him, and he commented, without excitement, that he had expected Japan to move the day before. Too bad he didn't think to tell the Navy.

I went from the office to the National Press Club to see what was doing and found Sir Wilmott Lewis, Washington correspondent of the London *Times*, in the bar pouring celebratory martinis for all and sundry. He warned us not to neglect the possibility that Germany and Italy would also declare war before morning.

After an egg sandwich and a glass of milk I took a taxi over to the War Department offices on Constitution Avenue for a press conference to be held by Secretary Stimson. We could see the flares of photographers taking pictures of uniformed officers rushing to their offices. When we reached the main entrance we got our first glimpse of war: troops with full field equipment on guard on the sidewalks, bayonets fixed, tin hats reflecting the street lights. I was told there were machine guns set up, but saw none.

Got inside all right with my White House press card, and went to the Press Section, where a number of top correspondents were waiting. Stimson did not hold the conference. General Alexander Surles took it. He is head of the Press Section, a thin, wiry man in civilian clothes. He looked tired, but unexcited. He told us that a new phase in press relations had begun and from now on news would be restricted. He didn't like the word censorship, but there was to be nothing printed about troop movements or activities or their materials or carriers, including transports in or out of American waters. Violation could mean a $10,000 fine or three years in jail.

This conference over—it produced no real news—I got in a taxi with Jim Wright and Dick Wilson and drove up toward the White House for the Cabinet meeting scheduled for 8:30 P.M. and one with Congressional leaders an hour later. Traffic was backed up so badly that I left the cab at 18th Street and walked the rest of the way. I didn't see any soldiers around the White House, but the White House police were on the job.

The press room was a madhouse. Hilmer Baukhage, Fulton Lewis, Ted Wingo and other broadcasters were set up there, typing scripts and then reading them into their microphones with the crowd talking and working in the background. There was a great deal of discussion as to what really had happened at Hawaii. Connie Brown had reports that [the battleships] *Oklahoma* and *West Virginia* were involved. Nobody could figure anything but that the forces in Hawaii had been caught napping. Secretary Knox is not popular with the correspondents, and there was considerable criticism of him as head of the Navy. There was no real idea as to the extent of the damage, but it was becoming clear that it was worse than had been first supposed. There was no doubt among the correspondents that Congress would declare war, or at any rate recognize the existence of a state of war. The difference seems to be between aggressing and being aggressed upon.

As the sleek Cabinet limousines rolled up under the White House portico, where fifty or sixty correspondents and photographers were waiting, the scene was spectacular. Across the street, in Lafayette Park, a crowd of perhaps a thousand men and women strained to see what was going on. Secretary of Commerce [Jesse] Jones and Vice President [Henry] Wallace arrived first, the former on foot. One by one the others went in, all of them declining comment. Stimson hopped out of his car and bounded up the steps like a mountain goat. Knox was last to arrive, and he was smiling faintly.

It was very cold, and a light mist somewhat obscured the moon. Lights blazed in the State Department, and clerks just called to duty kept running across the sidewalk past the ancient cannons into the building. We went back to the executive anteroom to await further developments. I heard that there was quite a crowd at the Japanese Embassy, with some hooting and booing, but no disorder. Someone said he had seen Baron Kato, the *Domei* correspondent, leaving his office, crying. He has good friends here. I heard that so many messenger boys had rung the bell at the Jap Embassy that they put up a sign advising those having business to go to the side door. The sign was in Japanese.

They were burning documents in the embassy. There was a story from San Francisco that the Jap consulate was taken completely by surprise. Naturally the diplomats could hardly be advised of what was planned, for any leak could have been fatal. Beyond that, their job was to cover up, and knowledge of the plan might make for insincerity obvious enough to be spotted.

It was the hard luck of [Ambassador Kichisaburo] Nomura and [Saburo] Kurusu [a special representative sent by Premier Tojo to help negotiate with Hull] that they were twenty minutes late for their conference with Secretary of State [Cordell] Hull, for by the time they had got inside he had been informed of developments. The Judge can really go to town when riled, and it seems he took all wraps off in telling the envoys his opinion of them and their country. He had kept them waiting an additional twenty minutes after they reached the State building, and Kurusu was hopping up and down like a grasshopper. When they left, the State Department press gang said, they were shocked and silent. Short of an eruption by Fujiyama, the Judge in action was probably tops for them.

Congressional leaders began arriving a little before 9 P.M. Most of them were silent. [Senator] Pappy O'Daniel came—uninvited—to see what was going on and to find if he could be of service and, I suspect, be able to tell his Texas radio audience that he had been at the White House that evening. Representative Charles Eaton of New Jersey said he wanted a constitutional declaration of war. Joe Martin (Minority Leader of the House) said he would talk later. Senator Hiram Johnson went in grimly. Senator Tom Connally had nothing to say, nor had Senator [Alben] Barkley, who had heard the news while driving up from Kentucky.

The crowd across the street began to sing "God Bless America" at about the time the Cabinet members came out, the Congressmen with them. Tom Connally acted as spokesman, and said the President would address the Congress at 12:30 the next day. Efforts to find out what had happened at Pearl Harbor were futile. Joe Martin announced unity in Congress and said there was now only one political party.

It was already obvious that nothing God could have planned could have unified the country as well as this. The cost of Hawaii may be high, but there is compensation.

We went back to the executive foyer, and I heard how the radio stations broadcast requests for correspondents and military and naval officers to go to their offices, and how similar bulletins were broadcast at the Redskins' football game. At about quarter to twelve Steve Early, White House press chief, announced that the lid was on for the night.

Charley Van Devander of the New York *Post* and I walked to the Press Club and had a glass of wine with Jim Warner and a couple of other chaps. I left about midnight and drove home, getting to bed about 1 A.M. Sylvia had had a busy time, what with listening to the radio, getting phone calls from Carl Brandt (my former literary agent) in New York trying to reach Hallet Abend and Forrest Davis, writers. Phelps had left word that we were going to press early. Some papers put out extras Sunday afternoon, but we did not.

————————

Monday
8 December 1941

I was up at 5 and took the car downtown, arriving in the office shortly before 6. Phelps was already there. I wrote a color story based on the events of Sunday night, and then went up to the White House. The first communiqué was issued by Steve and told of one "old" battleship capsizing and other damage. He admitted first reports had underestimated the effectiveness of the attack. Washington, including Congress, was buzzing as to how the Navy had managed to be surprised.

At the White House I arranged for a copy of the President's message to be rushed to the office and then took a cab down to the Capitol. There was a big crowd in the plaza, held back by cops. I should say that the streets on the the east and west sides of the White House, and the Ellipse behind it, have been closed off, and sentries with rifles are on patrol.

The House press gallery was packed by quarter to 12. At noon sharp Speaker Sam Rayburn banged his gavel. All galleries, occupied by special guests with passes, were jammed. Mrs. Roosevelt was there with some of her staff. The Senate came in after a brief recess, old Carter Glass looking pleased as punch. They were not yet seated by the time the Supreme Court entered in their black robes. The Cabinet came next.

There was silence as the President entered, under an escort of Senators and Representatives. As he reached the rostrum there were heavy handclapping, rebel yells and cat calls. We couldn't see him from where we were, but his voice was firm and his message just as determined. The old Rooseveltian trick of building a climax by repetition was obvious. The floor was silent until he referred to Japan's treacherous attack. Then there was handclapping. When he said the United States would win, he brought them to their feet. Isolationist Senator [Gerald] Nye sat impassive, his hands folded. The President got a big ovation when he finished, and left as rapidly as possible.

The Senate and other dignitaries followed suit, and the House received a resolution of a state of war from Representative John McCormack of Massachusetts. It was impossible for the House to act without some speeches, although cries of "Vote! Vote!" were heard right away. Representative Hamilton Fish announced his support and said he would volunteer at the proper time, preferably to serve with Negro troops. I believe he served with Negro troops in the First World War. Representative Jeanette Rankin of Montana tried to get recognition to make an objection, but was unsuccessful, Speaker Rayburn ruling that there could be no objection.

I stayed until the House was half-way through, with all enthusiastically voting "Aye." I rushed back to the office to write a sub for my color story. I learned Miss Rankin had been the lone "No" in House and Senate. The President signed the bill at 4 o'clock, and we were formally at war. Rumors were flying around town that Pearl Harbor had been the worst naval disaster in American History, and there were fears that the Japs now had naval control of the Pacific. The idea was sedulously nursed by Tokyo radio, but there was nothing more from the White House, the clearing house for news. I got home about on schedule, tired out.

———

Tuesday
9 December 1941

Rumors were flying on Capitol Hill and elsewhere. I got to the Round Table in the Press Club for lunch, and Jim West, who has good contacts, said we had lost four battleships, four cruisers, ten destroyers and 300 bombing planes. The discussion as to whose fault it was that we had been caught at Pearl Harbor was the topic of the day. Point was given to the discussion by a Chicago *Tribune* story that British intelligence had given the Navy warning of the time and place of the raid five days before the attack.

Washington was pretty calm, but there was a keen desire for good news. It had been announced that FDR was going to make a radio broadcast at 10 P.M. We thought this might mean no press conference, but it didn't.

I went to Steve Early's morning conference, where there was little news. Afterwards I suggested to Steve that the President take official notice of the rumors and tell people to wait for official news. He agreed. Whether that had anything to do with it, I wouldn't know, but the President dealt strongly with the subject in his talk.

I also attended Hull's press conference to find out what, if anything, was to be done about exchange of diplomatic representatives. He said arrangements were not complete. Hull told us that the country was on the alert, and that no surprise attacks by other Axis members would succeed.

The President at his press conference was perfectly calm. He had nothing to add to the Pearl Harbor story except that he was waiting for information. He was drawn into a discussion of news, and said it would be given out when: a) it was confirmed and accurate and b) when its publication would not give aid and comfort to the enemy. Bill Mylander [Cincinnati *Enquirer*] asked him if this meant bad news could not be made public. The President said that was not what he meant, and thereafter used the phrase "valuable to the enemy." It was the biggest crowd I'd seen at any press conference, and we were closely checked on entering. Our White House cards took us in all right. Pete Brandt [St. Louis *Post-Dispatch*] suggested that the attitude should be to give out everything that could be given out, instead of suppressing everything. The President agreed.

His talk that night was very good. It dealt with rumors, paved the way for war with Germany and Italy, and called for a united country. He also prepared the country for the loss of Guam, Midway and Wake Islands.

From such information as I could gather, the Navy was recovering from the shock of the opening blow, and was going about the business of putting into operation its prepared plans. Congress was aroused about Pearl Harbor, and Representative [John] Dingell was asking for an investigation and court martials. If the disaster was as big as it appears, heads are bound to roll. The Philippines, Guam, Midway, Wake, Hong Kong and Malaya are under attack. Japan is spread out some, but she holds the cards right now.

I suggested in a story that there were four aims in the raid on Pearl Harbor: 1) to do as much damage as possible without risking major forces; 2) to hold the American fleet in home waters, giving the Japs a free hand in the Far East; 3) to make a basis for propaganda stories about mastery of the Pacific; 4) to bring the war home to America. The reported presence of Jap planes over San Francisco, which I do not believe, would if true have the same objective as point 4.

Wednesday
10 December 1941

More bad news. The Japs have destroyed *Prince of Wales* and *Repulse*. This is a hard wallop, for *Wales* was a new battleship. *Repulse* was a battle cruiser, and Jutland showed this to be a useless type for modern battle con-

ditions. The Japs claim it was done by air action—torpedo planes and dive
bombers in a coordinated attack. It looks as though the battleship may be
on the way out. I cannot agree, however, that the surface unit is doomed.
Rather I look to see war at sea become truly three-dimensional, with air,
surface and submarine craft working as a closely integrated unit. The raid
on Pearl Harbor and the sinking of the British ships in the long run will
mean our security, for we will soon be paramount in the air in the whole
world. But right now it means a certain amount of difficulty.

I attended a conference at the British Press Service to hear a Colonel
Lockhard of the anti-aircraft service describe the work of defending against
air attack. He says A.A. fire is merely a deterrent, and that interceptors are
the real answer. However, he likes the Bofors 40 mm and says it is a real
killer for low flying planes. He said of 3,000 planes shot down over England
600 were destroyed by ground guns. That isn't such a bad deterrent. But his
point was that an interceptor unit could turn a squadron of bombers completely from their objective, while ground guns could not. He said it was
fatal not to hold fire until the last possible moment when defending against
dive bombers, but that it was even worse not to fire at all. Then the bomber
can aim, and will drop 'em on your neck.

Objective circles here are not particularly critical of Japan's strategy in
the Pearl Harbor attack. Figured we'd think it was pretty darned smart if
we'd done it to them. But they don't like the way we were caught. American
fashion, there is a good deal of joking on the surface, but underneath there
is absolute determination, mixed with a good deal of concern. We're in
something big, and it'll last a long while. The country is not in good shape
financially, thanks to the New Deal. But we're in, and we can take it. We
can also dish it out, a fact that will become evident.

———————

Thursday
11 December 1941

Germany and Italy declared war on us today. The President sent a
500-word message to Congress, suggested a postscript to Monday's action.
It went through both houses in record time, and unanimously. Miss Rankin
voted "present." Had she explained her Monday vote by saying that she
had conscientious objections and could not vote to put America in the war,
it would have been all right with most people. But when she explained that
there was no real assurance that there *had* been an attack on Pearl Harbor,
she reached a point where it seems to me she showed such absolute lack of
faith in her government's integrity that she should resign. The other top
isolationists are now in line: Nye, Wheeler, Lindbergh, etc.

The casual way in which war was declared on Germany showed how
thoroughly the country has accepted the world-wide problem. Willkie may
be right when he says isolationism is dead forever. Any man who, on

December first, bet that within two weeks Congress would vote unanimously for war against Germany (with one abstention) would have been hooted as a lunatic. But boy, would he have cleaned up!

Friday
12 December 1941

The President said little or nothing in the way of news at his morning press conference. He paid his respects to Senator Charles Tobey, who had sounded off in the Senate about losses, and accused him of stating rumors as facts, which he had no right to do.

New game in Washington: "Knock Knox, who's there?"

Monday
15 December 1941

At 3 P.M. Secretary of the Navy Knox held a press conference to discuss the Pearl Harbor attack. An enormous crowd turned out, the biggest he'll ever have. His office was packed, and it took a long time to get credentials checked out. He waited, puffing calmly at his pipe.

He gave out a written statement which gave the facts of what happened candidly and bluntly. Then the questions began. He said it was not true that it took an unconscionably long time to get steam on the fleet. He said the attack was the most effective fifth column job done in the war except for Norway. He doubted that a suicide squad manned the planes, although he said one Jap flew into a hangar, possibly unable to pull out of his dive.

He said there was no evidence of German planes being used, nor of four engine bombers. The raiders, he said, were of the one- and two-engine types used from carriers. There was no evidence that any new weapons were used.

Our losses in planes were heavy—on the ground. Naval air personnel loss and loss of naval aircraft were small. He then said two-man submarines took part in the attack. One of these was captured, another destroyed, as was a normal-size submarine.

He said the Japs had the most perfect possible information as to disposition of American forces. *Utah* was in the berth usually occupied by an aircraft carrier and received a terrific going over. He said they didn't know if the information was sent out by fifth column radios, but said this was suspected. An investigation is underway. He said steps to prevent leaks had been taken, but obviously had not worked. The attacking Japanese force was small—between 150-300 planes. Forty-one planes were shot down.

He said harbor facilities were not damaged, and that no oil had been destroyed, two most important points. He said there was no truth in reports that the Navy had been forewarned of the attack. There was a Navy patrol out that day, but it was not possible to follow the enemy planes to the carriers as they scattered in all directions. He said that material losses were less than feared, and personnel losses were greater. He admitted that the ratio of dead to wounded was extraordinarily high.

Tuesday
16 December 1941

I interviewed Samuel G. Hibben of Westinghouse, who believes the United States is being stampeded into a lot of air raid precautions that, while useful in England, are of no avail here. He believes blackouts are both unnecessary and dangerous. He does feel that prominent buildings, bridges and highways should be blacked out, but can see no advantage in blacking out suburban lighting, holding that it is of no help to enemy pilots.

He said there had been 10,000 blackout fatalities in Britain this year, many more than had been killed by German raiders, and that despite the blackout German pilots were able to find London any time they wanted to. He pointed out that enemy planes attacking Washington would have only to follow the Potomac up to the junction of the Anacostia, look for the bridges across the river and swing to the right, dropping flares if visibility were poor. New York would also be impossible to miss, blacked out or not. He also added that his conception of American courage was not to crawl into a hole and shiver in the dark whenever danger threatened.

America can expect hit and run raids, he said, and added that it takes the human eye half an hour to adjust itself to darkness. By that time the raid would be over, in his opinion. He seemed to make sense.

Wednesday
17 December 1941

The Navy has replaced Admiral [Husband] Kimmel and the Army General [Walter] Short [head of the two service branches at Pearl Harbor] with Admiral [Chester] Nimitz and General [Delos] Emmons. Washington reaction is that this is a smart move, and that public confidence will be greater as the result.

Sunday
21 December 1941

They had an air raid test in Washington this morning, and we couldn't hear the siren. Should we get any raids, I suppose we'll find out when the bombs begin falling.

Monday
22 December 1941

Churchill is here, with [Lord] Beaverbrook and a squad of military advisers. He arrived in Annapolis, presumably by boat, this afternoon, and was flown to Washington, where the President went to meet him.

Tuesday
23 December 1941

Steve Early was asked at his press conference whether Churchill would be at the afternoon Presidential conference. Steve declined to answer. Taking this as an affirmative, I got to the White House in the afternoon an hour early, and stood near the door to the Oval Office for three quarters of that time, in order to make sure of a good spot. I did, too, being in the second row directly in front of the President's desk. For what happened, refer to my story in the *Sun* the next day. It was a most impressive and historic occasion, especially at the end of the conference, when the Prime Minister clambered up on a chair in his blue jump suit and raised his hand in a V for Victory salute.

Tuesday
30 December 1941

We went to a cocktail party at the Brubakers, and while we were there they had the first blackout. It looked to be pretty effective except for the moonlight and the street lights. An interesting sidelight came when Senator Gerald Nye, who lives next door to the Brubakers in the Westchester Apartments on Connecticut Avenue, dropped in on the party. The blackout was still on, although near its end, when he raised his hand and said, "There is nothing to fear. You will not be bombed here. Hitler knows I live in this apartment." A mordant sense of humor, I must say. And a fit end for my war diary.

1942

HOW WE TRACED MacARTHUR'S TRANSFER TO AUSTRALIA

===

VIA BUREAU WIRE FROM NEW YORK

Mar. 17, 1942 10:08 A.M.

Adams or Perry

According to AP following message was sent to West Point in observance of 140th anniversay of Military Academy:

The sons of West Point on Bataan join me in renewed pledges of loyalty to our alma mater on its 140th anniversary.

The message was signed by Major General Jonathan Wainwright and not by MacArthur. I have a hunch that may mean that MacArthur has been sent to Australia. Do you think so?

Bartnett

Washington, Mar. 17

Bartnett, N.Y.

Congratulations on a nice piece of logic about MacArthur. Glen is sending the sum total of our knowledge on the subject and there may be something in it.

Adams 10:30 A.M.

Washington, Mar. 17

Bartnett, N.Y.

Story coming up on MacArthur. We certainly tipped that one off. I called Col. Fitzgerald at War Department and the following conversation ensued:

P. Who is in command of the Philippines now?
F. General MacArthur.
P. I wondered when I noticed General Wainwright had signed the congratulatory message to West Point.
F. I noticed that too. I don't know how Skinny Wainwright happened to sign it. We had a couple of messages from General MacArthur this morning.
P. Then he hasn't been hit or moved to Australia?
F. Well, he hasn't been hit, anyway.

Fitzgerald just called back to say we had a good hunch. He could not confirm because a 10:30 release here and a matching time in Australia had been agreed upon.

Perry 10:43 A.M.

Washington, March 19

Bartnett, N.Y.

That highly ingenious piece of deduction which led you to sense Mac-Arthur's transfer before it was announced has caused quite a bit of comment here. I took Parnell Thomas to lunch today and he brought up the subject himself, askng how it had been done and whether or not we had a beat on the story. Yesterday afternoon an official in the Office of Censorship told me you had given the War Department a nasty ten minutes while they in turn gave us the run-around in order to protect the secret. Only one other newspaper man—Constantine Brown—he said, had been equally astute in sensing the true significance of the Wainwright message, and he did not call the War Department until after we did.

It appears that the most elaborate precautions had been taken to protect the secret, and although—according to a dispatch in the *Chicago Sun* today—MacArthur spent seven days en route from the Philippines to Australia, two messages originating in Bataan and signed by his name came into the department the morning that his arrival in Australia was announced. These apparently had been prepared in advance for the purpose of diverting attention.

Adams 3:55 P.M.

To the best of my knowledge, Admiral Thomas Hart was the first American naval officer of flag rank to talk off the record to newsman after our formal involvement in World War II. He was, as will appear, the first of a goodly number. His comments were inferentially critical of Admiral Husband Kimmel, who appears to have been less aware of Japanese intentions than he.

ADMIRAL HART ON JAPANESE DARING AND ALLIED NAVAL FORCES

CONFIDENTIAL

Friday
3 April 1942

Dear Bart,

Admiral Hart spoke off the record at the Overseas Writers yesterday. It was extremely interesting. I'll go through what I recall of his remarks and then comment on them.

The first campaign of the Japanese War has come to a close, he said. It had as its objective the securing of oil, since Japan has no sources of her own, and since this country had shut down on sending American oil to Nippon. The question was whether Japan would try to cut through in a straight line to the Dutch East Indies, or whether she would make a broad sweep down toward the Malaysian Barrier (the chain of islands beginning at New Guinea and running up through Sumatra to Malaya).

As it turned out, the Japanese were very daring, and attacked along a very broad front. They of course got away with it in fine shape, using a type of warfare about which little has been written because there hasn't been much of it: amphibious war, combining land, air, and sea units to attack from the sea. This is the most difficult form of warfare, and was made possible by air superiority.

Admiral Hart, in command of the Asiatic Fleet, had only one surface vessel in his command that wasn't old enough to vote. He had, as I recall, a cruiser, some destroyers, quite a lot of submarines and some gun-boats, including those withdrawn from Chinese waters.

As long ago as last June Admiral Hart made up his mind that war was not far off, and he established his headquarters on shore at Manila. The reason was that in time of war a warship dares not use its radio, since it can be located by it. This means that an admiral on his flagship can direct local tactics by blinker but cannot cover broad strategy. Hence Hart established himself where he could send his orders to all ships.

By late November Hart was convinced that war was imminent, and he made his preparations accordingly. The Navy Department gave him all the information he required to reach this conclusion, and he acted on it. He had his ships at sea, commenting that admirals have been shot for allowing their ships to be caught in port at the outbreak of war, and that he didn't want to be shot. His plan was to use Manila Bay headquarters for his submarines as long as possible, preying on Japanese ship movements through the China Sea toward the Indies. It would also be used by surface ships as long as possible, but it was not believed that this would be very long.

He explained that under the American plan all shore installations, whether Army or Navy, are supposed to be protected from air attack by the Army. Unfortunately, the Army proved unable to do the job. When the Japs attacked, the American surface vessels were never able to get back to Manila Bay. Instead, they moved south. And the period in which submarines could work out of the Bay was far shorter than had been hoped and expected. This was a real disappointment, and the main upset in American calculations.

The Japs hit at Manila with land-based planes, apparently from Formosa. Hart hadn't thought this possible, figuring they'd have to use carriers. But it happened that way. He added that Japanese Navy planes did the bulk of the work. He also said it was his guess that the Japanese Navy had direction over the amphibious war.

Anyway, the Asiatic Fleet was driven out of the Philippines, except for the gunboats, which were left behind and are still in Manila Bay in American hands. Hart said they have been extremely valuable in protecting the shores of Bataan against the kind of Jap operations that were so successful in Malaya. The Japs will be able to knock these gunboats out ultimately, he said, but it will be a hard job. In the meantime, they are very much worthwhile. In addition a regiment of Marines, the 4th, is still in the Philippines with a detachment of sailors.

The Japs, having occupied Manila, by-passed most of the other islands in the Philippine group, jumping to Mindanao, where they established a base at Davao, bearing on Borneo and the Netherlands East Indies. The whole Japanese strategy was to advance in jumps so that they could always bring land-based air power to bear.

However, as the Jap lines of communications lengthened, they became more vulnerable, and their attack lost enough of its strength so that Allied naval forces could hit. They labored under difficulties, for Japanese control of the air gave the enemy complete observation facilities that enabled them to know all about what the Allies were doing. However, the Allies managed to keep some planes up, and through good luck and good management kept themselves pretty well informed as to what the Japs were doing.

The Battle of the Macassar Straits was the most successful example of Allied counter-action, but it was by no means the only one tried. A number of such attacks were projected, but could not be carried through. Once the Japs got word ahead of time of what was up, and when the American vessels arrived at the spot where they hoped to hit the Japs, there wasn't anyone around. In another case the American commander canceled his plans at 9:30 A.M. Hart said he was disposed to be critical of this until he found that the Americans had been shadowed all afternoon by Jap planes, that it was going to be bright moonlight all night, lessening the chances of surprise, and that the strength of the American force was known while that of the Japs was not. He then agreed that the cancellation was the correct move.

In the battle of Macassar, American destroyers were challenged by more powerful Jap destroyers and were pursued. But they spotted the main Jap body in another direction and changed course. The Jap destroyers did not see this, and steamed on right out of the battle. The American maneuver was well done, but it was not aided by luck, the Admiral commented, adding that you have to be both lucky and able.

Adding up the fighting prior to his departure, he said that in the aggregate more damage was done by American submarines than by any other arm, insofar as Jap naval and merchant units were concerned. He said it was his belief that the damage done had been so extensive as to make the Jap command very anxious about the success of future amphibious operations. Jap losses have apparently been quite high.

That was the end of his formal talk. In answer to questions, a good deal of interesting information came out. Commenting on the comparative value of carriers as against land-based aviation, he pointed out the mobility of the former, but offset it by the limitations imposed on the ship designer by the restricted landing platform and the vulnerability of the platform. One bomb can wreck it and make the carrier useless. Land fields, in addition to not being vulnerable from beneath the surface, are much larger. He made it plain that more efficient operations could be obtained from land fields.

On the success of the Jap drive to the south, he said they now had their objective: oil. The oil is *in* the ground, but the Japs are *on* the ground, and it is a question of restoring the destroyed wells or drilling new ones. Their first oil was captured in Borneo, where the fields are only a couple of hundred feet down, and where the oil quality is so high that it doesn't need to be refined, but can be pumped directly into the bunkers for use in ships. The second was in Dutch Borneo, where the oil was equally good, but deeper. The first field referred to was at Sandakan. On the whole, Hart believed a pretty good job was done of wrecking the oil fields.

On the subject of the Japanese being great copyists, he said it was overdone, that they were much more original than they were credited with being. If, he said, they had done this country the honor of copying our methods, he would not hesitate to borrow from the Japs, and he said we had learned much from them in the war thus far, particularly on the amphibious campaign.

He was asked whether our campaigns to reconquer territory taken by the Japanese in Malaysia and the Philippines would require the same amphibious warfare. "Yes, SUH," he said. He added that the Navy and the Marines (he couldn't speak for the Army) have been making a study of this type of fighting.

This Hart is a great little guy, and a fighting fool. He did not go into the reasons why he gave up his Far Eastern command. Nor did he discuss the loss of *Repulse* and *Prince of Wales*. You will recall, however, that he did talk a little about this at a press conference of which I wrote when he first got back to Washington.

I think that covers the highlights. I've probably not got it all down here, but we couldn't take notes, of course, so I may have forgotten something.

As for comment, it is clear that Hart gave Admiral Kimmel an awful going over without ever mentioning his name. His comment that admirals get shot for not having their ships at sea was one thing. His comment that the Navy gave him all the information he needed was another. Possibly his statement that an admiral must base himself on shore was another, but I'm not sure, as I don't know exactly where Kimmel based himself. But there was no doubt of the other two. They were whiplashes.

He also made it clear, it seemed to me, that he thought the Army fell down on the job of protecting installations around Manila. The Japs hit the air fields first, and the naval installations second, and the Army couldn't stop 'em.

Over all, I should say Hart was qualifiedly optimistic. And it was a most interesting session.

By the way, did I tell you that we are still maintaining some communications with Corregidor and Bataan by submarine? We are, but it is a very tight secret.

Regards

> Characterizing the memoranda reported thus far in this book, some might be tagged as coming mostly from corvettes, destroyers, light and heavy cruisers, and only rarely from one of the really big wagons, militarily speaking. To continue with the simile, this one is from one of the new fast battleships. It was the first off-the-record press conference with General George C. Marshall that I attended.

GENERAL MARSHALL TELLS OF REVIEW OF TROOPS WITH CHURCHILL, TOKYO RAID, TRAGEDY OF BATAAN, STILWELL'S TRIUMPHS

CONFIDENTIAL

Tuesday
21 April 1942

Dear Bart,

This is the off-the-record story of General Marshall. He, with two military aides, Harry Hopkins, and a Navy doctor, flew to Bermuda and from there to England. They went directly to London and saw Churchill. There ensued a whole series of conferences with military and other government people. Over the weekend Marshall and Hopkins went to Chequers, Churchill's country place, where they conferred until late at night with various high-ranking officials.

This worked quite a hardship on Marshall, who likes to go to bed as soon after 8 P.M. as possible, and they were up until 2 to 4:30 A.M. every night. There was so much to cram into the visit. What they talked about is a secret. It is my guess it was the question of a second front, but Marshall wasn't saying.

He and Churchill went to Salisbury Plain and Aldershot in the latter's special train, and watched field maneuvers in which live ammunition was used. Both of them were put in Bren gun carriers, and he said Churchill, in his bowler hat, was an amusing sight. They saw infantry work, backed by artillery fire, and supported by air force planes firing at real targets. He saw practice in transporting troops in gliders (this he hadn't meant to tell us, as it is a profound secret). He was impressed by the British troops.

Then he flew to Ireland to see our troops, whose movements are being conducted in great secrecy. He found them an excellent group of men, with high morale. He said the delicacy of the relations between north and south Ireland is incomprehensible to Americans, and great care is being taken to avoid treading on any toes. The men are kept in the north of Ireland, and no Irish-Americans were picked for this duty, lest they stir up some incident. He said there were a number of very amusing stories about the forces up there, but he wouldn't tell us any of them because, he explained laughingly, he just didn't trust us not to print them.

Next he turned to the raid on Tokyo. He confirmed absolutely that there was a raid, that American planes did it, and that it was very successful, coming as a complete surprise. He would not permit us to say that any American sources knew anything about a raid. This seems foolish, but that's no help, since the Army holds the cards.

He said the raid had worked greatly to our advantage, and that the Japs were very much worried over where the planes came from. He gave no hints, but he said that when the American announcement did come it would come from the Chiefs of Staff (Marshall, Arnold, King) which implies strongly that it was a joint Army-Navy action. My analysis of the situation indicates that B-25 bombers were put on carriers, which can just handle them, and were booted off when within reaching distance of Japan, dropped their bombs and continued on to some secret base in China. This has nothing to back it, but it looks pretty logical.

Turning then to the Philippines, Marshall said that the Japs were tightening their blockade all the time, going into the central islands. The United States managed to slip in a couple of shiploads of fighter planes, which operate from a secret base, and which can escort any bombers that come over.

As for Bataan, he said the plan was (when the place became untenable) to break through on the left and to escape into the Olangopo Mountains, there to continue fighting as long as possible. Had this operation been ordered a week earlier, it would probably have succeeded, but it would have meant giving up the peninsula. It was decided to wait, and then, after the terrible drain of two full days of fighting, with continual counterattacks, with heavy enemy artillery fire, and with constant strafing from the air, the American and Filipino forces simply didn't have the strength to break through. They failed, and are presumably prisoners. Some apparently did get through, though, and are conducting guerrilla warfare in the mountains.

General Marshall was concerned as to how much medicine the Americans were able to get to Corregidor from the peninsula. Medicine was for a long time a great shortage, but they managed to run a lot of it through the blockade, and it got to Bataan all right. But the Jap artillery ultimately hit the American field hospitals—he didn't say this was deliberate inhumanity, but merely remarked that the barrage ultimately got to that central section—and was the conclusive factor in breaking down the defense. Not that only the hospitals were hit, necessarily, but that concentrated fire struck that whole area.

He believes that if food can be gotten in to Corregidor, the fortress can survive for a long time—six months, perhaps. Efforts will be made, but the blockade is tightening and the hazards of war may make it impossible.

Rations on Bataan were cut to one-half in the middle of January, and were later still further reduced to fifteen ounces of food per man per day. The Department didn't know for a long time why this was done, but found recently that it was because of the large number of refugees on the peninsula. The original plan hadn't contemplated anything of that sort, but Marshall believes they were relatives of the Filipino soldiers, and he feels that had they been barred from the peninsula it would have had a very bad reaction among the Filipinos.

At this point he complained of the looseness with which American secrets are held. He didn't blame anybody, but he did say that publication of information as to how stuff was getting to the Philippines tipped the Japs off and enabled them to plug the holes more quickly than might otherwise have been the case. He said we find great difficulty in getting information from Germany and Japan, but he is convinced they know everything we are doing. Only in the case of such relatively small events as the Tokyo raid is it possible for us to keep secrecy. That one was known, he said, to only six men in Washington, so thorough was security.

He was philosophical about this difficulty in keeping secrets, and said efforts were being made to turn this to account in some way. My interpretation of this is that reports will be deliberately set in motion as to what we are going to do while we are actually planning something else in order to feint the enemy out of position.

He said the fighting record of American troops in the Philippines had very important effects elsewhere, particularly among the Russians. The Russians, he said, once they get going, are heedless of cost in human life, in material, in towns and villages, and they want their allies to be the same. They are critical of any lesser efforts, but they've had nothing but praise for the toughness of the American fighting man.

This war, he went on, is very largely one of tonnage. It avails nothing to produce munitions if they can't be transported to where they can be used. He referred any comments on this aspect of the matter to Admiral Emery Land, but he did link it up with Southwest Pacific. Convoys are moving there, and they must be protected. This requires naval strength, and diverts it from possible offensive operations. There is no help for it. The supplies have got to move.

He made very strongly the point that every time you establish a base or an advanced position, it means tonnage to carry to it the things you need to maintain it. At the same time, you have got to have tonnage for offensive plans. Thus the problem of allocation becomes acute.

He came back to the looseness of information, talking specifically of the reports of movements of the *Queen Mary* (none of which came my way, incidentally). She carried 9,000 American troops and traveled alone because of her great speed. He pointed out that you had to use her, and couldn't send her out empty, or only half full.

General MacArthur's difficulties, he said, have been political. In a military sense he has been in complete command ever since he got to Australia. In the military sphere things can be done at once, but dealings of a diplomatic nature between nations take time. They move slowly. But he is all straightened out now.

He expects to see a very vicious and bitter battle of islands in the Pacific. We hold many of them now. Each has its own garrison. In many cases these garrisons are small, and the Japs will attack them, chase our people off, and occupy them themselves. We'll be doing the same thing to their islands—he hinted broadly that we've already done so in some cases. These islands lie along the line of communication to Australia, and to have Jap planes based on them would be bad. So there'll be hard fighting all along that line. And Jap naval units will of course try to break the line, too.

As for the Japs, he figures they have got to take a crack at Australia sooner or later, because things wil happen to their flank if they don't. For the present, they have three potential courses of action: to crack Australia, to keep going in India, or to hit Siberia. He expressed no opinion as to which it will be.

Marshall spoke highly of the reorganization of the War Department that has been going on for a year and a half. I had a tip on that six months or more ago, and could never get anyone in the War Department to admit it. I think I mentioned it in a confidential memorandum. Anyway, it has simplified the set-up considerably, and has made possible trips such as Marshall has just taken. In fact, he said, the place seemed to be running better when he was away, and he figured he ought to take some more trips.

He discussed the Russian situation briefly, and said it appears almost certain that a major attack is planned for late spring on the southeastern front. He has no information as to Russian losses. Apparently nobody has but the Russians, and they aren't talking. However, he does not seem to think that Russian operations have been on as large a scale as the world believes. He says the Germans have taken real punishment, but more of it came from the winter than from the Russians.

On the other hand, the Russians maintained constant pressure, were always harassing the Germans, and they wore down many German divisions so badly it was necessary to take them out of the line and send them to Poland or France or where have you to rest up. This means that Hitler does NOT have at his command the long list of fresh divisions that he'd like to have to throw into a late spring offensive.

As for the Mediterranean, he paid high tribute to the defenders of Malta, and especially to the way in which supplies and airplanes have been brought in despite almost continual air attack from Sicily. Now, he says, there are indications that German air pressure against Malta is lightening, and he believes this means planes have been shifted to Russia. More evidence of a drive on the southeastern front.

Asked whether Italy is still in the war, he laughed and said he was glad she is no more active than she is. Then he was asked whether Hitler could move into Spain and Portugal. The answer was yes, but that it had its difficulties, such as having to feed the population. Beyond that, Lisbon is Germany's number one listening post, and is probably more valuable to her as it is than as a German possession.

Then, making a long jump, we came to Alaska. He said we are doing a great deal to fortify it, but that we have got to realize that it simply isn't possible to defend everything. It would take too much materiel. The Army fully expects raids on Dutch Harbor in the Aleutians and on Kodiak Island. As a matter of fact, he is surprised there hasn't been one there already. But there will be.

On this subject, the General made it very clear that there are going to be raids in various places from time to time, and that it is going to be up to the people to take it. That will be their contribution, knowing the stuff to protect them is being used on the fighting front.

The whole of modern war, he said, is a business of calculating hazards. You take certain risks, knowing you may lose out. Or you make an attack knowing it is going to be costly, but figuring it is worth the cost. I have long felt that a general is an economist dealing in men and material instead of money. And what this General said seems to bear out my theory.

The Japs, for instance, may be counted upon to raid certain Australian cities that lie along the coastline. They cannot all be made impregnable. To do so would be frightfully expensive, tying up stuff badly needed elsewhere. On the other hand, it is desirable to have some pressure on an attacker any place. The Japs would, as Marshall explained, calculate the hazard, know they'd have losses, and pay the price.

Raids on this side of the Pacific, he believes, will be chiefly to stir up the populace, and to try to break morale. He doesn't think such raids can be prevented. They are a part of the game. And, as I say, people will have to take it.

Then we came to Burma. He didn't express any opinion as to what is going to happen there, but he did say that two ships loaded with planes had been sent there, and had they arrived the British and Chinese would be sitting pretty. But they were sunk. It was a calculated hazard that went wrong, as some must, on the law of averages.

General Stilwell, he said, has done a magnificent job. But he cannot be given credit for it. In fact, the General asked that the newspapers refrain from mentioning Stilwell at all if it is possible. The reason is face. Chinese officers feel that they have lost face because they have to serve under an American commander instead of their own, particularly as he is riding them pretty hard. So he figures that while it will be possible to give Stilwell the credit he deserves later, it is better now to give all credit to the Chinese for what they are accomplishing.

Stillwell, he says, has great confidence in the Chinese fighting man. And Stilwell, without anything in his rear such as engineers, hospital corps or air support, has done great things. Or, to follow the line Marshall gave us, the Chinese have done great things.

Finally, he said that American weapons have proved very good in actual tests. The 105 mm cannon hasn't yet been tried. They didn't get any to the Philippines, and they didn't take any to Ireland, since the British could supply cannon, and this saved the tonnage that would otherwise be needed to carry our cannon and ammunition. You have to think about things like that when there isn't enough shippng to go around.

Our machine guns and our tanks have proved to be excellent. Our self-propelled cannon have been especially effective, being less noticeable than a big truck dragging a cannon along, and very mobile.

That's about all, except that General Surles stressed that nothing in the conference can be used, with or without attribution. I suppose somebody will violate his confidence, but I hope not. As you know, I have worked hard to bring about these seminars, and they will be continued as long as the boys keep the faith. The reasons for making it confidential are obvious from the context. There was, I think you'll agree, plenty of meat there.

Regards

GENERAL DOOLITTLE ON THE TOKYO RAID
AND LACK OF GRAND STRATEGY

CONFIDENTIAL

Monday
8 June 1942

Dear Bart,

Here is one that is so confidential I am almost afraid to put it on paper—the story of the Doolittle raid on Tokyo. The source is Doolittle himself, who told the story to Senator [Walter] George at lunch, and a third party at the table told a close friend of mine.

As I told you in New York, the B-25s were taken out on Navy aircraft carriers. I was guessing then, but I know now. I do not know how many carriers were used, nor how many bombers took part, but my belief is that one or at the most two carriers carried the planes out, and that between a dozen and twenty planes did the job.

It had been planned to boot the bombers off when they were within 400 miles of Tokyo—very daring. But the detectors picked up reconnaissance planes when the Americans were 800 miles off. It was decided to take off immediately, lest the carrier or carriers be spotted in the danger zone and the effect of the raid spoiled.

So they hopped off 800 miles from Tokyo, while the carrier or carriers skedaddled back home, getting away safely. This change in plan could not be transmitted to the Chinese, of course, since the operation was carried out in radio silence. This had important effects later.

Since the time required to fly 400 miles is so much less than the time needed to steam that distance, the planes got to Tokyo some hours before they had planned to be there. The raid's effects on Tokyo have already been described in the papers, so I won't go into that. But the early arrival in Tokyo meant that the planes also arrived over China earlier than they were expected.

One of the American bombers was forced to land in the China Sea. Its crew is believed to have been captured by the Japs. One other plane got lost and came down in Siberia, its crew being interned. The others got to China all right.

But it was dark when they arrived, and the landing field was not lighted, as the Chinese did not expect them until some hours later. It must have been the Chinese assumption that the planes were hostile, for it was not possible to make contact with the field or to get the field lights on.

The American planes cruised around in the darkness, hoping for a chance to land, until their fuel was exhausted. Then, one by one, the crews bailed out and parachuted to earth. All of them made it safely, but the planes of course were destroyed. This was too bad, as they could have been useful to China.

One pilot landed on what appeared to be a large expanse of flat rock. He lighted a cigarette, and when it was half smoked, threw it away. But he was surprised to notice that it didn't hit the ground. He hunched himself cautiously forward and saw a faint spark of light, still moving, far below. You can bet he sat still the rest of the night. When daylight came, he found he had landed on the very edge of a 2,000 foot precipice.

That's all I know about the raid, except that it scared the hell out of Japan, and was a powerful influence in what appears to be a profound change in Japanese tactics.

[Almost forty years after the raid described in the preceding memorandum, General Doolittle, eighty-four years old, spry and alert, spoke at a dinner of the Charles A. Lindbergh Post of the Air Force Association in Darien, Connecticut. I was present, and had an opportunity to raise with the General a couple of questions about the raid.

I asked him about the decision to boot off the planes from the carrier 400 miles farther from Japan than had been planned. He said the carrier formation was seen by some Japanese fishing boats. A cruiser sank them, but not before they had radioed news of their sighting. This gave the Jap high command advance warning that a raid was coming, but the Japanese assumed that carrier planes would be used, and calculated the time it would take for the task force to get within practical launching distance of the islands. This was of course a blunder, because the assumption that carrier planes would be used was invalid. The American planes were Army Air Force bombers, and they got to Tokyo some four hours earlier than the Japanese had figured.

He added that this time change also meant the bombers would arrive over China in darkness. Not all of them went there, as one pilot whose plane developed an oil leak decided it would be better to go to Siberia, where it landed safely and the crew was interned. They "escaped" later. Two planes landed in the China Sea and two men were drowned. The other fifteen planes cruised around over China until, one by one, they ran out of gas, and their crews bailed out. All landed safely.

Since the plan had been for the planes to land in China, I asked what use they would be to the Chinese, who would lack the gasoline to fly them. He told me there had been no intention of leaving them in China. The plan was to refuel there and then continue over The Hump to India, where they would be turned over to General Chennault.]

Our interview with General Hsiung [K'owu] made a big stir down here. It developed into a much bigger story than I had dared to hope when I went to see him. I gave the interpreter a dozen questions, typed out, and all of them were answered. Then, as we were getting ready to say goodbye, the General congratulated me on the probing nature of the questions. I replied that he had no doubt noticed that I had purposely omitted the subject of grand strategy, feeling that he would probably not care to discuss it.

He answered that this question was more important than the original twelve put together, and went on to say that he had come here to help plan grand strategy, and had found none. Then the General left, and Dr. Ho, the interpreter, said I could use everything the General had said, including the reference to grand strategy.

"He said it. It's true. You can use it," he said.

The United Press called up the Chinese Military Mission, confirmed the interview, and put out a condensed version which appeared in the *Washington Daily News* two days after we had it. The *News*, a Scripps-Howard sheet, played it under a three-column head.

Phelps said that a number of the boys mentioned the story at the luncheon of the Overseas Writers at which Henry Grady spoke. They seemed a little sore that they had been scooped on a story that any of them could have had for the asking—only they never thought to ask.

Regards

PS—Molotov has left the United States. He went to Hyde Park with FDR in the middle of the week, and left from there last Friday.

COMMANDER SMITH ADMITS PEARL HARBOR DAMAGE UNDERSTATED

CONFIDENTIAL

Saturday
20 June 1942

Dear Bart,

The Willkie dinner was one of the most interesting, as well as one of the most depressing, occasions I have known in Washington. Most of the information came, not from Willkie, but from Commander Paul Smith of the Navy Press Service. Paul is in civilian life managing editor of the *San Francisco Chronicle*, and was one of Willkie's chief advisers in the 1940 campaign.

We got talking with Smith about the naval situation. He went into the Stanley Johnson situation at length and in detail.* The report I mailed you yesterday is substantially correct, except that no naval officer has been arrested as yet in connection with the story. Two things must be added: 1) The officer responsible for allowing Johnson to go there will be shot by a firing squad for betraying his country in time of war. Or so Smith says on

---

*One of the Navy's most zealously guarded secrets was that its cryptographers had cracked the Japanese Navy's code. The victory at Midway, in all probability, would have been impossible without the information this piece of detective work provided. Then, a few days after the battle, Stanley Johnson of the *Chicago Tribune* came out with a front page story that the Navy had known in advance what the Japanese had in mind. The story contained Admiral Nimitz's covering letter and, verbatim, the Japanese order of battle.

Johnson was aboard the *Lexington* during the Coral Sea battle, and one of its officers had given him access to the documents. The officer was identified but not shot. Instead, he was punished by being blacklisted for promotion and resigned his commission in 1944. As for Johnson and the Trib, they were obviously in violation of the censorship code, but to try either or both would have meant going public and emphasizing that the Jap code had been cracked. And as it happened Navy fears turned out to be groundless, the Japanese did not change their code; that oversight cost Admiral Yamamoto his life some time later.

the basis of what the admirals have told him. 2) In addition to cracking our code and revealing to the Japanese that we'd cracked theirs, the story revealed to the Japanese our source of information within the Japanese Navy.

Now, about Pearl Harbor. I sent you a report on that some time ago—in January, to be exact. That report too was substantially correct except that the damage was understated. Of the seven capital ships in Pearl Harbor, five were sunk outright. All but *Arizona* have been raised and towed to the Pacific Coast for repairs. It will take from ten to eighteen months from right now to get them back into service. *California* had a hole blown in her side nearly as big as the *Sun* clubroom.

As for the reasons for secrecy, all the ships but *Oklahoma* sank on an even keel, and hasty pictures taken from the air while under antiaircraft fire made it appear as though they had not been hit at all. Naval Intelligence knows this because it got hold of Japanese propaganda movies shown to diplomats in South America. The Jap account was way off. They had no idea how much damage they'd really done, since their movies didn't show it. They wouldn't have known about *Arizona* if the Navy hadn't made a slip in announcing that Admiral Kidd had been killed. Twenty-four hours after that announcement *Arizona* was claimed by the Japs, who knew his flag was in that battleship.

Now, the Japs were forced to make their plans on the assumption that the damage they had done was considerably less than was actually the case. To tell the full story might have made a hell of a lot of difference to Hawaii, Midway, etc. However, the fact remains that Roosevelt lied to Willkie, full face and with a voluntary observation not evoked by a question from Willkie. He told Willkie only three battleships had been hit, and that one of them was already back in service. Willkie told me that himself a week or so after Pearl Harbor, and I so reported to you at the time.

Smith was asked why the sinking of a Japanese submarine in Pearl Harbor fifty-five minutes before the air attack did not put the defenders on the alert. The answer is astounding: they'd been fighting Japanese submarines there for the past four weeks, and just one more didn't seem anything to make a fuss about.

Another angle: Smith said Hu Shih, the Chinese Ambassador, was the last person to talk with Roosevelt before the news of Pearl Harbor was received. Roosevelt showed Dr. Hu a copy of his message to the Mikado, read it over with interpolations and comments, asked Dr. Hu to communicate its contents to his government, and added that if he had not received a reply from the Mikado within twenty-four hours he would tell the world the whole story of the Kurusu-Nomura negotiations.

FDR added that he did not feel easy about the Japanese negotiations, that he just didn't feel anything would come of them. In his opinion, it was probable that within a few weeks the Japanese would strike at Malaya, that it was possible they might strike at the Dutch East Indies, and that it was not beyond the bounds of possibility that they might strike at the Philippines. He did not mention Pearl Harbor. Dr. Hu told this story to Smith afterward.

There is quite a fight on in the Navy over Admiral King. He has many enemies who say he is a narrow-minded man who holds his place by telling FDR he is a great naval strategist, but that he lacks a grasp of the naval picture. I know something about King, and in my opinion he is the ablest officer in the whole Navy. I mention this so you'll have the background if you hear stories running down King. Don't believe 'em. King is all right.

As for Knox, he has been pretty effectively muzzled. You will note that he hasn't had a press conference in a long time, and that wasn't by chance. They planned it that way. He has been very unfortunate in his statements about the submarine situation, especially in his predictions that it would be under control by May 15, by June 15, by July 15. It won't.

The Navy is reporting only those sinkings in which the arrival of survivors on shore gets the story in circulation. Here are the facts: the Navy has reported the sinking of something like 270 merchant vessels. Actually, since the first of January, the Germans have sunk 700 merchant vessels, with a tonnage of about 8,000,000 tons. Yesterday they sank ten. Losses in May came to more than a million tons of shipping, and June will be no better. This in a zone of approximately 400 miles from Hatteras to Miami. The Navy's charts show that the Germans have about seventy-five submarines operating in these waters.

There is no evidence of a secret base, but it is known that submarines land people on our shores. For instance, recently a Coast Guard patrol of eight men was on duty on a Long Island beach. A submarine landed a number of people and a gun fight ensued in which six of the eight Guardsmen were killed as were seven of those landed. It is believed that three or four other Germans got away. Those killed were dressed in civilian clothes and had with them a number of thermite pencils—incendiary devices of small size but considerable effectiveness. If such landings can happen once, they can happen again.

In connection with this the FBI and ONI [Office of Naval Intelligence] expect a wave of sabotage in this country, breaking out of a clear sky when the proper time comes. However, the FBI believes it has got things pretty well under control. I hope they're right.

The Germans have come up with a new weapon, which the Navy calls an acoustical-magnetic mine. This mine renders useless the deGaussing equipment that has hitherto defeated the magnetic mine, because the new ones are exploded by sound vibrations emitted by a ship's propeller when they reach a certain volume. Such mines were responsible for the recent sinkings off the Virginia beaches which were announced by the Navy.

Now, as to the German submarines, of which 32, or better than one a day, were completed by the Nazis in May (our own production has been about forty a year, but is of course being stepped up). They are miles ahead of ours. U.S. destroyers recently captured one, catching it on the surface and shooting off its conning tower so it couldn't submerge. They captured another in anti-submarine nets at Hampton Roads. This has enabled them to study the German subs in detail. Several subs have appeared in Hampton Roads, the most recent last night.

They have a skin 1⅜ inches thick as against a maximum hull thickness of ⅝ of an inch in our subs. They can operate at 600 feet below the surface, and the safety factor is not strained until they get down to 750 feet. Ours have an operational depth of 250 feet and the safety factor comes in at about 350. Theirs can dive from the surface to 200 feet in 20 seconds. Ours can dive to 80 feet in one minute. They have sound locating apparatus so they can fire their torpedoes accurately without coming to the surface.

Obviously our depth charges in most cases have been ineffective. It is estimated that in the whole war we have sunk only some ten U-boats—as against published figures running as high as twenty-eight. Our modern destroyers can kill any sub they can track until they get into a good position. But we are using such craft to guard ocean convoys, and they usually can't spare the time to follow the tracks to a conclusion. They know there are more subs ahead that have to be fought off.

Our Atlantic convoy has been excellent, although we've lost quite a lot in the Arctic Ocean en route to Russia. I am informed that our most recent convoy went through very well there, loosing only seven ships out of thirty-five. They figured on losing seventeen on a factor of calculated risk. You know you're going to lose something, but you've got to take that loss in order to get the job done.

But there simply isn't the stuff available to patrol coastal shipping adequately. The Civilian Air Patrol is essentially a political gesture—or the result of political pressure, let's say. The planes can operate only in daylight. They can carry only a single 100 pound bomb. They are frequently in trouble and are, as a matter of fact, more trouble than they're worth.

The same is true of small yachts on patrol. They can't carry enough fire power to bother a sub. And the subs sink them by ramming them with their conning towers. Don't even waste shells on them. Even if the yacht has time to give the alarm, the sub is out of reach by the time help can arrive. Anyway, the problem is not to locate the subs. The Navy knows where they are from day to day within fairish limits of accuracy. The problem is to get the stuff with which to attack them. Blimps are effective because they have radar and carry depth charges. Also PT boats are being equipped with depth charge racks, and should help out quite a lot.

But the fact remains that the Germans are sinking our ships roughly twice as fast we can build them on a tonnage basis. This situation will definitely improve, due both to additional defense facilities and additional yards. But control of the submarine threat is not yet in sight.

To assess the difficulties, make this comparison: in the First World War Germany came within a hair of winning by unrestricted submarine warfare. Yet she was restricted to Kiel and other Baltic ports, and had to run through the Kattegat and the Skagerrak to get to the open sea. The subs had to face the menace of great submarine nets and mine fields. Opposed to them were the combined British, French and Italian navies. There was no war in the Pacific and Japan was on our side.

Today the American and British navies are doing the job alone. The Germans have bases from the tip of Norway down to Portugal. They have a third more submarines. The Italian Navy is aiding them. Britain and the United States have to fight in both the Atlantic and the Pacific. We have to protect a supply line of 3,000 miles to Britain, another of 5,000 miles to Russia and another of 10,000 miles to Australia. It's no picayune problem, and I'm afraid I've been much too optimistic about this war. We're going to win, all right, but we're not winning now and it is going to be tough.

Japanese submarines, approximately as good as the German, have been the big surprise of the war. It was thought they'd be excellently handled, but they aren't. The Jap sub crews are not very good, it seems. They don't carry through their attacks.

Our own submarines have done a magnificent job in the Pacific with comparatively small losses—ten. But you won't read any more about it at the request of sub commanders. They have found that every report of their exploits has led to greatly increased defensive measures by the Japs, making their job much more difficult. In a way this is too bad. For example, one of our subs recently torpedoed a 14,000 ton transport crammed to the gunnels with Jap soldiers. The sea was covered with their bodies. And then, when it surfaced, it found itself right next to two big Japanese I-boats—their long range subs. There ensued a surface artillery duel and our sub sank both of the Japs. A hell of a story, but not for publication.

Incidentally, we now know how the Japs transport their little two-man subs. They are bolted to the I boats. When the proper time comes, the crew goes aboard, unscrews the bolts, and goes off on its suicide mission. This was discovered at Sydney, Australia after recent raids there.

I think that covers the situation. I may have forgotten something—no notes could be taken, of course—but I don't think I've left out anything of importance.

I feel I must stress again the extremely confidential nature of this memorandum. I suggest that no one but Mr. Speed [Executive Editor of The *Sun*] and yourself see it, and that it then be destroyed. It is perfectly all right for you two to have this information, but no one else.

Regards

ADMIRAL CUNNINGHAM ASSESSES ALLIED-AXIS BALANCE OF POWER

CONFIDENTIAL

Friday
24 July 1942

Dear Mr. Speed,

I have acquired off-the-record data bearing on several subjects in the past few days. Most of it deals with various aspects of the naval situation.

1) The story of how a German submarine was destroyed in the vicinity of the Panama Canal. American planes spotted a place in shallow water in the Caribbean used by U-boats as a resting place. They would come in and lie on the bottom until it was time to put to sea again. The American command promptly declared this spot a U-boat sanctuary, giving strict orders that it was not to be bombed. Shortly thereafter an American submarine came into the sanctuary and came to rest on the bottom. After a while a German sub came in, and dropped to the bottom for a rest. The American submarine let loose a torpedo and blew the U-boat apart. I don't know whether they've done it more than once.

2) Admiral Sir Andrew Browne Cunningham of the British Navy spoke at the Overseas Writers luncheon a few days ago. He analyzed the fighting on four big fronts: Atlantic, Pacific and Indian Oceans and the Mediterranean. He said little about the Pacific, since that is mostly our baby, but did point out that the Japanese raid on Pearl Harbor completely upset the balance of naval power in that area, and profoundly affected subsequent events around Malaya, Singapore, etc. He conceded that the Coral Sea and Midway [battles] had done a good deal to redress the balance. But of course the harm had already been done in the Far East.

As for the Indian Ocean, he feels the British have this pretty well under control except for occasional commerce raiders. In the Mediterranean, however, the British, who had managed to hold control for a long time, lost it when Greece and Crete fell, since this completed a ring of Axis air bases around the central area.

He spoke quite highly of the Italian Navy, expressed the opinion that much of the damage done to its vessels by the British has been repaired, and added that it is possible that at least one Italian battleship has been added to the fleet, she having been unfinished when the war broke out.

He pointed out that loss of control of the Mediterranean had made it possible for Rommel to get supplies, with the results we have seen in Egypt. However, he denied that the British fleet has fled the Mediterranean. It is still fighting there. Finally, he said the British would never let the French ships at Alexandria fall into German hands intact. They'll be destroyed or removed, whether Vichy likes it or not.

The Atlantic, of course, he named as the chief problem, and stressed the urgency of controlling the submarine menace. He believes very strongly that there should be one commander of all anti-submarine operations, air and sea, with absolute authority. By concentrating on the problem, he believes it can be remedied. That it must be handled is axiomatic. We cannot, perhaps, win the war here, but we can lose it.

Sir Andrew believes there is enough shipping available now to open a major second front in France, due chiefly to the fact that our fighter planes could establish the necessary umbrella. As to Norway, he is not so sure our fighters can reach there.

It was clear that Sir Andrew doesn't think the Allies are handling the submarine question very well. He could be right.

3) Captain Miles Browning, aide to Admiral Halsey, whose carrier group in the Far Pacific raided Wake, the Marshall and Gilbert Islands, and, under Admiral Spruance won the battle of Midway, spoke at the Navy's off-the-record conference last Wednesday. Some of his observations were in contrast to what we heard the week before, and I put more faith in this fellow because he's been there himself.

He thinks we have gone overboard on the Zero fighter, that its novelty has given it a higher rating than it should have, and that anybody could have as fast and maneuverable a plane as the Zero if willing to sacrifice armor and self-sealing fuel tanks. He said it is very easy to set them on fire, or to shoot them down, and that their own weapons are too light.

He spoke interestingly of the Battle of Midway, in which the Japs had certainly four, probably five and possibly six carriers, against three of ours. They lost four carriers, while we had only one carrier hit, and didn't lose her. The great disparity in loss, he said, was due to the fact that the Jap carriers had committed their planes to an attack on Midway Island, while ours went after the Japanese carriers. The result was that the Jap ships had no planes with which to defend themselves. This makes sense, and is an explanation I've been looking for.

Furthermore, he takes the position that it was the Navy dive-bombers and torpedo planes that did the damage, and that the Army's high-altitude bombing was ineffective. This, of course, is a highly controversial subject. However, for what it is worth Browning said that high altitude bombing against ships is useless, as any vessel that is at all fast can maneuver to avoid such bombs.

The dive bomber, and the torpedo plane, which work in close, are in his opinion the planes that do the damage in naval warfare, using team tactics. They pay a high price, of course, but if you can sacrifice fifteen planes to sink a carrier—which means the end for the carrier's planes, pilots and crews, too—it is a good trade.

Browning feels that the carriers are supremely useful. Land-based aviation has great advantages, but the carrier on its side has mobility. It can boot off its planes and then run away, whereas the landing field is fixed. However, he did say that bombing of land fields is ineffective, since the holes can be filled quickly.

Incidentally, he said that when the Japanese attacked Midway they were careful not to bomb runways, obviously intending to take over the fields and use them once the island was taken. It is known—I don't know how—that the Japs had heavy bombers on Wake Island, all ready to fly to Midway and establish themselves. This little game didn't work.

As for our chances of attacking the Japs, Browning pointed out that we were two years behind the Japs when they attacked us, and that it takes time for us to get ready. Even if we've made up a quarter of the lost time, we still wouldn't be ready to go for another year, according to what he said.

When the time does come, it'll be tough going, for the Japanese Islands form an interlocking defense in depth of about 2,000 miles. If we attack and occupy an island on the outer perimeter, there are other islands within flying distance from which the Japs can launch counterattacks. Which indicates to me that when the drive comes, it'll be up from Australia rather than out from Pearl Harbor.

4) Tom Stokes has been writing a series for Scripps-Howard on nightly thousand-plane raids on Germany. It is a swell idea, but Phelps talked to Howard Mingoes of the Aeronautical Chamber of Commerce, who came up with the following figures:

A thousand bombers, assuming a quarter of them were four-engined and the others two-engined jobs, would make a total of 2,500 engines, in horsepower ranging from 1,500 to 2,000. The horsepower required for takeoff is about 1,500, and for cruising about half that, or 750.

This would mean a total of 1,875,000 horsepower for the thousand planes. Now, a gallon of gas weighs seven pounds, and one of these engines burns .45 pounds of fuel per horsepower per hour, or about half a pound per hour for each unit of horsepower. This would make a total of 843,750 pounds per hour for 2,500 engines, or 120,521 gallons per hour. A raid takes about ten hours, so the total gasoline used would be 1,205,210 gallons per raid. This is the equal of 21,913 barrels per raid, or about half of our total daily production of gasoline as of January 1 last. (This last figure is highly secret, by the way.)

England is not an oil producer. The fuel must be taken in. I don't know how great a burden it would be to carry in 21,913 barrels a day, which is what it would amount to. But it would be quite a chore, and it wouldn't be enough anyway, for other aircraft must be available to defend the British Isles at all times, and in quantity. And there are other areas.

I'm not saying it can't be done. I'm merely trying to indicate the magnitude of the problem. I believe we have the planes now with which to do the job. But the question of air fields, organization and coordination, supplies etc. are tremendous. It would take 6,000 men in the air and 60,000 on the ground to do the job at the start, not counting attrition, which might reach 10 percent per raid. Ten percent is supposed to be the top figure that could be stood over the long pull.

I hear we've been planning to put on such raids next spring. Apparently pressure is being applied to do it now. However, I think Stokes' articles, which raise the possibility of nightly thousand-plane raids on Germany, at this time, can too easily lead the American people to think there is a quick and relatively painless way to win this war, giving rise to an erroneous and perilous psychology. It isn't going to happen that way.

Regards

DEFEAT IN THE PHILIPPINES

CONFIDENTIAL

Thursday
30 July 1942

Dear Bart,

Some good news to start off with. Admiral King told Nelie Bull a couple of days ago that the Navy is getting the edge on the submarines. If such word came from Knox, I'd ignore it, but King is strictly a non-nonsense guy, and you can tie to what he says.

He says it looks to him like a long war, and that the Navy could use a lot more tools than it has now. But they're doing the best they can with what they have. And the submarine menace is gradually being brought under control. This is in some degree due to the fact that more boats with which to do the job are available all the time.

As I wrote before, the Navy has pretty good information as to where the German subs are, and as it gets the vessels with which to cash in on this information, the lot of the U-boats is destined to become increasingly hard.

The speaker at yesterday's off-the-record Navy conference was Colonel William Clements of the Marines. He was on Admiral Hart's staff in the Philippines, just got back, and was decorated in a big show at Marine Barracks a couple of weeks ago. He is just as good a talker as he is a fighter, which is tops.

He said the first word of the attack on Pearl Harbor came to Manila at about 2:30 A.M. on December 8th. He, Clements, got the first news, since he was sleeping in the Navy office. He called Admiral Hart and General

Sutherland, MacArthur's Chief of Staff, at once.

It was not until 9 A.M. that the first Jap bombers came over, and at that time just two bombs were dropped, at Baguio, where there is an officers' school. Little damage was done. It was not until noon that bombers hit Clark Field, playing hob with our planes, which were on the ground.

Later he was asked how come the Army's planes were caught this way, ten hours after they knew about Pearl Harbor and despite the fact that radar equipment was available to spot incoming planes. He said he didn't know, except that perhaps the Army felt it had to wait for a formal declaration of war.

Japanese planes struck at Cavite, too, and taking advantage of the densely packed nature of this base, wrecked it in a short time.

MacArthur had an army of about 100,000 Filipinos, some of them with six months' training, many with only a couple of weeks, and lacking uniforms and other necessary equipment, Clements' frank opinion was that this army was not much good. On the other hand, he said that the Philippine Scouts, a part of the American Army, were red hot fighting men, as good as they come.

MacArthur's first intention had been to resist invasion at the beaches, but later he decided against it, and concentrated on more tightly knit lines. This Clements approved, saying he believed MacArthur would have lost his entire army in a few days had he stuck to his original plan.

There were some 1,200 Marines available, and these were offered to MacArthur. It was first planned to brigade them with two regiments of Philippine Scouts, but this was never done. Then they were detailed to guard MacArthur's headquarters, a stunt in which the Marines weren't much interested. Finally they were given command of the beaches of Corregidor, Fort Drum, and the other island forts in Manila Bay, guarding them all against invasion.

In the meantime, unopposed Japanese landings made it evident that Manila could not be held, and it was declared an open city. The military were directed to be out of there by Christmas, although the Japs didn't come in until 2 January. Clements felt this was wrong, arguing that all military elements need not be removed at once from a city because it had been declared open, and that a great deal of materiel that was lost could otherwise have been saved.

Anyway, the Japs kept pushing in, and MacArthur finally moved to Corregidor and Bataan. A defense line was established across the point. In the center was tough, mountainous country which was left unprotected because it was thought that it was too tough to be used by either side. The Japs, however, dragged their guns up trails by hand, and carried ammunition by hand. They cut loose with an attack at the undefended center.

At the same time a small Jap force landed behind the American lines at Bataan and established a road block on the only road on the peninsula. It runs along the shore around the whole point. This cut the American left wing off from supplies for two days and, coupled with the center attack, forced the whole line back to new positions.

The Japs moved in behind them with landing attacks, putting 1,000 men ashore at Olangopo and 200 at Marivales. These constituted serious threats to the American lines, but ultmately both Japanese forces were eliminated. There is a hell of a story in the fight at Marivales. The 200 Japs chased American patrols off a strategic hill. An American Navy commander got together a force of about 350 men. They included some Marines, some sailors, boilermakers, sailmakers, civilians who had never handled rifles and who wore shorts and Navy caps. They chased the Japs back off the hill, and then followed them into a hell of a dog-fight. Reinforcements finally came up, and they killed the Japs to the last man.

The Japs had buried field guns in the sand on a point of land which had been lived on by a Japanese for seventeen years. The guns had been sneaked in some time before the war started, and were carefully wrapped in heavily oiled cloth. With them were firing and aiming devices, and caches of ammunition. We captured one of these guns when it was half dug out of the sand.

At Olangopo the Japs had lots of rock caves in which to hide, and it was found that the only way to get them out was to kill them. If wounded, they kept right on fighting. And they were tricky. They'd come out, arms upraised, announcing their surrender in English. When our people came up to take them, it would turn out that they had a grenade in each upraised hand. They'd lob them at the Americans. Or they'd have comrades hidden with rifles, to kill our men who came up to receive the surrender.

Actually, we took only fifty-two prisoners in all the fighting on Bataan. Twenty-seven of these were wounded. The wounded men were cooperative, and insisted upon being allowed to roll bandages and otherwise make themselves useful. The uninjured were less friendly. None wanted to return to Japan, the reason being that in the Jap Army a man missing is accounted dead, and the government pays a bounty to his family. For him to return to Japan after that would be a disgrace to him and his family. Clements said that as far as he knew Americans taken prisoner by the Japs were treated according to the rules of war.

The Japs attempted to supply their men at Olangopo by parachute, and our side picked up many of their drops. One contained an order congratulating the Japanese troops on their fight, and directing them to keep it up as long as possible. When no longer able to offer effective resistance, they were directed to go out into the water and swim some 17 miles to the Jap force. Pictures and graphs were given showing how the currents ran so that men could work their way by water from point to point. We picked up some of them actually trying to do this.

In the meantime the Japs, after a period of some quiet on the main front, got aggressive again. They found another weak point in the center of the line, and finally hammered through to break the front. The American and Filipino troops were by then too exhausted to offer effective resistance, and Wainwright's surrender followed.

Before this, the Japs used their planes a lot against Corregidor. They ran into superb anti-aircraft fire, and their enthusiasm for raiding cooled quickly. A squadron of nine planes would start with an early morning raid. Several would be knocked down. The others would return, and keep it up until only two or three Japs were left. They were aided in these bombing raids by numerous Japanese sympathizers who signaled by pocket mirrors, radio, etc., the location of strategic objectives. They caught one Jap using a radio to direct planes right into a naval installation. His case was not appealed to the Supreme Court. He was shot right then and there.

When Clements was ordered out, he made his escape by submarine and thence by slow stages back here.

He talked quite a bit about the Japanese soldier, beginning with the statement that he did not feel we had much to fear from him. He is tricky, but he is a poor shot and not very good with a bayonet. However, in jungle fighting he can see and hear things the white man can't.

Each Jap soldier is equipped with camouflage gear. He has inch-square mesh on his helmet, plus bundles of different colored grass about four inches long. He ties these into the mesh to conceal himself. He has a 6-foot square piece of cloth to throw over himself to blend into the scenery. He is adept at concealing himself. And when using natural camouflage, he does it right. If he intends to use a clump of bushes, he doesn't barge right into it. He'll tunnel for 30 or 40 feet, and come up into the clump, so there is no trail to be seen from the air. Or he'll dig a fox-hole between the roots of a tree, tunnel under the tree and dig another one on the other side.

Every Jap soldier kept a diary. Practically all of them had written that they hadn't expected what they got in the Philippines. They'd been told the Filipinos would join them, that they were hungry and poor. The Japs wrote that they were fed up with the fighting in the Philippines and would like to go home. But these same soldiers carried out orders to such an extent that they could be stopped only by killing them.

The Japs on Bataan were pretty well educated, and most of them spoke English. They'd jabber in English at night, luring our boys within shooting range. Then, bingo! And the Japs were good at infiltration, getting through and behind our lines. At night—and Clements said the best fighting men are afraid when they can't see—the Japs would set off firecrackers, yell, and shoot their guns whether there were targets or not, just to spread confusion. It worked well among the untrained Filipino troops. Trained troops got used to it, but never got to like it.

Each Jap soldier carries rations for eight days in a wicker basket about ten inches by four by two inches. It includes a lot of beaten biscuits, concentrated chocolate, squares of dried fish, etc., plus a bag of rice. Clements said it was excellent food, that our men would take it from dead Japs in preference to their own limited rations.

In addition, each carried a medical kit, which included disinfectants, powder for snake-bite, etc. Each soldier carried a tube about a foot long with a bell at one end. This bell was removable and a wad of medicated cotton was inserted. Then the bell was replaced, and the soldier could stick the tube into any water, dirty, foul or what have you, and drink in safety, since the cotton decontaminated the liquid.

Snipers carried a length of rope, and used it to get into trees. They'd stay in the trees, perfectly invisible, for three or four days, and not start shooting until the proper time on their schedule.

Clements believes, however, that one well-trained American soldier is the equal of five Japanese soldiers in anything but jungle fighting. He told of a Philippine scout, a fellow about 4½ feet tall, limping along a path. Clements asked him what the trouble was. He said five Japs rushed him. He shot four, but the fifth got in with his bayonet, and knocked the scout down. The scout regained his feet and shot the last Jap, but turned his ankle while doing it.

The Japs, Clements said, had a healthy respect for the Garand rifle, believing that all Americans were equipped with automatic rifles. Their scouts use .22 calibre rifles. The leader will have one on his back, and if he sees a target he bends forward, while the man behind him aims and pulls the trigger. They have heavier rifles, too, of course, and the usual artillery. They prefer to fire in short, rapid bursts, not being very good shots. The Americans and Filipinos, Clements said, are dead shots, and he found Japanese who had joined their ancestors via a single bullet through the helmet.

In Clements' opinion, the Japs never had more than 50,000 men on Luzon Island, and most of the engagements involved small forces in tangled jungle, at very close range. He believes that when any sizeable well-trained force of Western troops comes to grips with the Japs in anything but jungle country, the troop can handle them. Unfortunately, most of the fighting in Malaya, the East Indies, the Philippines or in Burma has been jungle warfare.

The Americans had no more than 10,000 or 12,000 trained troops on Luzon. The rest were raw Filipinos, two divisions of whom went over the hill in the last stages of the Bataan fight. He didn't blame them. They'd been on half rations since 1 January. More than that, they had believed firmly that relief would come, although the white troops knew it wouldn't. The Filipinos believed the American Navy would steam into Manila Bay, and would bring plenty of air support in six weeks. When it didn't come, they realized it wasn't going to come at all, and presumably figured there wasn't any percentage in holding out a month more when it wouldn't alter the ultimate result.

That's about all I can remember of what he said, except that the Japs bombarded them with propaganda, printed and radio, with surrender tickets bearing pictures of glamorous-looking white girls. When MacArthur left, the propaganda was that the General couldn't take it, so why not give up?

Oh yes, here is something else. Captain Lovett of the Navy P.I.O. [Public Information Office] told Phelps that the convoy to Murmansk, of which the Germans claimed to have sunk 35 of 38, took a bad pounding, more than 20 ships being knocked out. They were mostly British ships, for there were only five Americans among the 1,200 survivors of sunken ships. The others were British.

Elsewhere I have heard that convoys to Murmansk have been discontinued altogether. Too risky. That is, too much loss to warrant the effort. I do not have this officially.

You'd better tear this up after you and Mr. Speed have read it.

Regards

CONFIDENTIAL

Friday
7 August 1942

Dear Bart,

Here are three late specials I just acquired. All are from official sources.

1) The carrier *Yorktown*, reported by the Navy as damaged in the Battle of Midway, never reached port. She was torpedoed at sea by the Japanese.

2) The Murmansk line of supply has definitely been cut, as I reported unofficially a memo or so ago. Land-based aircraft and submarines operating from northern Norway, coupled with the presence of the ice pack to the north which prevents convoys from getting out of range, have made the passage impossible despite heavy escort. This means that if the German drive in the Caucasus cuts the line of supply from Basra, Russia is cut off from the Allies, since Japan blocks the approach by Siberia. It also gives me the idea that a second front may be opened in northern Norway, the purpose being to drive the Germans out and make possible the reopening of the Murmansk-Archangel line.

3) When the Japs raided Dutch Harbor recently, we had few men and no radar equipment up there. Both were in transit. They have now arrived. We have 50,000 men with full equipment in Alaska, and the Army believes this will be enough to hold it. At present, at least, no effort to drive the Japs out of Kiska, Attu and Agattu is contemplated.

Regards

Friday
21 August 1942

Dear Bart,

This will be my last memo before going on vacation. I expect to resume them on my return, of course. In the meantime, I thought I'd clean up a few odds and ends of information that have accumulated. Most of them relate to the Navy.

Here is some data about detecting devices. First, of course, is the sound detector for underwater use. This device projects sound waves through the water. They bounce off any object in their way, and are refracted to the detector, thus enabling the operator to tell the distance and compass bearing of the object. They call it "pinging," and a weakness is that it will work on fish, wreckage or what have you as well as on a submarine. A skilled operator can usually tell if he is pinging on metal, however. Another weakness is that the pings can be heard by the submarine, which has at least as good a detector as has the surface ship, and it can therefore take evading action. The sound devices on submarines are good enough so that torpedoes can be fired without using the periscope.

Next, there is radar, which cannot be used below the surface (although I've been told the British have found a way to do it). The principle is the same as the water detector, except that radio waves are projected. They bounce back in exactly the same way, but register on a plate instead of pinging.

I hear, too, that we've got another one in process of development, utilizing the principle of the electric eye, which can, in fog, darkness, rain, snow, and at great distances, reproduce on a plate the distance and bearing of an entire fleet of ships. The advantages of such a device in the Aleutians, where there is almost perpetual fog, is of course obvious. On dark nights, too. I hope it works out, and I'm told on good authority it does.

As for submarines, the long-shore convoys have proven very satisfactory. In the two months from May 15 (I think that is the date when convoying started in this area) to the middle of July, we took more than 1,100 ships in convoys between New York and the Virginia Capes. We lost just two—one of them to a mine—which is remarkable.

There is an estimate at the Navy Department that the Germans are using about 120 submarines—or more properly they are keeping that many at sea—in the Battle of the Atlantic, forty on station off our coast, forty on the way to station, and forty on their way home. It is possible that they are being refueled and re-equipped on this side, but no real evidence supporting that belief has been turned up. I am told that in the modern submarine, shortage of torpedoes is much more frequently the reason for leaving station than shortage of fuel.

You have probably heard that the Germans have a device for using their diesel engines below the surface, saving use of their storage batteries. Our

Navy says it has no information whatever to support this rumor.*

Here is an unrelated fact: our Army now has machine guns that can shoot at the rate of 2,000 bullets a minute. You can't hear any individual reports, just a continuous roar.

A funny thing happened the other day. I had, as you know, written an appraisal of the Solomons show, and I got a letter a morning or so later taking me to task. It started by saying it was evident from my story that I had assumed the Americans won the battles of the Coral Sea and Midway, whereas the truth was we got our ears beaten off. He went on to give all the Japanese claims, accepting them at face value, and went on to say that we had no chance of winning this war, and that the smart thing, as a naval officer, was for us to quit. It was signed something like Tomaso Dunnanzio, Captain, Royal Italian Navy.

I don't know if it was genuine or not. Somebody might have been ribbing me. If they are, they may regret it, as I gave the letter to the F.B.I. on the chance that it might be genuine. They were very pleased to get it, and are working on it. If it was the real thing—and I believe it was, since it doesn't seem like a very funny piece of ribbing, certainly not suitable in times like these—it might lead to something interesting.

It was not a crackpot letter. The man who wrote it knew something about the sea; he also knew something about drawing deductions.

Here's one for the book! I just had a call from McGuire at the F.B.I. saying they are going to town on this letter. They emphatically do not think it is a joke. As a matter of fact, it fits into a pattern of some other communications they have picked up. They hope ultimately to identify the fellow. When and if they get him . . . well, sedition is an ugly word, as the cigar ad didn't used to say.

Regards

SECRETARY KNOX REPORTS ON SUB AND AIR WAR

CONFIDENTIAL

Friday
21 August 1942

Dear Bart,

In company with five other newspapermen I had dinner last night with Secretary Knox aboard his yacht *Sequoia*. In the expectation that the

---

*The device, called Snorkel, was real and the Germans did have it. Whether the Navy knew this is not known to me.

rambling three-hour conversation we had together may interest you I am sending what seemed to me to be the highlights.

Sinkings. During the first ten days of August German submarines failed to sink any vessels along that section of the North American coastline for the protection of which the American Navy is exclusively responsible. Knox was careful to point out that this did not mean that we had licked the German submarine, but that it did indicate that we had licked it in this area, making it too hot for them to stay and driving them to other fields of operation.

He attributes our success to a number of factors, foremost among which is the submarine chaser. It is futile, he said, to try to fight a submarine with any ship other than one specifically designed for that purpose. The production of sub chasers was slow, and he designated an assistant as "expediter" to go to all the ship yards where sub chasers were being built to find the sources of delay and to secure for the ship builders concerned immediate delivery of material and parts needed in the completion of the work.

I believe Glen has probably written you what he learned through a friend of Admiral King of the manner in which blimps were operating close to the surface of the water and towing microphones under the water through which they could detect the presence of submarines without in turn making their own presence known to the U-boats. I asked Knox about this last night, and while he did not deny it, he said he had not heard of it.

Glen's source of information is so reliable that I am inclined to think Knox merely preferred to be cagey about it. He did say that blimps were proving an effective weapon for the spotting of submarines in areas where they were not exposed to anti-aircraft fire or fighter plane attack. He considers, however, that the only answer to submarine warfare of the type the Germans have been pursuing so successfully is to be found in the operation of well-protected convoys, and in this connection he pointed out an oversight that has been extremely costly to America to date: namely, the failure to design a navy properly integrated with the American merchant marine. He argues that since convoys alone provide adequate protection, the Navy should build convoy ships of appropriate design coincident with the construction of all new merchant ships. Thus, for example, he suggests that in the future it will be well to build an escort ship for each five or six merchant ships that come off the ways. Apparently this is to be our policy henceforth.

I asked him also about reports that I have had from a dozen supposedly well-informed sources to the effect that the Germans had discovered, and were using, a new kind of steel so hard that a plate half the thickness of ours provides equal protection and weighs only half as much. He denied this flatly, saying that the Germans were using exactly the same steel that we are, but are using a thicker protective coat than we have in our older submarines. Our new submarines, he declared emphatically, were the best in the world, and when the records of their achievements can be published, he said, the fact will be undeniably demonstrated.

He noted in confirmation of that statement the experience of *Nautilus*, which surfaced squarely in the middle of the Japanese fleet and saw a burning aircraft carrier dead ahead. *Nautilus* fired three fish into the carrier, destroying it, and then ducked with the entire Japanese fleet on top of it. The Japs dropped fifty-four depth charges around it, despite which *Nautilus* returned safely to port to tell the story.

He pooh-poohs Simon Lake's propaganda for cargo submarines, interposing these objections to them:

1) A submarine of the necessary size could proceed at a rate of speed of not more than 2 knots across the Atlantic,
2) It could not be adequately armed nor made sufficiently maneuverable,
3) It could not be equipped to dive to depths necessary for its protection and
4) It would therefore be at the mercy of enemy craft which with modern detecting devices could apprehend it readily.

He has little more faith in the present wave of cargo plane proposals. He said that he had dined night before last on his yacht with Alexander de Seversky, who had been enthusiastic about the cargo plane idea. Knox pointed out to him that the B-19-B—the Army's air leviathan—is impractical for cargo use because it takes a runaway two miles long to get it off the ground and needs a similar distance for a safe landing. De Seversky soared into the realms of Buck Rogers and suggested the use of rocket power in the wings to implement the take-off and cushion the landing. Knox brought him back to earth by asking: "Swell, but have you got it?" And de Seversky admitted, of course, that he did not. Obviously Knox was wholly unimpressed by de Seversky's wild dreams.

Australia. Among the newsmen present last night was Robert Sherrod, correspondent for *Time* and *Life*, who returned last week from Australia. Knox pumped him at length about conditions, and Bob opened up with unrestrained criticism of the failure of the United States to send adequate equipment in adequate quantity to that theatre of operations. Turning at once to his favorite thesis, Bob reported that among more than one hundred pilots to whom he had talked, not one had failed to say, "If they would only give us a Japanese Zero to fight in just once this war would be a pleasure." The Zero, Bob said, can fight at 33,000 feet while our own P-40s cannot fight above 16,000, nor our own P-39s above 19,000. He berated the government for its failure to equip our own fighters with superchargers that would add 10,000 feet to their fighting ceilings but would still leave the Zeros on top of them.

Knox took this criticism with good grace but remained unconvinced and began at once to "bore in" on Sherrod, as he described it. He pointed out that our pursuit planes were better armored, have pilot protection and self-sealing gas tanks, and that our pilots are trained in team fighting unknown to the Japanese. This, he argued, gives them superiority in the air even though our ships are admittedly less maneuverable and less speedy than the Zeros.

By adroit questioning he wrung several admissions from Bob that seemed to bolster up Knox's side of the case. Bob admitted that a single burst of American fire finding its mark would blast a Zero into matchwood, and that only once in all the Pacific fighting that has taken place has a Zero been brought down intact so far as we know. He admitted, too, that the Japanese pilots are not even equipped with parachutes and therefore never come back when a plane is hit, while American pilots in contrast are often saved.

In the only two instances of his own knowledge, Sherrod said, where American units had lost a number of planes, the great majority of the American pilots returned safely to their base. In one case fifteen planes were lost and eleven pilots returned, and in the second, eleven were lost and ten pilots returned.

None of our new P-47s has reached Australia. Knox observed that the production of these planes was coming along nicely. Sherrod retorted that there was a hell of a lot of difference between our production figures and the number of planes that were actually getting out in the fighting fronts in his experience.

Solomon Islands. Knox denied that we had encountered any unexpected opposition in the Solomons. We knew in advance, he said, what resources the enemy had there and what we would have to cope with. Our principal difficulty—which is still a matter of some concern in the mopping-up operations now in progress—is the fanatical refusal of the Japanese to surrender. On one island it was necessary to wipe out every Japanese. Not one would surrender.

An interesting sidelight on this was cited in the case of Guadalcanal Island, which is inhabited by a tribe of head-hunters, and which was the last place on earth where human flesh was openly offered for sale in the markets. The Japanese, when they occupied this island, continued to encourage head-hunting by the natives, thinking it would react against the British. But when our landing was effected and the Japanese themselves were driven into the brush, they rapidly fell prey to the head-hunters.

High Altitude Bombing. One thing that the Solomons battle has again demonstrated is the ineffectuality of high-altitude bombing to which General "Hap" Arnold is so strongly committed. Before the battle a squadron of our bombers reconnoitering over the area sighted an entire Japanese fleet. The surface of the sea was literally dotted with destroyers, cruisers, tenders and transports, the movement of which were easily discernible by the wake each vessel made as it zigzagged along, and pictures taken by the bombers prove all this. They also show that not one of the many bombs our planes dropped on this fleet found its mark. Knox is committed to dive bombers, which he says hit the target approximately 50 percent of the time, whereas a high level bomber is probably lucky if it scores a single hit in a hundred from 30,000 feet on a stationery target, and is completely useless on a moving target.

Torpedo planes are also extremely effective, but experience has taught that unless they are heavily supported by dive bombers and pursuit planes their mission is inevitably suicidal. Nevertheless, they are being used with increasing frequency and success, and it is largely for this reason that our consumption of torpedoes has increased approximately ten-fold since the war began. As we cruised past the Alexandria Torpedo Station on our trip down the Potomac, Knox pointed out that formerly we made only about one torpedo a week there, whereas we now make about six a day.

Australian-American Relations. One other interesting observation came from Sherrod. He reported that Americans and Australians are getting pretty thoroughly fed up with each other, particularly since the enactment of legislation increasing the pay of American soldiers to $50 a month. Australian soldiers seem to resent this bitterly, possibly because they were previously known as the highest paid soldiers in the world. Since that time six or seven Australian soldiers have set upon lone American soldiers on several occasions and beaten them badly with beer bottles or anything else that might come to hand. All of which is hardly conducive to international unity.

Best regards

Thursday
17 September 1942

I haven't any hot military dope, although I see they've announced the loss of *Yorktown* five weeks after I informed you of what happened via confidential memo.

Regards

RICKENBACKER LAUDS AIR FORCE CAPABILITY

CONFIDENTIAL

Thursday
15 October 1942

Dear Bart,

Here is what Eddie Rickenbacker had to say off the record at Stimson's press conference earlier today. Stimson explained that he had asked Rick to go abroad to look into the situation of our air forces, and to settle those "ignorant discussions" of our planes that had been indicating they were inferior. This, I should say, Rick has done. To me [his report] is most interesting, and is reproduced, in extenso and without comment of mine, as he said it.

The Ferry Command, which took him to England and back, has done a job that is simply amazing the British. There have been accidents at Botswood, but no serious accident involving the Ferry Command. This is a phenomenal record considering the number of planes that fly over daily.

In England, the American leadership in the Air Force, from generals down through squadron leaders, is amazingly good. Rick found many of his World War I colleagues on the job doing intelligence and executive work, and doing it very well. The morale of all concerned is very high. Health is excellent. The food, American rations, is very good.

The British at first were skeptical of our air technique, but events have demonstrated that the whole strategic conception of bombing by our air command has been sound. The British have now been completely won over and are very eager to obtain our equipment for their own use. Bombing results are remarkable, getting direct hits from 25,000 feet on specific targets in broad daylight while under fighter attack.

The Germans have put the heat on our bombers, and they pay no attention to our fighter planes. They will not even go up to oppose fighters, saving themselves for the bombers. This is sure indication of a shortage of fighter planes and/or pilots, and was noticed by the British in the Battle of Britain. Also, our bombers sometimes go on missions beyond the range of fighter protection, which brings them under intense fighter attack.

The battle over Lille showed how well able our bombers are to take care of themselves. The enemy lost many fighter pilots that it can ill afford to lose. The Germans are doing everything possible to conserve their fighter units, but they have to come up to attack the bombers. We sent 115 Flying Fortresses and Liberators into that scrap, and only four were lost. Of these, two crashed because of a collision, which means the Germans were able to shoot down only two. They lost about fifty of their own Focke-Wulf 190s, which with the Messerschmitt 159-Gs are their best fighter planes.

Are these figures optimistic? No. They are pessimistic and conservative. Unless there is ample proof, a plane is not credited as destroyed. A plane seen smoking and out of control is merely listed as a probable loss, or as damaged. There has to be positive evidence of the destruction of a plane for it to be so listed. The British, for their part, are astounded by our reports from the Pacific on our air victories, but they are just as conservative. Rick said he wouldn't believe them himself if he hadn't seen the actual reports and knew them to be true.

British and American bombers have not only played hob with airplane factories and other war plants, railroad junctions, etc., but have by knocking off fighter planes and pilots lessened the ability of the enemy to oppose our raids, and have also harassed the morale of the civilian population by round-the-clock bombing.

British bombers are mostly built for night use, and are not much good for daytime work because of their limited armor and limited firing power, limited speed, and limited altitude potential. Ours, which excel them in all these things (although not in bomb load) are excellent both for day and night bombing.

The English today have been won over to the theory of high-altitude precision bombing, and admit that if they had enough of our bombers they could do more damage with them than they are able to do with their night raids. They claim 50 percent hits at night—Rick considers this a highly optimistic figure—while our target bombing is about 100 percent efficient. When Rick mentions 100 percent efficiency he does not mean 100 percent hits, but 100 percent of a percentage of hits believed to be the maximum limit of practical accuracy.

The Germans have done an excellent job of camouflaging objectives and setting up decoys. They are likely to set up such decoys from ten to fifty miles from the actual objective. Here is how it works: In night bombing the difficulty of getting on the target is such that the very best navigating pilots are sent ahead to spot the target and drop incendiary bombs, so that there will be fires that the less talented pilots can spot and use to get over the place their bombs are supposed to hit. The Germans, knowing this, touch off decoy fires which sometimes lure the bombers into dropping their loads into unoccupied places where no damage whatever is done. This happens quite often, apparently.

Our daylight bombing can help out on this. Right now we have been confining our objectives to occupied France, for two reasons: one, we are seasoning our troops for combat bombing, which takes about two months; two, diplomatic relations with France are delicate and we cannot bomb indiscriminately. We have to hit at military objectives only. But when we get to the point where we are ready to do long-range bombing in daylight, we can send some planes out at night so they have the protection of darkness in getting to the objective, but do not get there until daybreak, so they can bomb in daylight. We can send others out so they will reach the objective just at sundown, and the fires they start can serve as beacons for the British bombers. They will be protected by darkness on the way home. Protected or not, however, our bombers make it extremely hazardous for any fighters that attack them.

In this connection, the British 8,000-pound bombs are really terrible on property and morale. They not only level everything in a square block, but blow out doors and windows over a radius of many, many blocks. This is tough on the nerves and also makes more work for German labor. Rick is convinced that if enough bombing can be done, the war will be shortened appreciably. In this Winston Churchill, with whom Rick talked, concurred.

Churchill told him it might shorten the war by years, or at least by months, if the supply problems could be solved so that really heavy and continuous bombing could be instituted. Incidentally, Rick finds Anglo-American relations excellent so far as the two air forces are concerned, which does not imply trouble elsewhere, but merely covers the limits of his inspection.

Contrary to his expectations, the British convinced Rick that the Germans have only about 4,700 planes for operational use (combat), of which 500 are not in use due to repairs, etc. The percentage of bombers is small. This covers the all-around situation: Western Europe, Russia, Egypt. This is a reduction of about 15 percent in the strength of the Luftwaffe, and the British swear they are not 5 percent off either way.

German plane production is lower than expected. This may show that our bombing is having results. But it may also be ominous, may mean that German plants are changing over to newer, better models. And of course the pace is so fast that to have the best planes for even a short time—thirty days or so—can make a world of difference. This means our designers have got to keep alert, and a step ahead of the enemy, as they are now.

Our bombing equipment is outstanding. This goes for heavy, medium and light bombers. The British have a wooden plane called the Mosquito which they use for "intruder missions" (sudden darts at enemy shipping, or nearby objectives, strafing, etc.) The trouble is it goes to pieces in heavy anti-aircraft fire. So the British are being more and more won over to our Douglas A-20-B, which they call the Boston. It is rugged, and able. It can absorb the flak and get home. You recall the plane that bounced off a German airfield in the course of a raid and came home on one engine. It was a Boston.

As for fighters, the British Spitfire 5-B, which saved Britain in 1940, is no longer good enough. The Spitfire 9 is equal to the Focke-Wulf 190 except that it does not accelerate as fast in a dive, and climbs slower at altitudes up to 25,000 feet, after which it is faster. (Remember my memo in which I told you the Germans outfoxed the British by turning out a plane that was better at lower altitudes. This proves that point.)

Our boys used the Spitfire, not because it was better than our fighters, but because it saved invaluable shipping space, because the British had plenty of them, and because using them saved confusion as to spare parts and repairs. Our P-38, the Lockheed Lightning, is about the same in relation to the Focke-Wulf 190 as the Spitfire 9, but its twin engines make it more reliable, and it has more range. It is a three-purpose plane, and has proved excellent for photography and reconnaissance in daylight at from 35,000 to 40,000 feet. Spitfires suffer in comparison because their cruising range is very limited.

The British and the Americans feel that the P-51, the Mustang, has shown itself to be better than any British or American plane in combat with the Focke-Wulf 190 even with the old 1150-horse Allison engine. With the new 1450 Rolls Royce engine it should be the world's best fighter beyond a doubt. We haven't very many of them overseas as yet.

And that's about all. He said in conclusion that our equipment was second to none, our personnel was without a peer, and that our theory of bombing was all right. And that adds up to a pretty impressive total.

Incidentally, it looks like really big business in the Solomons. Clark Lee, whose name you will recognize, came back recently, and he told Lyle Wilson, UP head here, that the Navy was kidding the hell out of us, that they didn't hold Tulagi at all, and only had a beachhead on Guadalcanal. I don't believe him. To withhold news is one thing, and is permissible. To distort it is something else, and I simply do not believe the Navy would be so stupid as to lose public credence that way.

Nimitz and McCain seem pretty confident, and neither is a pop-off guy. I think they know what they're talking about. And I hope my earlier information, that we set a trap for the brown brothers, proves well founded. In any event, the chances are good that this is the begining of the decisive battle of the Far Eastern war. Not that it will win it or lose it, but if we come out on top in this scrap we'll be in good shape to start moving north. And for strategic reasons, the best technique seems to be to keep on going instead of stopping to consolidate. It's going to be leap-frog ultimately.

Regards

GARDNER COWLES GIVES HIGHLIGHTS OF WILLKIE'S TOUR OF SOVIET UNION

The seeds of the off-the-record conferences with Admiral King that appear in this volume were foreshadowed in the following lengthy memorandum. Reference is to the first four paragraphs as well as to the exchange of messages between Bart and myself that follow the memorandum.

But the real meat of this memo is what Gardner Cowles, in time of peace one of the top figures in Cowles Publications, and at the time this memorandum was written an executive in the Office of War Information, told us about his trip to North Africa, Turkey, Syria and the Soviet Union with Wendell Willkie, who was sent to these countries as President Roosevelt's personal representative and observer.

Especially interesting was what the Willkie party learned in and about the Soviet Union. I was highly interested in Mr. Cowles' explanation that the mission was attempting to present the Soviet positions, and was not trying to debate the matter by presenting the British and American arguments.

I must have felt very happy about what I learned about Tulagi and Guadalcanal from two Marine colonels, for it nailed down my earlier opinion of the inaccuracy of Clark Lee's story to Wilson.

CONFIDENTIAL

Thursday
22 October 1942

Dear Bart,

A lot of material this trip. In the first place, I can tell you that the Germans have finally succeeded in sinking an American troop transport bound for England. However, I am informed that she sank so slowly that it was possible to rescue all those aboard, which is a magnificent—and most fortunate—feat. I don't know the ship's name, or details.

Second, here is the story on the way our three cruisers were sunk in the Battle of the Solomons. It was done by Japanese PT boats that sneaked in after the flares were sent up, and got torpedoes home. They pulled our own stuff on us and, I must say, did it damned well. Our boys never fired a shot, and the whole thing was over in ten minutes.

Apparently Japanese fifth columnists on the hills spotted our ships for the Japs. And the carrier *Saratoga*, sister ship of *Lexington*, was hit by one torpedo in the Solomons, but got to port safely.

Third, I am informed by those who know that the Navy is throwing a lot of curves in its communiqués. That is to say, they are holding back a number of serious losses. The idea, it seems, is that Admiral King believes the people can't take it. Losses in the Solomons, particularly, are considerably higher than any announced as yet. There is a great deal of indignation on Capitol Hill, and after the election there may be some real sounding off—also some new legislation designed to play hell with the present naval command. Whether this will come through is doubtful, but it may well be introduced if the Navy doesn't mend its ways.

Fourth, the same thing may be true of General MacArthur. I was disputing with Roscoe Drummond the superiority of our planes on the basis of MacArthur's communiqués, and Roscoe said Joe Harsch, one of the best military writers extant, had told him on his return from Australia that no one pretended the MacArthur communiqués on plane losses had any relation to the truth.

Being a simple sort of guy, who believes people in high places who say they are telling the truth ought not to kid the American people, this sort of thing is disturbing to me. Because when the people get onto the fact that they are being kidded, governmental credibility is shot for good and all.

Fifth, as Phelps has told you, Gardner Cowles, publisher of the *Des Moines Register*, the *Minneapolis Tribune*, and *Look* magazine, and now an executive in the Office of War Information, spoke off the record at the Overseas Writers Club yesterday. He had been with Willkie on his trip, and his talk was the most informative I've ever heard in Washington. He's an acute observer who knows how to tell his story once he's got it.

He explained that he was speaking for himself alone, and then turned to paying a tribute to the Liberator plane in which they made the whole trip. They didn't lose five minutes because of mechanical trouble, or weather too tough for the plane, in the entire course of the trip. There followed some light talk about Wendell, after which Cowles turned to their arrival in Egypt.

He said they were very much impressed by General Montgomery, and then told a story about Montgomery's interview with Churchill when he was given the African command. The two men had not known one another.

Montgomery announced, "I don't smoke, I don't drink, and I'm 100 percent fit."

"I smoke too much, I drink too much, and I'm 200 percent fit," countered Churchill. "That doesn't mean you're a good general."

He is a good one, and he enjoys definite air superiority, perhaps air supremacy, over Egypt and Libya. Cowles said he would be very much disappointed if there isn't good news from that front in the near future. It is his belief that Rommel is due to be smashed utterly, so that the Allies will control the entire north shore of Africa. Then the plan is to reopen the Mediterranean to Allied shipping, greatly simplifying and shortening the supply line to the Soviet Union.

This, it is believed, can be achieved by basing Allied planes on Malta, Gibraltar and the bulge of Africa at Benghasi. They believe that the planes we now have, with the ones en route to the Mediterranean, will be enough to do the job. In order to make this possible, though, the Axis forces must either be driven off so that Bengàsi can be counted upon as surely held, or better still so there are no more Axis troops in Africa to interfere. This would of course open the way for a smash at Italy.

Next the party went to Turkey, and Cowles is satisfied that Turkey will not go over to the Axis, and that she will fight all out if attacked by Germany. This tends to confirm other information of a similar character I have received. Then they went to Syria, where they had a long talk with De

Gaulle. Cowles said he was much disappointed in the General, finding him puffed up with all the publicity he has received. However, Free French people say he makes a most unfavorable first impression, but is all right when you get to know him. I wouldn't know. Anyhow, Cowles added that the Free French movement is not in good shape at all, with discord of one sort or another raising difficult problems.

Russia was the next stop. When Willkie got there, as elsewhere, he explained that he, as the head of the opposition, was the symbol of American unity, that he came to stress that point and to get information. He asked that he be allowed to see everything he wanted to see, and that he be told all he wanted to know. This was done, especially in the Soviet Union, where he got far better treatment and saw more than any foreign visitor had been permitted to see.

In a number of cases Willkie's hosts found it difficult to evaluate his exact position. The Arabs in particular found it hard to believe that the President would send the leader of his opposition as his representative. In some places it was obvious that Willkie was mistaken for Roosevelt himself. However, it was plain that Roosevelt stood out wherever they went as the outstanding world figure today.

Willkie and his party saw the plant in which Stormavik anti-tank planes, heavily armored and heavily gunned ships designed to fly low and fight mechanized forces, are built. It employs 20,000 men and women, and compares very favorably with the Lockheed plant in California, which Cowles had seen earlier. Phelps has written about what follows, but I want to include it just to have it in the memo: the workers are on a 60-hour week, and they are paid on a piece-work basis. This means that a man at one lathe may make twice as much money as the man next to him if he can turn out twice as much work. Thus the merit system has come into the Russian economy. Also, plant managers get about ten times the average pay of the highly skilled workers, perhaps $20,000 a year. He cited this as a comparison for those who believe all Russians get paid on a single wage basis, whatever their ability. It just ain't so.

Lawrence Todd, of *Tass* in Washington, told me one day that the old Communist slogan, "From each according to his ability, to each according to his need" had been changed, and now reads, "From each according to his ability, to each according to his work." I don't know how happy Lewis, Reuther et al would be in the Soviet Union.

Incidentally, Willkie asked Stalin about communism in the United States. Stalin said that was all over with, that Russia had learned at last she had plenty to do at home without worrying about the rest of the world. This, in case you are interested, is my idea of a very excellent grade of bologna.

Oh yes. In addition to getting higher pay, the more valuable men also get preferential treatment in the commissary. Thus their treatment of the war worker is diametrically opposite from ours, leading Phelps to conclude that the USSR is the last stand of private enterprise in the world.

Willkie and his party went to the front on the Rzhev sector, and their questions were answered fully, and as far as they could tell, frankly, by the general with them. Stalin had assured Willkie he could see what he wanted and get any facts he wanted.

The question of loss inevitably arose. The Russian high command estimates its losses at 5,000,000 men killed, wounded and captured, with German losses about the same. Correspondents in Moscow think both figures are too high. They put Russian losses at about 4,000,000, with German losses at something between 3,000,000 and 4,000,000. These figures deal with the military only. As to civilians, the Russians estimate that 50,000,000 are now the slaves of the Nazis, or at least in German-controlled territory, under German domination.

The food situation in Russia is very bad, and they are facing it with a realism that makes you shudder. The soldiers are going to be well fed on the food that is even now being collected and stored by the government. War workers will get next best treatment. And the drones will simply be allowed to starve. It is estimated by the Russian government that a million Russians will starve to death this winter because the war effort comes first. That is an acceptance of total war quite beyond anything of which we are capable, in my opinion. There is something terrible about it, but it is the kind of spirit that wins.

In this connection there are many Poles in Russia, due to the war's early stages. They will get no food cards, and their deaths will probably be numerous. The Russians, Cowles said, are just as intent as are the Germans on ending the possibility of a cohesive Polish nation on its border, and they are dispersing Poles all over the country. This, I might add, is in contrast to what [Polish] Prime Minister Sikorski said at a press conference I attended some months ago. Then Stalin said that after the war Poland would be larger and more powerful than before. You can take your pick, but my guess is Cowles is right.

Fuel for the winter is being obtained by sending large forces into the forests to chop down trees. These trees are stripped and brought into city squares, where residents can come and help themselves.

Cowles says it is his belief that Russia is so thoroughly aroused, and so committed to this war, that she will keep on fighting Germany to the bitter end, whether we give her any help or not. However, this by no means solves the problems of the United Nations, as will appear.

There is outspoken bitterness in Russia against the British, and to a lesser degree against the Americans. Stories are going around like these:

1) There are three things needed to win this war: blood, materials, time; Russia has the blood, America has the materials, and God knows Britain has time and to spare.

2) There are two ways to open a second front, the natural way and the supernatural way; the natural way is for the Archangel Gabriel to come down with his Heavenly hosts and sweep the Germans from the face of the

earth; The supernatural way is to make Churchill keep his word. These stories symbolize both the popular and the official feeling in Russia.

In Russia the Molotov-Roosevelt announcement was taken as a flat commitment to open a second front in Europe in 1942. As Cowles explained, American and British papers, and certainly Russian papers, so interpreted it. Maybe they were wrong, but no official voice was raised in London or Washington to dispute that interpretation, or to correct it. And so it was accepted by the Russian people that this was the correct interpretation. Now they feel that Britain and the United States have gone back on their word, and they are sore as pups. Cowles was asked if the Soviet government had also been misled. He answered that he did not think so, but it was taking the position that it had been, which was the important thing.

Secondarily, it is a fact that we are far behind on our commitments to the Russians in materiel, etc. This does not irritate the Russians so much, since they know the difficulty of getting supplies through both the north and south supply lines. However, they are very much annoyed by the large preponderance of materiel going to Britain, where it is not used to attack the Germans. They go so far as to say that there is no fundamental difference between the Russian policy of the Chamberlain and Churchill governments. The Chamberlain government, Munich-minded, wanted to turn Germany's might toward Russia and to keep England from being attacked. The Churchill government, they say, wants to turn Germany toward Russia and to keep Britain from being attacked. The Russians don't like either.

Well, as Cowles said, this doesn't mean the Russians will make peace. They won't. But it does mean that any plans and hopes we may have for a perfect post-war world will go down the drain if Russia wins this war without real assistance from us, enough of it so that Russia considers us as real allies. Stalin frankly said as much to Willkie. He said that if Russia won this war through its own sacrifices and efforts, it proposed to dominate the peace by natural right, or at least to dominate it in those areas about which it feels concerned.

Cowles did not say this, but I have got it from various sources, including Count Czernin of the Free Austria movement, that these areas include the Balkans (where it is very significant that the Russians are claiming Mikhailovich is not fighting the Germans, but is protecting the bourgeoisie against the proletariat, which is of course more high-grade bologna), Poland (recall what Cowles said about this), the Baltic states (which Russia took, only to lose them to Germany, and which she will take again—Sir Stafford Cripps as good as gave them back to Russia in an article in *Life* some time ago), and Scandinavia, beginning with Finland and working toward the Atlantic.

All of this reminds me that Willkie, way back last spring, told me one afternoon that in his opinion it would be disastrous for the democracies if the United States was not the chief figure in winning the war. Only if this country demonstrated the strength and virility of a democracy would the world run along democratic lines, he believed then. It looks now as though he was right.

To sum up this part, Russian relations, political and military, with Britain and the United States, are deteriorating, and steps must be taken at once to repair the situation. Cowles pointed out that he was merely presenting the Russian view, and was not making the American and British counter-arguments.

A real tribute was paid Willkie by the Russians when they allowed his party to fly up from Teheran to Kuybyshev, and from Moscow over Siberia to China. It was the first time any foreigners had been allowed to travel the latter route.

I'll interpolate here one brief paragraph about Iran. Britain and Russia are both highly unpopular there. As you know, they moved in and took over the country not so long ago. They both pretend that Iran is independent, but in fact it is not. For instance, in order to get onto the airfield at Teheran you have to have a Russian pass. In order to get aboard a plane you have a British pass, etc.

To get back to the Russian situation, the Russian high command is now convinced that Japan is most unlikely to attack Siberia. The feeling is that Japan has its hands full already. This being the case, Russia is in a much more willing mood to allow the United States to begin large-scale shipments of planes and material to Russia by transport planes via Alaska and Siberia. Deterrents previously have been two: 1) Unwillingness to risk a Japanese attack. 2) The fact that Siberian bases have not been prepared for any such transport.

Such a route would run some 350-400 miles north of Kiska, and would not necessitate clearing the Japs off there. Cowles believes such a route will get under way soon.

A few paragraphs about the Russians. They are immensely proud of their intelligence system in Germany. It reports that our bombings are having a terrible effect on the morale of the German people. Contrary to the results in Britain, where it merely stiffened the will to resist, it is breaking down morale a lot. The Russians call for more of this bombing, and still more. But they don't want America told this, since they believe America would assume there was an easy and painless way to win the war and would abandon thoughts of land action in western Europe.

(Czernin has suggested that German reaction traces to the fact that not since the Napoleonic wars has an enemy soldier fought on German soil. The Germans for the first time are finding out that people get hurt, and property gets wrecked, when your land is attacked. Of course, our isolationists would have us learn the same lesson, which doesn't make sense to me.)

Flying over Siberia, the plane was over the Trans-Siberian Railway for ten minutes, in the course of which seven long freight trains were seen under way. This is very heavy traffic, and shows the energy with which Russia is attacking her industrial problem. Incidentally, that Stormavik plant had been moved bodily to a new location outside the fighting zone and put into full production in nine months. The air fields the party saw in Siberia gave evidence of a great deal of work in the last ninety days, which shows that not until recently have the Russians been in a position to set up transport lines to Alaska. Incidentally, they get about fifteen feet of snow on the Siberian air fields, and they have rollers all ready to pack down the snow into a usable surface, and scrapers ready to take off new falls of snow. A thorough people.

When Stalin was talking with Willkie, he boasted of the progress made in education in Russia. In 1917, he said, less than 10 percent of Russians could read. Now 80 percent are literate. Willkie slapped him on the back and said, "If you don't look out you'll educate yourself out of a job." It took a little while for the interpreter to get this over to Stalin, but when he got it he laughed like hell and said he guessed Willkie was right. All of them were impressed by Stalin as quite a guy.

Cowles recalled that when their plane landed at Yakutsk, capital of the autonomous Soviet Republic of the same name (the second largest republic in the world, the largest being the United States), they found a public library containing 300,000 volumes. The town has a population of about 70,000. Des Moines, he said [a town of 42,000] had only 200,000 volumes in its library. Willkie claims to be able to tell a great deal about a town if allowed to spend half an hour in the town library. But of course the number of volumes doesn't tell so much as the velocity with which they circulate, and the number of calls for them.

And so we leave beautiful Russia, and head for China. The Chinese are just about as sore as the Russians at Great Britain and the United States. They feel this is an Anglo-Saxon war, and they haven't seen anything yet to reassure them that an Anglo-Saxon postwar world isn't in prospect. In consequence, they are burned up because no high-ranking officials have visited them. Cowles is convinced that we need to do a real job to show the Chinese and the Russians that we are on their side, and mean to have a real all-world peace after the war. This is of course true.

The Chinese are very proud of their intelligence service, too. They report that Japanese shipping losses have been very heavy indeed, much heavier than the Japanese high command had figured on. This is reported to be the only angle of the war that seriously worries the Japanese as yet. However, it is a major worry.

When dining in Chungking, Cowles, who had grown very ill on the food served them at the long series of banquets, noticed that ice cream constituted the seventeenth course of the fifteenth banquet. He mentioned his gratification to the mayor of Chungking, who sat next to him. The mayor said it was quite a treat, since six months ago cholera had been traced to milk in Chungking and the inhabitants were forbidden to use it. They made a special exception for the Willkie banquet, which may or may not have been a compliment.

And that is about all for Mr. Cowles. Quite enough, too. Willkie is giving a dinner here on 4 November for the boys who covered him in 1940, and he will tell his story of this trip. I'll do you a memo on that, too.

After the Cowles luncheon, I beat it over to the Navy Department to hear two Marine colonels just back from the Solomons. They didn't say much, but what they did say was very interesting. We hold, and have from the start, Tulagi Island and the small islands around it. We hold on Guadalcanal a strip of about 9,000 yards long by 4,000 yards deep. This includes the air field, which is all that is strategically important on the island. In the area we have about 20,000 Marines and 5,000 soldiers. This is about twice as much force as I thought we had. The Japanese seem to have about 23,000 troops on the island.

These colonels left there on 23 September. They didn't say so, but I gather they expect us to stay there. However, until we know just what out naval losses are, it is not easy to estimate the situation. It doesn't look too great, especially since you can't trust the Navy's announcements.

In any event, the two colonels had actually been there, and I am fully prepared to take their word against Clark Lee's.

Regards

EXCHANGE OF MESSAGES WITH BARTNETT

23 October 1942

3:04 P.M. Bartnett to Perry

General Eisenhower's statement on safe arrival of all U.S. troops in United Kingdom clashes a bit with opening paragraph of your memo.

3:31 P.M. Perry to Bartnett

I'll stand on my memo. Incidentally, Eisenhower's statement seemed to me very carefully worded. You will notice it denies only that "Several large ocean-going liners heavily laden with American troops" had been torpedoed. Heavily laden with American troops is a definite qualification of his statement. So are the words large and several. They lessen the message's force.

I suggest to you that our high command deemed it best to withhold news of the sinking of a transport, arguing that since no lives were lost no harm would be done thereby, and that it might be harmful to morale to have it known that a transport had been hit, even without casualties.

This last is speculation on my part. But it is a fact that these days communiqués and official statements have got to be read as the most literal of documents, meaning exactly what they say, and not always what they seem to say. *World-Telegram* of today may have an editorial on the weasel-wordedness of our communiqués. The *Washington News* (Scripps-Howard) has.

---

26 October 1942

10:20 A.M. Bartnett to Perry (Confidential)

Reported here carrier *Wasp* sunk in Southwest Pacific September 13 with loss of 300. Destroyer said to have rescued 900, including Rear Admiral Hugh Noyes. Can't trace source of report, but understand some survivors have reached United States. Do you know anything of such a report?

2:32 P.M. Perry to Bartnett (Confidential)

One carrier has been sunk and one carrier damaged in the Solomons fight. One is *Wasp*, and I believe she is sunk. The other—I may be wrong on this—is *Saratoga*, and she is supposed to have reached port safely. I cannot verify the circumstantial details about who was rescued etc.

---

28 October 1942

2:17 P.M. Barnett to Perry

Have you any private information to bear out the rather blue impression which everyone has after reading dispatches on Solomons?

3:17 P.M. Perry to Bartnett

The situation in the Solomons is critical as hell. As I pointed out in my story yesterday the Japs are going all out in their efforts to retake Guadalcanal and Henderson Field. People you talk to here who have good sources of information will tell you they wrote off our chances of holding on there weeks ago.

The chief difficulty is, as usual, supplies. Our lines are fantastically long and make it very difficult for us to get stuff in there to compete with the Japs, whose supply lines are very short. My personal opinion is that we will have to pull out pretty soon. That opinion is based on such information as I possess. I know that naval losses are considerably in excess of what has been announced. I've so reported in recent memos.

But pulling out doesn't mean we are licked in that area. This is a matter of how much we lose in comparison with how much they lose. This evaluation has to be weighted in our favor by our vastly superior replacement ability. Thus, if we lost five ships to their four we would still gain in the long run in the war of attrition that will probably set the stage for the knockout in the Pacific.

I do not say we want go get kicked out of the Solomons, or that it would not represent a definite check in our plans. There is, however, the possibility that we can stick it out down there. It's only a possibility and not a probability. But if it comes off, we've just about got Japan licked. That is, as the Germans like to say, the fate of the Japs will be sealed, even though it may take several years to consummate that doom.

George Fielding Perry

3:37 P.M. Perry To Bartnett

My information is that the carrier *Hornet* has also been sunk in the Solomons. This is not positive, but I believe my informant is accurate. This makes the following score: Sunk: *Lexington, Yorktown, Hornet*. Damaged: *Saratoga*. Carriers appear to be pretty vulnerable, eh?

Perry

KING BEGINS OFF-THE-RECORD MEETINGS WITH SELECTED REPORTERS

I first became aware of Ernest J. King—although not personally involved—when he was a four-striper in charge of raising sunken submarines. Several of these, in the period between the two world wars, went to the bottom through collisions or other disasters. Raising them was difficult and hazardous work, and Captain King, who quickly became known to the newsmen covering the events as a man who ranked them somewhat above bubonic plague as something to be avoided at all costs, proved to be very good at salvage.

Then, in the years between the outbreak of World War II and the ending of the cold war, Vice Admiral King surfaced again, this time as Commander, Atlantic Fleet, which was more or less in the war as what might be called an unofficial combatant. Pre-1941, beginning with the Spanish-American War, in which he was a midshipman, there had been a steady progression up the ladder.

It must have been evident to his superiors as early as World War I and the 1920s that here was a man who matched extraordinary dedication with decisiveness, intelligence, knowledge and an appalling directness when confronted with anything less than top performance by those reporting to him.

It was said of him that when some erring officer appeared before him, he was asked just two questions: What did you do? That was the easy one, setting up the second, which was one word long: Why? That was the zinger that reduced strong men to quivering hulks. The reasons, when advanced to that flinty, icy-eyed, grim-faced superior, usually sounded feeble and unconvincing, far from the standard expected from Annapolis-trained minds.

The rails on which Admiral King and I were running began to converge when my friendship with Nelie Bull suddenly developed a certain degree of importance in the war effort because of one military and one personal fact. The military fact was that our navy wasn't doing too well in the first three-quarters of 1942, for numerous valid reasons. The personal fact, as already mentioned, was that Nelie was Admiral King's personal attorney, as well as close and respected friend.

Over the years from 1937 to 1941, Nelie supplied me with a very full and complete indoctrination in the King character, personality, intelligence, knowledge of naval strategy, history and tactics, plus an approach to his job that placed him well down on any scoring list rating personal popularity. That was Admiral King, as seen by Cornelius Bull.

Then there was Ernie King, the man of wit, with a great capacity for friendship, considerate and loyal, a man who enjoyed a well-meant drink on suitable occasions. None of which was ever permitted to interfere with rigid concentration on accomplishing whatever mission was given him. When Pearl Harbor brought this country formally into the war, he restricted his alcoholic intake to beer. In the conferences in which I took part it was his unvarying custom to drink two bottles during a 2½ or 3 hour session, mount the stairs for a trip to the head, return to his chair for a question period and informal discussion with one more beer as a nightcap. The beer had not the slightest effect on him.

The post-Pearl Harbor housecleaning that saw Admirals

Stark and Kimmel put out to pasture brought Admiral King to the job known in service parlance as Comminch, an acronym for Commander in Chief. Formally his title was Commander in Chief, United States Fleet, and Chief of Naval Operations. Franklin D. Roosevelt had been Assistant Secretary of the Navy under President Wilson, and during that time he formed a respect for King that kept on growing. By 1941 that respect had reached full flower.

My friend Nelie, well aware of the King-haters in the Navy, the Congress and in the press, called on the Admiral to congratulate him on his promotion, and could not resist what might be called a leading question: "Ernie, how in the world did you ever land the top job with your platoons of enemies?" King's reply, which has become famous, was to the point: "When they get into trouble, they call on us sons of bitches."

Our paths continued to converge during this period, unknown to me, and for sure to the Admiral who, on getting his new job, installed his family in the big house on Massachusetts Avenue assigned to the nation's top-ranking naval officer, and then settled himself aboard a smallish flagship, U.S.S. *Dauntless*, a converted yacht, tied to a dock in the Washington Navy Yard, where he could be as close to the action as a fireman in his firehouse waiting for the alarm to sound.

The converging tracks met in the fall of 1942. The war had not been going well for the United States. Despite Secretary Knox's article in *Colliers* magazine entitled "The Navy Is Ready," which appeared about a week before Pearl Harbor in a masterpiece of horrible timing, the navy was *far* from ready for a two-ocean war against foes of the first rank.

German U-boats had been having a bloody holiday along the Atlantic coast, picking off tankers and freighters at night, when they were silhouetted against the shore lights that defied the blackout. The Japanese had effectively drawn the fangs of our surface forces at Pearl, and were threatening Australia after taking over the East Indies, which provided crude oil so pure it could be put directly into a ship's bunkers. The navy was doing the best it could with what it had, but years of public, and by corollary Congressional, indifference or actual hostility to the concept of preparedness could not be wished away in a few months. And at this point we became involved in an attempt to establish ourselves in the Solomons because the Japs forced our hand.

In such a case, it really didn't matter who was to blame. A public that has never yet accepted responsibility for improvidence or failure to plan ahead, finds it more comfortable to single out scapegoats. In Admiral King they had an alluring target. He was top man in the navy's picture. Beyond that, his enemies in the press, Congress and the navy rubbed their hands and warmed to the task of giving him the deep six.

There were, of course, King supporters in high places in the Navy Department, in Congress and in the executive branch, with special reference to the White House. The obvious approach was to "get to" the President, working on him in every possible way to convince him that the Navy's troubles would end very quickly if a new Comminch were installed.

Old Washington hands were quick to read the signs. The critical stories began to appear in the Washington papers. There were hints that he was a dead duck about to be fired. Nelie knew they were only the tip of the iceberg. He well knew with what shrewdness and ruthless mendacity pressure could be applied and made to seem plausible. He identified the news stories, columns and think pieces as intended, first, to smoke out public sentiment and, second, build a firestorm of outraged public opinion that would force FDR to do what King's enemies wanted.

The situation came to a head for Nelie and me in a discussion over a Press Club drink in a "Thank God it's Friday" session. It was far from the first time he had briefed me on what a catastrophe it would be for the United States if the anti-King forces had their way. But this time he excelled himself. He was in full stride as he reached his peroration, which took the form of a, for him, profane indictment of the public stupidity that could permit so disastrous a development as depriving the navy and the country of a man so perfectly qualified to tackle the Herculean job at hand.

As we stared moodily into our Tom Collinses, brooding over his pessimistic analysis, I was struck by an idea.

"Listen," I said, "if King is all you say he is—and by now you've sold me—and since we both know the press can quite possibly be decisive in things like this, why don't we get him together with some of the top Washington hands so they can get to know him and make up their own minds as to what kind of man he is? If he sold them the way you've sold me, it could set in motion a very effective counterattack.''

He shook his head. ''It's no use. Ernie hates newspaper men almost as much as he does Germans and Japs. He'd never agree. Even if he did, it probably wouldn't work.''

''Okay,'' I said, ''Maybe it's just an idea whose time hasn't come. Let's have one for the road.''

We met for lunch the following Monday, and as we sat down he said, ''Glen, I've got a great idea.''

''Hard to believe, considering the source, but what is it?''

''Why don't we get Ernie together with a bunch of Washington correspondents so they can see what a hell of a guy he is?''

It wasn't until many years after that I read that there was no limit to what one could accomplish if one didn't care who got the credit for it. I seemed to have proved the point even before I knew what it was.

''Gee, Nelie, where'd you get that idea?''

''I don't know. It just came to me over the weekend. What do you think?''

''I think it's a winner. Let's get going.''

And that is how it all started, in late October of 1942. The first move, of course, was the hardest, persuading King to play. That was Nelie's job. He got King at his quarters that evening. He found Comminch well aware of the delicacy of his position, and of the need to take effective counter-measures. He realized it was not the type of battle for which he was ideally equipped.

Even so, his initial reaction was ''To hell with 'em.'' But he was up against a very persuasive man and, even more important, a man he knew, respected and trusted implicity. Beyond that, he was sufficiently worldly to know that in a life and death struggle one cannot always pick and choose one's allies. As witness our alliance with the U.S.S.R., hardly a love match.

There were risks, too. The correspondents might be as tricky and unscrupulous as he had always thought them. They might take what he said off the record and then use it. Or he might not be able to convince them. Or the Navy's civilian brass, not to mention the White House, might be angered.

Still, it was a tight corner for him, and if this worked, it could save the situation. In the end, with considerable reluctance, he agreed to meet with seven or eight top Washington hands, to be picked by us, for an off the record discussion.

Nelie and I had decided that if the Admiral agreed, the meeting should be held in Nelie's house in Alexandria, across the street from the white-washed colonial jailhouse. We chose this locale partly so the atmosphere could be friendly and low-key, but mostly so that if anything went wrong, the Press Section could get out from under by saying it was an unofficial and personal matter between the Admiral and some press friends, with the navy not involved. I am sure it was a wise precaution, although the issue never arose, to the best of my knowledge.

The ground rules were simple. No notes were to be taken during the session, mostly to reassure the Admiral. I had found in my journalistic career that taking notes, even in an off-the-record session, put a man subconsciously on guard, wary and nervous, which was the last thing we wanted. It was permissible to make notes after the meeting, and to prepare memoranda for one's editors on a need-to-know basis. There could be absolutely no use of the material developed with or without attribution, in print or over the air. There could be but one man from each organization.

Why would correspondents be interested in information given them on so restricted a basis? I refer you back to the Bartnett preface. Suffice it to say that we had no declinations with no hesitation and no crossed fingers. I am sure the navy's war was reported to the American people more accurately, and in far better perspective, than was the case in any war, by reason of this and subsequent meetings with Admiral King.

As to the guest list, we decided to turn our duo into a trio, the addition being Roscoe Drummond, Bureau Chief of the *Christian Science Monitor* and my partner in writing articles for the *Saturday Evening Post* and *Look*.

Nelie deferred to Roscoe and me in this area, although he helped set up the criteria: absolute integrity and reliability were fundamental, which ruled out a few of the men who might otherwise have been brought in, plus high journalistic competence and a good rating on personality. There were, I might say at this point, fourteen conferences with Admiral King, involving twenty-six correspondents, to whom he spoke with sometimes frightening candor. There was never a single leak.

And so it was that, precisely at 8 bells on Sunday evening, 1 November 1942, the doorbell of the pleasant little colonial house on Princess Street rang. The men in the living room looked expectantly at the front door as our host opened it. Facing us was a tall, spare figure in regulation Navy blues.

He made quite a picture as Nelie took his greatcoat and uniform cap, bright with scrambled eggs all over the visor. Five-star rank lay in the future, but the broad gold stripe on each sleeve, topped by three narrower ones surmounted by a gold star, were sufficiently impressive. He wore three rows of ribbons—they had grown to five the last time I saw him—and I suppose that if he wore all the ribbons to which he was entitled they would have approached his waist. Gold aviator's wings were pinned just above the ribbons, and he could have worn the submariners' dolphins, too, had there been any place to put them.

He entered the room quietly, and what impressed me right away was that he was alone! No fussing aide or over-attentive public relations type to steer him past such reefs as might come up. It was just Ernest J. King, Admiral, USN, perhaps a little tense as one might be who has committed his fate to dubious hands. He was, none the less, completely poised, projecting an air of authority, of command, without having to make the slightest effort. Great men may enjoy the ruffles and flourishes, but they do not need them to win instant respect.

Nelie walked the Admiral around the room, presenting each correspondent in turn. He shook hands with each, a quick, firm pressure, repeating the name and accompanying the words with a keen eye-to-eye look. The eyes were not at all unfriendly, but it was no great trick to imagine that under less favorable circumstances they might look as though forged from the same steel that protected his battleships.

In a very few minutes the Admiral was installed in an easy chair in a corner of the room, a glass of beer on a small table beside him, with the correspondents and our host seated in a circle of which he was, paradoxically, the corner. I don't recall the exact words Nelie used to kick off the session, but he probably said something like, "You have the floor, Ernie." And so began King's first historic conference with the group which eventually became known as the "Arlington County Commandos."

CONFIDENTIAL

Saturday
7 November 1942

Dear Bart,

This is to me a memorandum of extraordinary interest, and the necessity for destroying it after you and Mr. Speed have read it will be apparent when I tell you that it covers an evening spent with Admiral Ernest J. King, Commander in Chief of the United States Fleet and Chief of Naval Operations, in which he talked freely and at length with a carefully selected group of correspondents.

To begin with, you will recall that in recent memoranda I have referred to the growing distrust of naval information and the fact that Congress was planning to make big trouble about the war situation. At the time I suggested to Nelie Bull, whom you have met, that it would be helpful to all concerned if a meeting could be arranged between Admiral King and some of the leading pressmen concerned with military and naval affairs.

The first one was held last Sunday evening. He, Roscoe Drummond and I arranged the guest list and all the rest of it. Those present were: Raymond Clapper, Scripps-Howard columnist; Ernest Lindley, chief of the *Newsweek* Bureau; Bert Andrews, *Herald-Tribune* Bureau Chief; Barnet Nover, military writer for the *Washington Post*; Ray Henle, correspondent for the *Pittsburgh Post-Gazette*; Marquis Childs, correspondent for the *St. Louis Post-Dispatch*; Nelie, Roscoe, me and the Admiral.

King, reputed to be ice-cold, hard as steel, emotionless, disagreeable, turned out on closer inspection to be a man who loves to laugh, a man with a keen sense of humor and a quick wit, an extraordinary intellect, a clear, lucid gift for explanation, and the most amazing grasp of the world situation in its military, diplomatic and economic phases. He made a profound impression upon the correspondents. By the time we said goodbye they were for him 100 percent.

In return, I believe he was equally impressed by the calibre of the men with whom he was talking. I judge this not alone by the increasingly relaxed way in which he conducted himself, but also because of the frankness with which he answered the questions put to him. I had met King briefly once before, but this was the first chance I'd had to measure him. He's all right!

Now, as to what he said: The conversation, with time out for a late evening supper, lasted for four hours, and while I pride myself on my ability to retain conversations until I can get to a typewriter, I'm sure I missed some of what was said, but I am quite sure I got the essentials. I'm going to try to weave them into a cohesive picture that emerged gradually, without pretending to present what he said exactly as he said it.

Let's begin with four definitions:

Theatre: This is the largest division of war activity. Thus the Pacific Theatre, embracing the entire Pacific Ocean, from Alaska to the South Pole, from Singapore to Panama.

Area: An area is a subdivision of a theatre. There are five areas in the Pacific. 1) North Pacific, the Pacific Ocean running north from a line dividing Oregon and California. The division is one of convenience, and was selected because the people north of the California border look to the north, to Alaska, for enemy attack, while those south of that border look to Hawaii. 2) Central Pacific. The area running directly west from the West Coast to Asia, with the northern border being the hypothetical extension of the Oregon-California border, and the south, roughly, from the border between Mexico and Guatemala extended. The reason is that all Central America is, for defense purposes, regarded as one country, and also because Mexico, abutting the United States and with its coastline a part of the Eastern Sea Frontier, presents a special problem. 3) Southeast Pacific, from Longitude 110 east to the coasts of Central and South America, from the Mexican-Guatemalan border to the South Pole. 4) South Pacific Area, from Longitude 110 west to the dividing line between New Zealand and Australia. 5) Southwest Pacific, the Australian area and its approaches. To go a bit farther with this, you will see that the North Pacific Area covers the Aleutians, Alaska, etc.; the Central Pacific Area covers the vital Midway-Hawaii-California supply line; the South Pacific Area covers the almost equally vital supply line to Australia; the Southwest Pacific Area covers the enemy's approaches to Australia; the Southeast Pacific Area covers the approaches to South America, including the Panama Canal.

Joint: This word is used to describe activities in which various United States forces take part. Thus, the Joint Chiefs of Staff are Marshall, King, Leahy, Arnold.

Combined: This describes activities in which various of the United Nations take part. Thus the Combined Chiefs of Staff are our four, plus Field Marshal Sir John Dill, and the British Navy and Royal Air Force chiefs here.

All right, then. With this as background, let's go. When Admiral King came to Washington and took over his command on 20 December, he sent two directives to Admiral Nimitz, Commander in Chief, Pacific Fleet (CINCPAC). They stated that the two chief and immediate objectives of the fleet, differing only in degree as to importance, were to maintain the Hawaii-Midway line, and also to maintain the supply line to Australia.

Now, it is important to realize that Admiral King and General Marshall, in their functions as commanders of their respective services, act as agents of the Joint Chiefs of Staff, which in turn derives its authority from the Commander in Chief, the President. Admiral King argues, and I agree, that this is the best form of unified command. I think that will appear on the following pages. I'll pause here to say that Mr. Roosevelt has at no time interferred with military and naval planning and activities. This is, I think, most reassuring.

As you see, the war effort—at least our war effort—is being run by the Joint Chiefs of Staff in consultation. That is the heart of our war effort, and it not only tells MacArthur, Nimitz et al what to do, but it has limitless authority. It can decide who is going to run what operations with what allocations of forces. Thus MacArthur's control over a job, and his power to handle it, will naturally be greater if Admiral Halsey is directed to place his fleet under MacArthur's command for a specific operation, or less if MacArthur is told to put his air forces at Admiral Ghormley's disposal, as was in effect done for the Solomons operation.

Well, the same thing is true of global war. The question arose as to who would handle Allied strategy and planning and allocation. Delicate feelings had to be considered, but a war had to be won, too. It was believed that those countries that had the forces with which to win the war should be the ones to decide what to do, and where and when. It would hardly have been satisfactory to have all the thirty-odd United Nations represented on the Combined Chiefs of Staff, and decide policy by a show of hands. That wouldn't be a unified command. This being the case, it was determined that Great Britain and the United States, as the two great powers of the United Nations at war with *all* the Axis powers, should constitute the high command.

Russia, you will see, is handicapped because she is not at war with Japan. Were she involved there, I am quite sure she'd be represented. However, there is no trouble here. Russia doesn't want to be on the Combined Chiefs, and has made this plain. As for China, the Netherlands, etc., their representatives are called into consultation when some operation is under discussion that involves their territories and/or forces. Otherwise they are not, and it is believed that this would offend them less than would having them seated at the table with no voice in the decisions.

Now, as to our Pacific Areas (I'll deal with the Pacific first and then swing to the Atlantic, Mediterranean, etc.): Directives to all commanders have made it clear that the borders of their Areas are set up for convenience, and are fluid. General MacArthur had this directive in his hands for thirty days before be assumed command in Australia.

Once in the war, we set up our plans. Hawaii was and is the key, but the next step was to assure the supply line to Australia. Samoa, Fiji and New Caledonia were turned into strong points. A division of troops was put into each of the latter two and nearly a division into Samoa. Then outposts were obtained and small forces put on them, so that we would have warning should the Japanese attack.

Once this was done, we were in much better shape to maintain our two vital Pacific tasks. However, there wasn't enough stuff to do a real job. You see, the Treaty of 1922 set up the 5-5-3 ratio for Great Britain, the U.S. and Japan, but we didn't keep our fleet up. It wasn't until 1935 that Congress authorized construction to bring us up to the mark, and not until 1936 that it appropriated the money with which to do it. Then, as things dveloped, the appropriations came thick and fast, ending with the decision to build a two-ocean navy. But to appropriate is not the same thing as to have the ships.

It was not until this year that our Navy reached Treaty strength, and it is only now that the beginnings are being made on the two-ocean navy. The carrier *Princeton*, and some others that have already been launched, represent the beginnings of our new Navy. It must also be remembered that we have very heavy commitments. The Russian Protocol is only one. Australia is forever wanting everything put aside until they can get what they want. The Chinese have a claim. The result is that our ability to supply ourselves suffers.

Anyway, we were doing our job. The Battle of the Coral Sea helped. The dangers of bringing our ships into that sphere of Japanese influence were considerable because of the air problem. *Lexington*, for example, tried to raid Rabaul and got within 300 miles before the Japanese spotted her. After that her commander had to decide what to do. His decision was to get the hell out of there. To remain might have lost us the *Lex* right there, with no compensating gains. It was a tough decision to make.

Then our sources of information brought us word that the Japanese had in contemplation an attack on Midway. We knew where their ships were getting together, what ships they were, and all that. At this point the matter of calculated risk came in. The Japs started on schedule, bringing heavy forces to bear with beautiful timing, the carrier striking forces left from one island and the transports from another, but as usual the fleets were right where they were supposed to be on the minute.

Our problem was what to do about it. There was always the chance that the Japs might double cross us and go south, toward the Solomons area, and the supply line to Australia, too. Also, the Navy knew everything about the Aleutians move except why it was made. I'll get to that.

The decision was made to put all the eggs in one basket. We got all our stuff together and brought it up so it would be available for the Midway fight. This left the Southwest and South Pacific Areas wide open if we got crossed up, and it also left the Aleutians open. But it was a calculated risk.

Then, three days *before* the first contact, our source of information was suddenly cut off. You can imagine that our high command was on tenterhooks for fear the Japs would go south. And word of our first contact with the Jap fleet right where we had figured it would be was welcome news indeed to our people.

As you know, we did well in that fight, and as soon as we had the edge, we shot some forces up to the Aleutians. Let's get that out of the way now. Admiral King pointed out to the President that the Japanese couldn't do anything to Alaska, couldn't even threaten it seriously, until they threatened Kodiak Island, which they were not threatening. The decision, then, was to let the Aleutians ride for the present, not because we wanted to but because we didn't have enough stuff for everywhere. Calculated risk again.

We got two breaks up there. The Japs, as it turned out, didn't know about our Army air base on Kodiak, east of Dutch Harbor, and at Umiak west of it. Thanks to these, we were able to stop the Japs at Attu, Agattu and Kiska. Thereafter, as the situation developed, we subjected them to heavy pressure, and things reached a point where we regarded Kiska as bait. They'd put ships in there, and we'd sink 'em. The Japs have paid a heavy price up there, and God knows they've got nothing in return.

One of their aims, as near as we can figure, was to get between us and Siberia. Another was to have a base from which to put on shows to divert our forces. Unhappily for them, we started diverting before they could. You can figure we aren't displeased to have the Japs on Kiska, since it is so costly for them to stay there. They are using Kiska for their small two-man submarines, but they aren't getting anywhere with them.

Well, in June the Chiefs of Staff began to figure on an operation in the Solomon Islands. At that time Guadalcanal was just another island. The harbor at Tulagi was the objective. This was definitely an offensive move that was in contemplation, and not a defensive move made necessary by the fact that Japan was building an air field on Guadalcanal. They weren't, at that time.

I suppose at this point I should say something about our grand strategy. It looks as though our best way to get at Japan would be to strike directly northward from New Guinea toward the Mariana Islands, to the westward of Japan's great installation at Truk in the Carolines. Guam, as King said, is the base we don't have in the Marianas, and Saipan is the base the Japanese do have. If we could drive northward through the western Carolines, and get ourselves established in the Marianas, we would be threatening the Japanese islands themselves so directly that we figure the Japanese fleet would have to come out and fight us west of Truk. One of our objectives, of course, is to get the Japs to stand up in a knock-down drag-out naval action. It looks as though we'd have to force 'em into it if it is to be done.

Well, the essential prerequisite for the implementation of such a plan is to drive the Japanese completely out of the New Guinea-New Britain area and from the approaches to Australia. The drive into the Solomons was to be—I imagine still is—the first step of the three-pronged drive aimed at kicking the Japanese out of the Australian area, including Rabaul, their big base on

New Britain. (It would help you, probably, if you read this memo with a map of the Southwest Pacific before you.)

Of these steps, the first was to be carried out by the South Pacific Command, then in charge of Admiral Ghormley. The fluidity of the area boundaries was shown then, when the line of demarcation between the MacArthur and Ghormley areas was moved to the westward so that the entire Solomons area was moved into Ghormley's command. The reason was that the main operation in this phase was to be naval.

The movement was thoroughly discussed by MacArthur and Ghormley in Australia, and they were in complete agreement. Wherever the Army and Navy may have been in conflict, it has not been in the Solomons. There, as Admiral McCain has put it, MacArthur's bombers were given a job to do, and they did it with increasing success.

The Navy urged the Army Air Force bombers to work at lower altitudes when attacking ships, arguing that they obviously weren't accomplishing anything from way up (c. 30,000 feet). The point finally registered, the Army went down to lower altitudes, and became very helpful indeed. It's one of those lessons that cannot be learned anywhere except in the actual crucible of war.

It had originally been planned to start the job in the Solomons on September 15. Then they moved it up to 1 August, on the theory that they could just as well be ready then. King was in London in July, and got word that it had been postponed a week, until 7 August. King does not believe in interfering with commanders in the field, but this time he thought it sufficiently important to advise Ghormley that it was not to be later than the 7th, and earlier if possible. The answer was, in effect, "You're telling me?"

They struck, as you know, on the 7th, and since then things have gone very much slower than planned. The reason was that while they expected the Japanese to react, they did not expect as violent a reaction as actually came. The Japs dropped everything they were doing everywhere else, and piled into the Solomons. You could see the result in New Guinea, where the Australians have moved well. The result was that our boys ran into a real scrap. The Japs will be back, and may be on their way back now. But King, asked what would happen, said succinctly, "We'll stick." Having stuck, I assume we'll resume our offensive.

There have been some heavy losses on both sides in the Pacific. The Japs, so far as we know, have two carriers—vessels built to be carriers, not converted—undamaged. So have we. But we don't know much about what else they have. They've been very secretive since the early 1930s, and we've been forced to estimate their construction from their plant space, and things like that. We are pretty sure they have two new battleships in commission, maybe as big as 45,000 tons, but we've seen nothing of them. We are, of course, going to need a lot of carriers to put on our offensive show when the time comes.

The American people are going to have to be prepared for losses. Heavy ones. That is war. We are in this as we've never been in war before. The First World War was for us a breeze in comparison. This means it's going to be very costly. It also means that we have no war-seasoned officers in the Navy. We're having to try them out in this war. You understand that tests, sham battles, etc., cannot really show the best officers. You find them only by taking your most promising men and putting them in the crucible. Some of them won't pan out. Most do. But you can never know until you've tried 'em. For example, Admiral Hart got twelve new submarines in his fleet the year before the war started. When the pinch came, the officer who was thought to be the best of the bunch had to be called home and relieved after six days. He couldn't take it. So you never can tell.

Our loss of three cruisers in the Solomons is by no means a closed issue yet. It is being investigated in an effort to find out what happened, and why. Incidentally, the sinking was not announced for a long time because the Navy, checking Japanese announcements very carefully, could not get any indication that the Japs really knew what they had done. King explained that the only criterion for releases being held up was that they might convey valuable information to the enemy. This rule will be rigidly enforced, and he expects the American press to understand.

King explained one misapprehension, namely that the Navy was holding bad news until there was good news to blanket it with. He said that the decision to release the news abut the three cruisers was made on a Saturday morning. Then, that night, came word from the Solomons that the Japs had been trapped in their turn, and a toll taken. This put the Navy on the spot. If they released the good news first, or the good and bad together, they'd be accused of blanketing. Knowing it was damned if they did and damned if they didn't, they decided finally to announce the bad news first and then the good. King convinced us that the Navy is playing it straight. He mentioned the fact that the Japs don't have to tell their people what is happening, which gives them an edge.

To clean up the Pacific situation as King described it, the Japs are strictly loners. The Germans really turned on the heat to get them to attack Siberia, but they wouldn't. Japan is in this war strictly for itself. Final point about the Japs: their air fighters ain't what they used to be. They've been reduced to using what amounts to second string pilots, the first string having been cleared out by heavy losses.

I might add at this point that the United States learned a lot in the original ABDA (Australian, British, Dutch, American) Command in the Pacific. For your information, Wavell was made commander in chief of that command chiefly so the British would play ball. This, of course, established the precedent for subsequent organization.

Finally in the Pacific, the Australian situation. MacArthur had a good deal of trouble with the Australian government, and is still having it. But he is handling it well. King once asked Walter Nash of New Zealand why Curtin of Australia couldn't keep his mouth shut. Nash explained that there was a very even division in the Parliament there, and that in order to keep control the Prime Minister had to blat his brains out.

Now we get to the Atlantic, where there are two areas. The line of demarcation is Longitude 26, curving so that Iceland is on the American side of the line. The U-boats have *not* been licked. They move into a district and raise hell for a while, and then pull out when the heat is put on. They'll be back on our shores when and if they feel it is to their advantage. The British figure of 530 [German] submarines sunk since the war began is thought to be pretty high, but possible.

One of the great worries is that *Tirpitz* will break loose and get into a convoy. If she should, she'd sink everything without ever being hit. There is some question why the Germans haven't sent her out. Probably they remember *Bismarck* too vividly.

Asked if our new battleships can take care of themselves against enemy planes, King said they sure can. *North Carolina* has been operating in the South Pacific, and has been attacked very heavily at times. Her anti-aircraft guns have done terrific work. She carries sixteen 5-inch 38 calibre anti-aircraft guns mounted in pairs, a large number of 40 millimeter cannon, and smaller guns everywhere a gun can be placed. She comes close to filling the air with a solid sheet of exploding metal. Our older battleships are being refitted. They took *Nevada* and removed all her upper works. They took away everything but her main batteries, and rebuilt her inside, too. When they got through she had everything North Carolina has, but on a smaller scale. She has, for example, only twelve 5-inchers. As to their ability to absorb punishment, he pointed out they are equivalent to *Bismarck* and *Tirpitz*, but also to *Prince of Wales*.

Incidentally, King discussed the charge that we have a lot of "battleship admirals" who have no use for air. He pointed out that for many years our battleships and cruisers have carried planes, and that all our men who have commanded such vessels are familiar with the advantages and uses of planes. King himself, of course, is an aviator and also spent four years in submarines. He is well-rounded, and regards submarine and air duty (both volunteer services, even yet) as on a par in importance to our Navy. He pointed out, however, that in all cases a man is a Navy officer first and a pilot or submariner second. This, he feels, contributes to unity of command.

As for the general progress of the war, King feels that Germany will collapse before Japan, and he thinks Russia, while suffering tremendous loses, is bleeding Germany white. He does not estimate when the war will end. King is a realist, and doesn't waste time speculating on things that can only be determined by the event.

Another point. He feels the RAF has not justified itself since the famous Battle of Britain. It has cooperated with neither the British Army nor the British Navy, with the result that there have been a lot of difficulties. In the present Egyptian campaign the RAF has done better, with obvious results.

Turning to Dakar, he says it cannot be taken by frontal assault from the sea. Too expensive. Thinks it'll have to be taken from the rear, but this is tough, too, for it would mean fighting through such people as the Senegalese, who in the First World War were feared more by the Germans than any other troops. However, if the Axis can be booted out of Africa, Dakar will be hopelessly cut off and will not be important very long thereafter.

In connection with the Mediterranean, King explained that he did not believe in combined commands, feeling the difference in habits, customs, traditions make it almost impossible to get good coordination. Although *Wasp* was lent to the British to take two loads of Spitfires in to Malta, as a general rule King has refused requests that he detach American ships for combat duty in the Mediterranean. He has, however, offered to substitute American for British ships elsewhere, thus releasing them to form a homogeneous fighting unit. This has been done many times, our ships forming a part of the British Home Fleet while British units went down to the Mediterranean to fight.

As for lend-lease, we are of course besieged by requests for stuff from the other United Nations. King's formula is to say we can't possibly decide what allocations to make until we know what the nation concerned can do for itself. Nine times out of ten it develops it isn't prepared to do anything. Russia has presented a difficult problem. In the first place, the Russians are exceedingly close-mouthed. We haven't been able to send observers to the front, and we haven't any information as to what the Russians have, what they are producing, and what they need more of. Beyond that, they have not been cooperative about helping us get the stuff in. Instead, they have in effect been standing on the dock with their hands out.

The route to Murmansk and Archangel, as you know, is very dangerous, and our losses have been heavy. Yet it has been the devil of a job to get any help out of the Russkies. Nowadays they are giving us some air and naval help—which they have always had available—and the situation is better, but it has been tough. For instance, the big problem is German aircraft bases on northern Norway. The Nazi submarines don't cruise around. They stay in port around Narvik, polishing brass and drinking beer, until the planes spot something. They they go out to do their job. We kept after the Russians to fight off those planes, and now they're doing it. The air fields in northern Norway are built over crevasses, having wooden bridges over them so the runways can be extended far enough. The Russians know they're there, yet have never bombed them. King doesn't know why.

He also doesn't know why the Germans haven't cut the Murmansk railway. Says he wouldn't out it past them to leave it open as a trap into which we keep putting our shipping, just as we are using Kiska as bait for the Japs.

And that is about the works. One of the chief delights of these memoranda is that there is no copy desk to say "Stop! No more space." I think you'll agree the material justified the length this time around.

Regards

WILLKIE'S VIEWS OF RUSSIA

The Willkie memorandum that follows covers the same trip described in an earlier memo on Gardner Cowles. It is reproduced here because it contains material that did not appear in the earlier memo, and because it is Willkie's own version.

CONFIDENTIAL

Monday
9 November 1942

Dear Bart,

After a description of flying arrangements to Africa, Willkie turned to his experiences with General Montgomery. He went up to Montgomery's field headquarters and spent some time on the actual battelefield. He saw some planes shot down, and also inspected numerous German tanks captured and destroyed by the British.

Montgomery told him straight out that Rommel was already destroyed, and that anything that happened in the future would be merely mopping up, or consummation of the victory. He said he had destroyed 150 of Rommel's good tanks, or about half of them. He did not capture and use them for two reasons: it takes too much time to teach one's men to operate captured vehicles, and the fluidity of desert warfare is such that Rommel might have recaptured them, and would of course have been able to use them at once, whereas if he took British tanks he'd have to teach his men to operate them. In addition, Montgomery said he had just received 305 of the best tanks in the world, our General Shermans. An additional 50 were lost in transit, but the ones he got were plenty to give him absolute superiority on the ground. He liked these tanks because the placing of the 75 mm gun high up on the tank makes it possible to hide the vehicle in a depression and still get effective fire power.

Rommel's fate having been thus jeopardized, the Allied blockade sealed it. Montgomery told Willkie that American planes based in Jerusalem and other strategic points all around the eastern end of the Mediterranean had clamped down so ruthless a blockade that only one of five vessels intended for Rommel were getting through. German soldiers were sent in by plane, and the figures there were not so favorable to the Allies by any means, but soldiers in Africa have to take with them what they want to use, and the cutting of supplies was the crucial point.

At this point in the discussion Frank Gervasi's article in *Colliers*, in which Willkie was viciously attacked, came up without being mentioned. Mont-gomery, Willkie said, told him that Rommel was through, and asked Willkie if he would announce it at a press conference called for 4 o'clock. Willkie asked why him? Montgomery explained that the censorship in Africa was so tight that he figured the story would have a better chance of getting out if Willkie said it, and that it was important for the working out of his, Montgomery's, psychological warfare to have news of the victory get around the Middle East. So Willkie announced it, and was criticized for not having adequate military backgound. It is just another example of how facts can be misinterpreted by desire or accident when the full story is not known.

After this, Willkie told of his conversation with Admiral René Godfroi, commander of the French vessels at Alexandria. These vessels, although Willkie did not say so, are the battleship *Lorraine* (almost obsolete), and the cruisers *Suffren, Tourville, Duquesne* and *Duguay-Trouin*. All have been demilitarized. In addition it is probable that a number of French destroyers also put into Alexandria, but it doesn't matter. If he tries to take his ships to sea the British will sink them, having made all their plans to do so. It is doubtful if they could get to sea with any speed because of fouled bottoms. Also, they have no fire power.

The Willkie party then went to Turkey, where he found the Turks intent on keeping neutral. They are also in food trouble, and Willkie cabled the President suggesting that he send 30,000 tons of wheat to Turkey. He doesn't know what, if anything, was done about it. For the rest the Cowles talk told the Turkey story enough to make duplication unnecessary.

Next came Syria, where Willkie talked with De Gaulle, whom he regards as an opera bouffe character, not worth taking seriously. De Gaulle is upset because he doesn't get equal consideration with the British and the United States in war councils, not because of his own prestige but because of the prestige of La Belle France. He complained about this to Willkie, who tried to convince him that he was wrong.

"Old man," Willkie said he told him, "you're a military man, and you should understand the situation. You say Syria is the most important military point in the world. It's French. But you haven't any soldiers with which to defend it. The British have. Now, if the cases were reversed, would you as a soldier waste time consulting those with no power to act?"

De Gaulle said it was different in this case, because it was French soil, etc. etc. Willkie told him that the only asset he had was a good reputation all over the world, and that he'd lose that if he didn't change his ways and come down to earth. De Gaulle agreed that this might be so, and commented that he thought he'd run up to London to talk it over with Churchill.

After this Willkie flew to Kuybyshev, where he was not welcomed as heartily as he could have hoped. It looked to him as though he wasn't going to get to see the people or things he wanted, although the supernumerary who talked with him (a kind of Soviet Grover Whalen) was pleasant enough. It wasn't until he met Stalin, and Stalin took a great shine to him, that he could get around in Russia. After that the sky was the limit. He could have anything he wanted.

Willkie characterized Stalin as a rough, tough little guy, who was smart, hard as nails, and knew what he wanted all the time. His sense of humor is somewhat on the earthy side, and I gathered he is quite a kidder. Willkie cited some of his jokes, one of which, with a real stinger in its tail, we'll come to later on. The subject of women came up, and Willkie remarked that he had reached the age where he didn't think about such things. Stalin expressed doubt about this, saying he was 62 years old, and he still thought of such things sometimes.

Before I forget, Willkie said Montgomery didn't make a very favorable impression at first. He is short, stocky, looks like an army officer. But Willkie came to like and respect him very much.

Although Stalin and Willkie talked through an interpreter, he didn't find that too onerous. Willkie had been in Russia a day or two before Stalin invited him to the Kremlin for dinner. He found the Kremlin magnificently impressive. The same was true of Stalin's office, and this reminded him that when John L. Lewis came to New York to negotiate with Willkie, he'd hire an entire floor in the St. Regis, because that was the swankiest hotel in town and he wanted to show he could do his stuff there. A trait of self-made men, Willkie thinks, and he commented later that Chiang Kai-shek's offices were very simple and unostentatious.

Willkie told Stalin repeatedly that he liked him, that he was, in Willkie's words, "My kind of fella." Stalin told Willkie he could see anybody or anything he wanted to. Willkie said he wanted to see two men, the head of the church in Russia, and the engineer who was planning power developments in Russia much larger than anything in the United States. If Willkie ever saw the latter, he didn't say so, but he did see the former. I'll come to that.

Willkie also said he didn't want to double back on his way home, that he'd like to fly over Siberia to Alaska. Why don't you? Stalin asked. Nobody'd said he could, Willkie answered. In the end Stalin explained he wouldn't have suggested the trip if he hadn't meant he could make it. This is pretty unusual. Until the Siberian supply line got set up, they even had Soviet pilots take command of lend-lease planes in Alaska and fly them over.

Willkie wanted to see a battlefield, and he went up to the front at Rzhev. He was escorted by a commander, a 37-year old major general whose father had been a peasant. Willkie throughout was impressed by the way Russians of common parentage had risen to positions of influence and importance. In view of the way the erstwhile ruling class had been liquidated, it could hardly have been otherwise.

Back in Moscow, he went to see the librarian of the Moscow Library, a place with 5,000,000 volumes. The librarian was English-speaking, intelligent, attractive. He asked Willkie what he could do for him. Willkie said he'd like to speak to him alone, where no one could hear. This being arranged, Willkie said he could understand how a working man might find the Russian regimen all right, but he didn't see how an obviously cultured man could stand it. The answer was that Willkie didn't understand. The librarian was the son of peasant parents, with no opportunity at all. Under the Soviets he was given the chance to become librarian of what he believed to be the finest library in the world. That, as he saw it, was real liberty. As to surveillance, what difference to a man who agreed with the regime?

Willkie also told of lunching with an attractive and cultured young woman. He deliberately needled her to get her to tell her true thoughts about Russia. Finally she hurled herself out of her chair and said, "My mother was a Moslemite woman in Georgia. She wore a veil. She was a slave. But I am free. I am free to sleep with you tonight if I want to." We gathered she didn't want to.

As to religion, Willkie said it was true there was freedom of worship in Russia, but that it didn't mean anything. He was taken to see the Metropolitan of Moscow, the head of the Russian Church. In Czarist days this man would have been a figure only slightly less powerful than the Czar. This time they had to look all around the outskirts of Moscow before they found the fellow in a small, one room place. Willkie talked with him, but he had already made up his mind as to how important religion was in Russia. On the way back he asked his guide why he hadn't come in with him. The answer was that he didn't want to see "the God-damned swine" and that he couldn't understand why Willkie should want to. Didn't they have enough like him at home?

Stalin told Willkie Russia was in a very tough spot. Stalingrad, he said, had little or no strategic importance, but it had become a symbol for the whole Middle East, and he was going to hold it if he could. Willkie figures Stalin is playing an opportunistic role as regards the United States, that he will perforce settle for what he can get.

He explained that Stalin wasn't on the outs with Churchill really, but that he was sore because Churchill was doing better than he was in getting material out of a sucker, the sucker being Roosevelt. A point that really bit was that 52 fighter planes destined for Russia had been grabbed by the British in Iceland. Stalin was burning about that.

As for the United States, Stalin said only 15 percent of the stuff promised to come over the northern route had left the dock in the United States, and 40 percent of the stuff for the southern route. He was not talking about their being sunk en route, or anything like that, but just that the stuff had never left this country. This, in his view, constituted a big letdown under the Protocol. He was also angry that the United States had not bothered to send any important figures to Russia. Churchill came because Stalin asked him to. The United States sent Harry Hopkins and Harriman.

Stalin believed the United States was in Britain's pocket, and the fact that Harriman, on arrival in Moscow with Churchill, said that the British Prime Minister spoke for both countries was the clincher on this point. Incidentally, he [Willkie] said Stalin wants to work with the United States in the postwar world, but won't unless it has cut absolutely free of British influence. Willkie stressed here, as he had before, that he was merely doing a reporting job, and not presenting his own views.

The Russian boss said that Germany now occupied the land on which 70,000,000 Russians lived, and that while it had been possible to get 10,000,000 of them out, the rest remained. The Germans took the men to Germany as slave labor. Stalin touched on German morale. He said it was still pretty good, but that air raids were helping to lower it, and high casualties had also had their effect. However, he is convinced that Germany must be beaten on the ground.

Stalin told Willkie he wanted to give a dinner for him. It was all right with Wen'll. On the morning of the banquet he was asked if it was all right if the British Ambassador was invited. He was to be the only foreign diplomat present (except, I assume, the top American diplomat). Everything was fine until Stalin got around to proposing a toast. He explained about the 52 American fighter planes consigned to Russia but intercepted by the British, and then, standing behind the British Ambassador, he raised his glass and said, "I give you the health of those God-damned thieves," Willkie got a personal translation from the interpreter.

It was evident to Willkie that Stalin had contrived this opportunity for exactly what he used it, some really hard-nosed ribbing. He also knew it would be reported in London the next morning, and also in Washington, which was unquestionably what Stalin had in mind.

The British Ambassador was called upon to offer a toast, and he uttered a few essentially meaningless words. Then Willkie got up, and recalled that there was a day, not so long past, in which Britain had been doing the fighting all alone, while Russia was playing footsy with the Germans, and he suggested that it might not be a bad thing if that fact was remembered now. He sat down, afraid Stalin would have him shot or sent to prison or, worse still, call off his trip through Siberia. Instead, Stalin leaned over and said, "Willkie, I like you. You shoot straight. You wouldn't steal 52 fighter planes."

There was an aftermath. The next morning the British Ambassador called on Willkie to express his profuse gratitude to the American for the way he had extricated the Ambassador from an extremely embarrassing situation. He added that if he could ever do anything for Willkie, to please call on him. Willkie promptly took him up on it.

"Here is something you can do for me," he said. "Answer just this one question: Did you steal the fighter planes?"

"Yes," replied the Ambassador.

Gardner Cowles referred to the stop at Yakutsk. Willkie went into somewhat more detail. Under the Czar Yakutsk had been the place to which exiles were sent. It had a basically Mongol population. It was ridden with tuberculosis and venereal disease. It had a population of about 20,000. Since the Soviet Union went to work, tuberculosis and venereal disease have been stamped out, and the population, which is now about 70,000, is 97 percent literate. Orders have come through, Willkie said, to liquidate the illiterate 3 percent, which is certainly one way of reaching 100 percent.

He doesn't see how this educational movement is going to result in any governmental change. He pointed out that Russian communists cannot be judged by comparison with the American variety. The latter group is composed of the have-nots, the ragtag and bobtail of the population. In Russia the communists are the big shots, the people in power. They have a vested interest in the state as it is, and they mean to keep it that way.

Russia, Willkie feels, is with the possible exception of the United States the most effective country in the world today in every way, and there is doubt in his mind as to whether it didn't rate first place. Incentive is a chance to win medals—the Russians love to give out medals—the chance to make money, and even to get membership in the Communist Party, restricted to 3,000,000 members, the cream of the country.

It is possible to make big money there, he said. He told of a composer who knocked out $100,000 in a year. But it cannot be built up into capital. It must be spent. Willkie inquired in a hundred ways, and all showed that it is impossible to acquire capital in Russia. One can own a house, or even two houses. But if one of the houses is rented, a state tax takes away all profit from the transaction. However since money can be made, it is spent in a big way.

The industrial system runs on a piece-work system, and would, Willkie believes, delight Tom Girdler. But the economic system runs on a no-capital basis, and would delight Norman Thomas. Whereas the economic system would not please Girdler, nor the industrial system Thomas.

As to proselyting, Willkie feels Stalin doesn't give a damn about it. The philosophy of Lenin demands that communism be spread, but he feels Stalin is more or less in the place of the Tammany boss. He wants to know how many votes there are in hand. He of course has to keep in touch with his district and what it is thinking, but he is mostly guided by materialistic ideas. He knows damned well Browder and his allied goons haven't a chance of overthrowing our government, and in consequence they are of slight interest to him. (This is my interpretation of what Willkie said.)

Summing up his ideas on Russia, Willkie feels there can be no lasting peace in this world unless the United States and the Soviet Union are friends. To this end, he believes all British influence on our diplomacy must be ousted. He says this while pointing out that he is a good friend of Britain, that he went over there when there were political costs to be paid for doing it. And speaking of risks, when he left the U.S. he went to Africa with the warning from FDR that there was a considerable element of risk, and that the chances were Cairo would have fallen by the time he got there. Somebody wasn't telling the White House everything, evidently.

Willkie also feels China must be friendly to us and Russia. He feels this friendship could be won by us by the exercise of no more than ordinary decency and courtesy. China, he says, is of course suspicious of Russia, recalling how Mongol territory was snaffled by the Russkies. But Chiang, he said, is a simple, able, hard-working man who is sincerely working to beat the Japanese.

Willkie said that when he was in China the United States had sent over just nine bombers and forty-one fighters, a disgracefully small number to a beleaguered ally. Chennault, Stilwell and Chiang all told him this. He hinted that Stilwell no longer stands high with the Gissimo, that Chennault is the fair-haired boy. Willkie, incidentally, is not high on Ambassador [Clarence E.] Gauss [U.S. Envoy in China].

By the time Willkie's discourse had got us to China it was very late, and he did not go into it nearly as fully as he did into Russia.

He said that when he returned to the United States the President asked him to call at the White House, and that after a playful exchange with Joe Barnes that was misinterpreted by an eavesdropping photographer as a quarrel, he went into the Oval Office.

In this connection, Willkie was plainly outraged by Roosevelt's comment that his second front remark from Moscow—or the comment thereon—was not of sufficient importance for him to notice. He said it was fortunate it did not come until he was in China, since in Russia such a throw-down by Roosevelt would undoubtedly have diminished Willkie's personal prestige, which in turn would have lessened his ability to do the job FDR had asked him to do, namely to sell the United Nations and the essential unity of the United States. I gathered that FDR's later kind words did not mollify Willkie in the least.

Anyhow, when he got to the White House, Roosevelt was frothy and effervescent, and soooo glad to see him. Willkie brushed all this aside, and told the President that few people around him dared to tell him the truth, but that he was going to. He then presented the Russian and Chinese complaints and his own reactions to them.

Winding up his talk, Willkie spoke with considerable heat, saying that in his opinion Roosevelt has lost his international grip, that he is not in touch closely enough to see when things are going wrong. He wondered what Roosevelt would do if the war should end next month, not that he believes it will. He figures we have got to think ahead and plan our postwar position, and he doesn't think it is being done. He figures we have got to establish good relations with Russia and China, and he doesn't think it is been done either.

I think this covers the salient points.

Regards

CORRESPONDENTS ACT TO SQUELCH RUMORS OF DISUNITY IN HIGH COMMAND

CONFIDENTIAL

Tuesday
17 November 1942

Dear Bart,

Sort of a potpourri this week.

To begin with, Bill Heinz's memo regarding service rivalries in Alaska is very interesting. However, by direction of the White House, sweetness and light is the order of the day between the Army and the Navy. This means that nobody in either service can pop off about the other. Nor can they verify material of this sort.

So we cannot hope, as I understand it, to get things of this sort totally cleaned up. Actually, jealousies are inevitable. But they crop up between naval officers themselves just about as often as between naval and army officers. And both services are making heroic efforts to do away with this sort of thing. So far as top-ranking officers are concerned they have succeeded, and it is gradually seeping down.

Incidentally, that incident regarding the mistaking of an American destroyer for a Japanese cruiser gives you an idea of the probable accuracy of our Pacific War table. I think ours is as good as any, and better than most, but that isn't saying much when you think of the Pearl Harbor damage we still aren't allowed to print, and the possibility that many of the cruisers we have claimed were in reality destroyers, etc. On the other hand, it is likely that some we claimed as damaged were actually sunk. I understand efforts to get the Army and the Navy to agree on a table of losses broke down over the Jap battleship *Haruna*. The Army says they sank her. The Navy says nuts. So they haven't gone any further.

As you say, parts of the King memo turned up later in my story, and also in Ray Clapper's column. There is a story behind this. You will recall that Representative Melvin Maas, from Minnesota, sounded off over the radio about the lack of unified command, and said we hadn't even begun to win this war.

When I found this covered in a CBS publicity release on my desk I called up Nelie Bull and told him the fight in the House over the high command had started, and that now was the time to squash it. Nelie called up Admiral King's aide, Commander Libby, and told him what I had found. Libby asked that I come over with the release.

So I grabbed a taxi and went to Admiral King's outer office. Libby read the release, and said he thought the Admiral should certainly see it. Just then Vice Admiral [Richard] Edwards [King's Chief of Staff] came in, and he too read it and agreed that the Admiral should see it and me. At that moment Admiral King came to the door of his office with Representative Edith Nourse Rogers, said good-bye to her, hello to me and asked me to come in.

He read the Maas release and turned to me. "You know this stuff is untrue," he said.

"I do know it. That's why I brought it over here," I said.

"Talk about giving aid and comfort to the enemy," King went on. "This does that to the maximum extent."

He went on to say that Maas had come in to see him when he returned from the Solomons, that they had been good friends for a long time, and that Maas had never mentioned any criticism or any intention of making criticism in public. This, King felt, was treachery. I suggested the following course of action

First, that the Navy take no direct notice of Maas, as to do so would build him up and also open the way for him to give a rebuttal. King agreed. I went on to suggest that the men who met with him at Nelie's would be delighted to do stories about the only really major charge Maas had made, that there was no unity in the high command.

This story, I added, would be based on part of what the Admiral had told us that evening at Nelie's, but would not be in any way attributed to King. However, we expected that if any question was raised he would back up our story. He agreed to this. The next step would be to get at least one of the stories into the *Congressional Record* so that there would be ammunition for Navy supporters to throw at Maas and yet not stamp the Navy with having furnished it.

He said, "Fine, why don't you do that?" I agreed. He said, "I want to thank you on my behalf, and on that of the Navy, for the interest you have shown.'' I told him anyone on our team would have done the same, and came back to the office.

Once there, I got in touch with Ray Clapper, Bert Andrews, Roscoe Drummond, Barney Nover and Ernest Lindley, explaining what was afoot, and added that timing dictated that it be an afternoon story as the Maas speech would break in the morning, and for them to appear together would be confusing. They all agreed.

Then I hammered out a story and sent it over to Admiral King for his approval. This done, carbons of my story, as corrected by King, went by messenger to all seven men. They wrote their own stories, based on the material in mine, and we got a good play. Senator [Warren] Barbour (N.J.) is inserting my yarn in the *Congressional Record*. And that, coupled with today's news from the Solomons, puts Mr. Maas right behind the eight ball.

It looks like a swell Christmas. Barring bad breaks, we'll have excellent news about that time from Tunisia, from West Africa, and from New Guinea. However, there is going to be real tough fighting in Tunisia. The Asix is going to make a big stand there. We'll come out on top, but it won't be easy.

Most significant fact from the naval front is that the Japs didn't bring any carriers down with them on their recent show in the Solomons. I'm basing my story on that tomorrow.

Here's an interesting item from the Pacific: *Saratoga* was damaged and went to Pearl Harbor for repairs. They rushed her through and the minute she was seaworthy shot her back to the Solomons. She arrived the night before the Japs struck, which was phenomenal luck.

One from the Atlantic: The coast of Morocco has such heavy surf that it can be used for landing only about seven days a month. As our fleet neared there, conditions got progressively worse for landing, since a storm was piling 15-foot breakers on the shore. But just as they were figuring they'd have to postpone, another storm came along from the south, hit the first one, and they both flattened out, leaving perfect landing conditions.

General Marshall explained about the Darlan [Admiral Jean Darlan, leader of the Vichy French government] matter. It is purely military, and not political. Our people did *not* know he was at Algiers, where he was visiting his sick son. They were surprised when he showed up. But they found that French officers in North Africa were bitterly hostile to De Gaulle [leader of the Free French movement], and were prepared to fight us as hard as they could, and then to sabotage. Our people wanted someone to call them off. ''We'd have dealt with a half-witted coon,'' Marshall said, ''if he could have done it.'' Darlan was willing to sell out. So they let him, and saved a lot of American lives.

The Free French are worried that Darlan's government will ultimately become the ruling power in France, and that is why they are raising such a stink now. But the chances are all in favor of their being 100 percent wrong.

What is happening now is rising above principle. It is hard-headed realism. Jean Beaube, Free French publicity man here, had a press conference yesterday in which he expressed his fears, and those of his friends. But the best idea, recommended by the Office of War Information (OWI), is to lay off until the military phase is over. Then there will be time enough to get into the political aspects.

Ambassador [Joseph] Grew (Tokyo) spoke at the Overseas Writers the same day all that King go-round was afoot. I managed to get to it. Grew repeated a good deal of the stuff he has said publicly, but added some other material of interest. I will add what I recall.

First off, he said that in January of 1941 he sent a warning back to Washington that if and when the Japanese struck at the United States it would be through a blow at Pearl Harbor. Then again, in November of 1941, he informed Washington that the situation had become so serious that it was necessary to be prepared for a blow-off at any time. He was asked when he himself concluded that there was no alternative but war. He answered that this was the kind of feeling a diplomatic representative could not allow himself ever to admit: that the situation was hopeless. To do so would be to end his usefulness.

However, in retrospect he feels that the situation became hopeless on 26 November. Without checking back, I believe that was the day the President sent his message to the Mikado turning down the Japanese demands. That date, Grew points out, would have given enough time for the Japanese Navy to put into operation the prearranged Pearl Harbor attack plan.

Grew does not believe that either Kurusu or Nomura knew of what was planned. He apparently has great personal fondness for Nomura. He has, for that matter, many Japanese friends, and is looking forward to renewing acquaintance with them after the war. His friends, of course, have been submerged and made powerless by the military clique that grabbed power. As you know, Grew believes the Japanese will not quit until they have been absolutely hammered to pieces.

He confirmed stories of torture of Americans, but said he did not believe top officials knew of the brutality of the police. The police, he explained, knew only one class of prisoner—criminals. And so the Americans were treated like criminals. He said that after stories about this were printed, and came to the notice of high government officials, the situation improved, especially in Hong Kong, where things had been pretty awful.

The point is that the thing about which the Japanese are most sensitive is being thought uncivilized by the remainder of the world. This is strange, in view of the way they run a war, but Grew says it is a fact.

He pointed out that for many years the Japanese have had such strict laws governing the restriction of information that nobody has been able to find out anything about Japanese war production. The United States, he said, had no exact ideas about what Japan had in the way of military strength, although our information was probably more complete than anyone else's. Actually, Grew said little that we didn't already know.

Ed Conroy tells me you are allowing 5,000 words for the war review. As I said, I plan to have the copy in your hands on the preceding Friday. It's going to be a white Christmas!

Regards

―――――――――

MESSAGE, PERRY TO BARTNETT

19 November 1942

Here is a story told about Alaska:

A Russian ship put in, fresh from its home port, bulging with champagne, caviar, vodka, etc. The American naval and army people felt lucky when they got water to drink, and their tongues were hanging out. The Russians sensed this, and threw a whale of a party and a heck of a time was had by all.

In return, the Americans felt they had to do something. So they threw a return party, and managed to get hold of a lot of rye whiskey. Since the Russians had been so open-handed, they felt they could do no less, and when the Soviet captain entered, the boys poured him a level tumbler full of rye. He sniffed at it a couple of times and then, with great aplomb, drained it.

A couple of stalwart Americans had got behind him to catch him when he fell, but he wasn't falling. He merely asked, "Do you have in your country much of this wine?"

Perry

ADMIRAL KING'S OPINIONS ON FAR-FLUNG WAR

The fact that the second King conference was held in the same month as the first is the strongest possible evidence of the impression the first one made on the Admiral. It is safe to assume that his priorities were such that he had not an hour to spare on trivia. Conclusion: he felt that it was worth the time he devoted to it, and that it was no mere social occasion for him. Actually, Nelie, the Admiral and I had felt that approximately every six weeks would be about the right interval between meetings. The fact that he requested another in less than a month was certainly indicative of his reaction. Not that we had been in doubt. The first King conference was held on a Sunday evening, as you know, and Nelie went to his office the following morning eager to phone the Admiral to find out how he felt.

He was too late. His phone rang before he had even looked at his mail. His secretary came in with the news that Admiral King in person was on the phone. When Nelie picked up his phone the Admiral, who seldom wasted words in business matters, used seven of them without bothering with the conventional "hello." They were: "When do we have the next one?"

The evening of the second conference was marked by something well nigh unique in Washington naval history, something that has never been revealed until now, even in our memo of the occasion. Admiral King forgot an appointment!

Had any officers junior to him been guilty of such a lapse, their bones would have been piled in front of the Admiral's office with a "Do Not Disturb" sign on them. But there it was. Nelie and his little band were there in plenty of time. Eight bells came and went. At eight fifteen Nelie called the Admiral's private number on his flagship, tied up at a Navy Yard dock. He didn't have to say anything more than "Hey, Ernie. . . ." "Give me ten minutes," said the Admiral, and to no one's surprise, he was with us in little more than that much time.

Walter Lippmann was at this conference, listening with great interest as the Admiral—"Skipper" to me," "the Thin Man" to Phelps—predicted that the Japanese would make a major effort to retake Guadalcanal, and that we hoped they would, because one of our big objectives was to force the Imperial Navy into battle.

Mr. Lippmann leaned forward, a worried expression on his face.

"But, Admiral," he said, "that would be to risk the fleet."

Admiral King had no objection to interruptions, although they were not numerous. His reply to the famous columnist was blunt.

"That's what it's for, isn't it?"

There was no reply, as Mr. Lippmann was brought up short with the sudden realization that a fleet was not something that won or lost simply by existing, but that it was something you actually fought with, if you could get the enemy to join the fray, and if you figured your chances of winning were good.

CONFIDENTIAL

Monday
30 November 1942

Dear Bart,

We had a most interesting evening with Admiral King last night. Present were Ray Henle, *Pittsburgh Post-Gazette*; Marquis Childs, *St. Louis Post-Dispatch*; Roscoe Drummond, *Christian Science Monitor*; Edward T. Folliard, *Washington Post*; Lyle Wilson, United Press; Walter Lippmann, Nelie Bull, Admiral King and myself.

In a general way the Admiral believes the war is going well. He subscribes to Churchill's description of the time as the end of the beginning. As for the Navy, it will be, comparatively speaking, on Easy Street in about six months, when new ships will be coming along with a rush. The program, with that of merchant shipping, was set back several times because of a vast program of construction of 35- and 50-foot invasion barges, which occupied all shipyards and Navy yards. The only way to end that program efficiently was to finish it, which is being done.

As pointed out in my last King memo, we were rated no better than 4 on the basis of the 5-5-3 ratio allowed us under the naval treaty, and it has taken time to build us up to treaty strength. But by next summer we'll be forging ahead rapidly. In the meantime, King estimates that we have destroyed approximately one-third of the Japanese Navy, which is a terrible rate of loss for a time when one is presumed to have the edge. And our submarines at the same time have taken a heavy toll of Japanese merchant shipping. It is King's view that we have forced Japan definitely on the defensive. He also believes Germany is preparing to assume the offensive despite the fact that she has yet to get hold of a satisfactory source of petroleum.

An interesting sidelight—King believes the Japanese even yet do not know exactly what they accomplished at Pearl Harbor. In this connection, he told us the permanent losses there are *Arizona*, two destroyers and the ancient *Utah*. Everything else has been or will be back in service, including *Oklahoma*. It is a fact that these rebuilt battleships are now far more powerful than ever before. I told you about the modernization of *Nevada*, which was one of the most seriously damaged. I assume what is true of *Nevada* is true of *New York, Texas*, all the rest of the line.

King's conception of the broad central strategy is that sufficient pressure must be held on Japan while Germany is being defeated. This is an exception to the concept of defeating the weaker partner first. In this case it is in all ways more logical to get Germany first. King does not know what exact proportion of our war effort must be kept in the Pacific in order to keep the pressure on. It may be one-fifth, perhaps one-quarter. But there can be no such thing as a status quo in the Pacific. If we don't pressure Japan, they will pressure us, and that means keeping them everlastingly on the defensive, pushing them back, now here, now there.

He is sure the Japanese will make one more last ditch attempt to get back Guadalcanal and drive us out of the Solomons. It'll be launched with everything they've got, and he says with absolute assurance that it will fail. It can be, and if we are lucky will be, turned into a catastrophic wallop at the Nipponese Navy.

Without pretending to understand Japanese psychology—King and the others of our high command were surprised by the violence and persistence of the Japanese reaction to our movement into the Solomons—King believes the Japs are committed to the campaign now. He thinks face may have something to do with it, plus the realization on the part of the Japanese that we intend to make this the springboard for an attack that will ultimately pave the way for the fall of Rabaul [on New Britain Island], key Japanese base in the Southwest Pacific.

King feels that it is very dangerous to give the Japanese time in which to consolidate their positions, and once we have our construction situation in hand—in about six months, as I said—I think we shall see some real activity in that area. However, as a practical matter, once the Japanese have been expelled from Rabaul, King does not think it desirable to press north from Australia into the Dutch East Indies.

The difficulties would be great, and we'd be exposing our flank to Japanese attack. I gathered King feels that when the time comes the best idea is to drive straight north from Rabaul, attacking Truk in the Carolines and Guam and Saipan in the Marianas. This would be a large and probably costly venture, but it would in all probability be less costly than the other possibilities, and would, once it was carried out, cut off the whole mandated archipelago from Japan and open the way to get back into the Philippines, which would in turn cut off the Dutch East Indies and make it impossible for the Japs to hang on there.

One of the most encouraging aspects of the Pacific situation is the steady deterioration of Japanese air quality. Their fliers aren't what they used to be, and we are now finding some army aviators among the casualties, where up to now naval aviation seems to have been doing most of the Grade A work. Jap naval air is rated well above that of the army.

As for the move into Attu, in the Aleutians, King is indifferent. He is not at all worried about the situation in the north, and you will recall that last time he expounded on the virtues of the Aleutians as a trap which is steadily consuming Jap ships and supplies. We, on the other hand, cannot take the offensive up there until and if Russia gets into the war with Japan, and that can't be until late next spring at the earliest, due to weather conditions.

The utilization of China's manpower is an important aspect of the Pacific situation. In this connection, King says that England is now scraping the bottom of the barrel on manpower, including the Dominions, and that this leaves China, Russia and the United States as the only wells of manpower left to the Allies. He feels it is important to utilize China's while it is still possible.

At the present time this situation is very unsatisfactory. Admitting the great desirability of getting more planes to General Chennault, King says it wouldn't do any good, because with the present supply line restricted to planes flying over very high altitude country, it is not possible to bring in the fuel and equipment needed to keep such a force in the air.

The reopening of the Burma Road is essential. In this connection planes flying supplies into China fly Chinese soldiers out to India, and General Stilwell now has three Chinese divisions in India preparing to attack Burma. These Chinese soldiers fly out without equipment, and are equipped with American stuff when they get to India. There is equipment available for more Chinese, but getting the soldiers out is a slow business. Also, it was not until fairly recently that Generalissimo Chiang consented to handling the thing this way.

To sum up the Pacific situation: Australia looks pretty secure. The Japanese are on the defensive, and it looks as though they'll be kept that way despite the British, who would like to see the Pacific left to drift while turning the full heat on Germany. Our own position in the Pacific has improved greatly. When the war sucked us in, we were greatly worried about the Hawaiian Islands, about the Panama Canal, about the supply line to Australia. As things stand now, it is most unlikely that any of these can be attacked at all, let alone with any chance of success. Not that we're taking anything for granted, but the fact is that we can rest much easier about the West Coast and the remainder of the Pacific theatre. Finally, we've been very lucky in that Japanese submarines haven't bothered us much thus far. We're knocking on wood.

Now, to skip around the world, I got the impression that King wasn't sold on the African campaign. It opened a ninth front of major character, tied up vast quantities of merchant and naval shipping, and in King's opinion doesn't promise much in a military way. He concedes, however, that as part of the blockade it is fine.

He does not think Churchill's theory of the "soft underbelly" of the turtle is too sound. The occupation of Sicily means only that it is necessary to occupy Sardinia. After that, a frontal attack on Italy, and when you bump against the Alps, what have you got? You still aren't in a position to threaten Germany directly, because the Alps block you.

While admitting that Italy might like to quit, he believes Germany already occupies that country as it does France, and that Germans would conduct the defense. The Pyrenees make invasion of Spain useless for the same reason the Alps do Italy. As for the Balkan Peninsula, that is possible. Turkey lacks equipment, and won't fight unless attacked. However, he concedes the taking of Africa—he thinks we'll kick the Axis out of Tunisia after a hard fight—will force the Germans to spread out a lot of divisions in South Europe that could be used elsewhere.

He discussed German strength somewhat. The Axis is supposed to have in Europe something like 300 divisions, of which 50 have never been definitely located. King wonders if these fifty ever existed, since he doubts that Germany would hang on to a reserve simply for the sake of having one, with plenty of places where they could be used. He estimates that Norway, Denmark, the Low Countries, France absorb about 50 divisions. Allied occupation of North Africa will force the placing of another 25 in the Italy-Sardinia-Sicily triangle and 15 to 20 in the Balkans. This leaves something like 150 for the Russian front, and that is the number King believes are probably operating on that front now.

Here is the background of the African move: when Churchill and Roosevelt had their second get-together, it was decided that a grand scale invasion across the English Channel should be launched in the spring of 1943. It was for this that the big invasion barge program was initiated. But the British finally decided that the fortifications along the Channel coast were too tough, and the effort was postponed. It won't happen next spring. The African move was decided upon when King and Marshall were in London last July.

The British figured they could have their cake and eat it. That is, they wanted to strike Africa *and* continue to prepare for the cross-Channel drive. The Americans took the position, and made it stick, that it was out of the question, that it had to be one or the other. The supply lines simply weren't available for anything else.

King believes the cross-Channel move will ultimately be made, although it might flank the defense by going around to Cherbourg, etc. One great virtue of either—or both—is that such an assault would make use of the planes and troops that have to be in England anyway, instead of leaving them comparatively inactive.

In this connection, King stated bluntly that Britain is hoarding war materials. He understands why. Britain is under the gun. If the Luftwaffe suddenly attacked her munitions plants, while the U-boats launched heavy attacks on the supply lines from the United States to Britain, England would be in a bad way. The result is that Britain is accumulating planes, tanks, guns, ammunition, troops, etc. Since Britain must be held at all costs, the Combined Chiefs of Staff now regard it as a citadel that must be treated as a war front like any of the others.

King feels there is still a good deal to be done in coordinating the Allied war effort. He points out that we send men to Britain, and from Britain to the Near East, instead of sending them directly to the Near East, thus saving duplication of effort. Also, we send fighter planes to Britain, and Britain sends fighter planes to Russia. Another waste of shipping space.

There are inevitable points of difference between ourselves and the British. King feels it would be smart if the British manufactured only fighter planes, which are needed to defend the citadel, while leaving bombers to us. The British insist on having Lancasters. King feels they could make out with B-24s or B-17s if they wanted to. But the British, of course, want to come into the post-war period with a well-balanced airplane industry. King feels we have a war to win, and that such considerations shouldn't count. Churchill, incidentally, impresses King as being for the British Empire first and for the Allies second.

There was some discussion about the completed invasion barges with the British. They wanted 'em sent to England and kept there until the time came to use 'em. We said the hell with that. We needed 'em to fight, not to store. So we're sending them to the Solomons, to Africa, to Alaska, to all sorts of places where American troops are stationed. We had to put our foot down on this particular piece of hoarding.

To get back for a minute to the African invasion, King said the Germans had heavy submarine concentrations along the route, but that we were very lucky. The subs got into a convoy coming north from Sierra Leone, sinking six or eight ships, but in doing so they pulled themselves out of the path of our attack convoy so thoroughly that there were hardly any alarms, let alone attacks, all the way over. A couple of transports and some freighters were sunk after they had got into the Mediterranean, but fortunately the troops had already left the ships. We know, however, that submarines will continue to be a problem, and a big one.

In this regard, King expressed the belief that Germany now has more submarines than at the start of the war, and that she continues quite heavy construction, although achieving a nice balance between submarine and plane construction that allows both as much latitude as possible. The submarines are very good, and while the original well-trained crews have been thinned down a lot, they are training new crews all the time. The submarine problem is far from solved.

To digress once more, our ship losses in the African adventure were pretty heavy, but nothing like as heavy as they might have been, or as we expected them to be. You can't make omelets without breaking eggs. I know. I made my first omelet at breakfast today. I ate it and I live. Banzai!

King expressed great satisfaction with the way the Combined Chiefs set-up is working out. He was here asked about the British dissatisfaction with the amount of information they get from us. He wanted to know what they'd do with the information once they had it, and dismissed their desire as natural curiosity that had no useful end beyond simply wanting to know. The truth is that we don't set up our naval command on anything like the centralized basis that the British have.

King said that when Churchill was at Argentia and in the White House he had his war room in which were charts showing the exact location of every British ship and, almost, every British soldier. This seems foolish to King, who believes in decentralization of command, letting the man in the field run his own show. He doesn't expect or want play-by-play accounts of every move. He prefers to have his commander in the field use his time on his own problems, rather than wasting it in formulating reports. As an example, a convoy is en route to the Solomons from the Canal. King doesn't know its exact position. He knows when it left and when it is due. Barring something unforeseen arising, in which event he would of course be informed at once, he doesn't give a hang where it may be from day to day.

Another observation: King attacked what he called, while admitting it was probably unjust, "RAF psychology," the spreading of propaganda that air power alone could win the war. He feels this is dangerous, for the reason that air power must always return to earth. Air enthusiasts are prone to forget that fundamental truth, that air-borne machines are fine in the air, but they can't stay there indefinitely.

Yet another observation: King believes that the German story that not all French ships were sabotaged is true, but he said he had no exact information. As for French ships at Dakar, Casablanca, Martinique, he supposed we might get them, but added that extensive overhaul would be neccessary, and he advised against delaying the war until we got those ships.

King talked about American manpower. The Joint Chiefs, after careful consideration, hit upon 10,800,000 as the ultimate size of all our armed forces: Army, Navy, Marines, Coast Guard, Air Force. He believes this is possible from an industrial and agricultural viewpoint once the country makes up its mind that it has to be done, and once women are fully utilized. The work week would also have to be extended.

While he doesn't think we will sustain any more severe reverses, and while he thinks we have good news ahead, he feels we must be prepared for eventualities, and that armed forces of 10,800,000 are by no means excessive. As things stand, he believes we are going to have the job of actually winning the war, and we might as well make up our minds to it.

Observation: there are four types of fighting in modern war: defensive (a prizefighter covering up); defensive-offensive (the fighter still covering up but looking for openings to strike); offensive-defensive (the fighter hitting with one hand and blocking with the other); offensive (the fighter swinging with both hands). In the Pacific we're in the offensive-defensive stage. Our position in the Atlantic was not defined. I gather, however, that since King views the African campaign as more of a holding action and a contribution to the blockade than as a springboard, he must classify it as defensive-offensive. Russia, of course, might turn the balance. As to this, King said Stalin knew why we can't get more supplies in—not enough shipping, too heavy enemy resistance.

And that seems to be about all. I've more material of a non-military nature, which I'll send along as soon as I finish my Review of the War.

Regards

PS—Lyle Wilson says he has it on the highest authority that there was no deal with Darlan prior to the invasion of Africa; that Darlan was a surprise and an embarrassment until it turned out [General Henri] Giraud couldn't deliver. More on this later.

CONFIDENTIAL

Wednesday
2 December 1942

Dear Bart,

Here are a few things that King told us but I remembered too late to include in my most recent memo.

First, as to Guadalcanal: King said, as I told you, that he believed the Japs would come back. He added that he hoped they would; that from a cold-blooded point of view their return could only mean further serious damage to the Japanese Navy, and a furthering of our war of attrition. He also remarked that the Japs came down last time with no signs at all of carriers, and that while they had some planes in the air, some of them were land based, flying at extreme range, and some with floats. He believes we have really hit their carriers very hard, so that they have to conserve them carefully.

King believes the Japs' last gasp attempt will bring down everything they have. He was asked if he thought the Japs had decided to win or lose the war in the Solomons. He said he doubted it, but that they had lost a lot of face, and were set on regaining it by hook or by crook. It is obvious, of course, that it may come to losing the war in the long run. I wish I could see you and explain with a chart before us, just what is in the wind, and why. I've already tried to do it in these King memos, but it's much clearer with a chart. And it's a fascinating study.

In talking about the Solomons, he said the Marines have been on duty there for a much longer time than we like to have our men serve without respite, and are about to be relieved. I imagine, although King didn't say so, that the force that just arrived in New Zealand will take over the job. This will of course enable the Marines to rest up for the next invasion. After all, the Marines are invasion, not holding, troops.

King said our biggest headache right now is cruisers. This is due to the fact that the invasion barge program threw our ship program off the track pretty badly for a time.

In connection with Allied manpower, King said the Australians have demanded the immediate recall of the division they have serving with Montgomery's Eighth Army in Libya. Obviously, it can't be sent back until the present show is over. But the Aussies have sent out no replacements, and the division's strength has dwindled from more than 20,000 men to about 16,000. When the division goes back, its equipment—guns, tanks, etc.—will remain behind. We will then have to equip it, presumably. Also, there are three Polish divisions in the Middle East, taken out of Russia, and I believe the British, who were supposed to be supplying them, want us to take on the job. They'll succeed, too.

I think that winds up King. Here is something I just found out . . . a little late, but it's still interesting. Lord Halifax and a party of important people flying to England came within an ace of being lost when three of the four engines of their plane conked out as they neared their destination. Fortunately the plane had enough altitude so that it could reach the landing field. It was a close thing, and the possibilities of sabotage are being investigated, since the law of averages does not figure on three out of four motors going dead. The big planes can, I believe, limp along on two engines, but one is hardly enough.

Here is what amounts to the official story on Darlan. It comes from a very high source. The story is that Giraud was approached as to his willingness to take part in the African expedition. He thought it over for quite a while, and finally consented. But he made two conditions. The first was that he be given supreme command of all forces, American, British and French, engaged in the operation. The second was that the landing be in France and not in North Africa. These conditions were turned down, whereupon Giraud said that while he would accompany the expedition, it would be only as an observer, a visitor, and he wanted this understood.

So the time came to go, and Giraud went along. He was convinced we would have ruinous losses, and he didn't want to be responsible for them, if we attacked North Africa. When the landings evidently were going all right, he changed his mind, and said he would serve in any capacity. The offer was accepted, and it then transpired that Giraud could not deliver. The French commanders in Africa would not come over to him.

Now Darlan enters the picture. He was in Algiers three days before our attack was supposed to break, and his presence was so embarrassing to our people that they were prepared to postpone the attack if he was still there with his son. But he left, as I say, three days before. Our people knew that.

What they didn't know was that he came back secretly, so when they hit Algiers, there he was.

Eisenhower didn't know what to do with him. At least, he didn't until it became clear that Giraud couldn't deliver, and that our information as to the reception we would get from the French when we came to North Africa was not accurate. That, incidentally, seems to me to throw some cold water on the paeans of praise for Mr. Hull's outfit. In getting wrong information, it seems to me they muffed the ball. Anyway, there was Darlan. He was ready to deal. Eisenhower wanted to deal. So they did.

Well, maybe so. I still think it stretches the long arm of coincidence pretty far. This is especially so now that stories are beginning to surface about how helpful Darlan has been, and how he is playing for keeps on this Chief of Staff business in North Africa, etc. I'm not giving up on the Klingenberg hypothesis, but it's better to give you both sides.

As for the future in the French situation, if it turns out that Darlan (and maybe Petain?) have been in our corner from the first, while appearing to work for the Axis [which was Klingenberg's theory], Darlan could be built up into a national hero to the Fighting French. Hell, let's be realistic. If they could make it appear that he had been doing this, whether he had or not, they could probably unite the French behind him. Ergo, they build up Darlan . . . or do they? I think they do.

Here is something that interests me. It relates to the ability of our officers. After the Army was allowed to go to seed at the close of the first World War, it grew very small, and had practically nothing to do except sit around the various Army posts. This meant that our officers had practically nothing to do but go to school. They did, at such places as the Army War College, a top grade school for officers.

The result was that when we got into the war we had a whole gang of high-ranking officers who had forgotten more about the high strategy of war, and particularly of logistical problems, than the British ever knew. This fact became obvious at once and was cheerfully admitted by the British, who are much impressed, and rightly so, with the knowledge of our general officers. Kill officers.

Here's a sidelight on the African show: Eisenhower is keeping a comparatively large force on the border of Spanish Morocco. He doesn't trust the Falangists as much as he might. In any event, he is taking no chances on a sudden and deadly change of weather. That is one reason, I take it, why we've not moved as fast as might be in Tunisia.

From Secretary Knox comes news that German submarines are more active, and that the greatly expanded supply problems we now face with the African campaign have put a terrible burden on our cruisers, destroyers and corvettes, particularly the corvettes. Knox believes the problem is too big for the escort ships we have available now, and that we may have a lot of trouble until building can catch up.

Regards

THE END OF THE LONG BATTLE FOR THE SOLOMONS

The battleship duel mentioned in the following memorandum was part of the climactic action that finally forced the Japanese to give up the battle for the Solomons. *South Dakota* was commanded by Captain Thomas Gatch. He was wounded by a fragment from a bomb that burst on the top of the Number Two turret, just forward of the bridge.

He was sent home, given his flag as a Rear Admiral, and was made Judge Advocate General of the Navy. He and I came to know one another quite well, and Nelie Bull quit his job with the American Veterans Association in 1943 to work under Tommy.

As a minor footnote to history, the Admiral told me that he saw the bomb leave the Japanese dive bomber, watched it descend, saw it hit the turret top—and the next thing he knew was when he woke up in sick bay, with a metal shard in his shoulder. He felt no shock, no pain, no nothing, just a blank. The pain came later, of course. It suggests that being fatally hit by such a fragment must be a quick and painless death. He also told me that the men in the turret were scarcely aware they had been hit.

Fortunately, the Admiral lived to continue serving his country. He told me, in another conversation, that *South Dakota* was once attacked by 22 Japanese torpedo planes that came through a gap in the hills as though sprayed out of a hose. The battleship's anti-aircraft weapons, 5-inchers, twin-mounted Bofors, and Oerlikon rapid fire guns, knocked 20 of them out of the sky before they even got close enough to release their fish, while the surviving two got no hits. He was making the point that capital ships had indeed been given adequate methods of defending themselves against air attack. Another officer told me he saw *South Dakota* in such an attack, and she was shooting so fast that he thought she must be afire from stem to stern.

CONFIDENTIAL

Monday
21 December 1942

Dear Bart,

This will be a right short memorandum, but no less interesting because of that. It deals for the most part with Navy matters.

In the first place, I am informed on excellent authority (Admiral [William] Leahy) that our new battleships *South Dakota* and *Washington* have had a battle with Japanese ships in the South Pacific Area recently. Since it was fought at night, we aren't sure what we did to their ships, or even just what ships were in the Japanese fleet.

However, we believe we sank a Japanese battleship. Our men could judge what was in the Japanese fleet only by identifying the types of shells that hit our ships. *South Dakota* and *Washington* were hit, the former repeatedly, by 14-inch shells, which means that at least one Jap battleship was along, since cruisers don't carry such heavy metal. We are quite sure we sank one.

But our people feel jubilant about the way our ships took punishment. The 14-inch shells of the Japanese were absolutely unable to penetrate the armor of the American battleships. They bounced off, or exploded harmlessly. At the end of the fight our ships were just as good both offensively and defensively as they were at the start. Some thirty men were killed on *South Dakota* and a few shells penetrated unarmored zones, but could do no damage where it was important that none be done.

As has been established previously, our naval gunnery is magnificent, even phenomenal, and we feel sure we got more hits than the Japs did.

However, there is a less pleasant side to the situation as it affects our Navy. When you come to think about it, half of our Navy has been bearing the full brunt of the Japanese Navy's weight for more than a year, and it has been an exhausting and wearing process. Our people are getting so they can do with some help from somewhere.

In consequence, the news that General Wavell had taken a poke at the Japs in Burma came as the best possible tidings to give the Navy a Merry Christmas. They don't care about the Jap ships if they can get the Japs to pull out some of their air power, and they believe the British push toward Akyab will help do this. In a sense, our Navy has been clamoring for a second front in Asia just about as much as the Russians have been seeking one in Europe. Now they have at least a token second front, and they feel good about it.

I talked to Joe Harsch of the *Christian Science Monitor* about reports of a German peace offensive. He has heard the same story, but doesn't see how it can be confirmed. He pointed out what is of course true, that the Germans would want to surrender to us because they believe we would protect them from the fate they have so zealously courted in their treatment of the Russians, the Poles, the Austrians, the French, the Italians, you name 'em. I cannot imagine either Britain or the United States going for any such plan, although I suppose it is also true that there are those in both countries who don't relish the idea of a Germany taken over by the Soviets enough to be impressed by the idea.

However, it seems to me that any true alliance between Germany and the Soviet Union is flat out impossible, no matter which is postulated as top dog.

Regards

GERMAN U-BOATS STILL RULE THE SEAS

CONFIDENTIAL

Wednesday
30 December 1942

Dear Bart,

At yesterday's Overseas Writers luncheon, the speaker was Admiral Sir Percy Noble, who has come to Washington to replace Admiral Cunningham as British naval representative on the Combined Chiefs of Staff. Also present were Admiral Land of the Maritime Commission, Sir Arthur Salter, head of the British Shipping Mission, and a whole slew of admirals, captains and commanders of both navies. It turned out to be a very interesting occasion. Part of it, developed in the question period, I was able to use, of couse without attribution, in my story today. A good deal more I had to keep off the record.

I was fascinated to learn that Admiral Noble was aide to the famous British Captain Chichester at the Battle of Manila Bay [in 1898]. He told us a little about that. For one thing, he informed me, and I think some others, for the first time that the French were ranged with the Germans in hostility to Dewey's fleet, and that it was a joint Franco-German delegation that boarded Chichester's flagship to say they didn't like what Dewey was doing, and to ask Chichester what he would do if they took active steps.

He answered, "Gentlemen, only two men know the answer to that question. They are Admiral Dewey and myself."

Then the German admiral said Dewey had said that if the German ships got in his way he would fire. Chichester answered that if Dewey had said he would do it, then Dewey would. Noble was asked if it was true that Chichester placed his ships between the Germans and the Americans. He answered that it didn't happen exactly that way. He said that Chichester's flagship happened to be under way, and that it just happened to get between them. Was it accidental? he was asked. He answered, with a twinkle in his eyes, "I very much doubt it, gentlemen."

But that was history. To come abruptly down to date, he said that the submarine situation was very serious indeed, and that if means were not found to solve the problem we might well find that our spectacular triumphs in Africa and elsewhere were worthless because of insufficient shipping.

What we must have are more long-range bombrs, more escort craft, more trained crews, and more teamwork. This last he stressed most heavily. Knox tuned in on this, since he had been hammering recently on the need for escort ships as the prime factor. Noble explained that he did not mean to underrate the importance of such craft, and that he wished they could double the present number by tomorrow, but that he still felt that coordination was the chief need.

He said that the First Lord of the Admiralty, Mr. Alexander, was very optimistic in his estimate that more than 500 submarines had been destroyed. He said he only wished that so many had been knocked off. As to actual German losses, he said we had not sunk anything like as many as unofficially claimed. He explained that the Admiralty is very particular about claiming sinkings.

In this connection a most interesting fact emerged. The British have prisoners from 90 percent of the submarines they officially claim to have sunk. The reason appears to be that the modern submarine, in contrast to its World War I sister, is not knocked to pieces by depth charges. Instead, when badly damaged, it comes to the surface, which gives the crew a chance to surrender.

This has not meant, however, that the British are capturing large numbers of submarines, for the Germans scuttle them. Only one was brought safely to port, and it is now being used by the British. Talking of the crews, the Admiral said that it was only wishful thinking to believe that the morale of German submarine crews was bad. On the contrary, they don't give a damn for anybody.

"They are truculent and filled with, you might say, hatred," he explained.

The modern submarine, it turns out, is much simpler to operate than the older ones. Men can learn to do it even in the dark. The result is that Germany is not suffering any appreciable shortage of trained crews. And, as I said in my story, they get five or six weeks of intensive training in the Baltic before going into the Atlantic.

He says the top estimate of German submarine construction is 25 a month, but he himself doesn't believe it to be that great. (You may recall that Admiral King put the figure at 30 a month.) He hopes our bombing has hurt Germany's construction ability, but he doesn't know.

Speaking about protecting against submarines, he said that the convoy system is the only sound one found thus far. The number of escort vessels needed for a convoy is calculated on the following rule of thumb: four escort vessels to a convoy, plus an additional escort for every ten merchant vessels. Thus a convoy of 40 ships would have eight escorting vessels.

The desirability of airplane support in defending against submarines is great, he said. He told of a converted merchant ship serving as a carrier coming up along the French coast with a convoy. Its bombers proved so effective that they destroyed four submarines on that convoy alone. That is marvelous hitting. Unfortunately a carrier, even a small one (7,000 tons would meet that description), makes a hellish big mark for submarines, and the one converted job the British had has been sunk. We have some, too, of course, of the Mooremac type.

German tactics at present seem to be to concentrate five or six submarines in a stretch of ocean through which they expect enemy shipping will pass. They are spread out so as to cover a considerable area of water. If one of the subs spots a convoy, it radios the others, and they form a wolf pack, stalking the ships. They stay with it for several days, attacking at night and keeping out of sight in the daytime. It is a mighty hard job to beat them off, Noble said. These tactics are made possible by two things:

1. A convoy consisting of 19 ships capable of doing 20 knots and one capable of doing eight must steam at eight knots. In other words, the speed of any convoy is that of its slowest ship.

2. The U-boats can do as much as 16 knots on the surface, although restricted to 4 or 5 knots under water. With their superior surface speed they can run circles around a convoy.

Noble spoke of the big convoys to Africa from Britain and the United States. He said his maps showed so many ships on the ocean that it didn't seem possible the submarines could miss them. But they did. Not a single ship was hit until they reached the African coast. This was a miraculous thing, a triumph of precision, organization, secrecy and good fortune.

He also referred to the Russian convoy lane. He pointed to the high cost of using it, but said that things have been better recently. Shortly before he came here a convoy of 31 vessels arrived in England from Murmansk without loss. It is, however, wise to assume that this was just a lull.

That is the essence of what he said in his direct talk. Then, in the question period, Sir Arthur asked if he might interpolate a remark. He then spoke his piece about ship sinkings being about what they were last spring, although our ships are faring better. He added that he thought the policy of secrecy was a big mistake. Knox spoke up to say it was only fair to add that the policy was not purely American, but was jointly Anglo-American. Noble said he thought the policy was based on the theory that to tell how much had been sunk was to give the enemy information that could be kept from him.

Well the truth is, as I indicated in my story today, that our Navy people began to get scared by the difference between actual sinkings and the American impression that the U-boat had been licked—as Paul Schubert, for example, said today in his column. They were afraid that the truth might come out all at once, to the detriment of American morale, and they have been casting about for a way of sneaking out some news to make the realization gradual.

I am sure that Sir Arthur came to the meeting determined to get the story out. He succeeded, although of course the off-the-record restriction on Overseas Writers' luncheons made it impossible to tell it all, or to name names. What was done was to use without attribution what came out in the questioning, and not to use what Sir Arthur said in his direct talk—in a general way, of course.

Today the Overseas Writers had another luncheon, this time with Leland Stowe as the speaker. Stowe has been in Russia, and he is very much impressed with what the Russians have done. He is a good speaker, and what he had to say gives you a new idea of what total war really means.

For example, Moscow. He told of a Russian woman and her daughter-in-law, a Spanish refugee, who were forced to live in the kitchen of their home because it was the only room that could be kept at all warm. The water pipes were frozen. There was no gas, and not much electricity. There was no food but some black bread. The temperature outside dropped as far as 50 below zero, and in the kitchen it got as low as 25 below. The Spanish woman explained that the Russians ate a kind of stew that looked like the slops fed the pigs. She had tried to eat it, but couldn't. Made her vomit both times she tried.

Then there was Leningrad, the story of which has never been told. It is a city of 3,000,000 people, and more than a million and a half of those people died of starvation and cold last winter. People dropped on the sidewalks and died there because there was no one strong enough to help. But Leningrad was held because the Russians had determined it would be held, whatever the cost. [A most graphic description of this siege is in volume two of Herman Wouk's *War and Remembrance*.]

Stowe said that most of the time civilians did not bury their dead in Leningrad last winter, because until they did so they got a small piece of bread for the dead person—about half a table roll. So the corpse, frozen stiff, was put in the closet or under the bed in order that the living might get more food. Grim stuff, God knows.

And Stalingrad, where the Russian troops were told there was no land behind the city, that they must fight where they were until they were killed. The individual Russian, he says, feels that his own life is unimportant. And they fought from house to house in a defense that all military observers in Russia had believed impossible.

Stowe believes that Russia's resistance has saved the lives of several million American boys. Russian casualties he puts at between six and seven million, with the Germans somewhat less but still very high. He has found that while the figures of losses put out by both sides are completely phony, the Russians have never claimed to have captured a place unless they had actually done so.

He says the Russians think we've had enough time to get going now, and that nothing but a second land front in Europe will seem to the Russians to be satisfactory. He finds the Tunisian action small, not a "blazing front," and comments that it has not gone as well as it should have. He says the Germans have much fewer than ten divisions there (as against 220 on the Russian front) and that if we haven't pushed them out of Tunisia in four or five more weeks it will show that we have an awful lot to learn about modern war before we can give the Germans a good fight.

Stowe is pretty indignant about American reaction to sending food to Russia. Who deserves it more? he wants to know. He also thinks we really don't know what total war is. The Russians know. However, he says the Russians like us, and that they get along with us much better than they do with the British. The average Russian, he says, would make a good Rotarian. The Russians have not been particularly critical of us about the second front, but they have been a little bitter about the British, since they figure there was no reason why the British couldn't start something in Europe. In this connection, he said Churchill and Stalin didn't get on too well when the Briton went to Moscow.

Stowe didn't see much American equipment while in Russia, although he did see some General Grant tanks, a few jeeps (but not nearly enough, for they are perfectly suited to the Russian roads) and some planes. He realized the difficulties of keeping the supply lines open, added that most of Russia's supplies are her own. Incidentally, he said the Russian soldier gets good treatment. He has much better clothing than the German soldier, for instance. The civilians suffer, but the troops are given every break.

On the other hand, the Russian command is very ruthless. It will, if necessary, deliberately sacrifice a division, allow it to be shot to pieces, if there is a compensating advantage to be gained elsewhere, or if supplies that can be used to defeat the Germans can be saved. The people, even those who don't like the communist regime, follow leadership of that forthright sort.

Stowe was asked about the Russo-Finnish situation. He has been on both sides of that front, and has affection and respect for both. He said the bitterness between them was so great that he feared a settlement was impossible. He believes Russia is going to take most of Finland as at present constituted, and that no one can do anything about it. None the less, Roscoe Drummond and I are going to apply the Cassidy technique to Litvinoff. We are going to write him a letter containing a number of blunt questions designed to smoke out some idea of what Russia wants from Finland. If we succeed—and Larry Todd of *Tass* believes we may—we shall of course have to give the material to the news services—with credit to the *Sun* and the *Monitor*, of course—but we will have the advantage of more time to handle the story.

Stowe is in favor of friendly relations, particularly of a commercial nature, between the USSR and USA after the war. He has an interesting argument, by the way, as to why we must really do our part in defeating Hitler. If we are afraid of a communist-dominated Europe, he says, we must realize that to let the Russians get most of the credit for beating Hitler will be to do much to bring that about. Right now, he estimated, occupied nations have more respect for the Russians than for anyone else because of the fight they are making, and he believes we shall get no more respect than we earn from such nations.

This ties in with Willkie's contention that the democracies have got to stand out as the dominant force in winning the war, since to let Russia's totalitarianism do it will mean that the world will be swayed to that system and away from democracy. There is, I believe, a good deal in this argument. It is interesting to think about.

Less sound are two other arguments advanced by Stowe. His contention that Russia will aid us in fighting Japan after Hitler is licked only to the extent that we help Russia to fight Germany ignores the fact that it is to Russia's interest—very much so—to lick Japan. They are realistic, these Russians, and they'll do what they must to solve their Japanese problem at a time of their choosing.

Secondly, he argues that Russia is drifting away from the world communist state idea—which may be so—and that even if she desired to conquer the world she is too shot to pieces to try it for a century. This is just not so. Nations come back very fast even after very severe costs in war. Germany, defeated and bled white in 1918, was able to come back strongly by 1939. A victorious Russia, even though also bled white, could come back very quickly. Whether it would matter a damn whether the Russian people favored conquering the world or not I don't know.

Stowe believes the success of the African campaign was predicated on Russian pressure on the Luftwaffe. He believes the blunders in Egypt were redeemed because of the Russian pressure on the Luftwaffe. Finally, he believed Russian battle claims to be about 80 percent correct. General Beaumont-Nesbitt (a Britisher here) tells me he figures their claims are 70 percent accurate. That isn't bad.

Regards

1943

ROOSEVELT'S TRIP TO CASABLANCA

Friday
15 January 1943

Dear Bart,

It seems pretty sure that Roosevelt is meeting with Churchill and maybe De Gaulle, but where is one of the prize mysteries of the day. Because none of his secretaries has gone with him, and even his regular telephone operator has been kept home, it is deduced that he is out of the country, and that he used an airplane at some point in the journey. Otherwise it is probable he would have taken Steve Early, at least.

Also Grace Tully, a secretary, went with him when he left Washington, but has since returned, which indicates he took her as far as they could travel on the ground, and then she came back. Churchill, I am told, is in the Western Hemisphere, but where nobody knows. De Gaulle is also missing.

The fact that Admiral King and General Marshall have been missing from Washington has been taken as meaning that a really major meeting is going on, but it now turns out that they were—and for all I know still are—in North Africa. Why they went there is also a mystery, but the presumption is they are talking about strategy with Eisenhower, Anderson and Giraud.

I can only repeat what I have said before, that this is the best-kept secret Washington has had in years. So far as is known, not even Steve Early and Bill Hassett know where FDR is.

Maybe in Moscow. Who can tell?

Regards

GENERAL HURLEY'S INSIDE LOOK AT WAR IN RUSSIA

Friday
22 January 1943

Dear Bart,

Brigadier General Patrick Hurley spoke at the Overseas Writers yesterday. He discussed his recent trip to the Soviet Union but did not go into the nature of the mission he performed for Mr. Roosevelt. In this regard, however, he said that satisfactory understandings were reached on everything he was instructed to discuss. I have some ideas as to what they were, and will come to that later.

Hurley, as you know, was Secretary of War under Herbert Hoover. He is an Oklahoman, and a real professional as an orator. My own opinion is that as an analyst he is perhaps a little shallow, but he is very much worthwhile just the same. And he had a story to tell.

He spoke first of his meeting with Stalin, whom he likes. His impression of Stalin checked rather closely with the one reached by Wendell Willkie. He finds in Stalin a first-class mind, wide knowledge of the world situation, and an absolute determination to win this war. He himself made a hit with Stalin by being exceedingly pungent in answering some needling by the dictator. Incidentally, he did not find Stalin the bombastic type, but rather simple and plain-spoken.

Stalin had remarked that if certain countries had taken certain decisions other than the ones they had actually taken in the past, the situation today would be different. The reference, I suppose, was to lack of trust in the Soviet Union by Britain, France and the United States.

Any ten-year-old child in Oklahoma knew that, Hurley answered, and added that if a certain nation had not made an alliance with the enemy, things would have been different too. At which Stalin laughed and said that Hurley was a real tough guy, and a man after his own heart. He asked Hurley what could be done for him.

Hurley said he wanted to see some of the actual fighting, that he understood no Americans or British had been permitted to do so. There ensued a good deal of palaver, but Stalin finally said it was okay. What else? Hurley said he also wanted to see what stood between the Russian oil and the German armies in the Caucasus. This too was approved after some discussion.

Before getting to Hurley's trip, I should say that Pat discussed the Far Eastern situation with Stalin. "I thought I knew that situation," Hurley said yesterday. But Stalin's grasp of it was amazing to him. He was thoroughly familiar with what was going on, and was able, with dates, to lay out the probable course of events.

Finally, as to Moscow, Hurley said that the red tape there was second only to Washington and London, but that once it had been surmounted he was wonderfully treated and was accorded every consideration. I am beginning to gather that once Stalin likes you, everything is clear sailing, and until he does, you get nowhere.

Well, Hurley and his party were loaded into a Red plane—the American plane in which they had been traveling was not allowed to go—and were given an escort of eight fighters. Hurley said they flew so low that the only time they gained altitude was when they went up to zoom over haystacks. It was a flight without incident, and they ended up at the headquarters of the general commanding the Stalingrad front.

It was a supply base, and Hurley confessed his heart sank when he saw the apparent confusion in which material and other supplies were piled up. He believed it would be impossible to get the stuff to the troops doing the fighting. But he was wrong. They were taken down the north pincer, which ranged from 40 to 100 kilometers in width and was about 160 kilometers deep at that time. The enemy was of course on both sides of them. But he said that the Reds, by using sleds with horses, wagons with oxen, and men carrying as much as 200 pounds on their backs, were getting the supplies forward in wonderful fashion. The men doing the fighting never lacked for supplies.

He got to the very end of the pincer in time to see an old-fashioned cavalry fight, in which some 32,000 Rumanian cavalry had been trapped on an open plain by five tanks on one side and Red artillery on the other. Then from a ravine the Red Cossacks debouched, and tore into the enemy. The fight lasted an hour and a half, until nightfall, and the Rumanians were smashed utterly. That night the temperature fell 40 degrees, from 20 above to 20 below. Sleet turned to snow, and in the morning there were thousands of dead horses and thousands of dead cavalrymen in the snow on the field. Hurley said it was the most grotesque and awful sight he had ever experienced.

While Hurley was there, the southern pincer met with the one from the north, completing the encirclement of the forces before Stalingrad. As soon as they met, the Red soldiers turned to the east and began the job of eliminating the pocket. Hurley spoke to a general, asking why the Germans had not been attacked instead of the Rumanians.

"Do you expect me to pick the strongest point?" asked the general in return. "We found a weak spot here, and smashed it. But there are Germans there (he waved toward the east), they are trapped and they will be destroyed.

His words are coming true now, of course. The favorite Russian tactic, Hurley found, was to probe until a weak spot was found, to smash through it and then circle behind the enemy. Then the Soviet forces in front of the enemy would launch an attack and crush the Germans against the encircling Red force. You might call it the riveting technique, and it works fine.

Hurley was worried about the possibility that the Germans might drive right through that northern pincer and cut off the Soviets, but it didn't happen. (Actually, there were other and larger pincers further to the north making this impossible, but Hurley didn't know that until later.) Pat and his party got out all right, much impressed with what they had seen, and went down to Baku.

He found that the Germans have not damaged the oil installations there in the slightest, although they've had planes over it at least twice. He then went up to the Georgian highway, the great military road through the mountains. The Germans were attacking, and he saw thousands of Russian women out digging trenches and gun emplacements. Before he left, a day or so later, the fortifications had been completed. Hurley does not believe the

Germans will ever be able to get to the Caucasian oil from now on. The fortifications are too heavy and the terrain too severe.

That, in essence, was his trip. Now, for the conclusions. The Reds, he said, do not have all first-class equipment. But second-rate equipment in the hands of able and determined men is doing first-class work. He says the Russians have good small arms, machine guns, anti-tank guns and light artillery, but that their tanks, transport vehicles and heavy guns are not so good. However, these are less important than ordinarily in the kind of fighting the Reds are doing, or rather because of the kind of fighting they are doing. Much of the Soviet heavy equipment is pretty badly worn down.

American equipment is very highly prized by the Reds. Our planes in particular are found to be excellent. They want light bombers, like our A-20, and are delighted with them. They are in love with the Airacobra. Our tanks are so welcome that Red soldiers burst into cheers when they see one. There are now a good number of them on hand. Hurley saw a great many, and he finds that the Reds are quite pleased with the stuff we are getting to them now. Not that they can't use more, but they appreciate the difficulty and hazards of the bottlenecks of Murmansk and Archangel and also of the southern route.

The Red soldier, he finds, is very good. He is a strong physical specimen, he can fight hard, and his morale is excellent. He inquired as to why the high morale, and was informed that it is due to the fact that the political commissars have been dropped. At first, it seems, the Communist Party didn't quite trust the Red Army, and insisted on the commissars. Now it is reassured, and those of the commissars who were officers have resumed their rank and the others have vanished. The result: excellent morale.

Hurley talked to prisoners. The Rumanians have no heart for this war in Russia. They don't like anything about it, want to go home, and surrender when given the chance. All they ask is good treatment while in captivity. Hungarians are not much tougher. German prisoners are pretty surly, and don't say much. But Hurley talked with one lieutenant who said he knew Russia was tough, but believed Germany could have licked them until the United States got into the war. That, he said, made the struggle hopeless in his opinion. Despite his belief that Russia could have been beaten, he admitted to the opinion that Hitler made a mistake in attacking the U.S.S.R.

Hurley commented that the prisoner was probably trying to butter him up when he said that British planes weren't much good, and that British pilots fled when attacked, but that the American Flying Fortresses did tremendous damage, and came on in despite all attacks. Hurley thinks the prisoner would probably say the same thing to a Britisher, knocking our planes and praising the British.

One of the questions several Red officers asked Hurley was, "What has become of the Luftwaffe?" It was said that there weren't as many in Africa as there had been, yet in Russia they didn't see one German plane where they used to see twenty. Hurley then laid out four possiblities:

1) That Hitler is pulling them in with the intention of going on the defensive on shorter lines of communication and is holding them for countering the big invasion attempts.

2) That Hitler intends to launch a blitz on England and is hoarding them for that.

3) That Hitler intends to launch a blitz on Russia and is hoarding them for that.

4) That the Luftwaffe has been shot to hell, and is no longer in a position to do as much as formerly.

My own opinion, since Hurley left it to us to choose, is the fourth. Against point one is the fact that planes get obsolescent very quickly, and that by the time he was ready to use them they might be just flying coffins. Against points two and three is the same objection, plus doubts as to Hitler's ability to make such an attack while holding firm on other fronts. Also, the initiative is in our hands, and the more strongly we hold it, the more difficult and dangerous it will be for Hitler to attempt offensive moves.

In favor of the fourth is the known fact that we are outbuilding the Axis in all areas. At the same time, Hurley says, the Reds believe the Germans are far from licked, and that they will make an attack in the Soviet Union next summer. Hurley too feels that it is far too early to be looking for Germany's collapse. In his opinion we are still going up-hill, although he realizes we are much nearer the summit than we were.

The Reds believe that Hitler has no serious oil shortages, since his synthetics, coupled with Rumanian and White Russian oil, take care of all his needs. Hurley doesn't agree. He thinks Hitler is pinched for oil. The Russians, to continue their thinking, believe Hitler was chiefly interested in depriving the Reds of Caucasian oil rather than in getting it for himself. Similarly, they believe that if Hitler had been able to establish himself at Baku he would not have struck by land at Iraq for the oil there, but would have contented himself with bombing the fields and putting them out of commission.

As for the present Red drive, he says the Soviets think it is good, but not overwhelming. They hope, he says, to be able to drive the Germans back to a line west of Taganrog, west of Kharkov, and correspondingly far to the west further to the north.

I have, since writing this part of the memo, recalled that Hurley said Stalin reminded him of Andy Mellon who, he said, could say only one word without stuttering, the word being "no."

Hurley, to conclude, said that the Russians can be worked with. He likes them and respects them. And, he said, they like us. He was speaking of the rank and file, I gathered, although I didn't infer that what he said is not also true of the higher-ups. He himself was asked by a general what he thought of communism.

"Well," he replied, "I am not a communist. I'm not even a New Dealer. I'm a Republican. But let's not talk politics. I didn't come here for that."

So much for Hurley.

Regards

"BULLDOG" EISENHOWER APPOINTED
TOP MAN IN AFRICA

CONFIDENTIAL

Monday
1 February 1943

Dear Bart,

Here is some extremely interesting material, which must be held in closest confidence. General Marshall and Admiral King are back in Washington, and the former held a talk with selected press representatives on Saturday afternoon. He talked very freely, and here is what he said.

In the first place, he was not appointed as Supreme Commander of the United Nations armies in the Casablanca Conference, nor was it planned for him to take that office at any future time. This, of course, does not mean that such a post will not ultimately be offered him. It means chiefly that the military situation now is such that a supreme commander would find his task impossibly difficult. I expect the subject to come to a head before the war is over.

Certain decisions as to command were reached, however. Here is the most important: as soon as General Anderson's British First Army and General Montgomery's British Eighth Army make contact with each other and with the American and French forces operating in North Africa, General Eisenhower is to be made supreme commander of all Allied forces in Africa. General Sir Harold Alexander, Commander of British Forces in the Middle East, will be Deputy Commander. Admiral Cunningham, present British naval head in that area, will retain that command and in addition will be given authority over the entire Mediterranean. Air forces will be under the command of Air Chief Marshal Tedder, who now commands Allied planes of the Middle East command.

One of the chief reasons for the selection of Eisenhower, Marshall said in a confidential aside, was that the British seemed unable to agree on any man of their own for the post. Apparently the Montgomery and Alexander backers got involved in a scrap. Anyway, Eisenhower, whom Winston Churchill, according to Marshall, calls "Bulldog," is going to be top man in Africa.

Incidentally, the importance of the African operations is such that the African theatre is to be divorced from the European theatre. Lieutenant General Frank Andrews, who has commanded American air forces in Europe—and who, if I remember rightly, did a great job in Cairo as air liaison with the British—is to take over the job Eisenhower formerly held, viz. commander of all American troops in the European area, including the British Isles. This will some day be a tremendously important post, of course, and my guess is that somebody like Devers or McNair will then fill it. At the present time, however, our chief activity in that area is air fighting, which explains why Andrews moved up.

Speaking of Africa, Marshall said that the Germans are suffering 200 percent attrition per month in keeping planes going there. He explained that he meant that in order to keep 200 planes in the air, 600 must be sent over. This seems to mean that two are lost for every one that survives. This is an unbearably high rate of loss for more than short periods of time.

Marshall also touched on Darlan. There are three points:

1) Darlan himself volunteered to give the orders to the French in North Africa to cease resistance.

2) After he had done so, Petain raised unshirted hell, and did it to such an extent that Darlan tried to rescind the order.

3) Whereupon Lieutenant General Mark Clark put Darlan under house arrest, and confined him to a villa guarded by two companies of American soldiers. He was held there until he changed his mind, and decided he didn't want to rescind the order after all. You can judge from this how stable things are around Africa in a political sense.

Hitler is getting about 700 men a day into Tunisia by ship and plane. He has, exclusive of Rommel's *Afrika Korps*, the size of which Marshall did not try to estimate, an army of about 60,000 men in Tunis. In this connection, the British are sinking three ships every two days on the average as Germany and Italy attempt to supply their forces in North Africa.

Getting back to the political situation there, Marshall said Giraud turned out to have no authority whatever with the French in North Africa. Even junior officers refused to pay attention to his commands. That gives you an even stronger idea of the ideological cleavages in that territory, and also the authoritarian slant of the French people.

One of the things that has been bothering us in North Africa has been the possibility of trouble in Spanish Morocco. We were, as I have reported earlier, forced to leave a large force of troops on the boarder of that territory in order to protect our rear from an Axis attack. There was also a danger that Hitler would strike through Spain at Gibraltar, and thence down toward Africa. Our high command was pretty worried about that a month or so ago, but Marshall says they feel much better about it now since the Spanish situation has improved greatly. Hitler, it is believed, has decided against a Spanish venture because his manpower is already a serious problem, because the transport situation would be very bad, and because there isn't enough food in Spain to feed the Spaniards, let alone a German army.

There was a word about Italy, too. Marshall said it was reported there were riots in Italy after Tripoli fell. It looks as though our people are hoping Italy will be knocked out of the war. However, I doubt if we much want her on our side, for whoever has Italy on his side has got to hold her up. It happened that way in 1917, and it'll happen again this time. However, it is hoped that large numbers of German troops can be tied up in Italy.

There is good news about our supply line to the Soviet Union by way of Basra, Persia. A year ago we were getting 240 tons a day over that route. Today we are sending 2,000 tons a day, and the time is in sight, in the near future, when it will be 10,000 tons a day. My private guess is that this last figure is predicated on chasing the Axis out of Africa altogether.

To turn to the Pacific, Marshall said that the Japanese are now engaged in making provision for a major offensive effort aimed at New Guinea, the Solomons, or perhaps the Fiji group. You will see that our people thus far aren't sure just what the Nips are up to, but they know damn well they're up to something.

That's about all I have now.

Regards

SECRETARY KNOX ON THE SOUTH PACIFIC, THE "FORGOTTEN" FRONT

CONFIDENTIAL

Thursday
11 February 1943

Dear Bart,

Secretary Knox opened his remarks by saying he was sore as hell as any newspaper man would be who had been scooped. (In civilian life he is publisher of the *Chicago Daily News*.) For some time, he said, he has been urging complete publication of United Nations shipping losses in an effort to awaken the people to the seriousness of the German submarine menace, but he has been overridden by the British government. Today, he said, Churchill scooped him by giving the whole picture in Parliament.

Questioned about the recent fighting in the South Pacific and the Japanese claims of sinking two American battleships and three cruisers, Knox replied that there had been no important engagements, and no significant losses on either side. Questioned concerning Japanese air power, he said that he believed the Japanese had probably sent carriers within about 500 miles of this area, and left the planes on several of their island bases there because there could be no doubt that Japanese air power encountered there recently was of a kind superior to any we had previously met.

He declared that our own crying need at the moment is for more planes in the South Pacific, and he appealed to the editors present to see that this need was not forgotten in the present tendency to concentrate public attention on the European theatre.

He also declared that in his opinion America should never again be without bases in the Pacific, because under any system of peace that may be established, it will be America's responsibility to defend against any threat of aggression there. He said these bases should be close enough together so that a fighter plane equipped with a belly tank could hop from one to another with ease, so that we would never again have to depend on surface transportation of our fighter planes. He made it clear that he believed we should take over all the Japanese mandated islands at the conclusion of the war, and said that, while leaving the governing of United Nations' islands in the hands of their present owners, we should insist upon the right to maintain bases on them at our convenience.

He told of the bombing raids that had taken place wherever he went, and said that they had only confirmed his contempt for high-level bombing, particularly at night. In any high-level bombing raid, he said, he preferred to be standing exactly in the middle of the target because in his experience this would be the last place to be hit. He professed to have no idea of what the Japanese plan to do next now that they have withdrawn from Guadalcanal. He pooh-poohed Australian fears and said that in his opinion Australia had never been in less danger of invasion.

He ponted out, however, that on his trip he had visited the entire series of islands that form a chain between Hawaii and Australia and that serve as key points on our supply line. One of these—Canton—he took as an example, saying that it had a strong and well-equipped garrison, a garrison as large as could be profitably maintained upon that island, but nevertheless a garrison that could not successfully resist an all-out attack if the Japanese decided to make it. The only thing our forces on Canton could do, he said, was to make such an attack extremely costly to the enemy. This is true of many of the islands of this area, including those held by the Japanese as well as by ourselves. It would not surprise him, he said, if the Japanese in order to save face were to take the losses necessary in attacking the American supply line at some point along the route.

In this connection he warned that the expression often seen in newspapers about "rolling the Japanese back island by island" had never been a military plan entertained by any branch of the United Armed Services. He said that, of course, it was the purpose to drive northward, constantly closer to the nerve center of the Japanese Empire, but that the drive would not be an island-by-island affair.

The evacuation of Guadalcanal by the Japanese leaves us with a tremendously valuable springboard for the launching of our next attack to the north. He did not say where or when. He said that we are building in the Guadalcanal area excellent facilities such as air fields with complete provision for dispersal of planes and completely camouflaged shops and housing facilities surrounding the fields.

One of the fields he saw was made of crushed volcanic rock, red in color, which was found to have the peculiar attribute of hardening like concrete after it has been rained on a couple of times. This field, he said, is now 1,000 feet wide, 6,000 feet long, is being extended for another thousand feet, and around it, completely hidden in jungle growth, are first-class housing facilities and all the repair facilities necessary for handling planes.

A quick once-over of the high spots of his trip are these:

Hawaii still needs some additional strength since Pearl Harbor, but is today by far the strongest garrison outside the continental United States. The oil supplies for Pearl Harbor have been moved from the tanks which the Japanese for some reason did not bomb, and stored in great rock caverns high in the mountains in the center of the island. What he described as "bottles" were hollowed out of the rock, lined with welded steel, and connected to the port by pipe lines through which they can be filled or emptied. Over them is a thousand feet of solid rock.

The entire island of Oahu is surrounded by barbed wire entanglements. Schofield Barracks, the main garrison on the island, is practically deserted and its men are living in pup tents close to the positions they would occupy in time of an alert. There are "numerous" air fields all completely equipped with dispersal facilities for the planes.

At Pearl Harbor itself, all of the docks which were under construction at the time of the Japanese attack have been completed and are in operation, including the drydock that the Japanese sank with the destroyer *Shaw* in it. The guns which were salvaged from the battleship *Arizona* when she was sunk have been used to strengthen materially the coastal defenses of the island. Beyond that, every sizeable island in the whole Hawaiian group now has airfields on it and is well supplied with planes.

At Midway he visited what he said was one of the finest hospitals he had ever seen. It is completely under ground, under eight feet of concrete with thoroughly camouflaged entrances giving the appearance from the outside of nothing more than sand dunes. It is excellently ventilated with a top-flight operating room, and is marvelously staffed. At Guadalcanal, the Marines have been fighting along the coast, where conditions are very bad.

It rains at least once every day, the muck is up to their shoe tops, the sun is intensely hot, and the mosquitoes are on all sides by the millions.

The men wear nothing but shoes and pants and most of them have grown beards, but their spirits are high and they don't seem to mind it. More dangerous an enemy than the Japanese, however, is malaria, which prevails throughout this region and which is keeping our hospitals filled to the brim. After his third attack of malaria, Knox said a man is no longer of any use to the Army or Navy and is sent home.

One thing of interest was the air transport system that has been inaugurated to take care of Guadalcanal wounded. Within 24 hours after a man has been wounded, he has been flown to a nearby island where an excellent hospital exists, has been operated on, made comfortable and is resting in bed.

Regards

THE SINKING OF THE *HOOD* AND THE *BISMARCK*

CONFIDENTIAL

Thursday
18 February 1943

Dear Bart,

I have, here and there, picked up some pieces of information that I think will be of interest to you.

First, Sylvia and I were invited to dinner by Hjalmar Procope, the Finnish Minister, last Friday night. Among those present was the Countess de Marenches, an old friend of my family. She is very close to the French people here, and is very anti-communist as differentiated from pro-Axis. That distinction, I think, exists in many people here, as in France.

In any event, she got to discussing the French situation. She told me flatly that the invasion of North Africa had been arranged between Petain and Admiral Leahy while the latter was Ambassador to Vichy, but that no time had been set. The general idea was that we would move this coming spring. When the plan was moved up, it seems nothing was said to Petain, but he got reports of concentrations of shipping at Gilbraltar and elsewhere, realized what was afoot, and cabled Darlan "You know what to do." Evidently Darlan's instructions were to play ball with us.

There are interesting possibilities here. It may be that Petain knew from the first that the double cross was France's only weapon in her condition, and that surface submission could cover deals with the United Nations.

[Pierre] Laval horned in with his pro-Axis ideas, but he couldn't spoil everything. It'll be fascinating to watch and see what happens.

So much for that. Yesterday afternoon Captain S. E. Porter, R. N. [Royal Navy], spoke off the record at the Navy Department. He had a good deal of experience on the Murmansk run, and was executive officer of the cruiser *Suffolk* at the time of her run-in with *Bismarck*.

Speaking about the Murmansk run, Porter contrasted the winter and summer seasons. Life in the Arctic, he said, is very lovely in the summer, with calm weather, bright sunlight 24 hours a day, brilliant blue sea, not a cloud in the sky, and not cold. Sometimes thick fog drops down very quickly. The ice pack moves to the north until ships can get within 700 miles of the Pole. Many of the officers who make the run have grown very fond of the Arctic, and hope to return—in summer and when the war is over.

For the Arctic summer means perfect conditions for enemy attack. Submarines, planes and surface units all combine to harass convoys, with the planes by far the most dangerous. They exhaust the crews of our ships, for the attacks come continuously for as long as seven days at a stretch without a break. Sleep is impossible, and the strain is frightful. There are always losses, but some ships make it.

In the winter the ice pack moves south, and is preceded by thin ice through which ships pass without even making a bow wave. Porter said it was somewhat eerie. You know you're getting to the ice when you see patches of the sea that look as though oil had been spilled. The winter in the Arctic is a period of complete darkness, except for a brief grayness at noon. But the stars are very brilliant, and in clear weather visibility is extraordinary. This is also true of the summer, when you can see as far as 50 miles. But the winter gales are frightful, with winds that get up to 100 knots, and make a very high, steep sea that deposits some 400 tons of green water on deck at every pitch.

Porter has sort of a poetic streak in him. He remarked that during these storms it seemed as though the old Norse gods were still alive and ruling that part of the world. He also spoke well of the aurora borealis.

Having laid this foundation, Porter turned to *Bismarck*. *Suffolk* was working along a stretch of fog that lay a little off the ice pack. When she worked out of it into the clear, she spotted *Bismarck* and *Prinz Eugen* about six miles away. *Suffolk* instantly ducked back into the fog. They were sure they must have been seen, for six miles at sea is a very short distance. But it turned out later they had not. However, *Suffolk* called *Norfolk*, another cruiser about 60 miles away, and that call was heard. *Bismarck* knew she had been spotted, but did not alter her course.

The concentration of British warships—a heavy one—made necessary by the menace of the small but powerful German Navy, went into action. *Hood* and either *Prince of Wales* or *King George* were in the vicinity, and they came along, guided by *Suffolk*. Those on Suffolk saw the fight that followed when, early in the morning, the three capital ships got together.

Wales (I assume it was she) was newly commissioned, and hadn't got the seasoning needed to whip a battleship into a really efficient state. She wasn't much use in the action that followed. Her plight was made worse by a lucky hit on her bridge that killed everybody there but the captain.

Hood and *Bismarck* opened fire at the same time at about 24,000 yards. The German splashes could be seen very close. Their fire control, Porter said—and this is borne out by technical descriptions of the Battle of Jutland in the last war—is always unbelievably good in the earlier stages of a battle, but it folds up and becomes quite poor after they have received a few substantial wallops. One of the German shells hit on that salvo, and those on *Suffolk* could see the glow where it landed, between the mainmast and the funnel. *Bismarck* was also hit once by *Hood*, and was set afire. But on the third salvo there came a mammoth column of flame some 3,000 feet high, with smoke shot through it, from *Hood* which never emerged from the column. German diaries, taken from survivors of *Bismarck* later, contained the account of a man who said he saw the bow emerge from the smoke, tilted way upward, with the guns still firing, and that then it sank back and disappeared.

There were just three survivors out of 1,800 men on the *Hood*. None of the three had the least idea what happened. A midshipman, 17 years old, said he knew nothing but seeing a vast sheet of flame and feeling an awful concussion. It was probably her high-angle fire ammunition that went.

As I said, *Wales* was pretty well knocked about, and *Bismarck* apparently suffered some damage, for she did not stay where she was, but broke off the action. *Suffolk* tailed her, aided by *Norfolk*. It was easy work, for she left a track of leaking oil half a mile wide. The weather was pretty thick at this time, and *Suffolk* went slinking along, some nine miles astern of her prey.

Bismarck ducked into a fog bank, and the skipper of *Norfolk*, a wily bird, feared the German intended to trap him. He took evading action, changing course, and was glad he did when *Bismarck* turned around, steamed out of the haze and headed for him. Porter said *Bismarck* was only about five miles off, and that it was no fun to watch her big guns swing around and train on them. Then came the flash of the ranging salvo. It was short. The next one was over. And the third would have been right on if *Suffolk* had held her course. But she didn't, and managed to avoid hits. One salvo burst 100 yards astern, and knocked men off their feet, so terrific was the concussion. She fired four shells at a time, three of armor-piercing type that threw up high columns of white water, and one of high explosive, which threw a black column. The latter is very deadly when it explodes near a ship, so far as personnel are concerned, as it sprays the deck with fragments. The armor-piercing shells go in before bursting, and if they miss, do little harm.

In the meantime *Suffolk* was firing her 8-inch guns and they believe they got a hit on *Bismarck*. Anyway, *Bismarck* turned away again, accompanied by *Prinz Eugen*, in the general direction of the *Brest*. It appears that *Eugen* too had been hit at some time, for she did not stick around, but kept on going. She might have been a decisive factor in the fight had she stayed. *Suffolk*, of course, made plenty of smoke screen and all that. Then the stalking was resumed. The arrival again of *Prince of Wales* apparently drove *Bismarck* to break off her action with *Suffolk*.

Some hours later some torpedo planes from a carrier showed up, and asked where *Bismarck* was. *Suffolk* was none too sure, but gave the general direction, and soon saw the flicker of anti-aircraft fire. It seems these planes got at least one hit. Anyway, *Bismarck* was slowed down. Earlier she had touched off her smoke at the stern in order to make a cloud behind which to escape, and for some reason the whole smoke apparatus went up at once. There were cheers on *Suffolk*, which thought the German ship had blown up. But she hadn't, and the chase continued.

It continued for some 60 hours, and then, in two minutes, *Suffolk* changed course and lost her., However, she had followed her long enough so that other Britishers had a good idea of where she was, and a Catalina flying boat caught her. Then, as you know, torpedo planes got her rudder. They came from *Ark Royal*. The earlier batch of planes came from the new carrier *Victorious*. *Bismarck* steamed in circles for a while. Then they got her going again, but she was badly slowed up.

This gave the British battleships a chance to catch up, and some of them did so with enough oil for just half an hour's steaming away from port in their tanks. In the fight that followed something like 1,500 shells went into *Bismarck*, and they couldn't sink her, although they reduced her to a shambles, afire from bow to stern. The British ships finally closed in to point-blank range, and you could see the shells leave the guns and streak into *Bismarck*, piercing her armor. She was finally finished off by torpedoes. About 130 of her crew were saved and another hundred had to be left because submarines were about. Some of the hundred were saved later.

Porter gave us some general conclusions about this action. One was the dislike of Germans for changing course. Even after they knew they were spotted they just kept on steaming in a straight line. Another was their failure to keep their fire control at a high pitch after a couple of pokes. The third was the fact that *Bismarck* had beat it after she sank *Hood*. They didn't dare to stick around. *Bismarck*, incidentally, was out on a pleasure trip, to show a lot of incipient officers how to sink merchantmen. They never found out.

Getting back to submarines, Captain Porter pointed out that they work best in a rough sea. The waves slow down surface vessels and also let the subs work in without being detected. They can get in close enough for sure shots. He also said that airplanes along with convoys help because they keep the submarines down. One of the ideas is to make them run as much as possible submerged because they are much slower that way, and because they use their electricity rather fast. Then comes an emergency later on, before they can surface to charge their batteries, and they are in a jam. On the other hand, allow them to travel on the surface in the daytime and they'll be in a perfect position to attack when darkness comes.

He commented on that action in which six British destroyers drove off a German surface fleet including a pocket battleship from a convoy bound for Murmansk. He says it is a peculiarity of the Germans that they'll run if you turn and head right for them.

Finally, he pointed out that German morale in 1918 broke in the submarine crews, and that the navy started the revolution. He also recalled that the Russian revolution started in the navy. He believes the same thing will happen to the Germans this time.

Regards

ADMIRAL KING EXPLAINS GLOBAL STRATEGY

What was Admiral King really like, as distinct from Ernie King the man? Well, he had a very limited tolerance for fools. Lay fools, who in his estimation cover quite a broad expanse of humanity, he handles by avoiding them as much as possible. Service fools do well to keep out from under foot.

It is my impression that officers who do their jobs never have much trouble with Admiral King, but that officers who don't never have anything else. I think he cultivates a manner of bleak efficiency, of a short fuse, of a cold and distant manner, as the face toward the world best calculated to enable him to do the best job possible, and to inspire the same in those working under him. An earlier Chief of Naval Operations (it may have been Admiral Standley) was given to saying that men were motivated by just two things: hope of reward and fear of punishment. I suspect E.J.K. accepts that doctrine.

But even on the job he is not always grim and taciturn. There are a couple of stories that illustrate the point. The New York *Sun* ran on its yachting page one Saturday during World War II a column-ender pointing out that while sailboats, however small, had right of way over power-driven craft of all sizes, including naval vessels, they should not insist on this right, but routinely give way.

Nelie Bull picked this up, pasted it on a buck sheet and mailed it to the Admiral, scrawling at the top, "Ernie: You should thank Glen for this bit of help." I received the slip in a Navy Department envelope. At the bottom King had written: "Glen: Thanks. E.J.K."

Another time I was in the Admiral's office in the "temporary" building given the Navy as its headquarters in World War I, and which it was still occupying for a couple of decades after the end of World War II before it was finally torn down. Vice Admiral Edwards had the adjoining office. He had a voice like the bull of Bashan, and since sound-proofing in those days was rudimentary, what he was saying was actually making it difficult for the Skipper and me to hear one another.

Finally the Skipper buzzed for his flag lieutenant, who had the outside office. He appeared as if by magic, and looked inquiringly.

"What is Edwards doing?" asked the Admiral

"Talking to New York, sir" was the reply.

"Tell him to use the telephone," was the King closer.

Another time, Nelie was in King's office on some personal legal business, when the Admiral's phone buzzed discreetly, and E.J.K. was promptly embroiled in a highly technical and, at least on his part, somewhat acrimonious discussion. It gradually became clear to the Admiral, Nelie and the unseen voice that this method of communication was not working well, if at all.

Apparently the voice suggested a personal meeting, for the Admiral grumped, "Oh, all right, come on up." In a couple of minutes the office door opened, and there was delivered on the threshhold a perky young ensign, a roll of blue prints under his left arm. The Admiral said nothing, following him with his eyes as he neared his desk. The eyes were doing the "forged in Pittsburgh" bit.

"I wanted to explain this to you in person, sir, so you could see what I was driving at."

"You'd better, son" grated the Eminence Bleu.

The Ensign, without further parley, unrolled a blue print on the Admiral's desk, whereupon the two launched into a discussion of an engineering point far beyond Nelie's comprehension or interest. The next thing he knew, the Admiral and the Ensign were on their hands and knees on an office floor carpeted with blue prints. The discussion continued until the King brow suddenly cleared.

"Ah, now I see what you mean. You're right. Go ahead and do it that way."

The Ensign got to his feet, rolled up his blue prints, put them under his left arm, and gave the first non-technical utterance since the one he'd delivered when he entered the office.

"I was sure you'd understand it when I explained it to you, sir."

With which he saluted, spun on his heel, and disappeared. King turned to Nelie, laughed, and said, "I like that kid. He wasn't afraid of me."

It is a safe bet that a note to that effect went into the Ensign's jacket, and that it didn't hurt his Navy career one bit.

CONFIDENTIAL

Tuesday
23 February 1943

Dear Bart,

Apart from the three super-confidential points of which I spoke to you and Mr. Speed on Saturday, the high points in the conference with Admiral King were his comments on the global war.

Casablanca Conference. It was the unanimous opinion of those attending the Casablanca conference that the number one task of the United Nations today is to defeat the Axis submarine menace. It was agreed that there are five ways in which this may be accomplished, all of them, unfortunately, involving the use of air power.

1) To bomb factories in Europe in which parts for submarines are made. The difficulty here is that if you bomb a plant which, for example, is making ball bearings for a submarine, it is still quite possible for the Germans to get ball bearings that are made for tanks in a factory some other place.

2) To bomb the assembly bases at which the submarine itself is assembled. This, in King's opinion, is the most effective known method of curtailing Axis production, which is now believed to be about 20 submarines a month.

3) To bomb the operating bases into which the submarines must put for refueling and supplies. Because of the thickness of the concrete roofs of the submarine pens (ranging from 12 to 16 feet) it is virtually impossible to damage the submarine itself, but it is possible to destroy the outlying buildings where supplies are kept and to blast the workers' homes, thus destroying the efficiency of these operations.

4) To track down the submarine at sea and sink it. The British Admiralty favors this above all other methods, but King believes it to be the least effective of all anti-submarine methods. We have, so far as we know, sunk only a handful of submarines in this war, and we believe the Germans now have anti-radar devices that enable them to detect the sound waves emanating from our radar detectors the moment they are put into operation.

5) To convoy all United Nations shipping so heavily that the submarines become useless. This probably is the most practical method of the entire five, but at the moment we do not possess a sufficient number of escort ships to do the job properly.

Convoys. Convoy escorts remain our biggest shipping problem today, for in spite of the fact that we have built a large number of new escort vessels, our convoys are no better protected now than they have been in the past because of the increased number of convoy routes we are now operating. Most important of these is the U.S.-U.K., through which we supply England. Then there is the U.S.-Murmansk and Archangel route, where our losses have been extremely heavy. Also, we operate U.S. to North Africa direct and U.K. to North Africa in addition. Beyond this, we have U.S. and U.K. routes around the Cape of Good Hope to the Persian Gulf, and finally a tanker route from Venezuela and the West Indies to North Africa to supply our operations there. These, of course, are entirely apart from our Pacific shipping operations.

For some time we were so lacking in escort vessels that we had to operate the U.S.-North Africa route over the U.S.-U.K. lanes, which made an extremely long journey and was wasteful of shipping. A slow convoy operates at six knots, while a fast convoy operates at nine knots, and this shipping so burdened the U.S.-U.K. route that we have to increase the intervals between convoys from the usual six days to eight days in order to get a supply of vessels sufficient to protect each convoy. Now this practice has been abandoned. Our convoys have already become so large and unwieldy that the danger point has not only been reached—it has been passed.

The escort ship construction program is lagging badly, which seriously increases the danger to our North Atlantic shipping. On the whole, this escort program is four months behind schedule, due largely to the fact that it was side-tracked to permit the manufacture of large numbers of landing craft used in the African operations, and also to the fact that the synthetic rubber and aviation gasoline programs, which require large quantities of brass and copper pipes and valves, interfered with it.

The destroyer construction program is six months behind schedule, yet King believes that by 1 January next we shall have about 60 percent of the escort protection that would be necessary to guarantee a reasonably high degree of safety to our convoy movements. Of importance in this connection is the question of aircraft carriers, because no convoy can be adequately protected which does not have an umbrella of planes above it at all times. On the U.S.-U.K. route, land-based aircraft can provide this protection for all but about 600 miles in mid-ocean, and King expects to station a couple of auxiliary carriers in the center part of this route to complete that air umbrella.

Regarding other routes, he is considerably more skeptical. The smallest carrier that he considers worth a damn is the 27,000 ton variety, of which we will not, in all probability, have a large supply any time soon. We are converting ten light cruisers (10,000 tons) into carriers, and while these will operate at 32 knots, and thus be highly maneuverable, there simply is no room on them for any adequate protection in the way of gun power. King says they can be sunk by a destroyer in any kind of weather that would prevent them from getting their planes up in a hurry. He says, further, that they will be sunk speedily in his opinion, and that some day the public will want to know why we do not have an adequate supply of 10,000 ton cruisers which we have sacrificed to build those carriers. He is no more enthusiastic about the fifty even smaller auxiliary carriers being constructed by the Kaiser yards, but he says that in this regard he has been overruled by higher authority.

Finally, he points out that one merchant vessel saved is worth two ships built, because whenever a merchant vessel is sunk, you lose not only the ship but its entire cargo. And the crew, even though some of them may be saved, is completely disorganized and must be reformed. For the past two months we have been very lucky. United Nations sinkings have been considerably reduced. Nevertheless, we can expect in April and May an increase in sinkings to new, unprecedented proportions, and it will not be until about December of this year at best that we can hope to destroy German submarines as fast as they are being built.

Blockade. One other important use for our escort vessels is the blockade which we are seeking to establish from Natal to Dakar. In the patrol of this line, we are getting substantial help from the French and from the Brazilian navy, which has finally been induced to go to sea, thanks to the heroic efforts of Admiral Jonas Ingram, who commands all American forces in South American waters. The problem of this blockade is to prevent Axis shipping between Germany and Japan. At present, Japan's ships are carrying rubber to Germany and returning loaded with ball bearings, which are badly needed in the Japanese war production effort. Some of this shipping proceeds around the Cape of Good Hope and some around Cape Horn, but by whichever route it follows, it must cross the Natal-Dakar line. We believe we can stop this shipping altogether. We have not done so yet. We think that about three Axis ships a week are getting through us.

The Global War. As he explained our strategy, every theatre of the war is linked with every other, and success in one theatre may profoundly affect the struggle in another. Here is how it shapes up.

Africa. The battle for Tunisia, of course, is important primarily because it must be won before we can come to grips at closer quarters with Germany. More immediately, it is important because by driving the Germans out of North Africa we will have done half the job inherent in opening the Mediterranean to United Nations shipping. The other half will not be done until we have likewise occupied the island of Sicily. With land-based aircraft both in Africa and Sicily we can bring our ships safely into the Mediterranean at all times. This would have two important results:

First, by making it unnecessary to operate around the Cape of Good Hope to the Persian Gulf in bringing supplies to Russia, it would release immediately 225 United Nations ships which could be used most advantageously elsewhere, to which I shall refer again.

Second, it might have an important psychological effect on Turkey. If Turkey could be persuaded to permit us to operate there, we could immediately launch a drive up toward the oil fields of Rumania, and with these in our possession we could eliminate one of our most serious supply problems.

Even before the battle for Tunisia has been won, however, it is proving to be of tremendous value to Joe Stalin despite anything he may say to the contrary, for at present it is estimated that Hitler has 200,000 troops in the Tunisian field and a substantial part of the air force.

Europe. The time and place of a second front are not mentioned by anybody. The key to European grand strategy, however, in King's opinion, is Russia, first because it has the manpower on the scene that is needed to defeat the German army, and second because it has the strategic geographical location through which it is easiest to strike across Germany's borders. For this reason, it is our purpose to fulfill to the letter 100 percent of our Lend Lease commitments to Russia. About 10 percent of total Russian arms and munitions will come from us under these commitments. King believes that Russia, in the last analysis, will do nine-tenths of the job of licking Germany, and as a wild guess he believes Germany's complete defeat will be effected in 1944.

Pacific Theatre. In the Pacific, King thinks the defeat of Japan will not be accomplished until 1946, but he is tremendously encouraged by the progress we have made thus far.

Taking a map, he pointed out the problem as it existed on December 7, 1941, and the extent to which that problem has been met today. Our chief accomplishment in that time has been the absolute protection of Australia, the safety of the east coast of which has been assured by our final victory at Guadalcanal. It is true that the northwestern coast of Australia, around Darwin, is vulnerable to attack from the Japanese forces based in the Dutch East Indies, but between Darwin and the populous area of Australia lies the entire Australian desert, and he thinks that a Japanese landing in Darwin would be completely unimportant.

Of course he concedes that it would injure Australian pride, just as it injures our own to have the Japs at Attu and Kiska, but it doesn't mean a thing. Throughout the islands lying directly to the east of Australia, we have completed naval operating bases which we believe are invulnerable to Japanese attack, and which will guarantee the safety of the Australian continent.

The most perplexing question in the Pacific is, what next? King believes the Japanese have some very definite ideas, and are preparing to strike a heavy blow at us somewhere. He has no idea where this may be. It could be in the Aleutians, but he thinks they can do no harm there and is inclined to guess that as a face-saving proposition they will strike at Midway. From our own point of view China is the key to the war with Japan just as Russia is the key to the war with Germany, and for exactly the same reasons. China has the manpower and the strategic geographical position necessary to crush the Island Empire.

Despite the President's smiling promises to Madame Chiang Kai-shek, there is no way we can get aid to China in the necessary quantities at present. This talk of 500 planes is simply ridiculous, he says. To supply any substantial air force in China will take tremendous quantities of transport planes, which can carry only light loads because they have to take in sufficient gasoline to get themselves out again. Making this problem more difficult is the fact that Russia is crying loudly for transport planes which are badly needed on the Persian Gulf route, where all our Lend Lease material to the U.S.S.R. must now be carried long distances over the desert, then loaded into ships, and then shifted to land vehicles again. The only solution to China's problem appears to be the reopening of the Burma Road. Because the monsoons are about to set in, it will be impossible to strike at Burma until next November, but when we do the Allies will fight there one of the major campaigns of the entire war in the Pacific. This is where we hope to use the 225 merchant vessels that will be released ultimately from Atlantic service when we get control of the Mediterranean.

Once we gain access to China, the whole Japanese force in the Dutch East Indies is automatically cut off, because Japan's supply vessels will have to operate within easy reach of our land-based aircraft. In this connection, we could also operate land-based aircraft from other points which I mentioned to you Saturday. Finally, our forces in China would be able to bomb Japan directly quite as readily as they could from Vladivostok or other northern bases where our problems of self-defense would be considerably greater than they would be in China.

Submarines. There are indications that Japan's supply lines to the Dutch East Indies are already beginning to suffer. Our submarine warfare in the

Pacific is producing highly satisfactory results. We are now turning out about three new submarines a month, and all of them are going immediately into Pacific operations. Through their activities and the operations of our land-based planes, we estimate we have now sunk about a million tons more of Japanese shipping than the Japs have been able to build, which means that her total merchant tonnage has dropped from a point somewhere between six and seven million last year to a point somewhere between five and six this year.

Moreover, we are doing better each day, and by the end of this year should have reduced her available tonnage by another million. This, in King's opinion, will cripple Japan's supply service to such an extent that she will have to shorten materially her own lines and thus release her hold on the Dutch East Indies.

Miscellaneous. The Navy has been instructed to check considerably more than it has in the past when it makes any claims regarding the sinking of Japanese war vessels. King said that if you total Jap losses as claimed by the Navy Department, not to mention Army claims (he said, nastily) you find you have sunk the entire Japanese Navy. As a matter of fact, he thinks the Japanese navy is considerably stronger than we had ever supposed it was, and that it is turning out new ships a good deal faster than we ever supposed it could. He seemed piqued at the way MacArthur's planes have concentrated on the bombing of Japanese air fields, and observed that if we could just persuade the Army to concentrate on bombing Japanese ships we would be a lot better off.

French Ships. Finally, he seemed to have a very low opinion of the usefulness of such French ships as *Richelieu* and others which are now operating with the United Nations. *Richelieu*, he pointed out, has only one of its turrets equipped with guns, and has to have a second turret so equipped. These guns do not use ammunition of the size we manufacture, and we must therefore start a whole new and separate production line to suppy them with shells.

In the meantime, we are equipping all these vessels with our own antiaircraft guns to avoid necessity for yet another line of munitions production. Moreover, he points out that even though the British and American forces speak the same language, problems constantly arise when you have to use them together. Different nations have different customs, requirements and taboos, and this is particularly true of the French.

To make matters still worse, the reconditioning operations will necessarily replace our own work in American shipyards. For psychological reasons and for purposes of morale, we have to make the French believe that we are extremely grateful to them. Nevertheless, they are expected to get a very low priority in American yards at the present time.

Regards

STRAINED U.S.-U.S.S.R. RELATIONS

CONFIDENTIAL

Monday
15 March 1943

Dear Bart,

This memorandum will deal with Sumner Welles, who has been Acting Secretary of State and whose star is very much in the ascendant these days. He had an off-the-record press conference last Friday afternoon at the State Department. The *Sun* was not advised, a matter which we are now taking up in a series of "aides memoires," consultations, conversations, etc., etc., with State's press head, Mike McDermott, feeling that we rate being in on everything down here. I called up and made a preliminary statement of our position. In return I was invited to attend the conference, and I did.

Welles told us in advance about the Giraud speech, about which he was well pleased. Then he talked about the French warships and their crew problems. He expressed the opinion that sailors deserting ships that are being repaired here for service with the United Nations are impairing the efficiency of the war effort, and that they are helping no one but Hitler.

He revealed that the Fighting French Navy, based in the British Isles, is also having trouble, that some 400 of its men are now under arrest on a charge of attempted desertion, and that some of them wanted very much to join up with the North African French naval force. So there's trouble on both sides.

He was asked about the chances of a rapprochement between the Gaullist and Giraud parties in France. He said that at the present time the prospects were not particularly encouraging. The difficulty is that De Gaulle wants to be the big shot politically, although not militarily. Thus it is apparent, as was hinted by Wendell Willkie when he returned from his trip, that De Gaulle is not much help to the United Nations. It is too bad that he is taking up this political approach, since he is a far better soldier than he is a politician. I guess he just got bitten by the bug and couldn't do anything about it. You remember Willkie called him a comic opera figure.

Welles also talked about Admiral Robert, in command at Martinique and Guadeloupe. Using extremely forthright language for a diplomat, he said that Robert was an absolutely typical reactionary French naval officer, with not a single idea in his head, and that he would have to be replaced before we can hope to get anywhere in that section.

Pressure is being applied to the people down there. We have sent in no food for four months, and Welles said that the temperature is rising rapidly so far as popular feeling is concerned. He believes that public pressure may get so heavy that by the end of this week there will be real developments. By this I take it he means either that Robert will quit or that he will drastically change his attitude.

Martinique cannot live without staple foods from the United States, Welles said, and the long period without such aid has resulted in considerable want there. Not to put too fine a point on it, we are starving Robert out.

That was about all of the off-the-record talk. But a friend of mine—you dined with us in New York recently—spent forty minutes alone with Welles the other day, and he was told some extremely interesting and very confidential things. This must be kept to yourself, Mr. Speed, and myself. I was not even allowed to tell it to Phelps, by specific direction.

Welles said that the time had come for an agreement with the Soviet Union, but that such an agreement could not be reached while Maxim Litvinov is Ambassador here and Admiral Standley in Moscow. The reason, astonishingly, is that Litvinov does not have the confidence of his own government, and that therefore what he tells them is not given as much credence or importance as it would have to have for negotiations to succeed. The reason for this lack of confidence I do not know.

As for Standley, it is true, as I wrote for the paper last Friday, that he is not to be recalled because of the violent attack he made on the Soviet government, in a Moscow press conference, for its failure to publicize our lend-lease aid to the U.S.S.R. Welles did not mind that, and it got such prompt results from the Russkies that our people are quite a bit reassured, and feel their position vis-á-vis the U.S.S.R. to be stronger than they thought it was. Actually, of course, what these people had in mind, I suppose, was Mr. Stalin holding out his hand in a gesture of refusal, saying, "Don't send any more planes, tanks and guns. I'm mad at you, so I won't take them." There was about as much chance of that as of FDR resigning in favor of Willkie.

To be serious, of course these people are afraid of the Soviet attitude in the post-war world, afraid that if we're not nice to them, they'll make trouble. Obviously Soviet foreign policy is completely chauvinistic. As long as it is in the interest of the Soviet Union they'll play ball with us. When it isn't, they won't.

There is another fear: that the Reds will negotiate a separate peace with the Germans, leaving us in the lurch. If they're going to do that, there's nothing we can do or say to stop it. I do not think they'll do it as long as there are Germans on Russian soil, and I doubt if the Germans will get off it willingly after the price they've paid.

My point is that Stalin is a tough guy who likes other tough guys, and we'll never get anywhere with the Soviet Union by making them think we are a patsy.

Anyway, to get back to Welles. Standley will not be recalled because of what he said, but sooner or later he will have to be recalled because he just isn't heavy enough metal. They would like somebody like Joe Davies, a capitalist, a genuinely able man, somebody who would be truly representative of this country. They emphatically do not want us to send a pinko. I think if Davies was well they'd send him back. As it is, I don't know who'll go.

Of course, the recall of Litvinov will be difficult, for he has become known as the Soviet diplomat above all others who stands for collaboration with the outside world. His recall would undoubtedly be interpreted as a sign of a drastic change in Red policy. But according to Welles it has got to be done, since nothing constructive can be accomplished while he remains.

Welles believes, as I said, that an arrangement must be concluded with the Soviet Union in the next six months if it is to be done at all. In this connection, he regards a settlement of the Finnish problem as of primary importance. This leads me to believe that our government will sooner or later try to get the USSR to offer Finland a fair peace.

Of course, the Reds are being unconscionably stupid about this. If they offered Finland, popular here, such a peace, and made a great fanfare about it, think of the popular reaction in the United States. It would do more to reassure this country about Soviet intentions than anything else they could possibly do. Think how it would set at rest the stories about Red imperialism. Why, they could get away with all sorts of murder in the Baltic states and Poland if they made such a gesture. (I seem to be venturing into the world of *realpolitik*. Maybe I'd better stop.)

Regards

THE WAR IN AUSTRALIA

CONFIDENTIAL

Thursday
18 March 1943

Dear Bart,

I had lunch yesterday with the Pan-American crowd, who produced for the occasion none other than Harold Gatty of Wiley Post fame, who is now a Group Captain in the Australian Air Force and who had some interesting and revolutionary things to say about the war in that area.

From the outset it was clear that he held a low opinion of General MacArthur, based principally on MacArthur's fear of the air, his refusal to travel by plane personally if any other mode of transportation was available, and his reluctance to agree to send 3,800 American troops to Port Moresby by air in the campaign that was waged there. MacArthur's observation when this was suggested was, "They'd all be killed."

But Gatty said that General Kenney, for whom he has the highest regard, spent several hours talking MacArthur into it. Actually, these men were transported in 44 bombers over a period of four days with full equipment, weighing in at some 290 pounds apiece. All during the show there, the air transport carried food, medical supplies and munitions at the rate of 120 tons a day to keep our forces supplied. Parachutes were not available for the drops, so they ripped the doors out of the bombers, and shoved the stuff out over the soft and swampy ground from an altitude of about 70 feet. At first they lost 60 percent of the stuff so delivered, but later improved things so that 70 percent was recovered. They have not found a satisfactory method, however, of dropping munitions without the use of parachutes because some of the shells are damaged in the drop and each one has to be tested before it can be used.

Three things about this campaign were extremely interesting to me: first, that we did not drive the Japanese out of Port Moresby, according to Gatty. He says that they did not use air transport for supplies, but depended on coolie labor, which could not take the malaria and dysentery and mud up to their necks through which they had to plow. The Jap supply lines thus collapsed completely, and the Japs had to withdraw.

Second, the 32nd Division, an American National Guard outfit, was a complete flop in this show. Its training had been wholly inadequate and it had ultimately to be withdrawn and replaced by the 41st Division.

Third, Gatty is inclined to believe that we cannot lick the Japs on the ground. He says that at no time were there more than 6,000 Japs in New Guinea and that against them we had 50,000 Australians and 3,800 Americans. He says the reason for this is that an American or Australian commander always wants to have a way out before he embarks on a campaign of action, whereas the Japs do not concern themselves with escape.

As an example of this, he said the Japs were teaching all their soldiers to say two sentences in English: "Come on in and get us, you Yanks. You're yellow." He says this is proving effective psychology, and that in one instance where three Japanese with a machine gun were surrounded and called upon to surrender, they retorted with that phrase and the Americans charged in on them and killed them, but lost more than twenty of their own men in the process.

In the air, however, the situation is reversed. He insists that the reports coming out of Australia now as to Japanese air losses are absolutely accurate. The P-38, he claims, is a better plane than anything the Japs have ever had, and the Jap pilot is deteriorating daily so our own seasoned men are coming up against the greenest sort of competition.

As he sees it, our only purpose in this area from the start was the protection of Australia, and this purpose, he says, has been fully achieved. While the Japs may land up around Darwin in the northwest in order to save face by actually invading the continent of Australia, he says they are powerless to do any damage there and that it is futile for us to try to drive them out of their own holes in an island to island campaign that would take many years and cost us ten times as many men as the Japs would lose.

Probably without knowing it, he advanced the same principle of campaign that Admiral King spoke of and that I covered in my last memorandum to you. He believes the answer lies in China and that the only way to get there is by recapturing Burma, although it might be possible to take some bases on the China coast through paratroop operations.

High level bombing, he says, is out completely, and no bombing operation is now conducted from an altitude of more than 4,000 to 5,000 feet at the outside, while most of it is being undertaken at masthead level. In our first low-altitude operations at Rabaul, he said, we so surprised the enemy that we got away with it fairly well, but the harbor is so well protected by anti-aircraft guns that though there are usually more than a hundred ships there, we seldom get more than two or three of them on a raid. He would not attempt to invade this Japanese stronghold, and points out that it's much easier to get their ships when they come out of port and are no longer protected by anti-aircraft fire than it is to go in after them.

He says that Australia is simply overcrowded with its own troops, most of whom will never see action anywhere else in the world and who are plenty strong enough to take care of any land operations that may now be in prospect in that area. There is no particular reason why the two divisions of our own troops stationed there should remain any longer. He claims we have plenty of planes down there, that the supply situation is excellent, and that the repair facilities and spare parts storage are adequate to meet any need now in prospect.

Regards

BRITAIN'S CONDITION IN EARLY STAGES OF THE WAR

Another world figure appeared on the Washington scene in the presence of Field Marshal Sir John Dill, key man on the British Joint Staff Mission. I was especially interested in his comment that although Dunkerque was a magnificent rescue operation, it was a success as to personnel only. The loss of weapons and supplies, all of which had to be abandoned, was enormous.

"There were not enough rifles to equip the soldiery recruited in Britain to repel the expected invasion. But help came from the United States at once. A shipload of rifles got through first. . . ."

I quote that passage because I had (at age 15) served in the New Jersey State Militia Reserve, less impressively but more accurately known as the Home Guard. We were issued Krag-Jorgensen rifles, which kicked so hard you could not lay your thumb across the stock when firing, lest it be driven into your eye. When we were mustered out, we were permitted to buy our rifles and bayonets.

I had forgotten about mine until, one day shortly after Dunkerque, I received a notice from the War Department that I should turn in these weapons, as they were needed. They even offered to pick them up, and did. I have no doubt they ended up in Britain, and I'm glad they never had to be used to repel an invasion because if they had been used, there would have been a lot of sore eyes in the defending forces.

And of course Darlan, who was shot by an assassin on December 24, just three weeks after my memo about him, is still a live issue—even though dead—as my conversation with Cedric Worth and subsequently with Admiral Raymond Fenard, who was based in Washington by the Free French, made clear.

CONFIDENTIAL

Tuesday
30 March 1943

Dear Bart,

Field Marshall Sir John Dill spoke at the Overseas Writers recently, and while he said, as you would expect, nothing sensational, he did give what amounted to an historical footnote on the British situation in the early stages of the war.

He pointed out that in the First World War he could remember how dire the peril to Britain appeared when it looked as if the Channel ports of France might be lost. It seemed then as though that would mean the loss of the war. But in World War II the Channel ports were lost, along with the rest of France, and the British, while despairing of their ability to withstand invasion, found that it wasn't as fatal as they had thought.

But there was more to the collapse of France than just the European aspects. In it the British saw the collapse of French Indochina, which would give the Japanese an open door for setting up a war to be conducted in Burma and Malaya. They saw great difficulties in the Middle East as the result of the possible defection of Syria. In Africa there were the three big French territories, Algiers, Morocco, Tunisia. All over the world the interests of Britain were affected by the collapse of France.

Worse yet, practically all of the equipment the British had that was worth a damn was lost. Men got out, but their equipment did not. There were not enough rifles to equip the soldiery recruited in Britain to repel the expected invasion, but help came from the United States at once (and for me, that was the minute we entered the war as an unregistered participant on the Allied side). A shipload of rifles got through first, old stuff taken from our arsenals, along with some French 75s that hadn't been modernized from the last war.

But gradually they got themselves organized. British war production picked up, and our help continued. And then came the need for a British choice. There was tremendous pressure exerted in favor of keeping British equipment at home, defending the citadel at all hazards. This was the British equivalent of our isolationism, I suppose. On the other hand, there was the more realistic school of thought which held that Britain could never win the war by sitting tight in the British Isles, and letting Suez, Gibraltar and the other key points of world strategy go by default.

As it turned out, the realists won, and despite the peril to England, large forces were sent to Egypt, to the Middle East, and elsewhere. In a sense, I suppose the collapse of British power in the Orient was something of a relief to Churchill, since it meant that there was one theatre of war that no longer had to be supplied, so there was just so much more for the other fronts.

Well, all this isn't particularly important now, but it's interesting background from a world figure, I think. I had a little private chat with Sir John before he gave his talk. He was optimistic about Africa, and we agreed that Montgomery was quite a fellow. Then I remarked that while Montgomery was unquestionably good, it seemed to me there had been a tendency to overlook his superior, Alexander. Sir John agreed, and added that this was diametrically the opposite of what happened in the first successful push to Bengasi, when Sir Archibald Wavell was given the credit, while General Wilson, who then occupied Montgomery's place, wasn't noticed at all.

Talking of present operations, Dill believes that we do not control the Indian Ocean at this time—this doesn't mean he believes the Japs control it either—but that we can get control of it as soon as we want to put the ships in. This is important because he says that Burma absolutely cannot be reconquered by land action. The job will be done, when it is done, not by striking in from Assam, nor yet by working down the coast toward Akyab, but by a big invasion force landing at or near Rangoon, taking that city, and working up the valleys. When we do that—maybe after the monsoon next fall—it'll play hell with the Japs if we can knock out their air force.

There has been a conference here, as I wrote this morning, of Pacific admirals and generals. They may get some additional stuff, but the basic strategy is still to get Germany first. The feeling is that the offensive-defensive we are pushing at Japan is holding them while our submarines and planes raise the devil with Nip shipping.

In other words, Japan is pretty well stymied now, and with the inroads being made on her shipping, cannot really exploit her conquests while we are licking the Nazis. Then, once that job is done, we can shift the whole British and American naval force, the RAF and the Army Air Force, and plenty of troops, into the Far East. That being done, Japan in the opinion of people who ought to know, simply won't be able to stand up to it.

Lieutenant Cedric Worth, USNR, called up the other day, and we had lunch. As you already know, he is now aide to Admiral Raymond Fenard, head of the French Naval Mission here. He has quite a lot of interesting dope on the French situation. He pointed out that while the Fighting French have sentiment on their side, and all that, the real fact is that Darlan promised the British that the Germans would not get a single French warship from his navy. And they haven't. The only ones the Germans may get are those now resting on the bottom at Toulon. [They had been scuttled by the French.] In other words, Darlan lived up to his word 100 percent. In this connection, I am still not convinced that, up to the rise of Laval, the Vichy regime was not a gigantic double cross on the Germans.

Worth also recalled what I know to be true, that the French naval people cordially dislike the English. The reason is plain. In the first place the British, in their usual tactful way, have let it plainly be known that they rate the French navy very low indeed. This is resented by the French, who aren't anything like as bad as the British think they are. In the second place, the British shot up the French Navy at Oran. The result is that the French don't want much to do with the British.

As for De Gaulle, most Frenchmen thought he was doing a worthy thing, and that he kept the spirit of revolt alive. But they also felt he was inept, and that he could not get to the heart of the ordinary Frenchman.

I'm afraid this has been a pretty light memo. But I promise you better things next week, for Admiral King is having another meeting of the Arlington County Commandos at Nelie Bull's house next Sunday. So I shall spend a gallon or two of precious fuel to listen.

Regards

PEARL HARBOR NEVER DIES—
NAVY LEADERS' BLIND SPOTS

CONFIDENTIAL

Thursday
1 April 1943

Dear Bart,

The Bureau seems to be inundating you with memoranda this week. However, I expect you can take it. This one, while it deals with the past and not with the future, is to me extraordinarily interesting. It is also extra-confidential, although it will be broken some day.

Nelie Bull and I had lunch with Captain [later Admiral] Ellis Zacharias, chief of the Office of Naval Intelligence, and the Navy's top man on all matters concerning information on and about the Japs. He commanded the cruiser *Salt Lake City* prior to Pearl Harbor. He is one of the few Americans who speak Japanese fluently, and who realize that, while Japanese logic may seem confusing to us, it is a frightful error to assume that because of this they do not think and plan. On the contrary, they plan everything they do to the last detail. In this they are much like the Germans. Zacharias knows the working of their minds very well, and the Navy planned it that way. Then, when the time came—well, that'll develop as we go along.

Some time before Pearl Harbor, Zacharias went to Admiral Kimmel and told him what he thought the Japanese were up to. At that time the chief fear in Hawaii was sabotage, and efforts were being made to combat it. Zacharias told Kimmel that in his opinion there would not be a sudden outburst of sabotage, but that the Japanese would attack the United States fleet by plane, wherever it happened to be, and that the chief aim would be to knock out four of our battleships (which would according to Japanese figuring give them control of the Pacific).

The attack, he continued, would come over a weekend, and probably on a Sunday morning. The general tip-off that the time was coming would be a sudden upsurge in Japanese entertainment of Americans (and such an upsurge was reported by Clark Lee in his book, *They Call It Pacific*). Specifically, the Americans would know that the time had come when Japanese submarines were located in the vicinity of the fleet, making final observations.

Well, an unidentified submarine was located in Hawaiian waters on 5 December 1941, but the contact could not be localized and the matter was never officially reported. Then, at 6 o'clock on the morning of 7 December, a Japanese submarine was attacked off Pearl Harbor and, if I remember correctly, sunk. Report of this went to Kimmel's office, but the man who received it said that Kimmel would be in his office at 8 A.M., and that there was no point in disturbing him before that.

And so Pearl Harbor happened.

After that, when the *Salt Lake City* was at Pearl Harbor, Zacharias was so disturbed by what he believed the Japs would do next that he voluntarily went to Admiral Nimitz's chief of staff, and told him that he believed the Japanese would make a large-scale attack on Midway. He expounded his belief at some length. The chief of staff asked him to write a memo which could be given to Nimitz.

Zacharias wrote it and it went to Nimitz, who circulated it among his officers. Then Nimitz did a strange thing. He got out of the file two earlier reports Zacharias had written, in which he had been bluntly critical of some officers and policies, and sent them to the Fleet Surgeon. The only possible explanation is that he wanted to make sure Zacharias was sane. Zacharias found out about it and asked the doctor about it. The doctor said it didn't mean anything, that he got lots of things like that from Nimitz, and that he (the doctor) had reported that Zacharias was all right, and that he was a very plain-spoken man.

Later Zacharias saw Nimitz in a hallway at headquarters. Nimitz said he wanted to talk to him about the report, but that he couldn't do it that afternoon, and that Zacharias was sailing the next morning.

Here I go back to Kimmel. When Zacharias told him what he thought would happen at Pearl Harbor—or wherever the fleet was—Kimmel asked him how it could be prevented. Zacharias said it could be prevented by maintaining a constant air patrol over a 500-mile radius from Pearl Harbor. Kimmel said he couldn't. He didn't have the stuff with which to do it.

To get back to pre-Midway, Zacharias had told the chief of staff that if the Navy wasn't on the alert, there would be a much worse disaster than Pearl Harbor. He meant Midway. And from the way the situation developed, and recalling my earlier memo on King, I think this time what he had to say was not ignored. After that, Zacharias was brought back to Washington by King to head up Naval Intelligence.

In the course of the luncheon I remarked that I thought that Army-Navy football games had done more than anything else to create a psychology under which the Army and the Navy found it difficult to work together. He differed, and said that in his opinion the Royal Air Force occupied that place. The reason is that the idea of a separate air force has raised all sorts of hell in Army-Navy relations. The Navy thinks naval aviation belongs under it. So do I. What may happen in the future when carriers are no longer needed, due to increased range of planes, is another question. In *this* war, the situation had better be left alone.

We asked Zacharias why he thought the Japs had kept on coming into the

Solomons with small forces that got knocked off, one after another. The reason, he said, was that the Japs who made the plan had figured the force they allocated for it could do the job. When the first one failed, they tried again, and again. Nobody, you see, was willing to admit that his plan could be wrong. Finally, when it became too obvious to neglect, they threw a big force into the Solomons. That one got knocked off, too. Then they changed the plan, having learned the hard way that it was no good. As I understood Zacharias, the Japs make their plans in Tokyo, and only Tokyo can change them, come victory or disaster. The men in the field merely do what they are told.

Zacharias does not agree with Ambassador Grew that the Japs will fight to the last man. Get to them with psychological warfare, and they will fall to pieces, he believes. He argued this out with Grew, who said it was impossible to get at them. That, answered Zacharias, is what you think. But what if we did get at them? Grew admitted that would bring up a different circumstance.

Well, Zacharias says we *are* getting at them. He wouldn't say how, and I'm just as well pleased, for if it is as secret as that, I'd rather not know how it is being done.

Incidentally, we asked Zacharias what he thought the Japs would do with their big battleships. He thinks they'll keep 'em in the Inland Sea until the war reaches the last stage, and maybe even then. The reason is that when the Japs struck at Pearl Harbor, they had no idea how destructive planes could be. That is one reason they weren't prepared to follow it up.

Anyway, when the pinch comes for Japan, Zacharias believes they will do one of two things: either take their fleet and attempt to bull through, perhaps at Guadalcanal, by sheer brute force, or hold it as a valuable chip to be used in bargaining. They reason that they could offer to surrender the fleet in return for certain concessions and, if we refused, bring out the ships and fight until they were all sunk, making it a pretty costly operation for us. They figure the American people would rather bargain. Zacharias inclines to think they'd adopt the latter course.

I told him about "Florence's" [a wartime predecessor to Jean Dixon] prediction that the war would end by August.

"That could be," he said. "Anything can happen."

But he isn't betting on it. Neither am I.

I guess that's the tops of it.

Regards

P.S. One last belated recollection. When Nimitz talked to Zacharias in the hall, he told him he ought not to be so critical of people, or he might have his head chopped off. Reflecting that it might as well be blown off by bombs out where he'd been, Zacharias answered that he did not broadcast

his opinions, that they were confidential matter forwarded to his commanding officer. Nonetheless, Nimitz told him, he ought to be careful what he
said.

GENERAL MARSHALL ASSERTS AMERICAN
SOLDIER IS BEST IN WORLD

CONFIDENTIAL

Wednesday
7 April 1943

Dear Bart,

Yesterday I was invited to the annual Army Day luncheon of the Military
Order of the World War at the Mayflower Hotel. The speaker was General
George C. Marshall, Army Chief of Staff, and the occasion was inspiring. I
was one of a party consisting of the Polish Minister, Mikhal
Kwapisczewski, a pal of mine who gets a bang out of the yachting songs I
growl to the accompaniment of a battered guitar; the Norwegian Military
Attache, Colonel Oskar Klingenberg; the Assistant Polish Military Attache,
Captain Count Stefan Zamoysky; Bob Sherrod of *Time*, just back from
Australia; Nelie Bull.

The place was bulging with generals and admirals. Seated at the head
table, with a stand of colors of the United Nations behind them, sat Presi-
dent Roosevelt, flanked by a list of military, naval and civilian notables that
read like a roll of honor: General H. H. Arnold; Brigadier General Albert
Cox; Major General Walter C. Baker; Brigadier General John Ross
Delafield; Brigadier General Richard H. Jordan; Admiral Ernest J. King;
Lieutenant General William S. Knudsen; Admiral William D. Leahy;
General Marshall; General Leslie J. McNair; Major General Hilton H.
Reckord; Vice Admiral Russell Waesche, Commandant U.S. Coast Guard;
Secretary of the Navy Frank Knox; Assistant Secretary of the Navy James
Forrestal; Harry Hopkins; Prentiss Brown; Elmer Davis; Senator Robert
Reynolds, Chairman of the Senate Military Affairs Committee; E. R. Stet-
tinius; Donald Nelson; Charles E. Wilson.

Interspersed with the khaki and blue at the other tables were all shades of
uniform color worn by Indian, Chinese, Polish, Norwegian, British,
French, Russian and other uniforms. So great was the crowd of notables
that the head table could not contain them all. There were in the crowd
Lieutenant General McNarney, Major General Russell Maxwell, Major

General Bethel, General Bricker, Major General Levin Campbell, Rear Admiral Cochrane, Senator Connally and a raft of others.

Confronted by this audience, General Marshall gave a talk that was something to hear. He lacks King's coldness and has, on the contrary, a great deal of magnetism. He is not a West Pointer, which is gall and wormwood to many of the stuffier graduates of that institution and lacks the stiffness sometimes encountered in them. Although what he said was off the record, he did not say anything I regarded as of value to the enemy. Quite the contrary, for he was bursting with pride in our new Army.

At the present time, he said, we have got one great advantage: we are now able to bring back from actual war zones officers and men who have been in combat, and know what it is all about. These men are being sent to units all over the country, so that their invaluable and unique experience can be transmitted to all sections of the Army. There is no substitute for battle, and this is the one ingredient that has been needed.

We are even bringing back Corps commanders, such as General Patch from the Southwest Pacific, to perfect our wartime organization. The results are very noticeable to the General, who said he was struck by the change in approach of the outfits he has seen. They no longer have to work on theory, or guesswork, for they have with them men who have actually been there, and know how things are done.

Second, our Selective Service Army—an army built from the beginning along lines the Regular Army has dreamed of for many years but has never been allowed to develop—is proving itself magnificent. The calibre of the men and of non-coms is, in Marshall's opinion, by far the highest of any army in this world. He said that when Anthony Eden was with him—and he had noticed the same thing among other foreign visitors, military and otherwise—he realized the Britisher was tremendously impressed with the quality of our personnel. He spoke, too, of the great results of our Officer Candidates Schools, the democratic way of obtaining officer personnel.

The products of these schools are now in combat all over the world, and the reports coming back on them from the area commanders are that they have measured up way beyond anything that had been considered possible. They really throw it at the boys. There are two reasons. First, time is a precious element, for we had to start at scratch with our Army, and not a second can be wasted. Second, it is desirable to weed out those who do not measure up before they are sent to the combat zones.

So successful is this process that it is estimated by General Marshall that 80 percent of those who would not make good officers are weeded out. Of course, it is never possible to tell how a man will react under fire. But if you can clean out 80 percent of the incompetents it helps a lot.

General Marshall, rapping out his words like machine gun bullets, imparted a great sense of urgency to his talk. He said the Army was being absolutely ruthless in getting rid of incompetent officers, and this has got him in bad with mothers and fathers, and even with Congressmen. But that is the policy, and it goes.

Our soldiers in this country, Marshall said, are doing a number of maneuvers under the closest possible approximation of actual battle conditions. This is one reason why so many of the unfit are weeded out before the real shooting starts. There are explosions, hazards of all kinds. People get hurt. There are bound to be casualties. But they save many more casualties later on. Dive bombers coming at you in practice prepare you for the Stukas—and don't let anybody kid you that dive bombing is obsolete.

Out of it all, Marshall said, is coming—and fast—the greatest army the world has ever seen. That, he concluded, was all he could say that would not interfere with military security, and sat down, leaving everyone who heard him convinced that if an army takes its tone from its commander—and it does—then indeed we are building the world's greatest.

While the listeners were still on their feet, applauding, generals, colonels, majors, captains, admirals, commanders, civilians, General Marshall picked up with his eyes the other three members of the Joint Chiefs of Staff (King, Leahy, Arnold). Without a word they hurried to a side door and vanished, hurrying back to their offices to discuss the conduct of the war as a group wholly unified and extraordinarily competent.

As I watched them go—few people there even missed them until they had disappeared—I couldn't help thinking how God has blessed this country in letting us have among us at this critical time officers of the calibre of these men. To know them at all, to see their minds work, is to realize that men like Colonel Kernan, who has just written another critical volume, are minor figures who simply do not compare in stature with these men who develop strategy, but who realize that the best plan has to be implemented by equally sound tactics.

They know all about calculated risk, and they take such risks. But they can be counted upon not to do the rash thing, and not to be timidly conservative. I have talked with all four of them, and I am sure of this. Bart, we're just blind lucky to have them.

After lunch I talked a while with Sherrod. He has a low opinion of MacArthur, but is interested in his area because he says there are 75,000 Marines out there, and they do not put those babies in a place just because of the nice climate. They go places to fight, and not only to fight but to attack. The $64 question is who and what and where and when they are going to attack. We worked over a map for half an hour without being able to decide.

Sherrod said bombing is hellish the first time, but that you get so used to it that you don't even duck into a trench when Jap bombers come over—this is probably NOT true when the Luftwaffe is around. Bob says the Japs are very poor bombers from high altitudes. Port Darwin was absolutely wrecked. There isn't a whole house or building in the town. But there they had no opposition, and they came in low. At Moresby, where we had great protection, the Japs have been kept high, and they haven't been able to hit a thing.

To go back to Marshall for a moment, he said that another great advantage of experience is that now we have been able to try out our techniques in actual combat. We don't have to argue or theorize, because we know without any necessity for talking about it what will work and what won't. We make improvements in technique in the field, of course, and then bring the results back for the training, so that new men have nothing to unlearn—at least, nothing that can be unlearned or never taught—in this country.

Here are a few comparatively minor items on the King conference that slipped my mind—it isn't easy to sit there for three hours of constant talk and be able to remember all of it the first time, I find. First, he got talking about the Dieppe show. He stressed the fact that it was not an invasion preliminary, no matter what the Germans say. It was a large-scale raid, and it failed to come off. It wasn't any more than that.

One of the probable reasons for doing it was that Canadian troops in England were going stale without actual combat, and this was one way of giving them something to think about. For the rest, Lord Mountbatten, head of the Commandos, is forever trying something. He has his men out on some job or other, from Norway to Egypt, seeing what they can get away with, feeling out the enemy's weaknesses and strengths, always probing for the weakness.

King talked about Kenney—General Kenney, MacArthur's air commander. Kenney, he said, has originated something in his fights out there, but it is not skip-bombing. That has been known for a long time, but so has the defense, which is to put up all the small-calibre ack-ack fire you've got, blowing the enemy plane, which must release the bomb at something like a hundred yards away, all to blazes.

What Kenney did was to evolve a system of teamwork in which two planes work together. One comes in from the bow or stern and rakes the ship with machine gun and cannon fire, the idea being to drive the gun crews from their stations and make it possible for the other plane to do the bombing without being attacked. The other plane, working in teamwork as delicate as is suggested by the fact that it must be in the right place just three seconds after the strafing plane does its stuff, comes in and drops its bomb, or torpedo, after which both planes escape. If the ship turns in an effort to escape, the roles of the two planes may be reversed by signal. It is quite something, and King stressed that it is extra confidential.

Finally, he was asked what made Halsey sound off with his brave—if zany—words about how we were about to beat the ears off the Japs. He denied reports that Halsey had been drunk, and said that the real reason apparently was that Halsey had become completely fed up with the assumption that the Japs were supermen. Worse, constant repetition of that idea was wearing down the morale of his men. So he decided to pop off a couple of times. And did, to the blank amazement of E. J. King & Co.

Regards

THE DIFFICULTIES OF WAR IN INDIA AND BURMA

CONFIDENTIAL

Saturday
22 May 1943

Dear Bart,

Field Marshal Sir Archibald Wavell spoke at the Overseas Writers yesterday, and got the biggest turnout that club has ever known, even though they raised the tariff to $2 a head.

We sensed a lack of decisiveness in the field marshall. He obviously has an excellent military brain, and knows war. But it was my impression that he is a better planner than he is an administrator. That is probably why he was sent away from the Middle East command to India.

However, he did give a very comprehensive picture of the difficulties of military operations in India and Burma. I think this would be most interesting for you in view of what Admiral King has told us about future plans.

In the first place, he said that the Indian Army at the start of the war was a force of about 200,000 men, thoroughly trained and able, taken from the comparatively few fighting races of India, with one English soldier to two Indians and with English officers. This army has since been expanded to just short of 2,000,000, and Indian officers are now being trained and many of them are in actual service. However, very few have advanced to a sufficiently high rank to hold major commands.

The training of this army is difficult. Urdu is the official army language, and not many of the recruits speak it when they are enlisted. The result is that along with everything else they have to be taught a new language, and it takes time. A man is not considered a valuable soldier until he has served a year and a half to two years. The same thing is true of British officers, who have to learn Urdu, along with the way things are done in India.

Wavell says the Indians make excellent soldiers when they are fully trained, but that the force he has now has too many men who will be all right as long as they have their tails up, and the fighting is going well, but not very reliable when the going is tough.

Then he turned to the geographical difficulties. In India communications are poor, and it takes a long time to move a force from one part of the territory to another. This is particularly true of Assam, the northeastern province that abuts Burma. It is cut off from the rest of India by the Brahmaputra River, which presents such a difficult engineering problem that it has never been bridged. It is deep, swift and the water level varies by as much as 25 feet in and out of the rainy season. Incidentally, he said that last April, one of the *dry* months, they had 22 inches of rain in Assam. You can imagine what it is like in the rainy season. Also, the river frequently shifts its course.

So they are forced to have railheads on each side of the river, ferrying material across. This makes things difficult. And once the end of the railroad is reached in Assam, one must still cover some 200 miles over which roads are just now being made before one even reaches the border of Burma. British engineers are hammering through one road and American engineers another, but it is slow work.

As for Burma, it has no communications whatever until one gets to the Mandalay area, far south even of Myitkyna. It is jungle country with one mountain range after another, and possibly the unhealthiest terrain in the world to fight over, due to the malaria mosquitoes. Both Allied and Japanese forces have suffered a great deal from malaria, which is discouraging to commanders, who find that nature knocks out at least as many men as does the fighting.

To get back to the strength of the Indian Army: as Wavell said, it amounted in all to just short of 2,000,000 men. But from this must be subtracted something like a hundred thousand casualties from fighting at Singapore, in Malaya and in the Middle East. Then subtract the force required to guard the northern frontier—the traditional route of invasion to India—which I suppose amounts to another 200,000. Take away also the men who are still in training, and are not ready for fighting, which also includes supply services.

You sensed as you listened to Wavell that he hasn't too much confidence in this army of his, although he spoke in high tribute of Indian soldiers of the old army who fought in Africa, and to whom, he said, Colonel General [Dietloff Jurgen] Von Arnim surrendered in Tunisia. You also sensed that the difficulties of campaigning against Burma by land are very nearly prohibitive.

As for the approach from the sea, it is very difficult because the rivers fan out into huge swamps, making it hard to land. Just the same, when the time comes, the attack will be seaborne and will probably be directed at Rangoon. At the same time Joe Stilwell's Chinese forces will smash in from Yunan Province.

Wavell then talked about the recent operations in the extreme southwest corner of Burma. He pointed out that it was not an invasion attempt, since that corner of Burma is cut off from the rest of the country by impassable mountains. The objective was to capture Akyab Island, and he stressed that he would never have tried it by land if he'd had the ships to mount a sea attack. The trouble was that the Japanese had easier lines of communication—as they do in the interior, where they can use the rivers to move men and material—and they got reinforcements from Akyab before the British-Indian force could make the grade.

Then the Japs put on a good counter-drive and pushed Wavell's people out. He admitted it was a set-back, but said that it had given valuable training, and that it had cost a number of Japanese casualties. He also referred to the raiding force he had sent out as an experiment, self-contained and not depending on lines of communication. Food was given it by air. News stories just came out about this force yesterday. Wavell believes much valuable experience was gained in this operation, too.

The Field Marshall says the Japanese are at their best in Burma. They are excellent soldiers in the jungle terrain. They are like savages in their ability to move about, and to subsist for days on a pocketful of rice. At the same time, they have excellent modern equipment and are also well disciplined. It makes a tough combination to beat.

Wavell was asked if the British had requested Chinese aid in Burma. He denied this, said he was offered two Chinese armies just after he took command. At that time he had one British and two Indian brigades in Burma, and believed that with another brigade he would be all right. But when he got back from Chungking, where he accepted the use of one of the Chinese armies and asked that the other be held in reserve until he could see how things worked out, his British brigade was taken away from him. The Chinese moved slowly and before his first army had taken the field a request had gone in for the second. But it was too late.

At the present time there are Chinese troops training in India, including those who escaped out of Burma and others flown in from Kunming.

Well, that's about the size of Wavell's talk. What he said about terrain and all leads me to wonder if Davies isn't trying to persuade the Soviet Union to come in against Japan now, for three reasons:

1) I think we have enough stuff to maintain an adequate air force in Siberia.

2) Japan is exceedingly vulnerable from Siberia.

3) Supply routes to China might be more possible from Siberia than from Burma.

To change the subject abruptly: this comes from Philip Murray of the CIO via Jay Hayden of the *Detroit News.* In January FDR had a meeting with his labor council, and in the course of it he kidded Bill Green about rumors he had heard that John L. Lewis was fixing to rejoin the AFL. Green and Murray both said they'd have no part of the so and so.

Whereupon the President dropped his kidding, and said, "Bill, I want you to know that John L. Lewis is Public Enemy Number One. If he comes into your organization that will be the end of friendship between the White House and the American Federation of Labor. More than that, I'll denounce it publicly.''

Opinion in Washington is that Green is very unhappy about Lewis coming back, but that he is a figure-head and can't do anything. Further, it is believed that Lewis, with one exception the most power-hungry man in the country, plans to take over the Federation. The dope is that Green would be retired on a good pension, leaving an opportunity for Hutchinson to combine with Lewis and take over. Could be.

And that's all from Washington at this time.

Regards

ALLIED MASTER PLAN, CHINA, AND
THE ORIGIN OF TOKYO RAID IDEA

CONFIDENTIAL

Tuesday
8 June 1943

Dear Bart,

Nelie Bull held another seminar with Admiral King at his home in Alexandria last Sunday night. In many respects it was the most interesting meeting we have yet held with him. Present were Paul Miller and Alan Gould of the Associated Press; Lyle Wilson of the United Press; Ernest Lindley of *Newsweek*; Ray Henle of the *Pittsburgh Post-Gazette*; Barnet Nover of the *Washington Post*; Turner Catledge of the *New York Times*; Nelie and myself.

King began by saying that the chief fruit of the recent Roosevelt-Churchill conference was the production of a master plan, laying out on paper the successive steps by which the war is to be won. The specific steps for the next twelve months were included and were turned over for implementation to the military and naval experts, who reported that the projected moves were within the capability of the United Nations.

The American Chiefs of Staff went to Casablanca to fight for the adoption of such a master plan, but were unable to get the British to get down to cases in the production of the plan. At Casablanca plans were made to be implemented after Tunisia had been taken, but there was no agreement on long-range planning. Now this has been accomplished, and all previous planning has either been canceled or incorporated in the master plan.

King seemed to feel better now that matters had been put down in writing. It was plain that he is now more confident that we shall be able to count on the British in the war against Japan as in that against Germany. I sensed in Admiral King a suspicion that the British had been loath to commit themselves before this, and that they had a tendency to forget what they had said before. Anyway, he is happy about it now.

It became clear in our conversation that no moves, however attractive, will be made in the future unless they give an affirmative answer to this question: do they further the fulfillment of the Master Plan? I'll have more to say about this later.

King then discussed world strategy for a while. The European strategy, he said, is very simple and very obvious. By its geographical position and its manpower, the Soviet Union is the inevitable hub of the attack on Germany. Our strategy is this: to implement Russian manpower by maintaining the maximum flow of supplies to the Soviet Union, even though it makes it necessary for us to forego attractive operations elsewhere; to undertake movements in Western Europe of a diversionary nature, so as to draw German forces off from the Russian front, thus making the Soviet task easier; and to continue the heavy air assault on German industry and transportation to reduce the German ability to make war. This is the grand strategy for Europe.

King believes that the Soviet Union, which has been thoroughly informed of what is going on, now understands and accepts our plans. Stalin, he comments, is a realist, else he would not be where he is, and he has finally come to have a realistic appreciation of the limitations and abilities of his major allies. By this you can understand through reading between the lines that Stalin now knows we are not presently in a position to mount a full scale invasion of Western Europe, and realizes the alternative action we propose is going to be valuable and helpful to him.

However, a large-scale action is imminent in the Mediterranean. The Allies at the present time are trying very hard to confuse the Axis as to where it will be, in Sicily, Sardinia, the Dodecanese, Crete or wherever. But it is coming, and soon. This led King to discuss the problem of Italy. There are, he pointed out, two schools of thought about that. One group favors knocking Italy out of the war by invasion, figuring the moral effect and the opening of the Balkan coast to invasion would be worth it. The other group, with which King sympathizes, feels that it would be wasted motion. Italy is a drain on Germany. To take it over would be to transfer that drain to our merchant marine. Beyond that, it would not bring us to grips with our major enemy, Germany, and would end with us up against the Alps. Hannibal and Napoleon crossed the Alps, he conceded, but added that times are different now. He was asked if this question had not been settled at the Washington conference. He said it had. Obviously the decision has been not to invade Italy.

He turned then to Pacific grand strategy. China, he pointed out, occupies an identical position with Russia, only vis-á-vis Japan. The problem, then, is to implement the great manpower and the geographical position of China. Nothing can be done about retaking Burma until the monsoons are over—and again I infer the attempt will be made then. Even after Burma has been retaken, however, the Burma Road will not be immediately open, as the British have been heavily bombing bridges and railroad lines between Rangoon and the beginning of the road proper. A good deal of rebuilding will have to go on.

In the meantime, then, air supply is the only route, and a major dispute over the use to be made of it was settled at the Washington conference. One faction, headed by Chennault, wanted the route used exclusively to bring air warfare supplies into China, arguing that with adequate air power Japan could be checked and driven out of China. The other faction, headed by Stilwell, admitted the importance of air power, but argued that military supplies for land troops must also be brought in.

Here is the point: in order to make the air route feasible, it was necessary first to locate bases in Assam, out of the reach of the Japs, bases that can be made very secure. The other end of the line is a number of bases around Kunming. Kunming can be attacked by the Japanese from any or all of three directions, from Indo-China, from Burma or from Occupied China. The fear is that if our air power becomes notably objectionable to the Japs they will end it by moving in on Kunming and, by blocking all air aid, making China worse off than she is now.

The answer, then, is to make Kunming untakeable by the Japanese, which can be done only by sending in enough land military supplies to enable the Chinese forces to set up an unbreakable defense. The ultimate decision was in favor of this, sending a certain percentage of air war supplies and a certain percentage of land war supplies. King said the amount of the latter needed was not so great.

At the same time, our strategy is to keep every possible pressure on the Japanese, by air, by sea, by submarines and other means. Every move projected in the Pacific is measured against this: does it increase the pressure on Japan? If it doesn't, however attractive, it will be scrapped.

In this connection, King said that a major move is being mounted in the Southwest Pacific, and that in his opinion it is being done much too slowly. He is obviously impatient with the failure to move more rapidly there, which I think means we can expect a big blow-off any time. He didn't say, but I am quite sure this means either clearing the Japs off New Guinea altogether, or taking a healthy sock at Rabual, which could have the same effect.

He was asked whether we know anything about the death of Admiral Yamamoto. He said we did, and that the story would break before very long. He declined to say anything more about it, except that the news of his death from Japan confirmed certain ideas of ours about what happened.

He then turned to a discussion of the operation of our submarines in the Pacific. They are doing a grand job, and are making the Japanese feel a real shipping pinch. However, he said that while we have been very fortunate about the way our submarines have avoided Japanese counter-measures, we have not been so lucky lately. There is bad news coming about our submarines in the Pacific—as to losses, that is. I gather it'll come out pretty soon.

King was asked why Attu was being attacked. He said it was because we found we had the stuff available to do the job, and that it increased the pressure on Japan, even though he added he did not consider Attu an effective base for offensive actions against Japan—the weather, presumably. He characterized the drive as remarkably successful, made possible by radar, which enabled us to go ahead despite heavy fog that grounded planes and brought into play old-fashioned naval bombardment as a preliminary.

We benefitted at Attu by the fact that the Japs did not cover the whole island, but only a relatively small part of it. Kiska is going to be much tougher, for the Japs hold all of it, and have something like 10,000 men there. In the meantime, we are trying very hard to cut all communications between Japan and Kiska, but the fog makes it difficult.

A sidelight on this operation at Attu is that we expected the Japs to send a task force to relieve the island, and laid a trap to take care of it. But the Japs did not bite. They let Attu go. We have, I gather, a similar trap for any big expeditions trying to reinforce Kiska. Radar will play its part if the weather is foggy.

King is evidently concerned about China. He said that if China fell, it would prolong the war in the Pacific against Japan for 10 or 15 years, since the Japs are well dug in all over the place. This led to a question as to whether he thought Japan could knock China out of the war. He answered that he thought it could if it made an all-out effort.

From this he went on to say that Japan was puzzling to Occidentals, who were not supposed to be able to understand Oriental thinking. Japan, that is, could do a number of things to hurt and embarrass us that are not being done. They could smack down China, but haven't. They could jump Siberia. King said that he was unable to understand why this hadn't been done, since in the long-range view Japan can never be secure while the Maritime Provinces of Siberia are in non-Japanese hands. And Russia is obviously all tied up with Germany. They could do things—unspecified by King—with their submarines that could hurt us, but haven't. He doesn't know why the Japs haven't done these things, but he isn't complaining.

He still expects the Japanese to do something big in the Pacific, and his bet still is Midway. He doubts that the Japs would have accepted the loss of face in cutting their losses in the Solomons without an alternative plan, and he is waiting for the blow-off. He says our margin is larger than it was in the first Midway attack, but that the Pacific is so big that it is impossible to be strong everywhere. He also mentioned Samoa again as a possible threat by the Japs, although now we have a base at Funafuti that they would have to get by, which would give us a little warning.

Our own concept of the war still involves getting back to the Philippines, but it won't be done tomorrow. Once there, the Jap supply lines to the south would be cut and the East Indies would drop into our hands like ripe apples from a tree.

King then turned to the story of the Tokyo raid. The idea originated with two members of his staff. They worked on it and then, finding they had no naval planes that could do the job, they brought in General Arnold. Next to be informed was Doolittle. Then, later, Admiral Nimitz and Admiral Halsey, who led the task force. Until 24 hours before the raid, these seven were the only people in the world (including, of course, King) to know what was planned.

At that juncture they told Roosevelt, who had been thinking about such a raid, and several times asked King questions, only to be requested not to ask at that time. So not even FDR knew about it until the day before.

Actually, not even the Chinese knew until then that the raid was coming off, as we had got the information about their air fields under the pretext that it was for future use. King commented that it was found that the fewer the people who knew about an operation, the better the chance of maintaining secrecy. King himself still feels sorry that the story of the raid was put out at all, explaining that it was hoped that it could be done again. He was asked whether it still wasn't possible. He said he supposed it was.

The Admiral discussed Wavell somewhat, giving his personal reaction. He doesn't think very much of him, chiefly on the ground that he is not adequately decisive. I infer that King felt more could have been done from his Indian base than Wavell did before the rains came this year. More important, he said he got the impression that Churchill shared this view. Hence, I am sure Wavell will be transferred before very long.

Which brings up Churchill. King said he thought Churchill had profited by his experiences in the First World War, and that he was now a first-rate military mind, with less inclination toward what King called "eccentric" operations, by which a military man means operations that may seem attractive but do not fit into a sound military program. That is, they do not further the Master Plan.

In this connection, he commented that in the nature of things the British had their economy under such satisfactory control that Churchill was free to devote himself to the progress of the war. Roosevelt, he said, was not free to do this, as our economic problems are not solved. This, he feels, works to Roosevelt's disadvantage.

Earlier in the discussion we considered the submarine situation in the Atlantic, which looks very good. King reiterated his belief that we would have the submarines under control within six months. He gave a new definition of this: keeping sinkings under 500,000 tons a month, against new construction of 1,500,000 tons a month, plus British and Canadian construction. March was a bad month. April and May were very good. But we'll have months that are bad. Breaks have a lot to do with it.

At the same time, we've made progress. The following factors are responsible:

1) Escort vessels. We now have enough so that we are able to keep at sea packs of such craft, ready to be rushed to any convoy that finds itself in difficulty. We are also able to give convoys more adequate protection, and our communications are such that we can, if indications are that one convoy is running into a group of wolf-packs, divert escort vessels to its aid from another convoy that seems to be safe from attack.

2) Air cover is proving a big help. We are getting auxiliary carriers into service to cover zones out of reach of land-based air craft, and they are helpful in spotting and attacking U-boats.

3) New weapons. All of them are variations of depth charges, which constitute the most effective weapon against submarines. For instance, instead of dropping one 300-pound charge, we may drop six 50-pound charges, using the shotgun principle as against the rifle. He didn't say so, but I infer the 50-pound charges use the new explosive of which Phelps has written.

4) Radar is also important. We are using it in planes now to spot submarines.

King expressed the opinion that morale in the U-boats is not what it used to be, and commented that in some cases green crews thought their submarines were more badly damaged than was actually the case, leading them to surrender when it wasn't necessary. The implications of this on morale are obvious. He also said he believed there was such a shortage of U-boat crews, and that it was so difficult to get replacements that the Germans were taking crews of Stuka dive-bombers, which are about obsolete, and putting them into the subs.

He also said that the bombing of German submarine bases and building yards was just beginning to make itself felt. We can't get at the pens, but we knock off everything else, making it very difficult to assemble or repair submarines. Construction maximum for the Germans is put at about 20 a month, and they have certainly not been able to pass that mark, if they have been able to maintain it. King estimates that there are about 400 U-boats now in action, which is more than Germany had when the war began.

In connection with this, King told us an amusing story about Churchill. Control of the submarine is of course one of the leading items in our Master Plan, and when this paragraph was formulated, Churchill suggested that the word submarine be killed when speaking of German undersea boats, and U-boats substituted.

"You see," he said, "the crews of the U-boats are those dastardly villains who sink our ships, while the crews of the submarines are those noble and heroic fellows who sink theirs."

King said that the recent staff meeting came about a month early, and that it was possible and desirable to advance it because of the progress of the war, in which we have been getting the breaks—such breaks as the sudden collapse of the Germans in Tunisia, the advance in the U-boat campaign, the deterioration of the Jap air arm, etc. The Chiefs of Staff, he said, have now come to know one another, they work smoothly together, and there is no time wasted in getting acquainted. Incidentally, there will be more frequent conferences—about every three months—in the future. I don't know whether this includes Roosevelt and Churchill, but it certainly includes the military and naval leaders.

The Russians, King said, while more friendly and understanding now, are still as secretive as ever—our observers are unable to get to the fighting fronts. In this connection, he stressed that the war was still being run by the Chiefs of Staff, although military leaders of other powers, notably China, were called in to talk during the recent conference. Such nations, however, are not completely filled in on projected moves. King conceded that this method of procedure was irritating to officers of other sovereign nations, but explained that somebody had to do the running of the war, and that it could not be done by mass-meeting, especially with many different nations represented.

There has been an upsurge of enemy blockade running. We are doing pretty well against it. The French Navy is already helping. The cruisers *Gloire* and *Georges Leagues*, which were at Dakar, put to sea even though not modernized, and the latter knocked off one blockade runner. King says the French Navy will be all right, that it is very eager to get into action, and that it is seeking ships from us. I gather it'll get 'em. The Brazilian Navy is still at sea, and feeling very cocky about it.

I guess that about tells the story, except for one thing. King predicted that Germany would be defeated in the early fall of 1944, and that Japan would be beaten in 1947.

Regards

MARSHALL GIVES SECRET INFORMATION ON ARMY CUTBACKS

CONFIDENTIAL

Wednesday
9 June 1943

Dear Bart,

Yesterday afternoon, in his office in the Pentagon Building, General Marshall held the second off-the-record conference since he returned from the Casablanca conference of last January. It was the first one since I was put on the list. I should say there were some 25 correspondents present, including David Lawrence, Earl Godwin, Richard Harkness, Roscoe Drummond, Richard Wilson, James Wright, Lyle Wilson, Bert Andrews, Ludwell Denny, Duke Shoop, Dewey Fleming.

Marshall, as you know, is a magnificent officer, well worthy of his command and of the respect in which he is held in all quarters. He seems to me to balance perfectly Admiral King, who is equally respected. In view of the nature of the conference, semi-formal, in his office, under Army auspices, he talked quite freely, although not as freely, I think, as the Admiral talks to a much smaller group in the truly informal atmosphere of Nelie Bull's home. It was a thoroughly interesting and significant conference.

The Army is very much concerned about the complete secrecy with which this conference is held. We are not even supposed to let anyone know we saw the General, let alone tell what was said. This memorandum, therefore, is even more confidential than ordinarily, and I hope it will be destroyed as soon as you and Mr. Speed have assimilated it. Without wanting to appear melodramatic, I suggest it either be burned or torn into very small pieces dropped in several waste baskets.

The most important and significant thing told us by General Marshall was that the development of the war has been such that they are now able on a tentative basis to "freeze" the divisional strength of the Army, although they have not been able to apply this to such special services as anti-aircraft and others. That still lies in the future, but may well come.

This freezing is desirable because expansion is weakening to the extent that it dilutes the quality of the existing troops, and makes necessary the grabbing of promising non-commissioned officer material for Officer Candidate Schools. The new system will make it possible for the Army to concentrate on training and perfecting the personnel it now has.

As I understand it, twelve divisions that were planned will not be activated this year. The result on Selective Service of this cutting back will be that between 500,000 and 700,000 fewer men will be inducted between 1 July and 1 January than was originally contemplated. The cutbacks are being made on a monthly basis. In July the original number set for induction was about 285,000. It will actually be about 150,000. The decision as to the number to be taken in August was decided last night, but I do not know the figure reached. The figures will be set a month in advance each time.

The background of the situation is this: when we went into the war there was considerable doubt as to whether or not the Red Army could stand up under the tremendous power of the German Army. If the Soviet Union collapsed, we were confronted with two choices: we could hold down the size of our Army and work toward winning a compromise peace, or we could go the limit for all-out war. We chose the latter.

Now, however, the signs are that the Red Army is going to come through triumphantly. Obviously this enables us to be more conservative in our plans. As I understand it, we are freezing the Army at approximately half what was originally planned, with a strength of approximately 5,500,000. The cutback plan, as I say, is experimental, and has not been carried beyond the first year, at which time the situation will be resurveyed.

The question mark is what will happen to the Red Army this year. If it can stand up to the German Army, and particularly if it is able to counter-attack by September rather than waiting for the coming of winter, the likelihood is that we shall continue to stand on our present divisional strength, calling on Selective Service only for replacements.

It is thought that the Red Army *will* be able to stand up. Marshall believes the Germans will attack, and says the time for such an assault is already overdue. But the Reds are much better off than at any previous time. For example, they are now telling us they do not need supplies in some categories, such as tanks, which shows that what we have given them and what their own plants are now producing are sufficient. This is very hopeful. Also, the Red Air Force is now comparably stronger than at any previous time, both in its own right, due to Soviet production and Allied aid, but also in relation to the Luftwaffe, which has been having a hell of a tough time.

Leading from this, Marshall went into a discussion of the possibilities of a German collapse. He refused to speculate as to time, but does suggest that when the military collapse comes, it will come very suddenly and very unex-pectedly. He turned to the First World War, pointing out that as late as July of 1918 the Allies were in a terrible state, with Paris being evacuated, with losses tremendous and with Germany holding the initiative everywhere. Yet by November it was all over.

He suggested three causes of German collapse. First, the continuation of the bombing of Germany. He said that our daylight bombing has been tremendously damaging and extremely accurate, and that the force is mount-ing. In April, when damage reached a new peak, we had 150 bombers in condition to raid—it takes about six weeks to get a bomber ready after it reaches Britain. In May we had 300, in June we have 500. In July we shall have 700, in August 900 and in September 1,200. It is easy to see what this is going to mean to Germany. There won't be one raid at a time, but several. The Luftwaffe, already strained to the limit, will be brought to the breaking point, and it is easy to picture a time when the German air force will be so completely overmatched that it is no longer an important factor.

This bombing is more and more cutting and hampering Germany's ability to make war. April was a particularly devastating month, but excellent bombing weather lies ahead, and we shall have the force to exploit it to the limit. At some time in the course of these raids, a sharp German reaction is expected. The Germans simply cannot stand the pressure, and the Luft-waffe will have to be concentrated on repelling the assault. This, of course, is one of our primary objectives, to force the Luftwaffe into the air where we can get at it and destroy it. We can stand greater losses then they, and we aren't having to. In some of our raids not a single plane has been lost.

At this point, however, I should say that Marshall is still of the opinion that Germany cannot be licked in the air. The man with the rifle has got to come in. But air can make it much easier and can prepare the way.

Second, if the Red Army stands up and if, as I said, is able to counterattack in September, the pressure on Germany, both as to morale and as to actual ability to carry on the war, would perhaps reach the breaking point.

Third, the collapse of Italy might well bring cracking pressure on Germany. I doubt it, personally, belonging to what might be called the King School as to Italy.

Marshall then was asked if he hadn't forgotten one point, an invasion by Anglo-American forces. He answered that he had referred to the collapse of Italy, hadn't he, and that he didn't suggest it could be done by waving a magician's wand. The implication is plain from this that Italy *is* to be attacked. So maybe I misundertood King, or at any rate got the idea that his position had been adopted when it hadn't. We'll have to wait and see, I guess.

Germany at the present time, he said, is involved in a damaging war of nerves, thanks to all the stories that have been coming out, and the German troop movements have shown this confusion. It is obvious that our hope of deceiving the enemy is not by concealment, but dispersion, so to speak, putting out all possible rumors and reports, letting the Axis choose which to believe.

Marshall talked about the Soviet Union. He told us that when he left here for Tunisia it was with the intention of going on to Moscow, but that the plan was changed when Stalin said he didn't want to see him. The Russian leader said there had been a hell of a lot of visitors, and that they could be an embarrassment, wanting to see this, that, etc. "If I went there, I expected to be damned embarrassing," Marshall commented.

This secrecy of the Russians is natural, he said, in view of the fact that they haven't always been too well treated. We have not been holding out on them, but have given them as complete information as to what we plan. We get no such information in return, but apparently our people have come to accept this as a normal state of affairs, and don't let it bother them. Sometimes the Reds give us information. More often they don't.

But the point is that we are in no doubt upon the essential point, that the Russians will fight, and keep on fighting. Our strongest assurance is the impossibility of making any deals that will stick with either Japan or Germany. The Reds know full well that it is impossible to deal with either, that pacts with them are without meaning.

In this connection, he said we have made repeated attempts to get a look at Kamchatka, so we can at least know what is there in advance for use if we ever have occasion to base units on the peninsula. No dice. Marshall said he does not think there is a chance of Russia attacking Japan while she is still occupied with Germany, that the Reds are making every effort to avoid any such outbreak. On the other hand, he is confident that once Germany is defeated Russia will come in against Japan. He thinks she is forced to by Japan's geographical position. When the time comes he thinks the attack will be forceful and mighty tough.

The Japs, he said, have been a little tougher with Russia. We have turned over some Liberty ships to Russia, and they go to Vladivostok. The Japs have stopped them to inquire as to ownershp of craft and cargo. He didn't know what happened after that, but King, who mentioned it, gave the impression the ships were allowed to proceed.

While on the subject of Japan, he confirmed what King has said about imminent operations in the Southwest Pacific area. He did not specify, naturally.

Turning to China, he told us essentially what King did about the resolution of the land-air controversy. He is hopeful that China will be able to hold, but does not put too much faith in Chinese communiqués. The Jap forces that operated beyond Ichang, for example, he put at 15,000 instead of six times that many. However, he did say the situation there looked hopeful, and that our air support has been very helpful. He stressed the difficulty of communications between Assam and China.

In the course of the conference he spoke of the German propaganda on the horrors of Allied bombings, and earnestly requested that the newspapers go all out on the thought that we must be very hard, and not allow ourselves to be city-slicked by what is, after all, nothing but psychological warfare.

He talked of his trip to Tunisia, and expressed great satisfaction with the way our boys became veterans under fire. He thinks we have a real good army out there, trained under difficulties. Many of them, he said, had the idea that once they'd driven the Axis out of Tunisia, they'd come home and let somebody else carry on. They didn't know that soldiers don't come home until the war is over, but they do now. They are, he repeated, real veterans.

He told one pretty amusing story. An American chaplain wandered over to a German prisoner enclosure, and a typical Prussian officer came up. He complained bitterly that the Americans were green, inexperienced, didn't know how to handle things, and didn't compare with the Germans they had licked. The chaplain answered mildly that we were new to this business, and that when we had as much practice as the Germans we'd be as good as they, probably. Then he pointed to the ornament on his tunic.

"Do you see this cross?" he asked. "It means I'm not a line officer. I have nothing to do with these things you've been complaining about. I'm a chaplain, and I just came over here to plant a few of you bastards."

Regards

MOUNTBATTEN'S NEW ROLE, CHIANG'S
BALKINESS, RAID ON PLOESTI

Thursday
26 August 1943

Dear Bart,

General Marshall returned from Quebec yesterday, and practically his first official act—or should I say highly unofficial act—was to call in about twenty newspapermen and give them an extremely hush-hush lowdown on the war in all theatres. He talked rapidly for more than two hours without using a note and without following any particular pattern, so that it is virtually impossible to give you more than the high spots. As I am sure Glen has told you, these conferences are so secret that no one who wasn't there is even supposed to know it ever happened.

He told us of the creation of the Southeast Asia Command under Lord Mountbatten, and that an official announcement would be made in the next day or two. Actually, it came from Quebec last night. The purpose of this move is to take the whole war in and around Burma out of the hands of the Indian government, and especially out of the hands of Field Marshall Wavell, whose "lethargy" has greatly disappointed the Americans. Conduct of the war in this area will not rest entirely with the Chiefs of Staff. The principal fly in the ointment is political, and centers in the person of Generalissimo Chiang Kai-shek, of whom Marshall apparently has none too flattering an opinion.

The most delicate task in the whole Burma campaign will be to sell the Generalissimo on this new command, for it is necessary in our plan of attack on Burma to have two highly trained Chinese forces—one operating from India, the other from China on the northernmost corner of Burma. General Stilwell has trained the India force to a high degree, but is having difficulty with the China-based force. Chiang has no interest in ground forces at all. To make matters worse, he dislikes and distrusts the British and will not cotton to Mountbatten's appointment. He is interested only in the creation of a big American air force in China—and he does mean American, not Chinese. Finally, he seems to be bitterly opposed to the creation of any well-trained Chinese army because the internal conditions in China are such that it is hard to tell from day to day who will control such an army. He therefore is expected to insist that the operations in Burma be carried out primarily by American and British troops.

We, on the other hand, think it is absolutely silly to send our men to an area where there are 400,000,000 available men of military age already on the scene. In this connection, Marshall pointed out that to transport one division from the Mediterranean to Burma would mean a reduction of two and a half divisions in the European Theatre when supply and transportation problems are taken into account. Marshall has a full and complete understanding with [Ambassador] Soong of the Chinese Embassy here on this question, but it may be necessary for Soong to return to China to enlist the support and cooperation of Chiang.

From what I heard at this conference, there can be little doubt that the decisions reached at Quebec will be translated into forthright action much more rapidly than has been the case in the past. Marshall pointed out with great care that thus far we had run no reasonable risk of defeat in any operation we have undertaken in the Mediterranean area. Sicily, he said, was pregnant with possibilities of a serious defeat, and we did not move against it until we had taken every one of those possibilities into account and had prepared effective counter-measures.

From now on, however, we cannot proceed with such caution. We are going to run risks, we are going to take chances, we are going to strike fast, and we are going to "get our nose bloodied" several times. He warned us of this, he said, so that we would understand when news of temporary reverses might come in. Inadvertently, I believe—for he was seemingly very careful not to tell us what our next target is—he used the phrase "when we have moved in on the toe and taken the southern end of the Italian boot." Thus there is no question but that we plan to occupy at least half of Italy by force. In Marshall's office is a topographical map table on which every detail of Sicily and the leg of Italy up to a point slightly beyond Naples is shown, with railroads, rivers, valleys and every other conceivable item of military interest clearly depicted. He invited our inspection of the map as we left.

He also pointed out that the Germans had recently bombed Palermo and Bizerta from their air bases on Sardinia, the Dodecanese, and Crete. Our next step, as he explained later, is necessary as a means of conserving manpower, if for no other reason, since it will enable us to remove the garrisons and anti-aircraft defenses that we must now maintain in every port that we have taken in Africa and Sicily.

He turned next to problems of supply and equipment. Our principal shortage today is landing barges. These, as you know, are large, complicated, self-propelled craft, capable in many instances of transporting our artillery and landing it on the beaches together with our men, so as to render them independent of cover by naval units during the beaching operations. These boats were developed largely out of our experience at Dieppe, and while the Dieppe raid was enormously costly in human lives, what we learned there has already saved many times that number of lives in the amphibious operations we have already had to undertake in Africa and the Mediterranean. One of the principal topics of discussion at Quebec was the rate of attrition upon which we had to count in reckoning our supply of landing barges.

Many of these were damaged in the beaching operation; others, of course, were sunk; and there was the inevitable percentage of engine failures, etc. We need more of these boats badly. The hulls afford very little difficulty—we can get these—but the engines are the bottleneck. Two or three times Marshall emphasized that any labor interruptions in any plant making power units for any purpose was a matter vitally affecting war plans, and he cautioned us to guard that in strictest confidence lest we alert the enemy to our greatest weakness at the moment.

His statements on this subject indicated bitterness toward irresponsible labor leadership and, to my way of thinking, a generous measure of disgust with administrative policies. It was obvious that he was pointing particularly at the threatened strike in Allis-Chalmers which, if it comes, will be due principally to the stupidity and bullheadedness of the National labor Relations Board.

Next item of interest in the supply problem is cargo craft, of which, for the first time, we have a superfluity, thanks to the virtual wiping out of the submarine menace. Up to the past few months we have had more transports and troop carriers in relation to our needs than cargo boats. Now the balance is reversed and we need more troop carriers to keep up with the supply of cargo.

This, he feels, is only a temporary condition that may be radically altered again when the Germans revivify their undersea activities, as he is confident they will. He displayed a secret chart showing for each week since the war began the number of tons of our shipping that has been sunk and the number of tons of new shipping constructed. While there were sharp variations from week to week, it appears that throughout 1942 we suffered on the average heavy net losses in shipping, while for the better part of this year we have had an absolutely enormous net gain. I noted, however, that there was no week during which we did not have losses.

He says that our success in the U-boat field is due to certain highly secret recent scientific developments. The Germans, he believes, are fully aware of these developments and can soon be expected to find the scientific means of counteracting them. It may be, he adds, that many of the submarines that have now disappeared from the Atlantic have been recalled to Germany to be equipped with counteractive devices. The lull, meanwhile, is giving us a splendid opportunity to get our stuff across the ocean and to supply a rapid succession of attacks if we can mount them soon enough.

As for airplanes, the picture is pretty good. We are getting 200 to 300 bombers a month over to England. The difficulty here is that we do not yet have enough crews to man them. From other sources I learned recently that for 600 of our bombers in England we had only 400 crews. Marshall points out that we shall need two complete crews per bomber to keep each plane in constant operation. He expects to have these crews in England by 1 October.

Far more important than our numerical superiority, however, is the way in which we have been using it. He declares we have literally terrified the Axis by our demonstrations of ability to strike at exactly the target we want, exactly when we want, without ever failing. He cited three examples: first, the ease with which we have selected fighter plane production plants, submarine assembly plants, small ball bearing factories, and other key German industries—even those that were moved to Vienna for safety—completely obliterating them. Of particular interest to him was a recent raid on a Baltic port [Peenamünde] during which we apparently dropped bombs upon a laboratory where certain scientific devices (probably associated with the submarine campaign) were in process of development.*

After this raid, the Germans announced the death of one of their greatest scientists, but Marshall declares that pictures in his hands show convincingly that we killed *all* the scientists at work on that project. This, he said, is ready calling your shots. The Rome raid proved the precision with which we could bomb from high altitudes and left the Axis feeling completely at our mercy. But by far the most devastating job we have done on Axis morale was the raid at Ploesti which, but for a tough break, would probably not have cost us a single plane or crew.

The oil fields at Ploesti lie just beyond the outskirts of the little Rumanian town, and our pilots flew unbelievably long distances, destroying the installations on those oil fields with staggering precision and accuracy, and without touching a civilian or a building in town. He told us that the first wave of bombers flew in low over the town and the pilots waved to the people in the streets, went on to the oil fields, where they shot down the gunners who were running to man the anti-aircraft guns, skipped their delayed-action bombs into the refineries and tanks, and turned homeward without suffering any casualties.

The tough break we had was that the second wave on its long flight to the target followed the wrong valley and arrived 40 minutes late. In the interim, many of our delayed-action bombs were going off and destroying our own planes, while the smoke and fire concealed chimneys, tanks and other obstacles against which our pilots cracked up flying at those low levels.

Nevertheless, reports from secret sources we have on the ground in those fields showed that three days later our bombs were still exploding, that we had destroyed 70 percent of the installations and the railroad facilities, blowing a whole train of cars up onto the station roof, and had not touched a non-military target, to the extreme delight of the Rumanian people in that area, who are singing our praises.

In connection with our air force, however, there remains one serious

---

*Although it was not learned until later, the raid on Peenamünde was designed to wipe out laboratories believed to be working on atomic energy. The rationale for the attack was super-super-secret. It turned out that the Germans had given up on the atomic project.

problem: an air force, paradoxically, is the most immobile branch of an army. As we move to each new advanced air base, we must undertake a tremendous amount of construction, building a complete utility system, pipe lines for aviation gasoline, electrical generators, water works, weather station, and communication lines, besides a network of roads and runways, hangars and planes. This is calculated to make our air advance slow.

The last remaining item is the problem of supply in manpower and the draft. The Navy still needs large numbers of men, but the Army is leveling off its demands with about 7,000,000 men in its ranks at present. It is activating no new regiments and it has highly trained reserves ready to replace our immediate casualties. Air force personnel is still not up to demand, and recruitment here will go on intensively until next June at least.

Meanwhile the Army will still have to make substantial calls upon the Selective Service System for "Specialized Units" to man the garrisons, operate the ports and staff the anti-aircraft and other defenses. At each step in our advance, large numbers of these special services are required and, by way of example, it is estimated that about one Army division—15,000 men—must remain in Sicily for these purposes. As soon as we clear the Mediterranean of all Axis air bases, we can take all our defense men from Africa, which will no longer be in danger of attack, but we must still leave men there to operate the ports and handle the supply lines.

On the Russian front, our information is still meager, particularly as to the strength of the German army, but we do know that most of the German divisions on that front are really at only about half strength, and at best no more than two-thirds. The skeletal structure is there, and if more men can be found for service, these divisions can quickly be built up to strength. But at present, when you read of 300 Nazi divisions on the Russian front, it means only about 150. Marshall does not believe the Germans are withdrawing voluntarily in Russia. According to his information, they are fighting desperately and brilliantly and will continue to do so until the home front cracks behind them as it did last time.

In the Pacific Theatre, things are going well but slowly. We could move much faster, but at much greater cost in human life, and there is no present necessity for haste. Our problem there is to move slowly enough to conserve human life and rapidly enough to prevent heavy losses from malaria, our greatest enemy. We have discovered two new Jap planes.

After all this talk about the superiority of the Japanese Zero, it develops that their new planes have some armor protection for the pilot and self-sealing gas tanks—tacit acknowledgement on the part of the Japanese that our slower, less maneuverable, better-protected planes were superior to theirs. They are also using a four-engine bomber which is new to them and about which we know little.

The withdrawal of the Japanese from Kiska has created a serious morale problem in Alaska, where our men were content to remain as long as a fight was in progress, but are now grousing to beat hell. Therefore, we are going to have to use a number of our none-too-plentiful transports to bring these men home and replace some of them with others.

And now for the politics of the present situation. Marshall is delighted with the way the two-power Anglo-American conferences are working out. The Canadians are sore because they were not included in the discussion at Quebec, but had they been included the Australians would have demanded a voice as would the South American republics, with the result that nothing would have been accomplished. Apparently there is trouble enough getting the Britons and Americans together as it is. He was definitely pleased by the absence of Russian representation, pointing out that Russia has no concern with anything other than its own purely land action on its western front, and has no knowledge of the difficulties inherent in the amphibious operations which we must undertake in our invasion of the Continent.

I gather that the absence of Chiang was even more pleasing to him, for he says when our Intelligence reports the concentration of a force of 125 Japanese planes, Chiang reports that the Japanese have 1,000 planes and that if half what Chiang says were true, we would have been wiped out of the Pacific months ago.

Indicative of some of Marshall's political troubles was our earlier raid on Ploesti when we tried to secure permission to land in Russia, thus shortening the journey by nearly 1,000 miles. He worked this all out with Litinov, who cabled to Russia for the essential permission. Weeks passed and no word was forthcoming, and finally we had to take off on the raid because the planes we were using were destined for Chiang, and he was growing impatient. So Roosevelt would not let Marshall hold off any longer.

About two hours after the planes had taken off Litvinov came rushing to Marshall to tell him permisson had been granted. Last time we tried to get permission to use Russian bases in that theatre, Stalin refused on the ground that our Army was so much better fed and cared for than his men that their presence would cause considerable trouble and possible revolution among his own troops.

In Japan, the one topic of conversation is the possibility of the Americans establishing an air base in Siberia. That is their great fear. Should this be done, or even seem to be in prospect, the Japanese would be forced into war with Russia in Siberia. They do not want this now, nor do the Russians. For that reason, they will not let any pilot of ours even see a Soviet air base in that area, but after Russia has licked Germany Marshall believes she must inevitably attack the Japanese in the Pacific.

This, he feels, is the greatest guarantee we have against a negotiated peace between Russia and Germany, because among the three nations, Russia, Japan and Germany, none can have any confidence in the word of the other, and all realize that any treaty drawn up would be completely worthless.

Finally, Marshall was asked: "Are you having any trouble with the color question in the Army?" After much concentration, he replied, "I'll answer that by saying that I would rather handle everything that the Germans, Italians and Japanese can throw at me than to face the trouble I see in the Negro question."

He was asked further if he could trust "colored" troops. Again he paused in deep thought and then replied, "Frankly, I cannot." He declared that the waste in connection with the training and equipping of these troops was criminal, and added his personal fear that the situation would grow much worse as the election of 1944 approached.

[General Marshall's shocking comments on the use of black troops afford a graphic measurement of the changes that have come about in race relations since World War II. Had the same questions been put to General Marshall today, it is inconceivable that his answers would have resembled those given in the 1940s in any way at all. These days black admirals and generals are to be found in our armed services, and black cadets and midshipmen walking the streets of our service academies create no notice, let alone comment. This is of course due to a profound change in national thinking, but also to the fact that blacks have been allowed to demonstrate that they can cut it as well as whites can.]

There is a helluva lot more, but this will have to hold you for a while. As it is, I suspect it will take you two months to read it.

Regards

CHURCHILL REVIEWS THE WORLD SITUATION

CONFIDENTIAL

Sunday
5 September 1943

Dear Bart,

Let's clean up some smaller stuff first.

As I told you in New York, the new battleship *Iowa* was piled up in a Maine harbor when the navigator's orders to the man at the wheel were misunderstood. It turned out to be not particularly serious. *Iowa* was repaired in sixteen days. The captain, who was at one time the President's naval aide, name of McCrea, I believe, and who is an excellent officer, gets off with a reprimand, while the navigator is to be broken.

Also, the Germans managed to get a torpedo into the battleship *Queen Mary* several months ago, but she got to port all right and was repaired at

Boston. She is back in service. The compartmentation of modern battleships is such that they can shake off one torpedo without even losing
much of their great speed.

In case Tom Headen [a *Sun* reporter] didn't tell you about it, he heard
some very interesting stuff about the underground in Europe. It is so
thoroughly organized that our people can get the answer to any question on
which they want information in 36 hours. This goes for Germany itself as
well as the occupied countries.

He cited one case in which OSS wanted the answer to something from the
Yugoslavs. Nothing was heard for three weeks. Then the Yugoslavs called
up and said they had the man who knew most about the situation. He had
been in Latvia, and had been brought by underground all the way across
Europe to Yugoslavia, was smuggled out and flown to the United States.
Apparently the underground can get people as well as news in and out.

The chief problem with the underground is keeping them down. They
want to break out into the open right away and start shooting Germans.
Our people don't want this, since it would only lead to useless slaughter and
deprive us of badly needed information. Our idea is to have the
underground stay out of sight until we can back it up by invasion.

Incidentally, the undergrounds have no need for weapons from us. They
have, one way or another, got all they need from the Germans. I am informed
that we are making ammunition in the German calibres in this country and
getting it to the underground, which takes care of transporting it.

So much for that. The Baruch party turned out to be a delightful occa-
sion, but was purely social. There was no news. The guest of honor was
Brendan Bracken, Churchill's Minister of Information. Other guests were
George Creel, who served President Wilson in much the same capacity in
World War I, Roy Howard, Mark Sullivan, David Lawrence, Arthur
Krock, Frank Kent, Felix Belair, Blair Moody, Sam Lubell, Marquis Childs.
I felt honored by the journalistic company I was keeping. I was certainly
junior officer present.

It was a delicious supper, cold salmon and cold meat, accompanied by
buckets of the famous Baruch Perrier-Jouet 1928, the best vintage year of
modern times. I'm not especially fond of champagne, but this was special.

Now, as to the USSR. There are those in Washington who fear that the
Russians are negotiating a separate peace with Germany. I personally do
not believe it, but the aloofness of Stalin has not made for understanding.
You know the story about Ploesti. Litvinov's departure also fed fuel to the
fire, although, as I reported before, he did not have the confidence of his
own government. Also, he had failed to get a second front in France. The
important thing, as Eugene Lyons explained to Roscoe and me at luncheon
last week, is that no Red ambassador is anything more than a messenger
boy. We'll come to more about Russia later on in this memo.

Winston Churchill, as the papers reported today, was guest of honor of the Overseas Writers, the National Press Club, the White House Correspondents Association, the Gridiron Club, the National Press Club and the radio press at luncheon at the Statler yesterday.

The hotel's sound system went dead as he began his talk. He eyed the offending microphone with complete contempt, said "A puling age" and adjusted his voice without strain to the new condition. He made a short talk and then answered questions for an hour. Here are the chief points:

In this talk he devoted himself chiefly to the thesis that our newspapers have been too specific in their analysis of our military plans. He stressed the value of surprise, and urged writers to be vague in what they said. Twitting Bracken on some Boy Scout crack he had made, Churchill added that any writer had done his good dead for the day if he wrote something that confused or misled the Axis. He did not mention that it might also be misleading and confusing to the British and American people, too. I expect that doesn't matter if the enemy is fooled. Then came the questions. I'll deal with them by nations.

Soviet Union. Churchill insisted that he and Roosevelt had made repeated efforts to get together with Stalin, and that one conference had been set for Khartoum, Egypt. It fell through. Stalin's plea has been that he is the leader of the Russian war effort, and cannot leave the country. This answer, Churchill said, was understood and accepted by Roosevelt and himself, since Stalin is a great psychological force in Russia, and his very presence bucks up the people and the Army no end. Incidentally, he added that the army is a growing political power in the Soviet Union. His first remark indicated that it was supplanting the party, but he corrected himself.

In the meantime the conference of foreign ministers is in the works, and Roosevelt and Churchill are still hopeful of getting together with Stalin. Churchill said he personally was ready to go any place at any time for such a meeting. He noted the difficulties involved for FDR and Stalin in leaving their own countries. Churchill also said he was perfectly prepared to back his policy with Russia in debate with Stalin or anybody else, that he thought the U.S. and Britain had an excellent case for every move they made. Liberal critics, he pointed out, had to face this dilemma: had an attack on France been mounted, there could have been no Mediterranean show. Thus, to criticize our policy is to say that the conquest of Africa and Sicily has been useless.

Basically, we have two aims in common with Russia: the elimination of the Nazis and the militarists. Once they are gone, the problems that remain can be handled with relative ease. He admitted frankly—and significantly—that Russia did not think America and Britain had spilt enough of their blood. He countered by saying that the object of war is to win victories, not to lose lives, and that he did not propose to lose a single British or American life in a political gesture to placate Russia. Our leaders are competent. They know what they are about. Selfish victories are better than generous defeats, he went on. He expressed great admiration for the way the Red Army has stopped the Germans but made it plain that this did not sway him from the path of logical development of our war effort.

Japan. He pointed out that Britain has at least as big a stake in defeating Japan as has the United States. He cited Hong Kong, the humiliation of losing Singapore, Malaya, Burma. Obviously we can count on Britain, once Germany is beaten, to swing everything she has against Japan.

He noted the bigness of the Pacific, and argued that the distances have the dual effect of spreading Japan thin and also of making it difficult for us to bring forces to bear against her. There are many more difficulties in the United States bringing 100,000 men to bear against Japan than there are for Russia, a land power, to bring 750,000 to bear against Germany, he said. He added that Russia, as a land power, found it hard to understand this.

However, he added that Japan is faced with increasing pressure, and that she is already paying for the pleasure of sinking five or six battleships at Pearl Harbor. On the other hand—this is top drawer stuff—he told us that Japan appears to have made quite a lot of progress in winning some native populations to her cause. I gather, although he didn't mention it, that the Philippines were one such place.

He expressed the opinion that the Japanese people, dragged into war by the militarists, were not immune to war psychology. He evidently figures we may ultimately be able to break down the Japanese war effort on the home front. Joe Grew of course does not agree. Anyway, Churchill cited the fact that at first we had to kill the last Jap, but that they have begun giving up in places like Kiska and New Georgia.

France. He defended our course of action in North Africa without going into details. He argued merely that Darlan had saved many British and American lives, and that he proved to be the only man who could give orders that anyone would obey. (Some day this story will all come out. From time to time I've advanced some ideas about our relations with Vichy, etc.)

Churchill also assailed those who criticize the French. They, he said, were in a terrible position, and we have no right to criticize them until we have gone through what they have gone through. We have worked with De Gaulle, and also with the military men like Giraud without whom De Gaulle could not hope to accomplish anything. Admitting De Gaulle had his faults, he nonetheles stood up and fought when others quit. As the result of our policy, he said, we hope that when the time comes to enter France we shall be received with rejoicing. In the meantime, he expressed the opinion that the French National Committee hd become more unified because it had not been recognized at home, and that this was a good thing for France's future.

Italy. Churchill assailed those who raised their hands in horror at the idea of dealing with anyone who ever had any truck with fascism. There is no-one in Italy who hasn't, he added. At one time or another every Italian has had to accommodate himself to the Mussolini regime.

As for Mussolini, he said he didn't know where he was, although he didn't think he was dead. However, he added, he would hesitate to write an insurance policy on Mussolini's life. (He got a laugh at that.) The fascist regime is gone, and Churchill indicated that significant events in Italy might be expected soon.

Germany. Still a powerful military force. The chance must be reckoned on that Hitler plans a powerful offensive in 1944 against overconfident enemies. Churchill doesn't think this will happen, but figures that the possibility cannot be discounted. He admitted that the Germans are valiant and powerful fighters, well equipped. He did not discuss their air strength, which is the crux of any question as to Germany's ability to counterattack.

However, he noted that the German's heart is ruled by his intellect, and that when his mind tells him he is licked, he is more likely than not to give up. This may happen in 1943, but Churchill doubts it. The British, he added, are ruled by their hearts and they do not think about quitting. Instead, when it looked as though the Germans might beat them, they merely said, "If we've got to get it, it might as well come now instead of waiting for later."

He likened Germany to a wild beast encircled by the hunters and beaters. Trapped, the animal nonetheless can strike out at some of his assailants, and may do great damage to the ones that happen to be in its way.

Turkey. Turkey has excellent infantry and artillery—some 40 divisions—but nothing else. Nor has she the manpower able to grasp readily the use of modern weapons. This means she has great limitations, and Churchill said he had always been very careful never to ask of Turkey anything that would turn out harmful to her, and make her suffer as other small European nations have had to suffer. This may not be candid. Turkey could be the key to Balkan operations, and Churchill here might have been doing his good deed to mislead the enemy, especially as what he said could be used if not attributed to him. I think what he said of Turkey's military power is undoubtedly true. But whether we don't expect to call on them, I don't know. Once we are placed so we can dominate military activities there, we might feel that Turkey would not suffer by throwing in with us.

United States. Churchill was asked if he thought a change of administration here would not hurt the war effort. He answered amusingly that he remembered the Declaration of Independence and knew that it would be wrong for him to butt into someone else's business. Going back to 1776, he said that maybe it was good for Britain that we rebelled, as the tail might have come to wag the dog, with the result that the dog might have been forced to rebel to get free from the tail. The idea of the British staging a revolution to get free from us tickles me.

So much for Churchill. He was magnificent, as always.

Regards

BRITAIN AGREES TO CHANNEL CROSSING—
ITALY SURRENDERS

CONFIDENTIAL

Monday
13 September 1943

Dear Bart,

Last night eight of our better newshawks (See *Time*, any issue) made the long trek to Alexandria to spend the evening with Nelie Bull and E.J.K. K talked steadily from 8 P.M. to 12:30 A.M. A certain amount of stuff is always repetitive from one conference to the next, but here are the high spots of new and interesting material as I saw them.

Contrary to the impression that General Marshall had given me, our relations with the British High Command have not been entirely smooth. Strong and vital differences of opinion have existed and still do exist, although they are being submerged more and more. For one thing, the British have favored the fighting of an "opportunist" war, striking wherever their fancy dictates, whenever the occasion seems propitious.

We have favored an overall plan, and insisted at Casablanca that we start drawing an exact blueprint of the methods by which we expect to defeat both Germany and Japan. That plan was started at Casablanca; furthered at the last conference with Churchill; and practically finished, in broad outline at least, at Quebec. Except for upsets, we now know exactly where we shall strike each successive blow, although the timing still seems to be vague. On the basis of this plan, K predicted that it will be another year before we defeat Germany and three before we lick Japan.

Mediterranean. He said he looked with great trepidation upon the prospect of going into the Balkans for a long, slow push which he thought would be unprofitable in the end. He does not want to be sucked in there as he feels we have been sucked into Italy. He does not feel that we ought to make any attempt to take all of Italy if it will take the time and effort that it now appears we must expend if we drive for Milan, Genoa and other northern bases. The airfields around Rome will give us an adequate base for operations in southern and southeastern Germany. The airfields further north would be better if we could get them cheaply and quickly, but even if we take all of Italy, we still have the Alps in front of us and no place to go.

He hopes, therefore, that the Germans are going to make their real line of defense in the valley that runs from Pisa through Florence to the Adriatic Coast. This is the narrowest point anywhere on the leg and will be easiest for the Germans to defend because it means the shortest battle line for them. It likewise means the shortest battle line for us, and if K's strategy prevails, we would not seek to press on beyond that point, but would hold that line, partly through the use of Italian troops, thus protecting our Rome air bases and the entire Mediterranean route, and leaving our men and material free for the major thrust at Germany, which must come, he says, through northern France.

French Invasion. Our major disagreement with the British has been on the subject of a cross-Channel invasion. The entire American High Command is united solidly in the opinion that the only way to strike at Germany successfully is through northern France—a Dunkerque in reverse. As long ago as last spring, Roosevelt and Churchill were agreed upon this strategy, but the British backed out. That was why Marshall and King made their sudden trip to England in July of that year. Churchill would still have none of it, and Roosevelt offered North Africa as a substitute, to which the British thankfully agreed. Now the British have once more promised to go ahead on the cross-Channel route.

It will take time—much time—and time is of the essence in view of the fact that Russia may conceivably drive the Germans back to their own borders in the east, and cease hostilities. That must not happen until we have a strong fighting force in France. To get this force we now lack three things: landing craft (see Marshall memorandum), troop transport, and seasoned troops. For the spearhead of this invasion we must use the troops that are now tied up in Italy and the Mediterranean. Once they have blasted their way in, green troops can follow in their wake. And these green troops, incidentally, will be virtually all Americans, for the British have no manpower left to throw into the breach once the drive is under way.

There are four French divisions, however, ready to take the field, and there will be eleven trained and equipped by the time the show begins. They are not battle seasoned, however, and cannot be used in the spearhead. We have altogether about 40 divisions in the Mediterranean area now. Thus, while Churchill looks longingly toward the prospect of a drive through the Balkans, K is bitterly opposed to it lest we tie up there the seasoned troops, delaying further the cross-Channel effort.

In favor of northern France, he argues that we have the greatest air force in the world based in Britain, and this air force, if it will concentrate on the French coast as it has concentrated on Germany, can blast an invasion avenue open for us so that we can take the rest of the German Channel defenses from the rear. As for the Balkans, he would merely have us establish beachheads on the Dalmatian coast once we have driven to the Adriatic, and maintain this foothold to insure a safe supply route for the equipment we are delivering, and will continue to deliver, to the Chetniks in Yugoslavia.

The shortage of landing craft and troop transport is a serious problem. We are concentrating on it heavily, with two immediate results: our destroyer escort program has been cut back sharply and is six months behind schedule; and many of the landing craft we had planned to send to Burma are being held in the Mediterranean, thus delaying the Burma action by about three months.

Another perilous problem in the cross-Channel effort is the fact that the rise and fall of the tide is extremely high, and the entire beach on the French coast slopes very gently, leaving great stretches of shallow water on which our vessels would be grounded We therefore have to set up special units which are now being trained to go in there and build long piers leading into the deep water.

Pacific. He is highly pleased with MacArthur's advance, and thinks things are going very well in this area. Rabaul will not be attacked. We hope to pinch it off by cutting its supply lines, thus saving heavy losses in men and equipment. He believes we may still be forced to make a separate frontal attack on Truk, but is clinging to the hope, obviously, that it, too, may be encircled and pinched off through the conquest of the Marianas. When asked about the prospect of a straight line drive to Wake, Guam and Saipan, he said, "Don't ask me these questions," thereby deliberately giving the impression that is exactly the course of action we plan to pursue.

For more than a week, we have had the report here that we have retaken Wake Island. When that subject was brought up, he played very cagey, repeating over and over again the single statement, "One island isn't enough. We have to have three, spaced at proper distances and well equipped with Japanese air bases." He did not say that we have recaptured Wake, but left the impression with us that the report is correct.

He also made it clear that we are about to raise unshirted hell in the Pacific, where we have 14 battleships today, eight of them Carolinas. In this connection, he said that the capture of the Italian fleet would release a number of British vessels for service in the Indian Ocean, but that he didn't think this would bother the Japs very much because by the time the British got there, the Japs would have plenty of trouble in their own front yard.

Burma. Our campaign in Burma apparently is to be concentrated on the northern end, from which we can make a quick link with the Old Burma Road without opening its entire length to southern Burma. We also plan another extensive operation to take place simultaneously within the area of the Southeast Asia Command, but he didn't give us any hints as to where this might be. My guess is a land attack on Singapore.

Significant, too, was his delight at the Marcus Island show which, he said, was a case of "coming events casting their shadows before." He stressed, too, when he said that, he did not merely mean attacks on other islands of that character. He was thinking, he said, of Japan proper. The Marcus Island show was a relatively small-scale rehearsal which would be repeated on an ever-increasing scale until all the complex and intricate mechanisms of carrier-based attack had been worked out to our satisfaction, after which the big drive on Japan itself would come. He said flatly that it was our purpose to use these carrier-based forces so extensively and so boldly against the Japanese that they would be forced to bring out their entire fleet where we could get at it.

Shipping. The Japs have not hit any of our submarines recently, and we, in turn, have had great difficulty finding Japanese targets to shoot at. We have so demoralized their shipping that they have instituted an entirely new system whereby they send their big cargo vessels under heavy escort to distribution points at Truk, in the Marshall Islands and elsewhere, where the stuff is transferred to small self-propelled wooden barges for redistribution.

Scientific Developments. The Germans have a new secret weapon which is a honey and which has us really worried. It is a rocket-powered projectile equipped with wings, resembling a small glider, and radio controlled, used for anti-aircraft and anti-ship work by the Germans. They send these into the midst of a formation of our bombers where they explode, creating a sphere of fire about a hundred feet in diameter and filled with fragmentation metal.

We have no defense against it yet, but on the other hand we have some honeys of our own in the works, he said. We are way out front in radar, and our scientists say that the room for expansion in this field is so unlimited that we can stay out front, many months ahead of the enemy, for the duration of the war. The Japs have radar, too. We found it at Kiska. But it is way behind ours. The Germans are now perfecting devices to neutralize our radar, and when their submarines are equipped with it we will have more trouble in the Atlantic.

However, we seem to have devised an unbeatable system of submarine extermination, and K is perfectly sure that we can sink 'em faster than they can build 'em. Our system is to use an auxiliary aircraft carrier with ten or a dozen escort vessels. Plane sights sub, loses same, but escort vessel picks it up on its listening and "pinging" systems. Escort vessel then sits down and waits for the sub to come up. Even if the sub dives "with a full can" (i.e., with batteries fully charged) it can stay under water only for a relatively short period. It then has to take its choice of trying to run, in which case we depth bomb it, or of surfacing and surrendering.

We have captured no submarines, but have taken the crews of many. Our depth bombs, incidentally, are now streamlined, so they sink much more rapidly than the old ones, and their depth fuses can carry them down as far as 500 feet before exploding. Moreover, they are equipped with "proximity" fuses, which explode them whenever they come within lethal range of metal.

Political. K is thoroughly mad at the RAF, which refused to function under joint military-naval command, and is determined to fight the war its own way by bombing Germany into submission. His complaints are twofold: first, that they will not bomb submarine pens in France, and this is going to cost us men and ships; and second, that they did not provide adequate air cover on the Sicilian landings.

Some revision has taken place, and at the Italian landings, the tactical air cover was under control of the joint command of the military and naval forces. But what he calls strategical operations of the air force, which should be mapped to destroy the enemy's communication lines behind the scene of the invasion, still remain under RAF command. He is dubious about Russia, but encouraged by the fact that we now have complete Russian, British, American liaison in working order, as is indicated by the fact that Russia joined in the terms of the Italian armistice.

He admires Badoglio, whom he knows personally, and says he thinks our press treated the Italians fairly shabbily. His contention is that Badoglio could not deliver Italy to us until he had formed his own government and built it up so that he would have something to deliver. We had hoped at some time to get to Rome this way, but that fell through. He believes, however, that when we have gone as far into Italy as we wish to go, we can rely upon the Italian Army to provide the garrisons there, relieving our men for northern France.

So far as the post-war situation goes, Churchill is enthusiastic about maintaining the present Combined Chiefs of Staff set-up exactly as it is now for a period of ten years, subject to the right of either nation to discontinue it on three years' notice. K, even more enthusiastic, asked Churchill why he didn't propose such a post-war set-up for a period of five years with the option of renewal.

Apparently the leadership of the British and American governments is bent upon keeping this arrangement, with all that it implies for as long as possible in the post-war era, the only flies in the ointment being the American Congress and the British Parliament. K emphasized the fact that the continuation of the Combined Chiefs of Staff after the war is only part of the story—it is a symbol and implies joint political and economic action as well.

That's not all he said by any means, but it's all you're going to get from me now except for one personal observation that I should like to make: it seems to me that the fundamental difference between the Americans and the British—and particularly between K and the RAF—lies in the fact that Churchill still hopes to bomb Germany out of the war without a major European land offensive, while K is proceeding on the traditional strategic concept that air alone cannot do the job, that ground operations will be necessary, and that air must be used as an auxiliary to these ground operations.

It seems to me highly possible, too, that Churchill may be right, and that it is certainly worth the chance for a while, because while it is true that Germany failed to bomb England out of the war, it must be remembered that

Britain's military supplies were not being made in the British Isles, but in the United States of America, where they were out of reach of the Luftwaffe, while the German sources of military supply are all subject to Allied air attack within the boundaries of Germany and her occupied territories.

Regards

RICKENBACKER VISITS RUSSIA AND RETURNS IMPRESSED

CONFIDENTIAL

Thursday
23 September 1943

Dear Bart,

This can be used as background but cannot be ascribed to Captain Rickenbacker.

When Secretary of War Stimson asked Rick to go to Russia to get all the military information he could, Rick said, "They'd never let me into that country, I have made too many speeches against communism. And I haven't changed my views and never will." Stimson suggested that the only way was to have Roosevelt make a personal appeal to Stalin. Evidently this was never done, for some time passed, and Rick decided to take the matter up with the Soviet Embassy here. They seemed glad to have him go.

The Russians showed him every courtesy, and he inspected many industrial plants, went to the fighting fronts, etc. He got the impression that they were not trying to conceal much. He said, "The Russians are great eye readers. They size you up, and if they think you are frank and sincere, they'll meet you man to man."

Rick explained the change in attitude of the Russians in the last quarter century. They lost the last war, including a lot of territory. Then they went through a revolution, and the whole world turned against them. They thought they were universally hated. They had a persecution complex, followed by an inferiority complex. Since they held Moscow and Stalingrad they have recovered their self-respect and now consider themselves the equal of anyone.

Russian communism today is very different from what we envision as communism in the States. When Stalin broke with Trotsky he lopped off a lot of heads. From time to time since he has lopped off a lot more. There has been an evolution in their kind of government and a swing away from international communism to state socialism.

Rick asked if men in factories received anything if they produced more. The reply was "Yes." They get more and better food. They get more privileges. There are no labor unions. All work on the piece system. They just don't understand when they hear of strikes and slowdowns in this country.

Rick said the Russians have lost 27,000,000 people since they entered the war, from battle casualties, starvation, murder, rape, etc. He said their deaths resulting from the fighting were 5,000,000. Then some 10,000,000 men, women and children have died of exposure, famine, disease, etc., in that part of Russia still held by the Russians. The deaths from starvation, executions, etc. in the part of the country held by Hitler amounted to 12,000,000.

It's amazing how the Russians moved whole cities and great industrial plants. He said Kuybyshev grew from a city of 300,000 to 1,500,000 in six months. Their method of moving industrial plants was to load machines from the factories onto flat cars or into box cars, and the men or women who worked the machines traveled with them. Many of them froze to death or died of exposure or starvation.

Every man, woman and child in Russia is geared to the war effort. Only the old and infirm have no place in it, and the Russians say frankly the sooner they die off, the better, for they have no food to spare. Rick said the Russian population was more universally engaged in the war than any other country, although he admitted he knew nothing about Germany.

Rick believes Roosevelt and Churchill should go to Moscow for a conference with Stalin. He said they would not lose face by such action. Stalin, he said, can't leave Russia—he has a war to win NOW—he can't win it next week or next year.

He thinks neither we nor the British have ever played exactly fair with Russia, and is not surprised that they are suspicious of us. He believes that if we do not reach an agreement with Russia and cement the alliance now, we may lose the chance for all time. And the danger is that after Russia has driven the Nazis off her soil, and finds herself isolated, she may turn to an alliance with Germany and Japan—which will mean World War III.

Russia, he said, wants not only the Baltic states, part of Poland, part of Finland, plus warm water outlets to the sea and the opening of the Dardanelles, but a sphere of influence in the Balkans.

"We must negotiate with her now, not wait until she has won her part of the war, and our bargaining power is gone."

Russia may also want to control an area down through Iran with its oil fields, and an outlet to Bushire on the Persian Gulf. We should be prepared to make some concessions to them—not everything they want, but something substantial. We must, if we are to hold their friendship and cooperation in post-war affairs. Russia will also want the port of Dairen on the Yellow Sea in southern Manchuria (Manchukuo) as a warm water port for Siberia.

Russia and Japan are natural enemies, and Russia will make war on Japan as soon as she disposes of Hitler. Then Stalin will allow most of Manchuria to be returned to China but will negotiate for Dairen with the Chinese. He says it is absurd for us to insist on Russia's taking on another front against Japan now.

Finally, he said the Russians get wonderful results with planes our men complain about.

My personal reaction is that it is amazing that a man like Rickenbacker, who hates communisn and believes ardently in the American system of private enterprise, should be so impressed by Russia. He went in expecting to be disillusioned and disappointed, but came out quite enthusiastic and believing thoroughly that we must take the Russians for what they are and do business with them if we are to avoid another world war.

Regards

ARNOLD BRIEFS PRESS ON AIR WAR; MARSHALL'S MOVE TO HEAD OF INVASION FORCE ANNOUNCED

When General Hap Arnold mentioned the Air Force's experiments with putting guns on planes in the following speech, I was reminded of how the use of artillery in planes first came to my attention earlier in 1943. I was one of a small group of accredited war correspondents flown to a Marine Corps air base on the North Carolina shore for a first hand demonstration. It seemed that Marine Corps B-25s used for this purpose had demountable noses, one for conventional weaponry and another in which a 75 mm cannon was mounted.

We were sent off, one to a plane, for a little target shooting. My fellow correspondents had the same experience I had, in that we had to crouch behind the pilot and co-pilot. They were seated and strapped in. We had no seats and nothing to hold on to. This was fine as long as the plane flew a straight course, and when we dove on the target, scoring a hit.

Pulling out of the dive, our pilot observed, "Now we'll take some evasive action." I had more or less expected that he would be unable to resist the temptation to scare the be-jabbers out of a newspaper reporter, and he did not disap-point me. I have no idea how long his stunting lasted. Probably two or three minutes. My only clear recollection is of looking out a port side window and seeing that the wing tip was pointed straight at mother earth.

But if the idea was to scare me, he missed by a mile. I felt like a grain of corn in a popper, and I was far too busy try-ing to hold on to be frightened. Actually, I doubt if I would have been frightened even if I *was* strapped into the co-pilot's seat, for two reasons: I assumed he must more or less know what he was doing, or he wouldn't be there, and second I assumed that he had no desire to die himself. As it happened, our only period of danger came after he missed his second shot and flew home some twenty miles at from ten to twenty feet above a beautiful sandy beach. The danger was that such a flight left no margin for error, and it was a no-no that might have caused him some trouble if I had told anybody about it.

As it was, I landed feeling exhilarated by the ride, with no damage but a pair of broken glasses and a slight cut on my forehead. We were entertained at cocktails in the late afternoon. Marine Lieutenant Tyrone Power was present, and it was amusing to watch generals and colonels busily engaged in seeing to it that he had a good time. Our guard-ian angel was Captain Louis Ruppel, an old friend from the days when Jimmie Walker was Mayor of New York, and Louis and I were covering City Hall.

At another point, when Arnold referred to the assault on Lae, I made a mental note that this successful attack, a triple envelopment, was something for the books. Es-pecially notable was the use by MacArthur, reputed to fear and have no use for planes, of fighters and bombers and troop carriers in such a way as to win a victory that might not have been possible at all without them, or would in any event have taken far longer and been infinitely more costly.

It is obvious in many of these memos that most of the officers who worked with MacArthur respected his ability, but didn't like him much. You might say they thought he had a big Swift's Premium Ham sign between his shoulders, but this is surely no novelty among the Great Captains of history. For sheer ego massage, who could match Alexander the Great's weeping spell because he had no more worlds to conquer?

There was large criticism of his over-blown rhetoric when landing on the beach at Leyte. I suggest it did not seem over-blown, but just right, to emotionally stimulated Filipinos. Whether he tailored his "I have returned" speech to his audience, or whether his audience was tailored to his natural oratorical style really doesn't seem to me to matter. It worked.

CONFIDENTIAL

Friday
24 September 1943

Dear Bart,

General Henry (Hap) Arnold, Chief of the Army Air Force, and member of the Joint and Combined Chiefs of Staff, spoke off the record at the Overseas Writers yesterday. As always, he was interesting, frank and profane. He is a good soldier. I'll go into what he said in some detail.

To begin with, he recalled congratulating the Secretary of War [Stimson] on his birthday recently. He had, he said, told the Secretary they had first met years before, when Stimpson was Secretary of War, and that on that occasion Arnold represented one-third of the Army Air Force, which consisted of only three pilots at that time. He recalled how, later, the Air Force had striven to get a force of 1,800 planes and never seemed able to make it.

Today we have 2,000,000 men in the Air Force alone. We have 67,000 pilots and thousands more in training. We are training 11,000 air gunners a month, or will be in October. We have 55,000 planes of all types in the Army Air Force . . . and it isn't enough. Our production of 7,000 planes a month is big, but it isn't big enough. He explained why.

He estimated before the war that our rate of attrition on planes would be about 25 percent per month. He wouldn't give the exact figure, but said they hadn't been far off. Apply this to a force, say, of 1,600 planes. That means 400 of the planes lost in a month. But it takes a month to get the planes established where they can be used. That doubles the number needed. Then deduct the planes given to our Allies, a considerable figure. Take out the enormous demand for transport planes. You haven't much gravy let.

With this preliminary, Arnold proceeded to discuss the various air fronts.

China. It is easy to say give Chiang 5,000 planes. We'd like to. We know the importance of China as the place from which to strike Japan. But there are only three ways of getting stuff in. China furnishes no fuel or ammunition. We can fly it over the Himalayas, a very difficult job. We can open the Burma Road. Or we can open a port on China's coast.

You will see there is no immediate prospect of getting real air strength to China. Despite this, we have managed to build up Chennault's force to fair size and have also helped the Chinese air force. We are still figuring hard, and intend to find a way to get planes and their necessities to Chiang, but we haven't got the answer yet.

The Aleutians. God, says Arnold, never intended this to be an air theatre, and man has been trying to make it one anyway. Ninety percent of the planes we lose there are due to the weather, and 10 percent to the Japs, who are not very numerous in this area. Special weather training is necessary before men can fly in this theatre and it is done in the back areas of Alaska. Our men have done a magnificent job of establishing fields on islands where it seemed impossible. They have repeatedly landed and hewn out a field on which planes were landing in 48 hours.

Australia-New Guinea. When we went in there, we were up against an enemy that had swept everything before him. Allied forces in this theatre had known only defeat, and the enemy had known only victory. In one year we have reversed this. It is Japan that has the bitter taste of consecutive defeats, and our people are riding high. It has been a tremendous job beautifully done. In Kenney and MacArthur, Arnold said, we have just about the best land-air command in the world today.

He recalled that the Japs were once only nine miles from the Port Moresby air fields, and that they've since been pushed back until their hold on New Guinea is seriously threatened. It was done by beautifully synchronized land-air operations. First, a puddle-jumper flew over the Owen Stanley Mountains and landed on a clearing. Its crew gave hand digging tools to the natives, and they cleared a space big enough for DC-3s to come in with mechanical digging tools, and mules. They landed troops on the strip, sometimes with Jap mortars dropping shells on it, and forced the Nips back so more planes could come in.

In the assault on Lae, we put on a marvelous show, timed so perfectly that not one plane had to alter course when it reached the rendezvous. First went medium bombers, with fighters overhead. Then came the big transport planes with 1,800 paratroops. Then came Flying Fortresses with supplies, weapons, and ammunition for the troops. Then came more bombers.

The first bombers hit the objective and then laid a smoke screen behind which the 1,800 paratroopers landed in a minute and 15 seconds, with only 30 casualties—broken legs and sprained ankles. The bombers went on to block off the nearest place from which Japs could attack with their reserves, while the Forts dropped the supplies. The whole operation was done, from start to finish, in two hours. That is modern war.

The Solomons. Fighting of a different sort, again with weather a big obstacle. We by-passed islands when the Japs were weak enough to make it possible, leaving them to starve. We hit 'em if they can't be by-passed. Frequently our men find the weather has closed in, and they go into the sea. It is surprising how many of them get back.

North Africa. A magnificent job by General Tooey Spaatz. He hammered at the Luftwaffe, forcing it to fight, and eventually beat it down to such an extent that we began catching their planes on the ground, which was the stunt they had pulled on their enemies with deadly effect earlier in the war. Late in the North African campaign it was not unusual for our strategic air missions to catch 60 to 70 German planes on the ground and ruin them. At the same time, our tactical air arm was giving our land forces cover that drew high praise from General Alexander. Now there are whole days when not a single German plane appears to contest our air operations.

Western Europe. This is the big fight. The 8th Air Force, working on principles that were ridiculed a short time ago, has established the usefulness of precision, pin-point bombing in daylight. It has proved more costly than was expected, but it is doing a job the RAF is not set up to do, and can't do. The pressure has become so heavy on the Germans that they have set up nine fighter commands in the area to meet our planes.

The Nazis have called up every long-haired scientist they have in an effort to figure out some way of stopping us. To date they have failed, but we have to keep on our toes, and stay a jump ahead. First the Germans tried to come in with fighters, but they couldn't take the terrific firepower from our big planes. They they tried to lay off and outrange us. But that produced little. Next they tried to get over our planes and drop bombs on them. That failed as they haven't got the technique to get hits—yet. Then they turned to rockets lobbed into formations of bombers from some 1,500 yards distance. The rockets throw large fragments of metal around, but we've stood up because our planes are so incredibly sturdy that they can take enormous punishment and still fly. Arnold says he has seen planes come home that he would have said could not fly, but they made it.

He told about a tail gunner of a Fort shot down over the Channel who drank a pint of brandy to keep warm. When he was hauled out by the Rescue Service, he was bobbing and weaving as well as shivering. The skipper of the boat brusquely ordered him below to change into dry clothes.

The tail gunner, offended, drew himself up, saluted, said, "I won't stay where one is not wanted," and jumped back into the Channel. They fished him out and sent him below.

The number of German fighters concentrated in this area is such that if we went straight in we'd run up against a stone wall. We had to devise some deception, and we went to the football field. Pilots in their briefing use football terms—end run, hidden ball, off-tackle plays. He explained how we use medium bombers as a feint at one objective to draw off some fighters, and then send our big bombers in from another direction at the real target. It works. He showed us one such show on the map.

We are equipping our fighters with belly tanks so they are now able to escort our ships clean over the Ruhr. Our raids are escorted out to the maximum range of fighters, and are picked up by fresh fighters as they come home. The role of the fighter has changed. Now it is an escort.

The 8th Air Force has two objectives. One is to smash German communications and industry. The other is to ground the Luftwaffe. We are looking to the day when we can send 1,000 to 1,200 Forts to Germany every day. When that time comes, we figure the way will be made very much easier for our land forces to move. Arnold wouldn't say when this would be, but admitted it was a difficult problem. Our losses being heavier than expected, we suddenly found we were having trouble even holding our own strength. It proved necessary to take away some trained men to plow back into the training program to increase the number of bomber crews coming out. That made for a lag. But now the situation is such that we are assured of enough big bombers and crews to maintain strength, or increase it.

To illustrate the difficulties Germany is having, Arnold cited the trouble we have when minor hitches come up in industry. There was a slowdown in a ball bearing plant. Not a strike. The men just didn't feel like working hard. It wasn't, but it slowed down engine manufacturers and cost Arnold 300 planes. If a minor thing like that hits us so hard, what does it mean to Germany when we destroy 50 percent of the buildings in a rubber plant, when we raze the Messerschmitt plant at Regensberg that makes 40 percent of their fighters? And when we keep coming back, it means unbearable dislocation.

We figure we can cripple German transport facilities, cripple German industry, break German morale, and eliminate the Luftwaffe by bombing.

Describing the general plan of modern war strategy, Arnold explained that the air force goes ahead and smashes up the enemy so our land troops can move in and establish more advanced air fields, which the air forces use to smash up the enemy so the land forces can move in and establish more advanced air fields, etc., etc. ad infinitum.

He mentioned several times the greatly increased demand for transport planes in all theatres. Planes on the ground are no use. They might as well not be there if they can't fly. And they can't fly if supplies, fuel, ammunition, bombs, aren't available. Land forces often can't move fast enough to keep up. Hence the growing need for transport planes. We simply can't get enough.

Germany. Has about 5,000 first-line planes and no reserve, which is their big trouble now. They have about 1,500 fighters in Western Europe, about a thousand in the Mediterranean (where Spaatz has knocked out 2,000 German and Italian planes) and about 1,500 on the Russian front. In addition they have some 1,700 bombers, and we wish we knew where they were and what is to be done with them. They've used only about 200 bombers in the last few months.

Japan. We are guessing, but we think they have about 4,000 planes. We think we know approximately their rate of production, but are puzzled by their ability to fill the holes left by losses. However, we notice that mostly they have to pull planes out of one theatre to bolster another, and there are other signs that Japan is scraping the bottom of the barrel. However, we're not yet in anything like a good position to bring the air war to Japan proper.

United States. Production of big bombers is okay. If we could get 4,000 transport planes tomorrow we'd still want more. Production of medium and light bombers not so hot. Our experiment of putting three-inch guns on planes is working well, and with them our pilots have been able to sink destroyers. He did not mention the B-29.

In summation, two points stick out, I think. First, his description of meteorological difficulties in the Aleutians lead me to believe we can't hope for much pressure on the Japs by air from there. Second, it is significant that Arnold does not believe the air force can lick Germany alone. He didn't say so, but it was implicit in his statement that the air force could make the task of invasion forces much easier.

Finally, he told us a colorful tale from the Sicilian invasion. In one of the harbors were moored four American ships. One contained high test gas. Two contained block-busters. The fourth was loaded with food and shoes. If one of the first three ships had blown up it would have rattled windows in Kansas City. And the German bombers came over. Thousands of rounds of anti-aircraft ammunition were fired at them. And those bombers got only one hit—on the ship loaded with food and shoes. What a close one!

Regards

SECRETARY KNOX ON POST-WAR WORLD

CONFIDENTIAL

Wednesday
20 October 1943

Dear Bart,

This is the first time I have had a chance to get to work on a memorandum covering a dinner which about a dozen of us had with Secretary Knox last Friday night following his return from the Mediterranean. He talked at great length, but I am not going to attempt to do more than hit a few high spots.

New Weapons. As he explained it, the glide-bomb which the Germans have been using against our ships is one thing, and the rocket-powered bomb which they are using against our aircraft is an entirely separate and distinct thing. This is at variance with the information given us by E.J.K. and with the statement that Winston Churchill made in Parliament. Knox says that we have found a satisfactory defense against the glide-bomb.

The sonic torpedo which the Germans are using is very effective, and goes directly to the propeller of the target ship. We also have the same torpedo and are using it. He believes we shall shortly have a radar torpedo that will actually "see" its target.

Pacific. Our submarines are still doing a swell job there, and some indication of the extent to which we have injured Japanese transport may be seen from the fact that the Japanese are using a constantly increasing proportion of wooden vessels in order to maintain their supply lines. He said that the war with Japan would be over when we succeeded in destroying the Japanese fleet and putting a Chinese army of occupation into Japan. Thus far, we have been unable to make the Japanese fleet come out and fight, but Knox says we can do exactly that by picking some island from 400 to 500 miles off Japan, taking it and holding onto it. That would place our bombers within easy range of Tokyo, and the Japs would have to eject us at any cost to themselves. For your information, there is a very handsome spot known as Rosario Island which would seem to suit our purposes admirably in this regard. It lies about 500 miles due south of Honshu.

Oil. Knox was angry at the suggestion that the British had been selfish about withholding their own oil suppy while they exhausted ours. He insisted that it was simply a matter of transportation and that it was much easier and quicker to get oil from the United States for our forces in Africa than to get oil from Persia and carry it 15,000 miles around the Cape, but now that the Mediterranean is opened up, of course it is possible to use the Persian oil advantageously. The British have now contracted to supply us with 100,000 barrels a day from the foreign fields. As we have been shipping 600,000 barrels a day from the East Coast here, it would seem that the British will henceforth give us about one-sixth of our supply. Beyond this 100,000 barrels, there is plenty of oil in Persia but not enough refining capacity to handle it, so we are apparently engaged now in an effort to create additional capacity in that area.

Russia. Knox made these interesting observations about Russia:

1) That when this war is over, the Russian people and the Russian government will be as anxious as we to achieve a world condition under which a long era of peace may be probable.

2) They will likewise feel that such a peace can be achieved only if they are allowed to establish boundaries that are defensible from a military point of view.

3) He is certain they will demand the Baltic states, some territory in the Balkans, and a warm-water outlet through the Bosporus. They will likewise

want about half of Poland to compensate for the lost territory.

4) He believes the odds are about five to one that when she has finished with Germany, Russia will turn to help clean up on Japan for the sake of her own future security.

Post-War World. These Russian aspirations bring up the questions of the Four Freedoms, the Atlantic Charter, and the self-determination of the peoples in the smaller countries of Europe. Knox takes the very practical view that we cannot guarantee the people of Esthonia, Latvia, Finland, Poland and other states bordering upon Russia the right to determine whether they shall remain independent or not, unless we are prepared to maintain a police force in Europe to protect that right, and unless, also, we are prepared to fight Russia right now. His own belief is that the best thing for us to do is to keep out of European land problems entirely, leaving Russia and Great Britain to police Europe in the post-war era.

As for the rest of the world outside of Europe, he points out that the United States and Great Britian will have the only two fleets in existence when this war ends, and he proposes that the American fleet undertake the policing of that part of the world extending from a line drawn somewhere through the mid-Atlantic, in a westward direction as far as Singapore, while the British would police all the other waters of the world—the eastern part of the Atlantic, the Mediterranean, the Red Sea and the Indian Ocean.

This would give us the task of preserving order throughout the entire Pacific Ocean and would necessitate our acquisition of as many islands in that area as might be needed for our air and naval bases. Any British ship coming into the sphere of American responsibility would automatically come under American command, while conversely any American vessel passing through British waters would come under the orders of the British Admiralty.

The Combined Chiefs of Staff as now set up in Washington would continue their operations as at present. Bases anywhere in the world would be jointly available for British and American use so that we could have our supplies to care for our ships and planes at British bases, and they could have their supplies at ours. This arrangement would be advanced as an interim proposal to be honored by both countries until replaced by a better one, possibly at the peace table.

Knox does not claim authorship for this proposal, which has come largely from active officials of the Army and Navy, but he is thoroughly sold on it and I understand that he has put it up to Churchill, Roosevelt and Hull, winning their enthusiastic support for it in all instances.

General Marshall. From what Knox said, it is apparently irrevocably decided that General Marshall is to go to London to command the cross-Channel invasion. Presumably this will not be announced until Marshall is already there and on the job. My understanding is that the plan now is to have Marshall retain his title as Chief of Staff while he is abroad, and to have the actual duties of the Chief of Staff performed by a deputy who will serve here in his absence. The Combined Chiefs of Staff will continue to make their headquarters at Washington as has been the case in the past. I gather that the announcement of Marshall's new job is expected any day now.

With best regards

THE MOSCOW CONFERENCE

CONFIDENTIAL

Friday
29 October 1943

Dear Bart,

First, there is something hot cooking in the Pacific. What it is I don't know, but my information is that in the next ten days one can expect some more trouble for the Japs.

Now, as to the Moscow Conference. The President at his press conference today said that things are going very well. The truth is that they are going far beyond our expectations. We were somewhat depressed by the *Pravda* attitude before the conference opened, but that fear has been swept away.

The following information comes from Mr. [Undersecretary of State Edward] Stettinius.

1) As Mr. Roosevelt said, the conference has gone very well indeed. The atmosphere has been friendly and cooperative. The Russians have gone out of their way to be helpful, and there has been none of the tension that Washington feared would obtain when the delegates got to Moscow.

2) Despite the attitude taken by *Pravda*, the Russians have *not* insisted on the Second Front immediately as a prerequisite for talks on diplomatic and post-war matters. Unquestionably the opening talks were devoted to an exposition of the Anglo-American military position, which we have felt the Red leaders, as heads of a land power, did not understand. That is, we felt they failed to understand the difficulties inherent in the sea phases of the war, the need for shipping, etc. However, all indications are that there is now no misunderstanding of our problem, if there ever was. Naturally the Russians want the Second Front as soon as possible. They'll get it if present plans hold, along about April or May of 1944. It looks as though the Red leaders accept that, whatever *Pravda* says.

3) The fears that the Soviet Union might make a separate peace with Ger-

many are absolutely groundless. The USSR is in this war to stay, and this fact has been made very clear in the Moscow Conference. There is no longer the slightest ground for worry on this point. Personally, I have never been worried about it at any time, for I have been convinced that no nation could do to Russia what Germany has done and not pay for it if the Russians had the power to exact payment.

4) While there is no specific information available, it can be said that Russia goes beyond merely setting up things for a future Roosevelt-Stalin-Churchill conference. The foreign ministers are making plans and agreements that stand in their own right as very important for the future peace of the world.

The Roosevelt-Stalin-Churchill conference will be held, all right. I'm sure of that. This fact is in itself a very hopeful sign, for had the foreign ministers not been able to get together there would have been no possibility of such a subsequent meeting. The future of the world looks better right now than at any time since we entered the war.

So much for Stettinius. Elsewhere, in military circles, I get indications that our highly placed officers are convinced that once Germany is finished Russia will come in against Japan. This too is a hopeful sign for the future, since a truly self-seeking Soviet Union—or at least one that intends to be isolationist—could sit back and let us spend ourselves against Japan.

And that's all from Washington for now.

Regards

HISTORIC STALIN–CHURCHILL–ROOSEVELT CONFERENCE IN TEHERAN

CONFIDENTIAL

Monday
20 December 1943

Dear Bart,

The following information has come to me over the weekend. I urge that after you and Mr. Speed have read it, it be destroyed in such a manner that it cannot possibly be reassembled.

Teheran Conference. Our people came out of these meetings much impressed with Stalin, who is appraised as a cool, calm, extremely realistic man who has no time for nonessentials. At the opening session the delegates were seated at a round table, Stalin flanked by Molotov and Voroshilov, Roosevelt by King, Marshall and Harriman, Churchill by Anthony Eden and his military leaders. Harry Hopkins sometimes sat at the round table, and sometimes stayed in the background.

At the beginning, Roosevelt spoke for perhaps fifteen minutes, pointing out that it was an historic occasion, and all that. Then he passed the ball to Churchill, who for ten minutes spoke words of like nature. Then all hands turned expectantly to Stalin, making it clear that it was his turn.

Stalin said, "The sentiments expressed seem appropriate to the occasion, and I endorse them. Now, let's get down to business."

I should explain that the protocol of these meetings was that when a Russian spoke, a Russian interpreter handled the translation. When an American spoke, an American, and when a Briton, a Briton.

Stalin, when general remarks were being made, doodled on a pad in front of him, occasionally looking in a pained way to the speaker. At the conclusion of the meetings, instead of tossing his doodles into the center of the table to be burned, Stalin carefully folded his chits and put them into his pocket. He forgot to do so at the conclusion of one session, and somebody got a souvenir. There were three sessions at which the military leaders sat in. The first two lasted for about three hours each. The third lasted three-quarters of an hour.

Questions as to why Roosevelt moved to the Russian compound elicited this explanation: the OGPU picked up information that German agents intended to create an incident. So Stalin suggested that FDR move from the somewhat remote American compound to his. This was done without incident after the Joint Chiefs of Staff had suggested that the secret service be restrained from running around like lunatics, tipping off observers that something was about to happen, and had also suggested that if guards were to be posted at street corners, they go on duty five minutes before the President was to pass, and not an hour before, as that would attract crowds. It worked smoothly.

Stalin is described as being of medium height and build. His uniform, when seen in the open air, was iridescent, and the understanding is that only he in the USSR can wear that cloth. Our informant doubted that anyone else would want to.

It is interesting to note that at one point in the meetings Stalin asked bluntly what was meant by unconditional surrender. He got no good answer. The truth is that the phrase was picked up as an afterthought at Casablanca to add drama to the final communiqué, and our people never have figured out just what they meant by it. I think you will find the phrase being dropped as gracefully as possible in favor of the Russian approach, which is to punish the guilty but not the innocent, and to try to make effective use of psychological warfare.

Russia made no plea for the Second Front, but made it clear that one is wanted, and in France or the Low Countries. No other place will do. Stalin told the conference that the first few days of the invasion might be pretty rough, as the Germans could move up reserves faster than we, but not to worry, that the Red Army would keep on punching and would take the load off our necks.

Our people came away convinced that Russia is in the war to stay, that Stalin took this conference in dead seriousness and regarded it as most important, that Russia will not go to war with Japan until Germany is beaten, being anxious to fight only one war at a time. The former unsatisfactory situation regarding exchange of information with the Russians was also ameliorated at the conference, and we have a military mission in Moscow headed by General [John R.] Deane, Secretary of the Joint Chiefs of Staff.

In this connection, our informant said the way to deal with the Russians is to turn on the heat. If you let them play you for a sucker, they will. If you don't, it's all right with them. Example: our naval attache in Moscow was anxious to see Russian shipbuilding. He got nowhere, and was finally told the Russians weren't building any ships.

Our attache then said he had been looking over lend-lease reports, and saw that we were shipping to Russia large quantities of materials that could be used only in ships. This being the case, hadn't he better inform Washington that the Russians were not building ships, so that the shipping space used for this material could be used for essential goods. He got the immediate answer, "What do you want to see?" and from then on had no trouble.

A significant aspect of the conference was that Stalin repeatedly used the words Russia and Russian, and only used the word Soviet once. This was taken as evidence of increasing nationalism on his part, as is news that only in the past few months have Russian schools been permitted to teach Russian history prior to the Revolution. Now Russian students get the whole picture of their country's history. It is the judgment of our informant that Stalin is not much concerned with proselytizing, and that the announced abandonment of the Commintern can be taken at face value.

As for Russian aspirations, they want free access to the open sea, both Atlantic and Pacific. The latter means they will want Dairen. The former may be settled by internationalizing the Dardanelles, and also the Kattegat and the Skagerrak, which connect the Baltic to the North Sea.

Cairo Conference. Like Stalin, Chiang stands as a great man on the record of what he has come through. He is a very demanding man, sometimes unreasonably so. The military people had one meeting with him. They feel, as to his demands, that we are a rather boastful people, telling the world of the miracles we can perform, and that Chiang wants us to perform a few of them for China. They don't blame him much.

Chiang is very much worried about the Chinese situation, and so are we. There is always the chance that Japan will decide to concentrate on China, and if that happens, China could hardly be expected to stand up to it. That, since we intend to defeat Japan by utilizing China's manpower and geographical position, would be a serious matter. I'll have more on that later on.

One of the good signs is that Lord Louis Mountbatten seems to have made an excellent impression at Chungking. I got the feeling that things are moving slowly in his theatre. The Assam Road to connect with Burma Road is making slow progress, and all signs are that we shan't be able to give real help to China until we can open up some China ports to our shipping. This puts it right up to our Navy, and it will take time.

In this connection, we were warned not to expect too much from Siberia when and if Russia comes in. We shall have to fly in everything for our air forces to use, as ground communications are very limited. It is, in a sense, another China problem. The Red Banner armies have their own stockpiles, but we need more than that by a good deal. But China still looks like the best bet, once we get in.

Mediterranean Theatre. As of 10 December, the Middle East Command was put under General Eisenhower, and thus comes under the authority of the Combined Chiefs for the first time. This consolidation will probably not be announced until January, when General Eisenhower leaves his command to go to London to head up the invasion forces. The command situation in the Middle East is described as "vicious," and apparently we are having our troubles there, symbolized by such things as the defeat in the Dodecaneses.

As I have said earlier, our objective in Italy is to get sufficiently north of Rome so that city is out of range of heavy cannon. We guessed wrong on what the Germans would do, thinking they would only offer real resistance north of Rome. However, we are diverting a considerable number of their troops from France, and also from their strategic reserve in Germany.

The Italian fleet has already proved itself of some help. It is escorting convoys in the Mediterranean, and took an active part in the landing on Corsica. However, we are not yet convinced of the real combat ability of that fleet. One Italian division has got into the fighting in Italy. The Germans found out it was in the line, and gave it a frightful mauling, but it stuck in there and kept on punching. Now we get news that it has taken the objective that it failed to take at such cost just a few days before. This is all to the good. But progress will continue slow in Italy.

Two points came out regarding Russia. One was the possibility of opening a direct supply line through the Mediterranean to the Black Sea as substitute for the Murmansk and Persian Gulf routes. The Russians said it was fine to open the Mediterranean route, but that it must be in addition to, and not instead of, the other two. The other was the strategic concept of opening a fighting line all along the south of Europe, linked up with the Russian Army. This was vetoed by our military people, as it would not force the Germans to move people clear across Europe, but would allow them to concentrate on one long front. The Russians showed no warmth for the idea, which by elimination must have come from the British.

There was some discussion about Turkey. The feeling of our informant, and of the Russians, was that Turkey would not come into the war until 5 minutes of midnight, being anxious until then to continue as a neutral. Interestingly enough, the Russians don't seem to care much one way or the other. This may be due to a feeling that getting the Dardanelles opened up after the war might be easier with Turkey as a neutral than as an ally. This last is my own speculation.

Second Front. There has been a great deal of squabbling about this between the British and ourselves. The British have always resisted the idea. Our informant pointed out that British policy has always been to have someone else do the fighting, and that up to the First World War this had always worked out. This was not mentioned in any critical sense, but as a realistic appraisal of a realistic policy. However, events have now brought the British to the knowledge that there is no alternative to the second front.

Our ranking officers have taken the position that the ability of the RAF and the 8th Air Force in Britain means that they could put frightful pressure on the Germans all along the invasion coast. This is especially true since our air power based in Britain is still growing, and since all southern Britain is virtually one huge air field.

This power, they believe, can be used to interdict absolutely German mobile reserves, and keep them, by a wall of exploding bombs, from going to the relief of the invasion centers. If they can't do it, then air power is not what its advocates say it is. It can hammer railroad junctions, road junctions, and all communication lines so that nothing can move. This will mean that our amphibious forces will have to deal only with those German troops actually in the invasion areas until they are well enough established to get along on their own. Our air people are now enthusiastically sold on this idea, and the British are also receptive to it.

As to the ultimate date, the weather makes invasion operations impossible until spring. However, the idea is to have the forces ready to move at any time if we should get a weather break. It is taken for granted that we cannot possibly achieve surprise as to the time of the operation. The Germans are bound to know that we are making the necessary concentrations. We can, however, achieve surprise as to where we are about to strike, particularly with an absolutely effective air cover. It follows, of course, that this invasion attempt is going to be preceded by the greatest air battle of all time.

Air Power. For the first time in this war, the relative value of the various weapons is being realized by all schools of thought. Even the rabid air enthusiasts are coming to see that their planes are tied to the ground by the necessity of having available fuel and supplies. They are realizing that air is just another member of the team in which there is no one supreme weapon. This is a very good thing, as the Severskys have done a tremendous amount of harm with their preaching that air power alone could win the war. It just isn't so, and even they are coming to realize it. Suppose, our informant said, that when artillery was introduced its advocates argued that it supplanted all other weapons, and that the infantryman was no longer of any value. What would have happened to the nation in which such counsels prevailed?

In this connection, our informant discussed the question of a Department of National Defense. Arguments in its favor are persuasive, especially in the economic field. This will be important after the war, when it will be necessary to maintain a considerable military-naval-air establishment at minimum cost. Through unification of such units as supply and medical services, considerable savings can be made.

On the other side is the possibility that having one Cabinet member in control of all the armed forces might be very dangerous. It was pointed out that in South America the first thing an incipient revolutionary does is try to get to be Minister of National Defense. This doesn't appear to be a problem to us now, but its future possibilities would have to be considered. In some ways, the Secretary of National Defense would be more powerful than the President himself.

It is certain that a good deal of thought is going to be devoted to this matter in high places. Our ranking officers, however, do not seem convinced that the presently-advanced divisions of sea, land and air are the right ones. In this discussion, the point came up that the time is near when our armed forces will level off on their demands for men, ceasing to build up and taking only enough to maintain the desired level.

Japan. It is important to realize that the Japanese do not regard their fleet as we do ours, as an instrument for carrying the war to the enemy. On the contrary, they regard it as an adjunct of the army, with the duty of enabling the army to do its work under the navy's protection. This is one reason why the Japs have not brought their fleet out, and why they won't until we can put such pressure on them that they've got to fight. This, our high officers believe, will not happen this year.

One of the possibilities that worries our people is that the Japanese estimate of the situation might convince them that they have bitten off more than they can chew, and that they might then, even at the cost of abandoning the Dutch Indies and the Philippines, swing everything they have against China in an effort to make sure of that much. As I have said, they could probably get away with it if they tried, and with short lines of communication and a well-consolidated position they could make it awfully hard for us.

Implicit in this is the damage we have done to Japanese air and sea power, reducing them to the point where the Nipponese high command has obviously got to consider giving up some of its conquests as a bow to the practical exigencies of the situation.

I gathered that there has been a considerable discussion between the

Army and the Navy over the possibility of by-passing Truk. The Navy appears to feel that Truk must be taken, as when you by-pass a place, you have to have some place to light. We haven't anything on the Japanese side of Truk, and could hardly get it with Truk on our flank. We felt that our informant was deliberately uncommunicative about the Pacific, and were quite satisfied to have it so, as about all he could have said was what is going to happen, and where and when, things we'd rather not know.

We were also told that Japan has adopted a moderate policy toward the Nanking government in China, and is making real progress. When the Japs were tough, they met nothing but resistance. But with a policy of bread and circuses, they are going places. This is something we must take into account, for we've just got around to offering the Chinese some real war objectives.

Finally, on the subject of Japan, this ties in: the Joint Chiefs have made a thorough review of the Canol project, and their recommendation is that it be brought to completion. They have so advised the Truman Committee, but refused to give that Committee access to the evidence on which the recommendation was based, taking the position that military security made it undesirable. It is our understanding that this oil would be very helpful, and would make long tanker hauls unnecessary in the event we went after Japan's Kurile Islands, or if it became necessary to supply planes flying to Siberia with fuel.

Truman Committee. The Truman Committee, under the guise of inquiring into matters of supply and demand, is interfering increasingly with the conduct of the war, and it is irritating our high officers no end. A typical example was the Committee's inquiry of the Marine Corps as to the cause of the high casualties in the Gilbert Islands.

In other words, the Truman Committee is getting out of its proper field, into matters with which it has, and should have, no concern. We paid a price in the War Between the States because of Congressional interference, and it would be tragic if we forgot the lesson we learned then. What will be done about this situation I do not know, but I judge some steps will be taken to bring the Truman Committee back to the performance of the duties for which it was established.

Unified Command. The Combined Chiefs have considered the matter of taking Russian representatives in, and have concluded to take no initiative whatever in the matter. If the question is forced on the group, it will take this position: that it is hard enough to get agreement between two nations, and that if three are represented it becomes a debating society, with the necessity for getting A and B, A and C, and B and C to agree, in addition to having to get ABC together. Every time you add one, it becomes more difficult.

Therefore, the idea is to continue present practice, to bring the representatives of a country into the counsels of either the Joint or Combined Chiefs only when operations are to be discussed that involve the territory and/or forces of that country. This has been done in some cases in the past, but will probably become routine procedure when and if the question is raised again.

Here is the story of General Marshall and the plan to give him command of the invasion of France. The ostensible reasons advanced by supporters of this plan were two-fold. First, he had from the very start argued for a cross-Channel invasion as the only way to crush the Germans against advancing Soviet armies, so it was logical that he command it. Second, there was a desire to see to it that his great contributions to victory be recognized in a way that could come only to one who commanded the victorious army in the field.

Apparently it was a closely held secret; the first that Marshall's comrades on the Joint Chiefs heard about it was at the Quebec Conference when Marshall informed them that he could no longer speak about second-front matters because he had become an interested party. He had been informed that he was to head the operation, leaving his position in Washington.

Shocked by this news, King, Arnold and Leahy each approached the President and pleaded with him to change his mind. Subsequently, when Mr. Roosevelt extended Marshall's term as Chief of Staff, they felt their pleas had prevailed, and that their highly valued associate would continue to function in the critically important area of high policy.

News of the positive decision to send Marshall to London came first to Marquis Childs of the *St. Louis Post-Dispatch* and to me from a high-ranking officer. There was no way such a major high-level story could be kept secret, and when it broke it precipitated a howl of public indignation that came as a terrible shock to the White House, which had anticipated no such reaction.

When the heat was really on, it was obvious that the move would be a major political issue in 1944 if something wasn't done—and done right away. A major difficulty was that the White House had informed Churchill that they would send Marshall to Europe, and backing out of such a commitment would be most embarrassing. And so an off-the-cuff solution was devised, it being to build up the new job so nobody (except maybe a Stalin) could complain.

Kirke Simpson of the Associated Press (close to Roosevelt), who had flown White House trial balloons before, wrote a story that Marshall was to become Global Commander in Chief. There had been no time to check this move out with the British, and Drew Middleton sent a dispatch from London saying the Churchill government had not been consulted and predicted strenuous opposition from the British.

In the meantime, Secretary of the Navy Knox, originally opposed to the transfer, had been persuaded to shift sides, as had Admiral Leahy. But the question of command was left hanging until the conferees met in Teheran. There Joseph Stalin, who had called loudly and often for a second front ever since the Germans marched through Poland into Russia, reached the boiling point as to when the invasion was to begin and who should lead it.

This brought matters to a head. Teheran was closely followed by the Cairo Conference, and there General Marshall informed his colleagues that he could again participate in second-front matters as he had been informed he was to continue on the Joint and Combined Chiefs. The British members, who apparently had not been involved in the conflict, were delighted, for they like and respect Marshall.

The General also informed his colleagues that General Eisenhower was to head the invasion force and that he would go to London at a date of his own choosing in January, presumably after Rome is taken. It seems that Mr. Roosevelt bowed to the wishes of his military and naval leaders, including General Marshall.

This became evident at one of the Cairo sessions at which the British were late in arriving. The President asked Admiral King if he wasn't going to thank him for keeping Marshall on the job. The Admiral stood up, bowed formally, and said "Thank you." So did General Arnold.

Our informant, asked how Marshall felt about it, said he couldn't put himself in the General's place, that Marshall would undoubtedly take the position that he was a good soldier and would do as he was told, knowing the supreme importance—even if not as spectacular as leading the world's greatest amphibious operation—of the work he was doing.

As a sidelight on Marshall, our informant mentioned that the General rarely swore, but that when his name was mentioned as a Presidential candidate, he really showed what he could do when he was aroused.

That's the long and short of that particular conference.

From another source I learn that the Army Transport Service has secured from Moscow permisson to establish a route from Teheran to Moscow for the conveying of lend-lease supplies. This is another sign that the Russians are loosening up more all the time.

Regards

There is a great deal of interesting information in this meeting with Admiral King. By far the most interesting part to me was the Skipper's account of the effort to make General Marshall commander in chief of the Second Front invasion. It was especially interesting because there was a story within the story involving myself and other members of the Arlington County Commandos.

The story began shortly after the Skipper's return from the Quebec Conference when I received a call telling me that Admiral King would appreciate it if I would come over to see him in his office. I went, and heard this story.

Prime Minister Churchill had for some time been trying

to get a change in the American membership on the Combined Chiefs of Staff. Reason? I was told that General Marshall and Admiral King made a stalwart team in opposition to what both men regarded as frivolous and/or eccentric projects put forward by the British members of the Chiefs, notable among them a move through the Balkans to attack the "soft underbelly" of Europe.

The Prime Minister, it was believed by my informant, thought that if he could get one of the pair transferred, a successor would likely be less rock-hard in his resistance to the Churchillian schemes. There was no valid reason for King's transfer. First, he was a naval officer. Second, his beat was largely the Pacific War, and there was no plausible spot to which to recommend his transfer. But General Marshall was something else. He was a military man and Europe would be a land war, making it perfectly logical that America's greatest soldier should lead the greatest amphibious invasion the world had ever seen.

The point was seductively made to the President that hardly anyone had ever heard the name of General Peyton C. March, American Chief of Staff in World War I, while General John J. Pershing, while subordinate to March, was the popular hero because he had led the way to victory in the field.

Naturally Marshall was tempted. However, he was a man of stern principles. He understood very well the difference between a single-front war like that of 1918 and a multifront global war like that in which we were engaged in 1943. He knew very well the importance of strategic planning in such a struggle.

Admiral King told me all this, along with most of what is recounted in the preceding memorandum. Then, getting down to cases, he noted that the target of the persuasion effort was not General Marshall but President Roosevelt, who had obviously been swayed by the British view, swayed enough so that a firm commitment was made.

Could the Arlington County Commandos, Admiral King desired to know, assuming they agreed with his thesis that it would be disastrous for the war effort if the American team on the Combined Chiefs was broken up so that General Marshall could head up one front instead of being part of the team responsible for them all, write stories or columns spelling out the danger? He asked me if I would talk to them and see what could be done, since the

President was always influenced by stories written by cor-respondents he knew and respected. I said I would be glad to, making a mental note tht Admiral King was a quick study in public relations as in everything else to which he turned his hand.

The Commandos needed only the statement of the prob-lem to grasp the situation, and the result was a string of stories strongly making the case for General Marshall's retention on the Joint and Combined Chiefs while General Eisenhower, who had already brilliantly demonstrated his talent for managing a mixed operation, would command the cross-Channel invasion.

I have no way of knowing how much influence our stories had on the final outcome. I do know that, embar-rassing as it must have been to the White House to draw back from its commitment to the British, the ultimate deci-sion was that Marshall stay where he was, to the vast satisfaction of General Arnold and Admiral King.

As is obvious, I did not put this story in my memoran-dum, then or later, and Admiral King never referred to it in any of his conferences with us or with me in private conversation. I am sure he felt, as I did, that there was nothing to be gained by talking about it. To the best of my knowledge, this story has never seen the light of day until now, when I don't see how it could hurt anyone.

HARRY HOPKINS'S VIEW OF THE CAIRO AND TEHERAN CONFERENCES

When I was invited to Wilmington in mid-1944 to have lunch with the members of the Du Pont Company's Ex-ecutive Committee, who thought the job for which I was being considered—Assistant Director of the Public Rela-tions Department—was of sufficient importance that they should look me over before deciding finally, I was not especially nervous, maybe because I loved what I was do-ing at *The Sun*.

The private dining room in the Hotel Du Pont was smallish and comfortable, and I thought things were going well enough when the financial vice president, Angus

Echols, described in a subsequent *Fortune* article as having "the frosty warmth of a mint julep," asked me how Harry Hopkins was regarded in Washington. I didn't have to think about that one.

"He is the most valuable civilian in Washington with the possible exception of the President himself."

My boss to be, Harold Brayman, was obviously stricken with a sudden fear that this answer might prejudice against me a group of very conservative businessmen who abominated the New Deal and those who ran it. So he cut in with an escape hatch.

"Well, now, Glen," he said, "don't you mean to say that he is well regarded by the New Dealers?"

"No, Harold," I replied, "Hopkins is regarded by everyone in Washington who knows what is going on as the most important civilian in town. Partly because he is an extremely competent individual who is completely dedicated to the war effort and can get things done when they have to be, but maybe even more important because he is the only man alive who can keep papers from burning holes through the President's desk and never getting acted upon. He can get action from a man who instinctively puts off making decisions."

As it turned out, that answer clinched the job for me, because this committee consisted of men who didn't let personal political views warp their professional judgments with a preference for straight answers. But I couldn't have made any other answer. I never met Hopkins personally, and heard him speak only on this occasion at the National Press Club, but I heard plenty about him from people whose opinions I respected, and all of it was good.

His "tax and tax, spend and spend, elect and elect" didn't help him any with the conservatives, myself among them, and I'm very sure his social and economic views would never have squared with mine. But we were in a war, and there would be no second prize. There was no time for politics, and Hopkins was too good a man not to be kept on. The memo that follows gives an insight into why this was the case.

Hopkins was in miserable health through most of World War II. He had such a highly selective digestive system that he very nearly starved to death before doctors and dieticians could devise a diet he could use. The experts who solved that riddle deserved well of their country.

CONFIDENTIAL

Thursday
30 December 1943

Dear Bart,

Harry Hopkins spoke off the record at the Overseas Writers, Phelps and I both heard him, and both of us found what he said extremely interesting and informative. It will perhaps surprise you to know that our top military people rate Hopkins as one of the most useful people around in the prosecution of the war. It is a fact that when the palace guard of far-out New Dealers come around trying to put over some of their more controversial reform measures, Hopkins boots their tails out of there with the stark admonition that we've got the war to win, and all else is subsidiary.

As to the wealth of information at his disposal, there can of course be no question. No one outside of Roosevelt knows more about what is going on. However, Hopkins was discreet in what he said. He said nothing to which anyone could take exception. On the other hand, when you are listening to Hopkins you have to listen to intonations and inflections. You have to fit what he says against the background of how he says it, of your own knowledge, against the logical pattern of the situation as you know it, and it becomes most revealing. Phelps and I came away feeling that our knowledge of the world situation had been increased by what he said.

It is implicit in the above that interpretation plays a considerable part in evaluating his remarks. I am going to do some speculating, therefore, but will note the occasions when it is done.

First, Hopkins devoted himself to the Cairo Conference with Generalissimo Chiang Kai-shek. There was a very thorough review of the war in the Pacific, both as to what has been done and to what is going to be done. It was observable that Chiang was inclined to view action in the Solomons and the Gilberts as pretty remote from China. Intellectually he could see the reasons behind it, but emotionally he was interested in matters nearer home.

Hopkins discussed the hardship brought to China by the cutting of the Burma Road. It didn't carry much, but what it did carry was vitally necessary. The air route from Assam to Kunming is very hazardous. We are paying heavy penalties for keeping it open, and the time is coming when we are going to have to have pretty considerable fighter protection for the route, which in itself presents difficulties and puts a new drain on the gasoline supplies.

The logistical situation in India is none too good, with few roads and railroads. However, we are stepping up the amount of supplies carried. At the present time the division between the Chinese land forces and their and our air forces as to allocation of supplies is about 60-40.

He discussed the fighting in China, and what could be done there. At the conclusion of this discussion, Hopkins said that the Generalissimo was "reasonably satisfied" with our plans. Nothing could fully satisfy him except a plan that would kick the Japs out of China in the next six months, Hopkins added. Such a plan does not and cannot exist, of course. Hopkins said he didn't blame Chiang for his feeling, for China has been in this war for a long time.

Hopkins also referred to the enormous problems involved in switching the forces being used against Germany into the war against Japan once the Nazis are beaten. He mentioned particularly the great air forces in the Mediterranean area. We deduced from what he said that a good deal of study has already been given to this problem, and Admiral King ratified this belief at his press conference today.

Chiang, Hopkins said, is badly worried about China's internal condition. It is very serious, although not critical at this time. Inflation is very bad, and getting worse. Nothing can alleviate this except making goods available to sop up the inflationary money, and we can't get anything to China now, or in the immediate future. Any available space is needed for military supplies.

We gathered from the way Hopkins spoke that Chiang's position is by no means secure. He once said, "If Chiang controls China. . . ." The exact context is less important than that he felt impelled to make the point at all. In this connection, Hopkins expressed the firm conviction that while Madame Chiang is influential, the Generalissimo is the real boss. However, one must again bear in mind Hopkins' reservation, which I take it indicates that if China's situation is not improved within a reasonably short time Chiang may be in for serious domestic trouble.

There was thorough discussion with Chiang as to the policy to be followed once Japan is beaten. They talked about who would occupy Japan, and how it should be done. They discussed the kind of government to be given Japan. They discussed the island and mainland bases that would be used to keep guard on Japan. What the decisions were, we were not told, but it is evident that conclusions were reached, and that they were satisfactory to all hands. General conclusions, that is. Some matters, such as sovereignty of land on which bases are to be located, must wait. Hopkins gave the impression that this will be a matter for the American people to decide later.

As to who shall occupy what bases, Hopkins said that if they could, the Chinese would unquestionably prefer to deal exclusively with the United States. Evidently this will not be possible, as Britain and the Soviet Union, both intensely interested in Pacific affairs, will have to be consulted.

They discussed Chinese feelings toward the USSR and Britain. They learned what Chiang felt China should get out of this war, and the Declaration of Cairo, including Formosa and Manchuria, grew out of this. It discussed China's commercial needs in the post-war period, including what industries now located in Germany might be moved to China. Again we were told nothing as to conclusions. They discussed free ports in China.

All in all, the Cairo sessions were regarded as very productive, and at the same time as disquieting. Disquieting because of the hints of China's extremely difficult position, and the possibility of the overthrow or collapse of Chiang's government.

Then Hopkins turned to the Teheran Conference with Stalin. First he dealt with the social side. He described the custom of drinking toasts at dinners, and said that the President was very glad to have him along, as some of our boys couldn't stay the course of a Russian dinner after one o'clock in the morning, whereas Harry could. There is a technique to it, he said. You don't have to empty your glass on every toast, which is just as well, since Molotov would give some twelve or fourteen toasts, and Stalin from nine to twelve at each dinner.

It is all very jolly, even though sometimes in their toasts the Russians will stick a verbal knife into you and turn it around. When Stalin decided to give a toast, he would walk slowly from his place to the man he was about to toast, and they would click glasses. If it was serious, he seldom spoke long. If he was ribbing somebody, he might speak at some length. Then he would click glasses with whoever was handy and drink the toast.

Roosevelt moved to the Russian Embassy, of course, after the discovery of the threat to assassinate one of the Big Three while traveling in the city. FDR had a guard of American soldiers, of whom there were some 5,000 in and around Teheran, but this wasn't significant to the Russians. They had their own guards, both military and OGPU. There was even a guard at the bathroom used by all the Americans except Roosevelt, who had one of his own. The Russians were taking no chances.

The first dinner was given by Roosevelt, he having asked Stalin if he might. Army food supplies were used—except, I gather, as to liquid refreshment. The next dinner was given by Stalin, in the same room. Stalin insisted on the same seating arrangements with Roosevelt in the center seat of honor, Stalin at his right, and Churchill at his left. Stalin got the right hand seat because it was decided that Churchill had become Prime Minister after Stalin had become something or other—Hopkins' exact words, by the way. Roosevelt felt that Stalin should sit in the middle at the Russian dinner, but Stalin refused. Roosevelt said, "But this is *your* party." Stalin answered merely, "And this is *my* house," and carried the day.

Hopkins said that sometimes serious matters were discussed at these banquets. But he discovered that nothing said at the parties, however serious, was binding the next day. However, it should not be thought that they were purely frivolous occasions. The Russians like lots of "dog"—paradoxically, they go in for it more than do the capitalistic states. Their parties are valuable for breaking down reserves and for measuring people.

The business sessions were entirely serious, and nobody was, kidding in them. The discussion fell into two divisions, military and post-war. As to the first, there was complete exchange of information, and decisions governing the entire future course of the war were reached. As to the second, there was complete exchange of information, and no decisions of any sort were reached.

On the military side, the first business was to fill Stalin in on the Japanese phases of the war. He was both very interested and very well informed. This was in contrast to the first time Hopkins saw Stalin, in 1941, when he wasn't much interested in the Pacific, being preoccupied with the war against Germany.

They discussed the Mediterranean Theatre, and again Stalin was very much interested, but not very well informed. However, he began asking questions about it that speedily elicited the full information available, and showed that Stalin has an extremely competent military mind and background.

Stalin appreciated the value of the Mediterranean Theatre, but it was apparent that he wanted attacks from other directions too and chiefly. Hopkins never specified second front. He didn't need to. Stalin was continualy asking about landing barges. Three or four times Hopkins referred to questions by Stalin on this subject. When an operation was mentioned, Stalin wanted to know how many landing barges and other supplies would be needed, how long it would delay certain other moves, and matters of that sort.

Now, as a pure shot in the dark, I suggest that we are planning further action in the Mediterranean, probably directed against the Balkans, and that Stalin was interested in knowing whether such moves would delay the second front.

As to Russia, Stalin, flanked by Molotov and Voroshilov, gave a very complete picture of what the Soviet military position is. He told what divisions he has, what divisions the Germans have against them, and the quality of enemy divisions. He told what he expected to accomplish in the war against Germany, and convinced our people that he can make good.

The result of all this was the most thorough integration of Allied war plans, and the exchange of information will be continued and kept up to date by Red military delegations in London, Washington and the Mediterranean, and by British and American delegations in the same places.

Hopkins said that the Red Army insisted that Stalin assume the title of Marshal. Stalin, he said, is the absolute and complete boss of the Red Army. It does not advance or retreat without his approval. All along the lengthy front he is responsible for all the strategy and most of the tactics.

It was apparent, Hopkins added, that Stalin not only intends to win the war against Germany in 1944. He must win it. Our deduction is that Russia has taken such a frightful beating and is strained to such a pitch that she simply couldn't carry on the war in an effective way beyond next year. Going a step further, it is not inconceivable that there might be revolution in Russia if the war were prolonged unduly, or in any event a general collapse that would have the same effect.

As a final sidelight on the military phase, Hopkins said he himself had asked Stalin the significance of the Free Germany Committee of German officers that has aroused some concern here. Stalin, he said, shrugged it off as mere propaganda.

Now, as to the non-military and post-war aspects of the conference: here we got little of a tangible nature from Hopkins. Yet it was possible to fill in the gaps in a very interesting way. First, Stalin made it very plain that he intends to raise drastically the Russian standard of living after this war. Through its whole course, the army has got everything and the civilians nothing. Once the war is over, the people have got to get a break, and a darned good one. Here again is the implication of trouble in Russia if this isn't done. This is an inference, but, I think, justified.

As to the German part in the post-war world, there was a thorough discussion of what kind of government the Germans shall have, including whether they shall have any, or whether there shall be a straight-out military occupation. There was talk as to who should occupy what in Germany, whether a joint force should occupy it all, or whether Britain would police one part, we another, and Russia a third.

Here I should say that Hopkins said there was no suggestion from anyone at this conference that the Allies should disarm. On the contrary, the decision was that Japan and Germany were potential world enemies, and that it should be made physically impossible for either of these to wage war again. But the Big Four will maintain their military power, and Hopkins believes that as long as they stand together there will be no war. Obviously this is true. The question is how long they can stand together. I'm not suggesting anything one way or another, but that is the $64 question.

Now, we asked for and got the most explicit answers from Stalin as to what he wants in the future in regard to Poland, and Baltic States, Finland, China, free ports, access to the open sea, air and naval bases. He stated his position fully and concisely.

Also, we learned more from Britain in this conference as to what she expects in the post-war world—deduction: that Britain in the past has been holding back on this subject.

It was clear from what Hopkins said that we did not get beyond the statement of war aims and objectives. There was evidently no attempt to reconcile the various views. However, Hopkins expressed the opinion that the conference had been very much worthwhile if only for the fact that we now have from their own lips the desires of Stalin and Churchill for the post-war world.

I believe Hopkins made the statement that in his opinion there were no irreconcilable differences among the Big Three. Phelps does not recall it being said specifically, but in any event there was the atmosphere of such opinion in the way Hopkins spoke. Without going deeply into the question of whether he actually said it or not, it seemed that he felt that way about it.

Hopkins—this was interesting—remarked that he came home from the conference feeling that we were much better off because it was held. The way he said it indicated to Phelps and me that there were those who did not feel that way about it. But Hopkins didn't say so, and it is purely inferential on our part. I haven't any idea who would feel that way. Possibly the British. I don't know.

Analyzing what Hopkins had to say, and putting it together with our own background, and also the pattern of events, Phelps and I feel that Stalin is steadily veering to the right. His preoccupation with raising the standard of living in the USSR suggests it. So does the abandonment of the Comintern and the Internationale. So does the whole Russian picture as it shapes up.

This is a two-way proposition. It indicates that in Stalin the allies will be dealing with the right-wing leader in Russia, and that the advantages of dealing with such a man can be counted upon by Stalin to call forth our strong support. It also suggests that Stalin realizes that only by continuing this trend to the right can he satisfy his people and maintain his position. It is an interesting development—and of course Sokolsky has pointed out that the USSR is today the only truly capitalistic country in the world.

I have some material from other sources about the Japanese situation, but this has already run overlong, and I'll save it for another day. (Imagine me feeling that way about a memorandum that ends on page 10! I can only think the tight papers we have these days is weighing on my subconscious . . . and, to beat you to the punch, on my conscious, too.)

I'm planning to come up to report in mid-January, as you suggested. And a Happy New Year to all the *Sun* gang in New York, and especially to you and KS.

Regards

1944

GENERAL MARSHALL AND THE LABOR STRIKES

As time went on, it became increasingly important not to bandy names about in our communiqués to *The Sun*. The secret conference discussed was given on New Year's Eve by General George Marshall—the character variously referred to as "our host," "our man," "our informant," and "The Presence"—one of the most quietly impressive men on the volatile Washington scene.

CONFIDENTIAL

Saturday
1 January 1944

Dear Bart,

The secret conference at the Pentagon Building about which I wired you yesterday was notable chiefly for the astonishing charge against Labor about which you have already read in today's papers. The stories, however, do not—and indeed could not—give a true picture of the dramatic earnestness of the speaker. I doubt that I can either. You have to know and see the man to get the full effect.

Twenty-eight of us were present, not counting the half dozen of our host's own aides and advisers. It was a slightly larger gathering than that which attended the previous secret conference in the same office immediately following the conference at Quebec. It was also a thoroughly representative group covering all the press associations, the leading metropolitan papers, and at least two of the radio chains. We were all checked into his office with great care and formality, and there we had to wait about five minutes before he himself arrived with a simple and sincere apology for his tardiness, explaining that it was the first time during the day that he had had a chance to go to the bathroom.

Every time I see this man I am more deeply impressed by him. There is no man in Washington in either party or in any office whom I respect more highly, and I believe that feeling is shared generally by those in the capital who know him. Despite his high rank there is nothing of the swashbuckler about him. He *never* makes a show of authority. He doesn't throw his weight about. He is as unassuming in manner as the simplest private in the ranks. Both in speech and manner he is a gentle person, kindly, sympathetic and thoroughly reasonable. He smiles readily and frequently. He has a delightful sense of humor and a great facility of speech that enables him to talk rapidly and interestingly, using the exact words that he wants without ever stopping to grope for one. He speaks with utter frankness and has an obvious contempt for diplomatic doubletalk. He says exactly what he means in simple, direct phrases that cannot possibly be misunderstood or misinterpreted; and what he doesn't say in this direct way, he doesn't say at all. There is no use trying to read between the lines—there's nothing there but space.

His outstanding characteristic probably is his avoidance of profanity or vulgarity in his speech. Few among his most intimate friends have ever heard him swear. The only previous occasion on which he has been known to cuss, so far as I am aware, was when one of his colleagues was twitting him about some newspaper stories advocating his candidacy for the Presidency on the Democratic ticket. In that instance he went about it efficiently and effectively, turning the air a deep indigo for some distance beyond him.

That is why his remarks of yesterday were so impressive and so dramatic. From his lips they fell with shocking force upon our ears. For sheer emotional effect about ten minutes of that conference outdistanced anything I have ever heard or experienced in my fifteen years in Washington.

He talked for an hour or so about the progress of the war in every theatre of the world, prefacing his remarks with an apology for calling us out on New Year's Eve, when we doubtless had had many other things we wanted to do. He had hoped, he said, to schedule the conference for next week. He didn't say why he had had to change that plan. He simply made it clear that he regarded his talk with us as a matter of greater urgency.

Then, after rambling in a leisurely fashion, as I have said, he came to what he called the principal topic he had wished to discuss with us: the railroad strike threat.

"I cannot tell you," he began, "how I felt when the Army was ordered to take over the railroads."

"That—and the steel strike—was the God damnedest crime ever perpetrated in America—a crime that will cost us hundreds of thousands of casualties and billions of dollars."

He spoke in measured, even tones, devoid of any note of hysteria or fanaticism. Just flat, unhurried words and phrases that fell in a steady stream upon a deathly silent room.

"I want the American people to know that. If I could, I would tell them that myself, and let them throw me out—but I can't. I can't explain the meaning of it to them without revealing our plans. I can't talk about it anywhere except to you in this room. Not while there is any hope.

"People think that because there was no railroad strike, and because there was no interruption in war production, no damage was done. In God's name don't let them think that—don't write your stories that way. You don't know what it has done to us—what it's going to cost us.

"For months we have been hoping for, and working for, an explosion in the Balkans—in Turkey and all through that part of the world. The effect of that explosion would profoundly influence the course of the war in the Pacific. What its effect upon Europe would be is incalculable. The people in these countries are ready to revolt. They would quit Germany in an instant if they could bring themselves to defy the Gestapo, to revolt against the Gestapo and risk the consequences. They were beginning to understand that that course of action was less dangerous than going the rest of the way on the Axis side.

"We have been planning heavily on that explosion, and doing everything we can to touch it off. You have noticed that planes, badly needed in the Italian campaign, have been used instead to make long flights into the Balkans to accomplish this purpose—like the recent bombing of Sofia. We have spread pamphlets and propaganda throughout this area and we had been hoping that the explosion would come in late February. That is what we were aiming for.

"I think we had a fair chance of getting it by the end of February." (Here for the first time he paused, weighing the situation a few moments.) "Yes, a fair chance—perhaps an even chance. Then came the news that the Army had taken over the American railroads—that the steelworkers had walked out on strike. The German propaganda agencies poured this news into the Balkans through every possible channel. They said America was in a chaotic condition—it was falling apart. All Germany and her satellites had to do was hold on a little longer and America would be ready to negotiate for peace. Hold on! Hold on!

"And there went our hopes. At the critical moment we had given the Germans the only weapon they could have used effectively against us. Analyze the situation for yourselves. See what it means:

"Cities all over Germany are destroyed. Berlin is more than half destroyed and the rest of it is badly pockmarked. In a short time our American daylight raids will be going out over Germany in 1,000 plane missions. Germany's cities will be wiped out at the rate of about one every ten days. The smaller cities won't stand up that long. I do not see how the High Command of the German Army can stand by and see their cities wiped out in that way.

"The only hope that the German government has had of preventing collapse has been to keep the hope of victory alive in the German people and the people of the satellite countries. To do this they first said that the United States and Britain would split. That hope has forever gone. Then they held out the hope of a split between Britain and the United States on one side, and Russia on the other. That hope too has been completely wiped out now. The only thing they had left was their secret weapon—their rocket gun—and that is wholly a vengeful thing that may cause us suffering and damage but cannot, so far as we can see, influence seriously the course of the war.

"Now we have given them new hope—the hope of complete chaos in

America, and ample evidence to support the propaganda that such chaos does exist here. By that act we have prolonged the war for six months, for if Germany lives through this winter, it will not fold up until the coming of the next winter. We must undertake our invasion, and that will cost us hundreds of thousands of lives.

"Yes, the railroads are running, and war production is going ahead undiminished, but that is of small importance. The damage has been done. That is why I say that this is the damnedest—the God damnedest crime—ever perpetrated in America. I want the wives and mothers of America to know that, and understand it. It is too late to do anything about it now, but I want them to rise up and see that it can never happen again."

(You will understand that anyone who ever tried to pull a pencil out of his pocket or take a note at one of these conferences would be instantly expelled, never to return, so the above quotes are wholly from memory and are not intended to be exact beyond their general content.)

He was asked if the Railway Labor leaders were ever told of the situation. Was it ever put up to them this way? He said he did not think so, that our Administration officials did not seem to understand the true importance and significance of the thing. He said he had talked to [Director of War Mobilization] Byrnes about it on the telephone that very morning, and that the military aspects of the situation had never even occurred to Byrnes. When he fully understood them, he was furious about it, however. Our informant himself, of course, was not in the country at the time the negotiations were undertaken.

To me it seemed that his attack was directed fully as much at the Administration as at the labor unions themselves—and intentionally so. His principal complaint appeared to be not so much against the threat of a railroad strike as against the seizure of the roads and turning of them over to the Army to run. I think that those who view this merely as an attack upon labor are completely overlooking the real target at which this man was striking: the New Deal Administration.

I myself reached some very firm conclusions, which may be entirely wrong—but I don't think so:

I believe that our military High Command is firmly convinced that our chances for victory are being seriously jeopardized by the quick nostrums of "Dr. Win-the-War" on the home front. I believe they have determined to try to correct the home front situation, though this forces them into conflict with the most powerful dictator the country has ever known. I believe this program has been definitely planned and deliberately launched with the full consent and approval of Secretary of War Stimson. My beliefs are based on the following highly circumstantial events:

1) Just before we were ushered into The Presence, and we were leaving the Public Relations office in which we had foregathered, Secretary Stimson himself walked in and wished us a Happy New Year. Then, smiling, he said

he thought we were going to hear something *very* interesting at our conference. Whereupon he left. It was apparent that he knew exactly what was going to be said. It was apparent that he approved of it heartily.

2) Next was the apology of our host for the suddenness with which the conference had been called, and the implied plea of urgency.

3) Then came the unprecedented circumstance that we were not only permitted to write the story, but were implored to do so, and were told in the most helpful possible way how we might give the story full coverage without transgressing the necessity for military secrecy.

4) Then, too, there was the character of the group itself—clearly designed to cover the newspaper and radio field like a tent.

4-a) He made it clear he *still* might go on the radio to arouse American wives and mothers.

5) I am impressed, too, by the fact that our informant during the past few weeks has talked with virtually every commanding officer in every theatre of the war—not only in the Army high command but in the Navy as well. To do this, he came back from the Cairo and Teheran conferences by way of a 35,000 mile tour through the Pacific. It is possibly significant that he did this without the knowledge and consent of the President. He told us yesterday that if the President had known about it, he would not have let him go.

I would not stress this point because of other things said at the conference which I shall not take time to discuss, but I suggest that our man had excellent opportunity to discuss the home front situation and its effect upon morale both of our forces and the enemy's with every high officer in both branches of the service, and may well have done so.

6) Finally, there was the incident of the suppressed press release upon which he dwelt at surprising length before reaching the main feature of his discourse. Here it is in a sketchy way:

Congress, in discussing the "draft fathers" legislation, has shown considerable concern about the high percentage of rejections among inductees on medical grounds and about the number of medical discharges that have been handed out in recent months.

Always responsive to Congressional sentiment, our host immediately ordered a full investigation to be made on a nationwide scale by some of the best medical men in the Army. When the results of the investigation had been reported to him, he put them into memorandum form and sent them to General Surles with the suggestion that they be put out in the form of a press release. The General turned thumbs down, so it was never put out, and never will be. But our informant, in General Surles' presence, read it to us in full yesterday.

It seems that 40 percent of the men called up for induction are rejected on medical grounds, and some 200,000 have received medical discharges from the Army in the last six months or so. So far as purely physical ailments go, steps have been taken, he said, to substantially reduce the number of rejections and discharges. But from 25 to 35 percent of all these cases are in the realm of neuropsychiatry, where there are no means of measuring exactly the seriousness or falsity of the disorders complained of.

Men who are unable, unwilling or slow to adjust themselves to army life consciously or unconsciously develop symptoms of illness and report for sick call. They go to the hospital where they have their meals brought to them, receive all kinds of special care and attention, are entertained by the "Gray Ladies" and also have the advantage of discovering other effective symptoms in their conversations with fellow patients.

None is ever convicted of malingering because no doctor can ever take his oath on an opinion that the patient is *not* suffering the pain of which he complains. So these men are not only of no use to the Army, they take up precious room in the hospitals and the time and attention of the overworked and all too meager staff of doctors. The line officers are only too happy to get rid of them. So is the hospital. So they receive medical discharges, bonuses and disability pensions for the rest of their lives. About four cases out of five are sheer fakes, the report indicated. This makes it doubly tough and unfair for the one-fifth whose difficulty is genuine.

Up to this point I thought he was leading up to a defense of General Patton, but instead he came abruptly to the conclusion that the fault lay generally with the system of education and the environment in which the youth of this country have grown up during the past twenty years. While Axis nations have been training their youth to endure all kinds of hardship, he said, we in this country have taught our youth to believe it is their *right* to live in luxury, and to be supported and pampered by their government, if necessary.

This direct slap at the New Deal and the National Youth Administration surprised me, but proved, of course, only to be a mild forerunner to the main attack that followed.

So there it is. As I say, I could be wrong.

———————

Now for the rest of the conference—rather sketchily:

Pacific. Here we have evidently made real progress. Each new advance gives us great new air bases and naval bases from which we are bombing Java and the Dutch East Indies, destroying oil refineries and other installations of the Japanese. These are the longest bombing flights being undertaken in any part of the world.

He spoke of our feat in establishing an air base behind the Japanese lines in the Lae campaign of which Perry has already written in detail in his story in the paper; but he pointed out that the crowning achievement was the serving of ice cream for dinner to the men on the very first day that the air base was set up.

Our principal problem here is in rolling up the installations behind us as we go. We are virtually through with Australia now. Our ships—even our biggest transports—can go directly to Lae and other bases in New Guinea, saving precious miles and ships and saving all the work of trans-shipment in Australia. Guadalcanal is a summer resort now, and we are trying to take our men and supplies out of it as quickly as possible.

Our greatest achievement probably is the conquest of malaria. We have got it licked. At the latest word, only 8 percent of our troops now develop the disease, and in some places it runs as low as two percent.

We are trying to arrange for rotation of men so that they can get back home once in a while as new men go out. Where men are actually fighting this is not so important, but where the fighting is over, morale suffers badly. That is why it is so important to roll up our rear rapidly as the advance goes on, and to get these men back into action or give them a furlough home. Not many of them will ever get the furlough because every ship used for this purpose must be taken out of the supply line at a time when we can't spare any ships. Still, about one percent a month may be accommodated under plans being worked on.

MacArthur and our man had a thorough discussion and found themselves in complete agreement. MacArthur is fully satisfied with the equipment and supplies he is getting, and understands why no more are now available. He resents bitterly, so he says, his injection into the Presidential campaign and burns up every time a new news dispatch reaches him about it. He is not coming back to America in the near future, so far as is known.

Clearly our host was well satisfied with everything in relation to the attack on Japan, which has now been fully planned and integrated in every detail. He was likewise impressed with what he saw in Hawaii, which is our central distribution and training point for troops in the Pacific Theatres. Here there is a complete school for the training of men in jungle warfare. The men can be put through it at the rate of 5,000 a week, and "when they come out, they've been somewhere." A general watching one man wriggle his way through a jungle patch noted that he avoided a clear space and went through some dense growth instead. He asked the soldier why. The boy replied, "I wasn't taking any chances. These sons of bitches are tricky and you never know what they're going to do to you next." The general was much amused.

Invasion. Our informant is deeply worried about this—particularly about what is being published about it. He registered no complaints against the press, but is disturbed by the fact that we have fully advertised our exact intentions to the enemy. The only element of surprise that we have left is the matter of timing. He would like to prevent the wholesale publication of news about that, frankly admitting that he did not know just how to do it, and asking us, if we had any suggestions to offer on the subject, to send him a brief memorandum. He himself, for the first time, uttered no word about the wheres and whens of our future actions in any theatre.

I noted with interest that he has two great plats [a plan of a piece of land with actual or proposed features] in his office with topographical maps. The one at the wall to his left is of the Pacific. Last time I was there the one at the right was of Sicily and the southern half of the Italian boot. Today the one at his right is of the east coast of England, and the full length of the English Channel from Holland on down through France. Every hill, stream, road and railroad is shown.

General Patton. He explained why the General Patton incident was veiled in secrecy: the time of its occurrence coincided almost exactly with the invasion of Italy proper. In Italy we were faced with a serious problem and ran a long chance. We needed air fields. We needed them badly and quickly. We didn't have enough transport to take the necessary men and equipment for construction purposes and at the same time take any substantial military force across. There were only six divisions of Germans opposing us in this area, we knew; and we had only a thin skirmish line of our own thrown across Italy against them.

Our purpose was to prevent other divisions being sent down by the Germans to wipe us out. The Germans we knew were worried about the whereabouts of Patton and the Seventh Army. Any news as to where Patton was was therefore of the utmost importance and significance to the Germans. Actually we sent him ultimately to Corsica—apparently with great secrecy—thus confirming the fears of the Germans that we were going to strike at Northern Italy with an amphibious operation, probably in the neighborhood of Genoa, and cut off the entire German force to the south. The Germans were therefore required to maintain strong forces in Northern Italy, thus giving us the chance to build up our own forces in the south, laboriously and with painful slowness.

The correspondents fully understood this, and our host of yesterday expressed his gratitude for their cooperation.

Conferences. He had little or nothing to say about the conferences at Teheran and Cairo. Asked if our invasion plans were fully integrated with the Russian attack, he said he had gone to Teheran prepared to tell Stalin exactly what we wanted, but before he had a chance to do so Stalin told *him* exactly what he intended to do, and that Stalin was going to do considerably more than we had expected of him.

He characterized Stalin as "quite a fella" and told of an incident at a dinner at which one of our people was paying high tribute to the bravery and courage of the Russian soldier. Stalin interrupted to say that it wasn't bravery so much as fear of being cowards. The ambition of the Russian soldier was not so much to be at the top of the pile of heroes as it was not to be caught at the bottom. [Later on, Admiral King told us this same story and, I must say, got a lot more flavor out of it than the General did. Ernie quoted Stalin verbatim.]

Apparently our man had quite a little fight with Joe when Joe tried to tell him how to run an amphibious attack. Our man responded that when it came to running a war on land he would be glad to take lessons from Joe, but when it came to a landing operation he thought the shoe was probably on the other foot. Joe insisted that his men had crossed lots of rivers—very wide rivers—and were tops in amphibious warfare. Our man replied:

"There's a big difference, no matter how wide your rivers are. If you try to cross a river and fail, you have suffered a reverse. If you try an amphibious operation and fail, you have suffered a disaster."

He said he never convinced Stalin, but that they had agreed in good spirit to disagree.

He added that he spent two days in a cold sweat before we undertook a landing operation. Nobody, he said, could fully comprehend the awfulness of the consequences that could occur should one of these go wrong. He was thinking about a big one, of course. About *THE* big one, I imagine.

Under the heading of the Pacific, I meant to tell you that the most numerous and most serious casualties he saw in our hospitals out there were burns—indescribably hideous, he said—and caused not by swimming in burning oil or by airplane crashes, but by lighting fires with gasoline in sand. The same was true in Libya, he said.

He undoubtedly said a lot more, but this has got to be mailed sometime, and I've got to eat dinner, so to hell with it.

Regards

CHIANG, THE CHINESE COMMUNISTS, AND CHINESE WAR PRODUCTION

CONFIDENTIAL

Tuesday
25 January 1944

Dear Bart,

Ten or so of us had lunch today with Donald Nelson [head of the War Production Board], who as you know recently returned from his second mission to China. Let me stress that everything he said was off the record, and that his account of the falling out between Chiang and Stilwell was in the strictest confidence. I think all of us were amazed at the utter frankness with which Nelson answered some of the highly delicate questions we put to him.

He and Pat Hurley went out to China together and were there during November and December. Together these two are completely responsible for the remarkable improvement which has occurred in our relationship with Chiang, and in the capacity of China to defend itself against further Japanese incursions. For this he gives Hurley the lion's share of the credit. He thinks Pat is a helluva fellow, with tremendous diplomatic capacities and a fine sense of humor. Hurley's job was to deal with the military aspects of our problems with China, Nelson's with the economic side. They worked as a team.

They went to the Burma-India theatre, where they combed Joe Stilwell's problems over with him (of which much, much more anon) and then humped over to China.

On the way they drafted a three-point program which they believed Chiang should agree to before they even discussed anything else:

1) The Chinese Army should be placed under the command of "Vinegar Joe" in its entirety, so that Stilwell, reporting to Chiang, would be in approximately the same capacity as General Marshall is in relation to Roosevelt.

2) Chiang should make his peace with the Chinese communists and bring them fully into the war effort, arming them without reserve and using them to the fullest possible advantage.

3) Chiang should settle his differences with Russia, obliterate the difficulties of which the Russians had complained, and establish himself on a basis of full friendship, cooperation and confidence with Russia.

Chiang agreed unhesitatingly to point number one. His attitude was: "I don't like Stilwell. He and I don't get along. But if you say he should command the Chinese Armies, he shall. If that's what you want done, I'll do it."

On point two Chiang declined to agree fully. He sincerely hates the communists, but nevertheless expressed a complete willingness to reach an agreement with them. He would see what he could do about it, anyway. On point three he agreed fully and readily, interposing no objections or reservations. Chiang, in short, was damned tractable any way you figure it. Hurley and Nelson were well pleased.

Hurley then turned to one of the most delicate problems of all: the little matter of getting 25,000 more trained Chinese troops to join the fighting down in Burma where the Chinese forces were pressing down from the north to join Stilwell's troops coming up from below.

Chiang moaned. He pointed out that in the campaign thus far, Stilwell had lost 65,000 of the 75,000 trained and armed troops Chiang had provided for him. (Stilwell admits to 56,000 lost.) The Generalissimo complained that he could not sustain such losses. The force which had been lost, he said, constituted the major part of his well trained and fully equipped forces.

But when he got all through groaning about it, he agreed fully. Stilwell should have his 25,000 men, he said, although he could scrape together no more than 17,000 rifles. The troops would be sent down by air, under American command.

And this was the situation when the blow-off came. Chiang had agreed to absolutely everything that Hurley had asked for, except for the further negotiations to take place on recognition of the communists. And with the military aspects of the problem thus disposed of, he received Nelson the following day to go over the economic picture.

While he was talking with Nelson, a message was brought to him. He read it, apologized and excused himself, explaining that Stilwell had arrived and wanted to talk to him immediately, and that he would be glad to resume his conference with Nelson as soon as he had complied with the General's request. Nelson was quite satisfied and went out of the room to find Hurley in a great dither.

Now right here let me do a movie flashback to give you Nelson's reappraisal of Vinegar Joe, Chiang and their relationship with each other, as he had given it to us during the desultory table conversation between courses at the luncheon.

The two men, he said, simply hated each other thoroughly. Stilwell never referred to Chiang except as "that old son of a bitch," and he used the term quite as freely in Chinese company as he did in private councils with his fellows. Likewise Stilwell and Chennault hated each others' guts. Chennault, of course, was the darling of all China and was widely regarded by the Chinese as their savior. To his air force they attributed the fact that China had not yet been conquered by the Japs.

Nelson made it plain that he liked Stilwell very much, that he was a fine general, that his campaign in Burma was a masterpiece of military strategy, that the Chinese troops he had trained adored him, and that he, in turn, regarded them as the finest troops he had ever commanded, fully on a par with his own American forces.

Hurley, Nelson reported, had been a little worried by his assignment to China, feeling that Stilwell might resent his messing into the delicate situation with Chiang, and in a conference with General Marshall Pat asked what Stilwell's reactions would be. Marshall grinned and assured Pat that Vinegar Joe would have no objections whatever. He had already heard from Stilwell on this subject, and that Stilwell said he was fully aware of the fact that it took oil as well as vinegar to make a salad dressing.

Nelson added that Stilwell's entire military organization in the Burma theatre had been magnificently perfected, but that the same was unfortunately not true in China. Stilwell had done nothing to strengthen the Chinese forces there. Except for the two hours he spent with Chiang while Nelson and Hurley waited outside in anguish, he had not been in China in eight months. And that was the way the score stood when Nelson found Hurley tearing his hair and biting his nails.

Hurley explained that Stilwell had gone in to show Chiang a telegram he had just received from President Roosevelt. (Nelson insists that from the language of the message he is convinced that Roosevelt never saw it, and that it was sent by the War Department at Stilwell's request.) The telegram bluntly ordered Chiang to accept Stilwell as full commander of the Chinese troops, and to give him 25,000 men for the Burma fighting. In other words, the telegram sought to force Chiang, under threat, to do exactly what he had just promised Hurley he would do—a promise that he had made quite willingly in a spirit of cooperation and understanding.

Pat pleaded with Stilwell not to show the message to Chiang. He explained that the Generalissimo had already agreed to everything the telegram "ordered" him to do. He pointed out that it would be an unforgivable insult and would jeopardize the whole relationship between Chiang and the United States, and might greatly facilitate the Japanese conquest of China. He poured it on, to no avail, Stilwell saying: "I'm going to show that old son of a bitch he can't push me around." And he did.

When the conference between Stilwell and Chiang was over, the Generalissimo did not send for Nelson as he had promised. Instead he sent word that he did not care to continue the conversation. He had invited Hurley and Nelson to dinner that night. He canceled the invitation. Chiang was through—all through, and he made no bones about it.

Nelson was scheduled to leave Chiang's cottage the next morning and go back to town. Before he went, however, he insisted upon seeing the Generalissimo. He says he never saw a madder man in his life; but for all his anger, Chiang was the courteous Chinese throughout. He apologized for his anger, and for his failure to fulfill the dinner engagement of the evening before. He was sorry, he said, that he had lost his temper. Then, by way of extenuation, he added: "I don't mind being treated as a slave by the military, but I refuse to be treated like a crook."

Nelson saw that Stilwell would have to go. Hurley hoped things could be patched up, and worked on it for three weeks before giving up. Then Stilwell went, and normal diplomatic relations with Chiang were resumed. Hurley, with Chiang's blessing, went up to see the communists and to find out upon what terms they could be brought together with Chiang. He found them quite willing to make a deal. Their demands, he felt, were reasonable if not modest. He worked out an agreement with them under which they would give their full cooperation to the Government if Chiang in return would give them one place in his cabinet, one place on his military council, and one place on some other body the exact name and purpose of which I do not recall.

Chiang promptly agreed to these terms, but warned Hurley that he was very much afraid that the communists would boost the ante the minute they found he had acceded to their demands. Hurley promptly dissipated his fears: "Oh no," he said confidently, "They won't do anything like that to me." Chiang smiled.

No sooner had Chiang's concurrence been communicated to the communists than they doubled their demands. They must have two members on each of the bodies named, instead of one, they insisted. Otherwise it was no go.

Pat Hurley was enraged. "The God damned New Dealers," he roared to Nelson. "The blasted Democrats!"

The thing is still hanging fire, apparently. When Nelson left China, he urged Hurley to come back with him, but Pat refused. As long as there was any hope of bringing the two factions together, he was going to remain, he said, and he still felt optimistic.

"My birthday is January 8," he told Nelson, "and I'll be with you in Washington on that date."

But he isn't back yet. The last Nelson heard of the negotiation, Chiang had agreed to put two communists on each of the governmental bodies in question, and the communists had upped their demands to three. There's no place like the Orient, except possibly a Democratic National Convention.

Now, while Pat was up north dickering with the commies, Don Nelson got down to economic business with the Generalissimo. He wanted to build up Chinese industry. The fundamental obstacle was capital. He had to get the Chinese banks to put up the money. Chiang sought to be helpful.

"Tell me exactly what you want the bankers to do," said Chiang, simply, "and I'll just order them to do it."

Nelson demurred. He explained to us that he had had bitter personal experiences with cases wherein the government ordered somebody to do something, and he had found in general that somehow it never got done. All he told Chiang, however, was that he would like to hold acceptance of his generous offer in abeyance and try to work the thing out with the bankers on a voluntary basis. Chiang called a conference for him.

That conference must have been a dilly. The bankers were all smiles—they hadn't seen an American sucker for years.

Now you should know at this point—as we were instructed—that the interest rate in the government-owned banks in China is 3.2 percent monthly, compounded monthly. In addition, there are insurance charges and auditing costs which must be borne by the borrower. In the end it works out that he pays upwards of 60 percent annually for loans from government banks and as high as 75 percent on money borrowed from private banks.

This of course is not so greedy as it sounds. Inflation being what it is in China today, the value of money is dropping steadily, and by the time a loan is repaid, the principal sum is worth a great deal less than it was when the bank advanced it. The high interest rate is designed to compensate for this deterioration in the value of the principal sum.

Nelson outlined his problem to the bankers. He had discovered among other things that even Chiang did not know, that the reason why the Chinese ground forces were not properly equipped with trenching tools was because the factories had had to shut down for the lack of money with which to continue their operations. Now a trenching tool, he explained, is one thing an army cannot fight without in the average Chinese terrain. Without it, they cannot dig themselves in for protection against mortar fire, machine gun and rifle fire, and bombing and strafing from the sky. Confronted by these ever-present elements of modern warfare the only thing they can do is run. Trenching tools therefore were a number one necessity.

Rifles were next. Until recently the Chinese had been producing only about 5,000 rifles a month, and they were losing more than that number each month. As for Chinese steel production, which could be used in the making of mortars and shells—about the only kind of artillery the Chinese use—it was only about 10 percent of capacity. Moreover, as Nelson explained, there was no reason why the Chinese should not manufacture replacement parts for trucks. He explained that he had brought with him to China five of America's outstanding experts on the fabrication of steel, plus one fuel expert. These six men could, he said, build up Chinese production to the necessary levels in short order.

The bankers were much impressed. He could count on their help and cooperation unfailingly. Of course, they couldn't drop the interest rate much. They might shave it a little.

The bargaining proceeded on this high diplomatic level for some time until Nelson, getting warmer and warmer under the collar, finally burst out with, "Look here. You fellows are putting dollars ahead of Chinese lives. I don't give a damn about that. That's *your* business. But you are also putting dollars ahead of American lives, and that's *my* business. As far as I'm concerned you can all go to hell."

(Isn't it surprising how much profanity manages to creep into our diplomatic negotiation with these cultured, soft-spoken Chinese?)

The bankers climbed down off their high horses promptly. The interest rate came tumbling down precipitately. An agreement was struck in no time at all.

"What interest," I asked Nelson, "did you finally agree upon?"

"Well," he said, with a slight show of reluctance, "we agreed on 20 percent, but I slipped a little joker in the deal. The contract has a renegotiation clause in it."

As a result of this deal things are really looking up in China. Rifle production is now 11,000 a month and will reach 25,000 ultimately. Steel output will be stepped up to about a million tons annually—a small figure, indeed, but large enough to meet virtually all the requirements of the Chinese Army. Within three more months the entire Chinese armed force will be fully equipped with trenching tools—and none of this stuff will have to come in either over the Hump or along the new Ledo road.

If the Japs will hold off for three months longer, Nelson insists, the Chinese will be able to handle the situation. In this connection the work done by [General Albert] Wedemeyer as successor to Stilwell has been amazing. For the first time, China has a real military organization. He has worked wonders in beating the rough-hewn Chinese manpower into a trained fighting force. Also his prompt action saved us loss of all our work on the Ledo road. By hastily taking a couple of divisions out of the Burma show, Wedemeyer prevented the Japs from capturing Kweiyand after they had swallowed up Kweilin. The latter was a distressing loss, but the former would have cut us off completely from the Burma end and made the whole Ledo project futile. There were no Chinese forces to stop the advance, but thanks to Wedemeyer's prompt action, the Japs were turned back and Kweiyand remains safely in Chinese hands. Wedemeyer has replaced every officer who was under Stilwell, thus setting up an entirely new organization with which everyone from Chiang to the Chinese privates is delighted.

Nelson reported further that Chiang is in full agreement with the view that has been expressed so often by EJK in our conferences with him: namely, that once Japan itself has been invaded and defeated, it will be up to the Chinese to mop up the Japanese army that will then be sequestered largely within China. Chiang does not want American troops fighting in China any more than we do; and he is particularly fearful lest the Red Army come in to "help."

Both Hurley and Nelson played adroitly upon this fear of Russian military intervention in winning Chiang's full, and almost abject, cooperation with our plans. All agreed, however, that China cannot drive out the Japanese army until our Navy manages to take some Chinese seaport through which to bring the necessary mechanized equipment and munitions.

Finding Nelson in such a frank and communicative mood, I was prompted to ask him at the conclusion of the luncheon if he would tell us just what it was that Henry Wallace was sent to China to do, and just what he really accomplished there. Nelson didn't like it much. He thought it over quite a while, and then said, "I don't want to answer that question. Henry is a friend of mine."

He said Wallace went to China chiefly to study the agricultural and food problem and see what he could do about it. He took along with him some new kind of hoe which was infinitely more efficient than the primitive hoes used by the Chinese. Thus he thought to modernize Chinese agriculture and was deeply disappointed and chagrined when the Chinese tried it out, discarded it promptly and went back to the familiar instrument of their forefathers.

One story that he had picked up in China, Nelson said, revealed better than anything else the true character of Henry Wallace. Nelson got it from a co-pilot who flew Wallace over the Hump on his way into the country.

As the plane approached the mountains, it seems, the co-pilot was instructed to go back and see that the oxygen masks were properly adjusted on all the passengers on board. He got along beautifully until he came to Wallace, who had made no move to put on the mask.

"Mr. Vice President," said the co-pilot with proper deference and respect, "we are going upstairs now and you'd better put on your oxygen mask."

"Thank you," said Mr. Wallace. "I don't intend to use it."

"But Mr. Vice President," explained the co-pilot patiently, "we are going up to sixteen or seventeen thousand feet. You must use oxygen to make up for the deficiency in that rarefied atmosphere."

"It will not be necessary," said our hero. "I have always felt that a man of sufficient courage and willpower could overcome those atmospheric deficiencies, if he would simply put his mind to it. I assure you that the oxygen will not be necessary."

The co-pilot, bewildered by this sudden flight into the mysticism of Yoga, went back to the pilot to report. The pilot sent him back with instructions to see that Wallace donned the mask. But Wallace would have none of it.

"I believe strongly in this mental power," Wallace explained, "and I am determined to put it to the test."

The co-pilot gave up and returned to the cockpit. The plane started climbing, and about half an hour later, when they had reached the ceiling, the pilot asked him to go back and check again.

"I lost a man once who wouldn't wear an oxygen mask, and I'm worried about this one. Geez, he is the Vice President, after all."

The co-pilot found Henry stretched out on his berth. His lips were blue and he was gasping painfully for breath. The co-pilot reached for the mask and adjusted it.

"You really must wear this, sir," he said firmly. "This is an Army plane under Army orders. Our orders require us to see that everyone aboard wears an oxygen mask at this altitude. Remember, sir, that you are the Vice President, and if anything happens to you, it will not be your fault, but ours. We will be court-martialled and drummed out of the Army. We would never live it down."

About five minutes later our Henry managed a reply. All he said was, "Well, I guess I was wrong that time, wasn't I."

Nelson said that Wallace did accomplish one thing in China. He wangled permission from Chiang for us to establish diplomatic and military relations with the Chinese communists. As a result of his negotiations we sent a mission of six—three military men and three from the Embassy—to act as a permanent liaison between us and the communists.

To this act on our part Chiang now attributes the independent attitude of the communists and their present action in constantly upping the price of cooperation. Nelson disagrees. He thinks Henry done good.

From where I sit at the moment, it just looks like Henry is done, period. I'm done, too.

Love

BRITISH AIR MARSHAL FOSTER WARNS
OF HEAVY CASUALTIES

CONFIDENTIAL

Tuesday
8 February 1944

Dear Bart,

Yesterday afternoon I was invited to attend a background conference held at the British Information Service by Air Vice Marshal W. F. McNeece Foster, former Deputy Head of the RAF Delegation here, and now assigned to the British Joint Staff Mission (the British half of the Combined Chiefs of Staff). The conference was the first of a series, which will from now on be completely off the record and will be held on the first Monday of each month. I should say that when the speaker can talk freely on an off-the-record basic, he will be quite as valuable to us for background as the King Marshall conferences, assuming speakers of comparable metal.

At the conclusion of the session I discussed the situation with Jack Winocour, head of the British Information Service here, and am conferring further with him today, making suggestions as to how the sessions can be most beneficial to all concerned. It looks very promising, as we have been lacking a real expression of British facts and opinion on military matters, put to us in utter candor.

Even on the background basis, Marshal Foster was extremely interesting. You will have realized by now that he is the source for the Berlin bombing story I filed today. There was other material which I shall cover here.

First he spoke about the Italian situation. Some of this the A.P. picked up so incompletely as hardly to present his true evaluation of the picture.

He began by stressing the importance of weather in that picture, especially as a limiting factor on air operations in the tactical field. We had excellent weather for the first few days, and things looked very rosy (I'm referring to the Nettuno beachhead, of course). Then the overcast shut down, and we had great difficulties in keeping our air show going. Fortunately, on the other hand, we had no gales which might have made it impossible for us to maintain sea-land communications.

In any event, what looked extremely promising ten days ago looks less promising now. The Germans have wrested the initiative from us, although if the weather clears we may be able to get it back. The Marshal referred to criticism of the command as over-cautious, and suggested that it might be better to wait before making judgment, so as to have the complete background. This background he did not, probably could not, give.

He admitted that bold action at the start might have got us across the two main highways we were trying to cut, especially since we caught the Germans completely off guard—the first Germans we saw were five drunken staff officers in a limousine.

The Marshal does not think that we shall be pushed into the sea, or anything like it. However, we are unquestionably in for some very tough fighting, and are in fact now getting it. He referred to characterization of our position as a trap. This he denied, and then went on to make an interesting observation.

German and Japanese commanders, he said, have a military advantage over us in that they can spend their manpower resources as they wish. They can put a division in a dangerous spot, and tell it to stay there until it is wiped out. They have no one to explain to except the high command. The peoples' feelings are disregarded.

British and American commanders, on the other hand, are responsible to the people as well as to the high command, and they are, both because of this and because of a humane concern for conservation of life and avoidance of casualties, impelled to avoid such sacrifices.

Stalingrad, he commented very soundly, was not a trap at all, in the sense that German troops were not caught there involuntarily by the Red Army. The German command knew what would happen to them, but the Nazi force there was deliberately sacrificed in order to get troops out of their perilous position elsewhere. I imagine there would be all sorts of hell raised in Congress if General Eisenhower deliberately sacrificed 200,000 men in order to extricate other forces from a bad spot.

However, the Marshal made the point that there are times when heavy casualties are unavoidable, and that such times lie ahead. People have simply got to stand up to them.

One other point. Talking of the Italian venture, he said our commanders must often take daring risks in the hope of large gain, and that some of these chances may not come off. If they don't, the people have got to understand that this is part of war.

My reaction was that the Marshal was delicately getting across the point that we may get pushed off at Nettuno, and that if we do it has got to be accepted as one of the ventures that failed.

The Marshal was asked if he thought Italy could be the decisive theatre of the war against Germany. His answer was that there can be no one decisive theatre. All of them combined will ultimately defeat Germany. Then the historians can debate which was the coup de grace.

Further, the Marshal referred to the calibre of our foe. In Italy the Germans are fighting virtually without air cover, and they are not too well off for ammunition. Yet they are putting up the staunchest resistance. I make this parenthetical observation: it looks like a fair—not a good—bet that Japan will be beaten before German, judging from developments in both wars.

The Marshal spoke very briefly of Burma. He pointed out the tremendous demand for landing craft all over the world, suggested that no major operations could be staged in Burma without amphibian operations necessitating large numbers of such craft, and said flatly that no such operations are to be expected until the end of the next monsoon season—say in November. However, we of course don't want the Japs to know we aren't going to do anything, so we are trying to give the impression of imminent activity. It is important, however, that our own people realize the truth, which makes things complex.

I asked him what had happened to the British expedition that was recently reported as moving toward Akyab, on the Burma coast. He was most guarded in his answer. So much so that nothing came of it save the hint that there might be news later.

As for China, he mentioned the magnificent job done by the American Transportation Corps in keeping supplies flowing in, and let it go at that.

Then he turned to the bombing of Germany, and especially Berlin. Most of this I got in today's story, but some had to be omitted for reasons of security and some because of space limitations. He said that if it were not so grim, the development of the air war would be a fascinating game, with blow and counter-blow coming along swiftly. Tactics similar to those on the ground are being developed. We will feint at one city with our bombers and then, having drawn fighters to it, swing off to another, finding it comparatively undefended. We will send several hundred Lancasters over Germany, and shoot a handful of them at one city and the remainder at the real objective.

The Germans, who have a path of searchlights all the way to Berlin, sometimes concentrate their anti-aircraft guns in some location that is left dark. Our raiders, thinking that looks safer than the lighted part of the sky, fly over it and get the hell shot out of them. And so it goes.

The Germans have come up with some new weapons, such as rockets controlled by radio, but have, fortunately for us, thrown them in on an experimental basis, thus giving our scientists time to figure out an answer for large-scale use. Thus far we have managed to find answers for everything they have.

The Marshal also said the fighters were much more of a menace to us than flak, and that while block-busters sound romantic and are effective, we use mostly incendiary bombs, having found them to produce the best results. A large percentage of the bombs dropped on Germany are incendiary.

He then turned to our air force results. The Germans, he said, dislike our day bombing so much that three-quarters of their fighters have been brought to the western approaches to Germany, and many of them have been shot down, while our precision bombing had produced great results. The Germans have been forced to cut production of bombing planes—the offensive weapon—to make fighters. Even so they have not been able to enlarge their fighter force, although holding it even.

Our objective, of course, is to hit the Luftwaffe so hard and often that our bombers will meet only slight resistance on their missions over Germany. When that time comes, Germany's finish will be near. However, I suggest that the time is still remote, although we are of course increasing the rate of attrition all the time.

Regards

KING REVIEWS OUR STATUS IN WAR

CONFIDENTIAL

Friday
18 February 1944

Dear Bart,

Present: Dewey Fleming, *Baltimore Sun*; Bert Andrews, *New York Herald Tribune*; Lyle Wilson, United Press; Paul Miller, Associated Press; Marquis Childs, United Features; Felix Belair, *Time*; Barnet Nover, *Washington Post*; our host [Nelie Bull], our guest of honor [Admiral King], myself.

Our host was his usual congenial self. Libations flowed liberally, as always. Our guest was convivial as he unfailingly is on these occasions—and even more informative than usual—yet the evening was far from a cheerful one. Things were definitely on the pessimistic side. Here are the headlines of our two hour talk:

• We no longer think we can beat Germany in 1944.
• When we do, it will take several years to beat Japan.
• The Germans outsmarted us in Italy.
• We outsmarted the Japs in the Marshalls.
• The war as a whole is not going so well for us.
• We are way behind schedule.

- The British have let us down badly in the Pacific.
- We will not start the Burma show this year.
- We may not get it started next year.
- China is weakening; we fear collapse.
- The obstacles we face in the Pacific seem almost insurmountable.
- We fear a Japanese trap and a bloody nose.
- We do not seek to take Rabaul or Truk, but hope to pinch 'em off.
- We fear the public will demand peace before we really lick the Japs.
- Siberia is not practical for an attack on Tokyo.
- Washington to the contrary, we WILL invade Europe.
- We have plenty of landing craft.
- Anti-submarine war in the Atlantic goes well.
- Our submarine war in the Pacific goes marvelously well.

All of the above statements were made by our guest in approximately these words during the course of the evening. His discontent with our British allies was noticeably marked, and figured in his conversation at frequent intervals. There was to my mind a suggestion that he is likewise discontented at the failure of our Commander in Chief to exert pressure on the British to give us more aid and cooperation than we are getting from them. Some of the others present did not get this impression; some agreed with me. At one point, however, he said, "The British had to be pitchforked into the coming invasion. And for God's sake keep this extra off the record, but it was Pal Joey [Stalin] who applied the pitchfork."

Now, to get down to the regular order.

Pacific. We are disengaging from the battle at Truk, and it will be some time before we are able to repeat the attack on so lavish and overwhelming a scale. We found about 25 ships and two aircraft carriers there—not a large score. The Japanese Navy is elsewhere; either in home waters or in the Philippines. We do not expect them to come out and fight for some time yet.

Our Strategy. We shall make no attempt to invade either Rabaul or Truk. It is our purpose to pinch off these strong points and to neutralize them. Rabaul is being rapidly reduced—so much so that we were able to send four destroyers there the other night to carry out a direct bombardment of Jap installations under cover of darkness. We still would not risk it by day. Truk would present a terrible problem if we had to take it, and would be far more expensive than Tarawa or anything else we have seen in the Pacific.

It is completely encircled by a coral reef projecting from four to six feet above the water and varying in width from a few feet to several hundred. This is pierced by narrow openings which provide our only method of getting at the island cluster within, and which can easily be defended at all times by the enemy. Our purpose, therefore, is to hammer away at Truk as we have at Rabaul, thus preventing the Japanese force there from escaping, and preventing them also from receiving any outside aid.

To accomplish this pinching off process we will head next for the Marianas, but we don't yet know what we will be getting into there. We must reconnoiter first to discover exactly what the Japs have done in the way of fortifying Guam and Saipan. Thence our course would be to the Philippines and our ultimate objective, a port on the Chinese coast to the south of the Luzon-Formosa line.

Japanese Strategy. We wish we knew, of course. We are somewhat puzzled by the fact that the Japs are not resisting our advance as strenuously as we believe they could. The Admiral who succeeded Yamamoto (I forget his name) is by no means the enterprising gentleman that Yamamoto was, our guest asserted.

We know that the Japs are very patient people, and will spend years, if necessary, laying a trap for us to walk into, and we fear we may wake up one of these bright mornings with a very bloody nose. However, we are attacking only the Japanese outer defenses at present, and the Nips have apparently determined to let us do this without risking their fleet. Meanwhile, we believe they are working effectively to make their inner ring impregnable.

This inner ring is formed by the island of Formosa, Korea and Japan on one side, and by the Yangtze Valley and Manchukuo on the other. The Nips are building huge stockpiles inside this region, of rubber, tin, oil in apparent anticipation of the day when we may cut their communication lines with the Dutch East Indies. We cannot win the war without breaking this ring, and our guest frankly admitted that he does not know how we are going to do it.

In his opinion it can be done only by means of a land offensive, through China. He is confident that Russia has a score to settle with Japan and will turn to the job as soon as Germany is out of the way. In this connection, he discussed at length the problem of logistics in Siberia, and without attempting to report his conversation fully, let me say merely that his conclusion was that any force we bring into Siberia will face exactly the same difficulties that Chennault is now experiencing in China. Everything we use will have to be brought in by air, and we can't do the job that way.

Hence his conclusion that we must take a port on the China coast, where we can bring in our supplies by the shipload and make northeastern China the base of our operations. Even if we could open the Burma Road it would not be a drop in the bucket. Since Formosa constitutes the southern arc of the Japanese inner-ring defense, the port we must take must be below the Luzon-Formosa line. A corollary advantage of this strategy on our part is that by this action we will cut squarely across Japanese communications to the south and keep them from using "the wealth of the Indies."

Of course this does not mean that we ourselves will be able to exploit the oil, rubber and tin resources of the Indies for some time to come after that unless we are prepared to engage in an island-hopping campaign and actually recapture the islands. Cut off from Japan, these strongholds will wither, but slowly. The Japanese garrisons on them will never lack for food since it is to be found in abundance all around them. They will find it impossible, however, to maintain a military organization, and ultimately we should be able to move in without using major attacking forces.

Our chief difficulty is, however, that if the Japs correctly estimate our strategy they can turn all their efforts to an immediate conquest of China—an all-out attack on Chungking, for example, which if successful would virtually end organized Chinese resistance, or at least render it wholly ineffective. This would just about stymie us.

Now at best this all adds up to a long, plodding, costly war that will stretch out for years to come. Our guest believes that we must fight this war to the bitter end—that we must lick the Japs so thoroughly that they will never again be able to attack anyone. His fear is, however, that the American people will weary of it quickly, and that pressure at home will force a negotiated peace, before the Japs are really licked.

He admits that an important consideration will be the extent to which American industry may be permitted to return to civilian production after the cessation of hostilities in Europe. Today almost all our Navy is in the Pacific, but apart from that, about 85 percent of Allied personnel and equipment is in the European theatre, with only 15 percent in the Pacific. He estimates we can lick Japan with about 50 percent of the present combined strength of the Allies. More than that we cannot use. We could not deploy it effectively.

Here, however, his suspicion of the British asserts itself again. He simply does not believe that we will get much help from them. They will contribute far less than their 50 percent, which means that we must use correspondingly more than our own 50 percent. He does not think, therefore, that we can return anywhere near 50 percent of our manpower and production facilities to civilian use, and he hazarded the pessimistic guess that it might be as little as ten.

We could materially shorten the Pacific war through the use of poison gas. He would like to, but feels that the American people would never stand for it. (Many of those present vigorously dissented from his estimate of present-day public opinion. The consensus was that the American people would willingly use anything against the Japs.) We have no agreement with the Japs against using poison gas, and we are fully prepared to use it at a moment's notice as a retaliatory measure if the Japs ever use it against us. Apparently we carry large supplies of it wherever we go in the Pacific. The use of gas, however, poses two immediate problems:

1) it might provoke Germany to use it against England, and

2) it might cause the Japs to use it heavily on the Chinese.

Miscellany. We outsmarted the Japs in the Marshalls. Reconnaissance flights have shown that a couple of the islands we did not attack are much more strongly fortified and heavily manned than Kwajalein, which we took. Apparently these were the islands the Japs expected us to attack. As it is, we have neutralized them without going anywhere near them. The garrisons on them have plenty of ammunition, but nothing to shoot it at; and ultimately their food must run out. Then they starve. They can't get out, and no surface vessels can get to them to save them.

Our own problems of supply in the Pacific are becoming terrific as we extend our lines. We have only Pearl Harbor as a base, and it simply isn't big enough to do the job. We are licking the problem, though, and will continue to stay on top of it. Sea trains are helping. For instance, we took a little island called Majuro in the Marshalls. As you know, about the first thing we do, on moving in, is to set up an air field, and we did so here, but also brought in a sea train almost coincidentally with our attack on Majura. The island has a wonderful deepwater lagoon, and the Seabees moved in at once with dynamite, underwater bulldozers, mines, etc. to clear away the coral, blast passages, and set up a first class naval base. In the sea train, of course, are a complete repair ship, tankers, a commissary ship, a munitions ship and all other facilities necessary to establish a permanent outpost in an advanced position. We are doing these things wherever we go, but we will not move up our main supply of naval stores from Guadalcanal and other southerly points until we have pinched off Rabaul.

Submarines. We cannot understand why the Japs have not been more successful against our underwater attacks, in view of the fact that we had such excellent results with our defensive methods in the Atlantic. They are making it hotter for us than it was. We are having to put considerably more anti-aircraft on our subs than we used to, just as the Germans have been forced to do. But while our losses have mounted numerically in the Pacific, the ratio of loss has not increased. We are turning out five or six subs a month, and all are going to the Pacific.

Burma, the British, and China. From the foregoing discussion of our strategy and objectives in the Pacific, it might appear that the campaign to reopen the Burma Road is no longer of vital importance to us. That is NOT so. Our guest was merely becoming resigned to the prospect of doing without Burma. He was also downright sore about it. Here is the situation as we piece it together:

China. The Chinese are becoming very weary of the war. There is surprising evidence of what almost amounts to treachery among the men surrounding Chiang Kai-shek. The natives of the country are starving. The inflation problem has reached disastrous proportions. Every so often one reads dispatches boasting that the Chinese have repelled a Japanese attack upon the great rice bowl country. These dispatches are true enough, but the whole purpose of the Japanese is to destroy the rice crop, and this is done quite effectively before they retreat. Thus more Chinese starve and the price of rice shoots further skyward. I gather that we fear the possibility of a total collapse of Chinese resistance. We fear, too, a Japanese drive on Chungking.

The opening of the Burma Road would be of tremendous importance to us. It would not enable us to supply an attack of our own on Japan. It would enable us to strengthen the defense of Chungking; to bring in large quantitites of badly needed food and supplies, and thus to reverse the inflationary trend which is impoverishing even the most substantial citizens of the land. Chiefly, however, it would be a tremendous psychological shot in the arm, which should put new hope and courage into the Chinese. So what are we doing about it? Well, practically nothing.

Burma. The monsoons are about to set in again. All our hopes for a real drive into Burma have definitely been crushed. "We've gone about as fur as we kin go," to quote from Oklahoma. And of course we haven't gone anywhere at all. The worst of it is that we have no assurance of doing any better in the fall, when the weather again permits. I asked how it happened that this energetic, courageous, devil-may-care Lord Mountbatten has managed to peter out in such a fizzle. The answer, succinctly, was. . . .

The British. Mountbatten is being held strictly under wraps, and despite his fine reputation and his blood relationship to the Royal Family, he cannot move a muscle. The whole defeatist strategy of Wavell pervades India, and nothing can be done about it until the whole mess—Wavell, Auchinleck, etc.—is cleaned out from top to bottom. Churchill simply won't do this. Our guest asked me if I knew how many men the British had under arms in India, fully equipped and trained. I didn't, so he told me: 750,000.

Question: What are they doing?

Answer: They're eating regularly.

Wavell, as Viceroy, is still in complete control of the military, although his office is purely political. Auchinleck, as Commander in Chief, controls supply and personnel. Mountbatten asks for this or that, and is told, "Unh unh. We need that stuff here. You can't have it." So two puny forces go piddling along through the jungles of Burma at a rate that is laughable to the Japanese, and that causes the Allies to lose face daily, thus contributing to the dangerous unrest within India, and doing much of the Japs' propaganda work for them.

Question: Don't you think the newspapers could help you out a little if they could get across this idea that we do not have to be so all-fired nice to our dear Allies?

Answer: Well, let me indulge in a little double talk here. Perhaps you are familiar with the record of Winston Churchill in the last war, with special reference to the Dardanelles disaster. Then, remember that the leopard hasn't changed his spots. Churchill fancies himself as a great and subtle strategist, and he fancies that he can win the war without bloodshed. Now of course he can't, and the British Chiefs are having a sweet time with him.

Our guest also suggested another point, that the British probably figured that when they had let *us* lick Japan, Burma would fall naturally back into their laps without any effort or expenditure on their part.

Mediterranean, Turkey. We tried to get Turkey into the war. Their price was too high. If we had given them all the equipment they wanted, we would have had nothing left for the invasion. So we couldn't pay the price. They knew it, and that is why they demanded so much. They mean to come into the war at five minutes to 12, to share in the plums of peace without sharing in the costs of victory.

Italy. The Germans outsmarted us here. We had expected that our amphibious action at Nettuno and Anzio would force them to fall back from Cassino to prevent the danger of encirclement. Instead, they merely strengthened their line at Cassino and prevented Clark from moving north to aid the amphibious forces. Meanwhile, our landing forces were extending their beachheads over an ever-expanding perimeter and were being spread thinner and thinner, thus becoming more and more vulnerable to attack. The weather, of course, was the pay-off. We've heard so much about "Sunny Italy," but we've seen nothing but rain and fog which have hampered our actions tremendously.

German glide bombs have been hampering our shipping in this area to some extent, and may have been responsible for the loss of the transport, the sinking of which was announced last week.

Invasion. For the past three or four days Washington has been pervaded by "hush hush" reports "from the highest authorities" (always unnamed) that we are not going to invade across the Channel. The reason invariably given is that we can't get enough landing barges.

Our guest says flatly that we WILL invade, and that we have enough landing barges for the job. We are behind schedule, nevertheless.

Atlantic. The U-boats are becoming much more cautious. They don't bore in on our convoys as they used to. Therefore we are not getting as many of them as we formerly did. The new tactics are ascribed to the fact that the Germans are scraping the bottom of their personnel barrel—that neither for their air force nor for their submarines can they get the type of men they used to have. Actually, we believe that the Germans are now building submarines faster than we are sinking them, yet we find fewer than ever in the Atlantic.

We "count" their submarines daily through the use of cross bearings by radio. A sub "peeps." We hear it, and instantly chart its position. It may not peep again for several days, but a trained staff of experts that follows German sub movements day and night can tell with an amazing degree of accuracy whether a sub that is peeping tonight is the same one that was somewhere else three days ago, or a new one we had not previously charted. These days we "count" about 60 to 70 U-boats in the Atlantic. Six months ago we counted 115 to 150.

Personnel. Our Navy is experiencing some of the difficulties just mentioned in the above paragraphs. Since it began taking inductees instead of volunteers, it is having just about as much trouble with psychoneurotics and malingerers as The Man told us recently that the Army is having.

Late in the evening the following conversation took place as nearly as I can recall:

Q. What about the rocket guns on the French coast?

A. They're still there. You may have noticed that we're bombing this part of the coast much more heavily now.

Q. Why haven't the Germans started to use them yet?

A. They're smart. In the last war, you remember, we tried out the tank experimentally and gave the show away before we were ready. The Germans aren't making that mistake. They aren't going to use those guns until they can do it with maximum effect and at the time when they think it will be most disastrous for us.

Q. Do you think they might use gas in the projectiles from these guns?

A. There are things worse than gas. (Pause while most of us looked puzzled.) Well, I mean bacteria.

Q. But aren't our men inoculated against most of the disease germs they might use?

A. No. They could use bacteria that our medical men and research laboratories would still have to find the antidotes for. Some day we will be able to tell the story of what these medical men are doing. They are working day and night to examine every possibility, and to prepare and protect against it.

Q. What do they think the Germans might use?

A. Botulism.

Q. Would our defense against this be to retaliate in kind?

A. Yes.

Q. But wouldn't that mean killing our own friends in the occupied territories as well as the enemy?

A. Yes.

Q. If the Germans do this thing are we now prepared to retaliate at once? Do we have the bacteria ready?

A. I shouldn't answer that question. But the answer is yes. (Note. This is one of the reasons I'm afraid we will not be able to end the European war in 1944. The Germans are not through by a long shot.)

At this point our guest excused himself, I thought rather abruptly, and went home. The whole exchange could have meant nothing more than that we were making far-sighted preparations to meet any and every contingency that may arise in connection with the coming invasion. I think all of us present, however, were led to the belief that we were acting on definite information that we have somehow obtained concerning German intentions. It also occurs to me that if we are forced to wage a medical war of this kind, we will be poisoning and infecting the country which our own troops must invade, thus exposing them to all the dangers that helped rout the enemy from the territory into which we are moving.

Regards

HOW THE PRESS KEPT JAPS IN DARK ABOUT U.S. LOSSES

CONFIDENTIAL

Thursday
24 February 1944

Dear Bart,

I figured the enclosed would be of interest to you.

Here is something confidential. We did better at Truk than the Navy reported, sinking one aircraft carrier that wasn't mentioned. The idea seems to be the Japs don't know we know we sank it, which might be valuable to us some day.

Also, we lost 40 planes, and not 17, as announced. The 17 apparently crashed in eyesight of the Japanese, and the others didn't. So we are keeping them guessing.

Regards

ARMY PREPARES FOR THE INVASION— CHINESE FORCES IMPROVED

CONFIDENTIAL

Tuesday
14 March 1944

Dear Bart,

Another Marshall conference, which went as follows:

Army Students Training Program. His main concern was to explain why the War Department had begun to transfer the A.S.T.P. Corps from college to active service in the Army. The prime reason was that the draft boards have, since last September, been falling behind in meeting their quotas, as far behind as 200,000 several weeks ago; and that it ws imperative to get these men into service if we were to mount the invasion on time.

The percentage of rejections and the fact that so many had to be turned back were also factors, as well as the need for specialized groups. This type of man is particularly needed to fill the specialized phases of combat, especially engineers, harbor masters, anti-aircraft units and index of supplies—in fact the whole Service of Supply personnel.

It has become necessary to decimate certain numbers of divisions to make up the gaps; also necessary to send out large numbers of men who have not been adequately trained for their jobs—so much so that investigation made of every unit about to embark has caused as high as 40 percent of the units to be turned back in a recent period.

Great Need for Infantry and Riflemen. The need has arisen for several reasons: a) The other divisions of the Army are more glamorous and attract more soldiers, and b) the replacements have to be maintained at an exceedingly high level. Replacement runs as high as 70 percent. That is, 70 percent of the replacements going to the Army are required by the Infantry, which comprises only 11 percent of the entire Army.

The Infantry has to get in and lead the way, to be followed by tanks. He emphasized that the role of the tank now differs from that of the time when the German Panzer divisions overran France, because today, unlike France in 1940, the tank is met with almost equal opposition and no longer has freedom of range and movement. A particular difficulty is presented by land mines and anti-tank guns which the Infantry has to clean out.

He was specifically asked whether the shortage of draftees and the problem of gathering enough Infantry was affecting the time schedule of the invasion. He answered "No," but that it would have if they had not interrupted the A.S.T.P. [Army Student Training Program] program.

Originally the units were set up with 10 percent additional replacement—this should be 20 percent for infantry and 5 percent for others. The extra men are called basics. Largely the shift in strategic position made the tank less effective and required the way to be cleared by infantry so that that branch takes the greatest weight of casualties, and he thinks the arrangement of percentage replacements is out of line.

Air War From London. We have 2,200 heavy bombers in England and 1,000 heavy bombers in Italy. A month ago, according to the best information, it was believed that German fighter production reached 2,200 a month. Bombing has now reduced it to 300 a month, according to combined American and British Intelligence. Three weeks ago German production was 650 a month. In a period of 18 days we had destroyed 1,112 German planes in the air and on the ground. It was reported that the Russians claimed destruction of approximately 300 planes in four days. As a rule, we cut the Russian estimates in half, so he wasn't sure about that figure being right.

Our objective of raiding is not only to cut down plane production—we are looking for fights. The purpose of the air offensive is both to destroy the German capacity to produce and to destroy the existing Luftwaffe. The main reason for raiding Berlin is that such a raid is always able to get a fight—it does get German planes off the ground, which is essential to the accomplishment of our ultimate purpose. It is believed that the ball bearing works are wiped out entirely.

Bombing priorities: 1) Fighter plane production, 2) Synthetic oil, 3) Rubber production.

We are continuing to attack the invasion coast, but we don't know how extensively we are damaging the targets because they are so camouflaged and because there are so many dummy gun sites, etc. We don't have to waste bombing expeditions on the invasion coast because this target is used for practice bombing and when bad weather makes it impossible to carry the raids further inland.

He said it was likely that in the next three weeks the Germans would be using radio-directed planes from the Channel coast.

Ireland. He disclosed that he had G-2 for a long time investigating every conceivable method of bringing pressure on the Irish Free State; and was surprised and gratified that action was being taken without any suggestion from the War Department on a high level. He said that the situation was vicious; that it was much worse than Argentina, and that they had information that gives them great concern as to the thorough and continuous activities of Axis spies in the Irish Free State.

He compared the situation to that which would exist if we had American representatives at Kyushu and a few others some miles north of Berlin who would be free to come and go as they wished, to interview travelers fresh from enemy territories and to send to their headquarters by radio what they had learned.

Italy. He emphasized again our main hope in Italy is: a) to gain airfields north of Rome, and b) to make the Germans fight to hold Nazi divisions on that front.

He placed special emphasis on the need for holding as many German divisions there as possible; then emphasized the danger that the Germans may shorten their lines and merely fight a defensive war requiring a relatively small number of divisions.

In the Anzio beachhead the Germans are already fighting a defensive war, as far as our best information now indicates; and have withdrawn all of one division and part of another, presumably to the Russian front. Actually, our position on the Anzio beachhead is very good.

One German division from the Cassino front was sent to northwest France, indicating what they are expecting. Our purpose wasn't only to engage as many German divisions as possible in Italy, but also in the Balkans and through a threat to southern France.

Air Power. The advocates of air power are beginning to realize that you can only fight in the air on certain days of the week, but that war goes on seven days a week, Sundays and holidays included.

For more than three weeks we have had something planned on the Cassino front, and weather has prevented us from bringing our bombers into operation. For some time, when Eisenhower was still there, they had planned two beachheads rather than one; they had to postpone them because the Germans had too much strength in that area and we had too few landing and assault craft. The objective of the Italian operations remains the same—ultimately to establish an Allied line along the Po.

Russians. He believes that press coverage of the Russian campaign is generally complete and accurate. In the south the Germans are retiring in good order. It was his impression that the Germans are putting up a much stronger defense along the northern front than in the south. In support of that, one reason was the feeling of what effect a fast retreat in the north would have on the Finnish situation. On another track, he said that one of their fears was that the Germans may eventually pull back to the Riga line.

The Bug line didn't amount to much; it would not enable them to shorten their lines much and is not very important. He ended the brief comment on the Soviet front by saying that the Red Army is doing a grand job, and "God give them strength."

German Morale. He was certain that the German Army would fight a disciplined and effective war until it received word from the top to stop; and that the military necessity was to convince not the Nazi officials, but the Army High Command—the Junkers—that it is hopeless from a materiel and manpower standpoint to continue the war. Their problem does not seem to be production of material as much as its distribution over the few important rail junctions that embody their distribution system.

While the Germans apparently are short on meat and potatoes, they have ample supplies of other types of food and expect good crops this year. The public morale is a factor, and damage to it could seep up from the bottom and affect the military judgment of the High Command, but in the last analysis it is not considered a major factor. The imponderable is the Gestapo. We have never fought an army before which has a Gestapo driving on the civilian home-front.

Palestine. Asked for his views on the Wagner-Taft Resolution, which calls upon the British to withdraw the White Paper of 1939, reopen Palestine to unlimited Jewish immigration, and favor the establishment of a Jewish state in Palestine, he replied somewhat whimsically that he had expressed these views to what was supposedly a closed session of a Congressional committee, but he discovered that it had none the less gained currency.

He pointed out that it is essential for us to use our troops in active positions under present circumstances and that to this end we are withdrawing all our forces in the Middle East as rapidly as possible. Furthermore, French officials in North Africa are having considerable difficulties with the Arabs.

Finally, a very large section of the population of India is also Moslem. Therefore, any action that we take now which will anger or arouse the whole Moslem world may have serious repercussions on our war effort and force us to scatter our strength through North Africa, the Middle East and perhaps India.

Asia. He declared that news stories purporting to show that Stilwell and

Mountbatten, his superior, were at odds were a particular pain in the neck to him. There have been stories recently that Stilwell is still disputing the strategy of Mountbatten, who has been pictured as a playboy and whose appointment was allegedly designed to stall off American enthusiasm for an early offensive against Burma.

Our informant holds an entirely different estimate of Mountbatten. He considers Mountbatten a dynamic military man who was appointed to inject some life and enthusiasm into the lethargic Indian government, namely Field Marshall Wavell. That is exactly what Mountbatten wants to do and is beginning to do.

He read a private communication from Mountbatten reporting that Stilwell's forces in the north of China, made up primarily of American-trained Chinese soldiers, together with an American regiment, had wiped out the famous 18th Japanese Division which attacked Singapore and successfully frustrated the ill-starred attack that Field Marshall Wavell had led at Akyab. The Japanese who escaped the attack were driven off into the jungle and dispersed. He read another message from General Stilwell which went into more detail, paying high tribute to the fighting ability of Chinese soldiers, and making it clear that an encirclement operation performed by an American column provided the keynote of surprise that turned the tide of battle in our favor.

The important job we have now is to try to bring into full participation in the Burma campaign American-trained Chinese forces in Yunnan. Of course it is still difficult to do this because everything these forces will need has to be flown over the Hump. But one of our major difficulties has been cleared up since Chiang has given Stilwell sufficient latitude and authority to develop and officer the Chinese troops under his command. He also said we have American officers in the higher ranks of these Chinese troops working to try to keep things in shape. He predicted that all of this was going to have tremendous effect on the entire Chinese Army.

Pacific. He said that as far as he was concerned the Washington newspaper correspondents could invade Paramushiro at any time they wished, but he preferred that we didn't all do it the same night. He said the Japanese were considerably worried about an attack at that point, and it was his purpose to keep them so. He also said the Japanese were deeply worried about possible attacks by our naval forces at other points in the Pacific—notably out of Northwest Australia, and to that end had strengthened their garrisons on neighboring islands.

He likewise reported that the Japanese were concentrating ships near Singapore, primarily for defensive rather than offensive purposes, and added that possibly the plenitude of oil in that region and the growing difficulty the Japanese are having in transporting that oil to their home quarters had something to do with the movement.

He said we could look forward to some interesting action on Bougainville, where we have sewed up 22,000 Japs who are slowly starving to death, and whom he believes will prefer to go down fighting. He looks for similar suicide attacks at Rabaul and on New Britain. He pointed out that wise strategy on our part would be to thin our defensive lines, permitting Japanese infiltration at whatever point they may select, while building up a mobile reserve to resist such attacks successfully and at great cost to the attackers.

Our strategy remains to get more air bases from which to attack Japan. One of the fruits of that strategy is that we are forcing the Japanese to use their aircraft carriers for the purpose for which they were not originally intended. Recently they have been using carriers to transport land planes to the theatres of operation, and have used their crews to fight those planes in land action, sustaining heavy losses. Now the Japanese are finding it difficult to man their carriers with trained crews capable of flying carrier based operations.

Regards

IBN SAUD, IRAN, PALESTINE, DISAGREEMENTS WITH THE BRITISH, GOLD AND OIL

General Patrick Hurley, in the talk described herewith refers to the Atlantic Charter drawn up at the Teheran Conference as it concerned Iran. During the interminable months that the Ayatollah Khomenei was playing his deadly game with American hostages and blaming the United States for everything that went wrong in his country, earthquakes not excepted, I could never understand why nobody took the trouble to point out that had it not been for the United States, his country would have been a Soviet province after World War II. It was President Roosevelt at the Teheran Conference who initiated the decision by the conferees that their troops would pull out of Iran once the war was over. Had he not done so, the chances that the Red Army would have moved out were so slim as to be microscopic. Making the point would hardly have moved the Ayatollah, who was not geared for rational thought, but it might have affected world opinion.

CONFIDENTIAL

Wednesday
15 March 1944

Dear Bart,

Major General Patrick J. Hurley, who has just returned from the Middle East, with way stations reaching as far as Chungking, spoke at the Overseas Writers today. Phelps and I were both present and this is a joint memorandum comprising our recollection of what he said. General Hurley is, as you know, the President's special representative in the Near East.

General Hurley struck both of us as combining bursts of oratory with profound observations in a fashion that was somewhat bewildering. I think we felt that his second appearance before the Overseas Writers was perhaps less effective than his first, which I recorded for you at the time. However, this should not be taken as meaning that he was anything but very interesting indeed.

On this occasion he seemed particularly sensitive to newspaper stories and other public references to his work in Iran, which made him feel that he was under attack. He seemed, therefore, to be very much on the defensive, while at the same time his bursts of oratory at frequent intervals suggested that he might be entertaining some political aspirations.

It interested us that Paul Leach, Bureau Chief here for the *Chicago Daily News* and Frank Knox's right hand man, reached the same conclusion about General Hurley's political ambitions. Leach also talked to Representative Allen of Illinois only yesterday, when Allen said that he had the ideal candidate for the Republican keynoter, and that that candidate was Pat Hurley. Asked about this today, Hurley said that he was not sure that he could accept that honor under the rules governing political activities of American Army officers, but that there had been quite a bit of discussion about it. Paul asked him if he was a Republican still, and Hurley replied, "Well, not so still." The impression that Leach got was that General Hurley is President Roosevelt's candidate for the Republican vice presidential nomination, but personally I am not at all sure that General Hurley is looking that far down the scale.

So much for preamble. General Hurley began with the statement that he could not understand why the people of the United States seemed puzzled as to our foreign policy. He thereupon proceeded to define that policy as an implementation of the belief that the maintenance of the British Empire and the Commonwealth of Nations was absolutely essential to the continued welfare of the United States. We have bent every effort to sustaining the British Empire, he said, commenting "And as the girl said, 'Buddy, it's been a hell of a job, too!'."

He added that he was convinced that we had a sincere and necessary friend in the Soviet Union and that we must deserve and earn that friendship. At the same time, however, the General strongly denied that this implied any communistic bent in his own thinking. He thereupon launched into a defense of the American system of private enterprise and what it has meant to this country, concluding with a statement of confidence that 135 million Americans could determine what system they wanted much better than any clique of foreigners could do it for them.

Then General Hurley pointed out that although he had been a member of the English Speaking Union for many years, although he was convinced that our foreign relations policy relative to Britain was sound, he never hesitated to go into any difference in detail that arose between the two countries. He stressed the fact that such controversies were only surface differences, and he compared them to the differences that frequently exist between the Republican and Democratic Parties in this country. Such rows are often extremely heated while they last, but are quickly over and do not affect the sound basis of mutual agreement. He defined his position as saying he hoped he could qualify as as strong a champion of American interest as Winston Churchill is of the British Empire.

Next, the General turned his attention to the Atlantic Charter, with particular reference to Iran, with the plain implication that he believed both Winston Churchill and Joseph Stalin did *not* have their fingers crossed when they signed this document at Teheran, and that its principles would guide the post-war world. His whole discussion of this subject seemed to us to be extremely unrealistic in view of present-day events, except as it applies to Iran, which has already gotten a specific individual guarantee.

Then he outlined our fights with the British:

1) Lend-Lease—General Hurley said that when lend-lease material was first sent to nations in the Near East, we had no distributive organization there, and that it was therefore perfectly logical for us to ask the British to handle it for us. General Hurley said, however, that when he arrived in the Near East all we were getting out of it was the privilege of paying for it, with no credit among the native countries at all. He said that he had raised a row about that and that it had now been straightened out.

2) Saudi Arabia—He said that when he visited King Ibn Saud he found that American companies as long as ten years ago—long before the war—had acquired the oil properties in that country which promised to be most productive and that, therefore, he felt very strongly that we should get full credit for any lend-lease supplies going into Ibn Saud's kingdom. We had a pretty tough fight with the British on this one, he indicated, but we finally got it fixed up. He didn't say how.

3) Pipe Line—The General next mentioned the question of the pipe line from Mosul to Haifa. In general, his position was strikingly similar to that

detailed by Justice Byrnes in his talk of last night. It would be duplicative to go over that aspect. He boiled it down to a very simple, common-sense statement which was about as follows:

"I am opposed to government ownership on general principles. But the British have already applied for lend-lease steel with which to build this pipe line, and it seems to me that if any government is going to build it and that if the American taxpayer is going to pay for it, the American taxpayer might just as well own it. I don't think the American oil companies who have been opposing this project really understand this."

The General pointed out that he has represented the oil companies whose property was recently expropriated in Mexico and he felt very strongly the desirability of starting some kind of a system of governmental participation in foreign economic developments to an extent that, while preserving the full rights of private enterprise and the profit motive, would protect against the improper exploitation of foreign citizens by selfish American operators on the one hand, and on the other hand would protect decent American operators from expropriation. He made it plain that in the case of pipe lines he thought this might provide the desired solution.

4) Palestine—He said frankly that the effect upon the citizens of the Near East would be very serious if the Wagner-Taft resolution were adopted by Congress. This, as you know, would call upon the British to withdraw the White Paper of 1939; reopen Palestine to unlimited Jewish immigration; and foster the establishment of a Jewish state.

Hurley, in some anger, said that he had been greatly misrepresented on this issue by Congressman Celler of New York, who recently put into the Congressional Record a statement attributed to General Hurley and purporting to discuss a conversation between King Ibn Saud and the General as reported to President Roosevelt. Hurley denied that there was a word of truth in Celler's charges. He said that King Ibn Saud had made no such statement to him; that he had made no such reply; and that he made no such report to the President.

He said that what he did report to the President was that King Ibn Saud had already sent to our State Department a letter fully explaining his position on Palestine and that it was therefore not necessary for General Hurley to try to acquaint the President with the King's views. He made no secret of the fact, however, that he strongly believed that passage of the Wagner-Taft Resolution at this time would incite a war in our rear, and that as a military man he opposed doing anything that would have such an effect before we had at least disposed of the war on our front.

General Hurley quoted a prominent English gentleman as saying to him that Britain did not desire to establish a Jewish state in Palestine, but that the United States was pressuring her to do so. Hurley expressed the opinion that the United States and Great Britian should get together on the question of Palestine and present a unified front rather than differing among themselves. He said he told the Britisher that he thought "you folks" should make up your minds either to set up a Jewish state or not to.

5) World Economics—General Hurley said that in his opinion there were four economic factors in the world today:

a. Gold—Some people believe that, since we have so much gold buried at Fort Knox, gold is no longer a factor in the world. The General said that if we knew how much gold was being mined in Russia and elsewhere, we would realize how false this impression really is. Gold is still the number one economic factor.

b. Oil—He said that we had been depleting our natural oil resources at a terrific rate and giving them to Great Britain and our other allies as a contribution to victory. He made it clear that he heartily approved of this practice to whatever extent might be necessary, but that he felt we had a perfect right at the end of the war to say to the world, "Now let us obtain oil properties in other parts of the world to make up for that which we have given you."

c. Water—General Hurley pointed to the importance of water transportation both in the war and also in the post-war world. He stressed Britain's dependence upon shipping, and he pointed to the obvious fact that at the end of the war the United States will virtually dominate world shipping. He believes that it would be a far-sighted development if the United States would see to it that British shipping is maintained to a major degree in its prewar position so that our task of sustaining the British Empire will be simplified by just so much. He also said that the small maritime nations had contributed their shipping to the war effort and that it was up to us to see that their lost ships were replaced. However, in both cases, General Hurley was opposed to giving ships to anyone. He wanted us to be reimbursed for them.

d. Air—(General Hurley left it at that.)

6) Turkey—General Hurley was asked if he cared to comment on the present situation in Turkey, and replied, significantly, that he thought it would be better if he did not. He then went on to explain that the Turkish situation was a matter of controversy among the Allies, and that it would not be proper to say anything until this argument has been resolved. We might add that this was the first thing that had been said in Washington to indicate that the controversy was not wholly between Turkey on the one hand and the United Nations on the other, but also among the United Nations themselves.

Finally, General Hurley commented briefly that in his opinion the Battle of Stalingrad, part of which he personally saw, would prove to have been the turning point of the land war, just as Midway was the turning point of the war at sea.

Regards

THE U.S. AIR FORCE AND ITS PRESENT POSITION

CONFIDENTIAL

Friday
14 April 1944

Dear Bart,

The Thursay Evening Supper and Study Club met with General Hap Arnold last night at the Statler. Those present included Major General Kuter, Air Chief of Staff; Herbert Bayard Swope; Jim Wright of the *Buffalo Evening News*; Paul Wooton of the *New Orleans Times-Picayune*; Dewey Fleming of the *Baltimore Sun*; Ted Alford of the *Kansas City Star*; Tom Stokes of Scripps-Howard; Dick Wilson of Cowles Publications; Frank Kent of the *Baltimore Sun*; Walker Buel of the *Cleveland Plain Dealer*; Bill Murphy of the *Philadelphia Inquirer*; Pete Brandt of the *St. Louis Post-Dispatch*; Turner Catledge of the *New York Times* and a visiting fireman from the *Milwaukee Journal*.

General Arnold was extremely interesting and frank. In his dinner conversation he talked quite a lot about the Indian situation, and it is very obvious that he has little faith in the British out there. Their outstanding characteristic is "It can't be done" and the civilian government he believes to be slow, inefficient, and of little use to the military. Wavell and Auchinleck he finds defeatist. He thinks well of Mountbatten, but feels he is up against a very difficult proposition.

There are plenty of British and Indian troops on hand, but they don't seem to be putting out the requisite effort. What, asks Arnold, are they fighting for? They lack fire, and the big question is whether Mountbatten can instill the fighting spirit in them. If he can, well and good. If he can't, it will be just too bad.

Arnold referred to last year's abortive expedition toward Akyab. In that one, he said, a British division, followed by a brigade, was surrounded by three Japanese battalions. This would be the equivalent of three men surrounding twenty. The answer is plain: it couldn't be done if the surrounded force had the will to fight.

This pessimistic feeling about the British in India is fairly rife in Washington. Arnold, continuing to discuss Mountbatten's problems, asked who controlled the railroads in India. The answer is the civilian government, which is so bogged down as to be useless, from Mountbatten's point of view. He also talked very briefly about Stilwell's troubles with Mountbatten. Stilwell, Arnold said, figured his campaign in north Burma was vitally important, and he couldn't understand why the British didn't pitch in and help the drive on Myitkyna.

Typical was the building of the Ledo Road. The defeatist attitude of the British about this project had an adverse effect on the builders. In three months they completed 14 miles. Then we brought out fresh people, and insulated them from the defeatist talk. They made good three times the distance in the same period of time. Arnold, incidentally, wonders if the British care very much what happens in Burma, to which the Chinese might lay claim.

Arnold believes that according to the way things are going now, we shall have established our vital port on the southeast China coast long before the land route to China from India is finished, and he looks forward impatiently to the day when we can dismiss India from our calculations.

After dinner the General really got down to cases. He began with a defense of the Air Force policy of giving decorations in a liberal manner. It is true, he said, that we have given out 117,000 Flying Crosses. We'll give out 100,000 more. The boys earn them. And that ribbon and bit of tin are very good for morale. Beyond that, the Air Force is the only American fighting service that has fought every day since Pearl Harbor. The boys know that if they keep flying in combat long enough, the percentages will catch up with them, and it is little enough to give them or their widows a medal.

Then the General started at the beginning. Thus far in history, he said, there has never been an air force. There won't be until we have one, which will come to pass in the next couple of months. The Germans didn't have one. Their planes were tied to operating with troops, a field in which they were very effective. But when they tried to bomb Britain, they took a terrible licking and had to give it up. The Russian air force is not a real air force, for it too is tied to ground forces. The RAF is not a real air force, for its bombing is wholly on an area rather than on a precision basis.

The American Army Air Force does not yet qualify as a real air force with the necessary striking power and the necesssary reserves to implement its strategy and tactics. It will in about two months. Don't tell the Germans, he said, because he thinks the Germans believe we have a real air force now.

Until such a force exists, he went on, nobody can say what an air force can do. The only real air force operation the enemy has staged was the Jap strike on Pearl Harbor, but the enemy lacked the knowledge and the imagination to follow up. Their thinking was tied to our fleet. Had they gone ahead and struck at San Francisco, Los Angeles, Seattle, Portland, they could have done so, for we had neither the sea nor the air power to keep them off. But they didn't realize what they had, and we got out of it all right.

Ever since then, Arnold has tried to build up an air force, but always something has happened. Some area commander has screamed that he had to have air support or he would be annihilated. And, Arnold commented, they don't want plane for plane. They want four to one, five to one, ten to one. He didn't blame 'em for feeling that way, but it did prevent him from building an air force. As an illustration he cited the Aleutians, where the Japs never had more than fourteen planes in the air at once. We had to put more than 250 planes in the area to make the local command happy.

Despite these interruptions, Arnold and his people went ahead. For the first six months after Pearl Harbor they took an awful beating at home. Planes, engines, men all were criticized, but the only thing that saved the morale of air force personnel was the spate of strident arguments by air fanatics who, he admitted, promised too much. But the command's faith never wavered, and gradually we established very high morale in what Arnold calls the greatest bunch of young men ever gathered anywhere.

He cited the Zero, which was held up to us as the ideal fighter. Some of our best pilots flew in a captured Zero and they said when they got down that it was the best Sunday afternoon airplane they'd ever seen, and God help the poor Jap who had to fight in it. He recalled that General Kenney, MacArthur's chief air officer, recently let out a squawk that he was being given insufficient planes in a vital category. And what do you think it was? The P-40, which all the "experts" were writing off as obsolete years ago.

He told about the Eagle Squadron boys, who fought for the RAF and then transferred to our air force. These men could see nothing good about our planes, our tactics, our personnel. Arnold got them all together and asked what was the matter with our stuff. When they got through he told them they were criticizing in so general a way as to make it clear they were criticizing our country and not just the planes. If they felt competent to do that, he invited, let them stand up and do it. They saw the point, and discovered finally that our stuff was good, and that our men were, too.

He cited the Spitfire, which is said to be the world's best fighter. For fighting what? he asked. It carries enough fuel only to get to the invasion coast, stay there a very few minutes, and then come home. It is good, that is, only for defending England against German bombers, and he wanted to know how that would help carry the battle against Germany itself. In other words, every plane has to be considered in the light of what it is supposed to do.

Then the General got around to the various fronts. I'll take them in order:

China. We realized early in the game how important it was to keep China supplied. At the time, with the Burma Road cut, the only outside help China got was from CNAC, which was flying 300 tons a month over the Hump. Arnold promised that if all went well, we should be flying 10,000 tons a month by next December. Generalissimo Chiang Kai-shek, a true military man, demanded 14,000. So we flew in 12,000 last December, and more than that for each of the following three months. In each case it was more than the Burma Road ever carried. We did this despite the fact that the stuff had to come up over a single-track Bengal-Assam railroad, being lightered over the Brahmaputra River and then reloaded onto cars.

We are very much interested in Stilwell's drive on Myitkyina, for if we can take it before the monsoons and get established there, we can double the tonnage flown into China. I might also mention that our planes flying in there have to carry the gas to fly themselves out, and that sometimes they find that a west wind of 40 miles per hour when they flew to China has a velocity of 100 miles per hour when they try to come out, and they lack the fuel to do it.

Pacific. Our air forces have led the way in all operations in the area, and will continue to do so. The Japs have one track minds; they do stupid things like leaving their planes lined up along air strips for us to knock out; their pilot quality has declined.

The Mediterranean. When we got in the war the Luftwaffe had some 2,600 planes in the Mediterranean area, and controlled it from Gibraltar to the Bosporus. Every Allied convoy entering at Gib was under air attack all the time until it got to its destination. We proposed to change all that. So since that time we and the British have destroyed 5,000 German planes in that area; we have shepherded the army and navy forces of both countries through North Africa; we have taken Sicily, Sardinia, southern Italy, and have reduced the available German air force to something like 300 planes.

Europe. Our design was to smash right into Germany with our precision bombing and knock out the Luftwaffe on the ground and in the air. We were told it couldn't be done. Why not? They wouldn't let us. Who wouldn't? The Luftwaffe. How would they stop us? By putting up too many fighters. But we *wanted* their fighters to come up.

We started in a small way, with a hundred heavy bombers. We developed long range fighters to accompany them. The Germans realized as well as we did what was going to happen, that if they couldn't stop us, we would knock out the Luftwaffe and leave Germany open to all sorts of attacks. So they came up to meet us, and there has ensued, as you know, a terrific battle.

When we started the Germans were producing about 1,300 fighters a month. By last March 1, we had knocked that production down to 300 a month. Bad weather in March allowed the Germans to restore some of that production, getting back to perhaps 400 a month. But we have knocked it down again, and we know positively that their losses run much higher than that. This means in the long run that we are sure to knock them out. They can either stop fighting us or expand their production. Since they can't do either, the ultimate result is plain.

The force of our air attack is still increasing, and as I said before, in a couple of months we shall have enough forces everywhere we want them, with sufficient replacements, to go to town and really find out what an air force can do.

The Army Air Force now has some 34,000 combat planes, and some 17,000 are overseas, including 5,000 heavy bombers. These figures are extra confidential, by the way. At the start of the war we figured our loss would be 20 percent of planes and personnel engaged in combat every month, which would mean 100 percent replacement every five months, or better than twice a year. We cannot say what our casualties actually are, but they have come to a point considerably less than we estimated. Here is an indication: since 1 January we have lost about 860 heavy bombers. That is a lot, but divide it by three months and it works out at an average of about 280 a month. On the basis of 5,000 heavy bombers in combat duty overseas, this is a small rate of loss, since the original 20 percent figure would have indicated losses of approximately 1,000 a month. Thus we estimate our losses of heavy bombers run to something like 5 percent a month, which is bearable.

These bombers have, as I said, done terrible things to German plane production. The Germans have deconcentrated their production facilities into what they call "complexes," in which motors will be produced in one plant, fuselages in another, landing gear in another, all within an area of some 40 square miles, with an assembly plant in the center. To knock out the assembly plant delays them for maybe three weeks. But if we can hit the engine plant, we are knocking out machine tools, and that means a long delay. Our intelligence as to the location of the various plants is excellent, and our bombardiers can hit them, and do.

We have specialized on ball bearings, and have so reduced production that they are getting them from Sweden. This ties in with Cordell Hull's warning to the neutrals and with subsequent developments in the diplomatic field. If the Germans can get ball bearings and machine tools for producing them from Sweden, the work of our bombers is to a considerable degree negated.

Now, as to specific questions. He was asked about Cassino, and his answer seemed to me to be critical of the morale of our ground forces in Italy. He showed us pictures of Cassino, and said the Air Force has wrecked the town utterly, but that it could never fix things so the troops could simply walk in and occupy. If the ground troops aren't willing to pay the cost in blood, the objective simply won't be taken. He made it clear that the same thing is going to be true of the second front when it comes. We know we can destroy the German fortifications, but we also know that we cannot knock the Germans out of the ruins. Our ground forces will have to take them by fighting for them. They won't be able to walk in without cost.

As to German replacement ability. They can rebuild a wrecked plant in three months and have it back in operation. Arnold contrasted this unfavorably with the apparent delicacy of our own industrial setup. It is natural, once you think about it, for our mass production scheme goes all to pot if one cog is knocked out. So we watch the German plants, wait until we see that the roofs are rebuilt and planes are coming out of the assembly door, and go back.

He told of one raid on Bucharest recently in which we knocked out 1,460 railroad freight cars. Imagine, he asked, the howl that would go up if we lost that many freight cars in Chicago, and then estimate the effect on German communications in the Balkans.

As for the B-29, he asked us to be patient. I have been told it will not be used at all in Europe, but will do its job in the Pacific, where its great range will be of more use. Specifically, when we take the Marianas, B-29s based there will be able to hit Tokyo at will.

And that covers it. We are meeting at Nelie Bull's in Alexandria Sunday night, which should produce a most interesting memo. You know who.

Regards

KING'S OPTIMISM—INVASION PLANS OUTLINED

CONFIDENTIAL

Monday
17 April 1944

Dear Bart,

Present: Raymond P. Brandt, *St. Louis Post Dispatch*; Turner Catledge, *New York Times*; Marquis Childs, United Features; Ernest Lindley, *Newsweek*; Paul Miller, Associated Press; Richard Wilson, Cowles Publications; James L. Wright, *Buffalo Evening News*; our host [Nelie Bull], his guest [Admiral King], myself.

As the invasion day draws near, the actual news budget of these conferences grows smaller and smaller. What interested me most was an almost complete change in the general atmosphere since the last conference with this speaker. At that time, you will recall, I reported a distinct note of pessimism that pervaded the entire evening.

Last night no vestige of that note remained. Our guest contemplated the future with apparent equanimity, and not even a discussion of the situation in Burma quenched his enthusiasm for the general prospect. From all of which I am led to the conclusion that the British haven't been annoying him much recently. Also, he has just returned from a ten day rest.

Headlines of the evening would be as follows:

MORE BIG NEWS FROM THE PACIFIC
IN ABOUT TEN DAYS
Still other developments to come later.

INVASION PLANS FOR SECOND FRONT
"SHAKING DOWN NICELY"

Date picked at Teheran remained unchanged, but attacking force doubled in size. Disposition of German defense forces adroit but indicates they do not know place selected for attack. They believe invasion will come earlier than we plan it.

ITALIAN OPERATION HAS BEEN BUNGLED
BY ALLIED COMMAND
Deadlock, however, will be broken.

GERMANY'S COLLAPSE IN 1944 AGAIN SEEMS PROBABLE
Thanks chiefly to Russia's magnificent drive, which has amazed Allied command.

WE WILL ATTACK AND TAKE THE MARIANAS,
BY-PASS PHILIPPINES
Guam is key island in this group, not yet strongly fortified by Japs. Recapture of Philippines sentimentally desirable but would be "eccentric" operation. Might take Mindanao, but will be delayed from three to six months if we have to seize Luzon. We may head straight for Formosa.

HOPE IS VIRTUALLY ABANDONED FOR
REOPENING BURMA ROAD
Expect to reach China coast and open port there before Burma campaign succeeds. Japs now face great victory or great catastrophe in Imphal attack. Mountbatten is in serious difficulty but should be able to triumph. We cannot hope to reach China before 1945.

NEW B-29 DEVELOPS MORE BUGS,
DELAYING ITS USE
Motors are overheating. That has been cured, but new difficulties have arisen. Should now be in use in Pacific but won't be for some time yet.

Invasion. The date was fixed at Teheran within narrow limits, depending wholly on weather forecasts at the time. We must have good weather for our planes. While the Germans think the attack will come sooner than it is coming, they will know pretty well when the time comes because it is impossible to conceal our preparations. They will not know, however, where we intend to strike until we actually do it. Our information as to the disposition of their forces indicates that they have no inkling yet as to our immediate objectives, though their forces have been adroitly disposed to meet any contingency. Several weeks ago the British apparently gave up trying to postpone the invasion date. They have committed themselves at Teheran, and they're stuck with it. The conversation there went something like this:

STALIN: All I want to know is when.
CHURCHILL: (Talked for 20 minutes)
STALIN: But when.

CHURCHILL: (Another 10 minutes)
STALIN: When?
CHURCHILL: Oh well . . . (naming date).
STALIN: Good! That's settled, then. And don't worry. When the time comes I'll take the pressure off so you'll have plenty of time to get set. The Germans will be very busy.

It seems, as a matter of fact, that the Russians are already taking the pressure off us, for the Germans have been forced to withdraw one division from northern France, to our knowledge, and another from the Italian front. The Red Army's sustained drive is regarded by our command as the most magnificent in history, and its ability to maintain its lines of supply is nothing short of incredible to us. Thus our guest's abandoned hope for victory in 1944 has been reborn.

Our situation as to landing craft is good. When the invasion comes, it will be practically possible to walk from England to France, so crowded with boats will the Channel be. That attacking force on D-Day will be nearly 100 percent larger than that originally planned at Teheran. We are counting on the overwhelming force of our attack to ensure its success. For days in advance, our planes will darken the skies over the objectives, bombing out gun and rocket emplacements, supply depots, every highway and rail line, and every junction.

The spearhead of the attack will be American and British divided about fifty-fifty, with a token force of French. Once a beachhead has been established, we will fan out, cutting off the entire peninsula of Brittany from Brest to St. Nazaire, making it possible for our troops and their equipment to land directly on the soil of France thereafter. We will then pour in a total of 50 to 60 American divisions (all we have) and expect to form a battle line along the Seine. A glance at the map will convince you that this page should be burned very promptly. All of southern England during this period will be one great airfield.

How much havoc the Germans can cause with their rocket guns we do not know. We know very little about them, except that we have noted with increasing frequency in reconnaissance flights the appearance of certain installations having an identical pattern and deeply shrouded in protective concrete that may be impervious to our bombs. We suppose these to be rocket gun emplacements. We presume these guns can wipe out London, which will not seriously impair the invasion, since it is not starting from London. If it is possible, however, for the Germans to control the range of their rocket weapons they can play hell with our invasion forces. We assume further that the Germans may contemplate the use of gas in these rocket projectiles and we will be prepared for it.

Arnold has stepped up the tempo of air raids greatly now.

Italy. The belief is that this show has been bungled from the beginning. The commanding general, going into Anzio and finding none of the opposition that we expected, stuck to his orders to the letter instead of improvising in the light of conditions as they existed. If he had marched on in boldly and cut the road to Cassino, he would have played the devil with the Germans, and the whole story might have been different, even though he would have extended his perimeter far beyond the ability of the suply lines to support it in the face of concerted attack.

To make matters worse, both General Clark and General Alexander were present and could have amended his orders had he requested, but neither he nor they took such action, and he has been relieved from his command. Likewise the command at Cassino has not been good, particularly among the low ranking officers whose work and decisions are so important in actual combat.

This will be changed, however, and the deadlock ultimately broken, although we expect to replace the present fighting unit with fresh troops before this is done. Our particular concern is to maintain so much pressure on the Germans that they cannot withdraw to the invasion area without risking in Italy the same kind of debacle they are facing in Russia.

In any attempt to get at our supply routes along the Italian coast, German submarines have recently been attempting to sneak though the Straits of Gilbraltar. We have taken effective measures to stop them, and have sunk three, capturing parts of their crews. We capture some survivors from almost every submarine we sink these days. The men are green and unskilled in comparison with the crews that used to man these boats.

We sink an average of two subs every three days. We have expected that the Germans would ultimately give up trying to get past Gibraltar and start concentrating their forces at the entrance to the Straits, to prey upon our shipping there. Apparently they are getting the same idea. So far as we can discover, the Germans now have not more than 60 submarines in the Atlantic at any one time.

Burma. Report received from Mountbatten yesterday indicated that the Japanese threat to Imphal was serious but that he expected to beat it. Our guest seems to feel that the British would succeed in doing this in their own sweet time and their own peculiar way. British forces there outnumber the Japs substantially, but the Japs have the jungle to use for cover. The Jap attack is daringly planned, and they have managed, somehow, to get two whole divisions up to the plains of Imphal without being discovered in time. They have no supply lines whatever, and can use only the food and munitions they have with them. Their hope is, apparently, to dig in around Imphal for the period of the monsoons, and cut off Stilwell's supplies. If they succeed, Stilwell is sunk, and it would add greatly to Japanese prestige in India. If they fail, they will have taken a heavy loss, both in personnel and face.

Stilwell on his part entertains no hope, apparently, of reopening the Burma Road, but is bent primarily on taking three Japanese air fields from which Zeros are now harassing our flights over the Hump. It's just like sitting ducks for them to bump off our transports. But with these fields taken over, we can fly at much lower altitudes on this route and increase our payloads correspondingly. We are now getting from 12 to 15 thousand tons of stuff a month to Chiang. Of course he always wants 5,000 tons more than we're getting to him.

The opening of the Burma Road itself has ceased to be of great importance, since it cannot be accomplished before we can reasonably expect to take and hold a seaport on the China coast. But the air route will continue to be of tremendous importance, since we have to get supplies to Chennault, upon whom we lean heavily in our plan to occupy a portion of the China coast.

Also, we have to maintain Chiang, who is walking a kind of political tightrope, which makes the situation there every bit as complicated as the one in India, where Wavell and Auchinleck seem to be able to retard all of Mountbatten's efforts despite London and the King. Mountbatten, as you know, has already set up headquarters in Ceylon, chiefly in order to get out of New Delhi and its defeatist atmosphere.

Pacific. Nothing was said about our objective in the next big attack in the Pacific, scheduled in about ten days. More will come regularly thereafter, unless and until the Japanese fleet decides to poke its nose out. Our strategy there is developing rapidly, but only up to a point.

That point is the Marianas. We are by-passing Truk, Rabaul and other Japanese strongholds that could be taken only at great cost. But in doing this we have to take and hold strong bases somewhere. That somewhere is the Marianas, and is presumably Guam, which was described last night as the best island for our purposes in the entire group. Our most advanced bases now are at Kwajalein and Eniwetok.

We hope the Japanese fleet will come out to defend the Marianas. We think they will have to. If they don't, we'll just have to go into the Inland Sea and dig them out. From the Marianas our course is uncertain. The possibility of staging a direct frontal attack upon Japan proper is under consideration now. The temptation to go into the Philippines and clean them out for sentimental reasons is strong, but it would be an "eccentric operation" in the view of our informant, who favors a bold course aimed directly at Formosa.

In this connection, it would be advantageous to take and hold Mindanao, which could be done, we think, with relative ease. We hope we will not have to go after Luzon because of the delay that would be entailed. Our occupation of Mindanao might be expected to come about this year.

Whether Formosa or the Philippines, however our 1945 objective is the coast of China. Picking a spot is exceedingly difficult, because the Japs have torn up most of the scattered railways lines that existed, and there never were any roads or highways. Once we land, therefore, we will have to proceed up the coast in a series of amphibious hops until we get to the point where we can really obtain an avenue of supplies into the interior, where we can successfully exploit Chinese manpower and get a vantage point from which to strike at Japan with our air power.

B-29s. These planes are expected to do marvels in connection with our Pacific operations. They will not, as you know, be used elsewhere at present. They are being turned out now in large numbers, but little faults in the design—inevitable in all new models—are still showing up and delaying their combat appearance, which was scheduled for 1 February, I believe. An unusual number of these faults or bugs have developed under actual operating conditions.

Our guest observed that there is something about service personnel that no test pilot can duplicate. Time after time, he said, he had had new models of planes tested out under every conceivable condition, and in the hands of several different test pilots. But when these planes were given a clean bill of health and turned over to service personnel to fly, the bugs began to show up. The B-29 is in that stage now, he added. He indicated, however, that nothing serious was wrong with them.

The operations of these planes will be controlled by the Joint Chiefs of Staff.

Odds and Ends. Our submarines in the Pacific have been extremely fortunate recently in bagging Japanese tankers right and left. They also sank a convoy trying to get through to Truk, which has been isolated fairly effectively. The Japs, in desperation, have materially strengthened their escorts and are making things hotter for us, particularly through the use of planes. Our new subs, as they come out, will carry heavier anti-aircraft weapons. I suppose we can expect an increase in losses. Nothing was said about it.

Jap plane pilots continue to deteriorate in skill. Moreover, we are taking quite a few more Jap prisoners than we were able to get formerly. This is construed to indicate a letdown in Japanese morale, and a growing realization that they can't win.

While the Army continues to call for more men, the Navy will not. It will stand on its present quota, which will be full in September, probably—and thereafter will ask for no more manpower despite the fact that new ships are coming along all the time. Admirals at sea are already squawking and are expected to squawk some more, but to no purpose, even if it is necessary to retire some of the older ships.

Something is distinctly rotten about the Battle of Savo Island. In that encounter, you will recall, we lost three ships and the Australians lost the cruiser *Canberra*. Admiral Hepburn was sent out to make a full investigation, and he questioned virtually everyone connected with the affair. His report went to Nimitz, who commented on it and passed it along to King, who commented on it and sent it along to the Australian government and to the British.

The original intention was to release the findings when they were available. Now, however, they have been locked away in a safe, and will not be released until after the war. I don't know the dirt on it. Maybe I will later. Meanwhile the report has been going around that these ships fired upon and sank one another. This was flatly denied last night.

Regards

PATTERSON TALKS WITH REPORTERS

CONFIDENTIAL

Thursday
4 May 1944

Dear Bart,

As you know, the Thursday Evening Supper and Study Club met last night with Judge Robert Patterson, Assistant Secretary of War. Present were Pete Brandt, *St. Louis Post-Dispatch*; Paul Wooton, *New Orleans Times-Picayune*; Walker Buel, *Cleveland Plain Dealer*; Dewey Fleming, *Baltimore Sun*; John O'Brien, *Philadelphia Inquirer*; Jim Wright, *Buffalo Evening News*; Dick Wilson, Cowles Publications; Bert Andrews, *New York Herald Tribune*; Ted Alford, *Kansas City Star*; Roscoe Drummond, *Christian Science Monitor*; Herbert Bayard Swope, and myself.

Some of what was said can be printed without attribution. I intend to write the manpower angle myself tomorrow morning. However, to retain cohesiveness, and have the whole thing together, I shall cover the high spots that Judge Patterson touched on, both on and off the record.

Manpower. The Army as of today had 3,300,000 men overseas. By the end of the year it will have 5,000,000 overseas. We do not as yet know what our replacement needs will be in the European push. It is possible that our casualties will not be as heavy as we expect, just as our Air Force casualties have not been nearly as heavy as we had feared. However, we are up against a very tough business, and they may run even heavier. We just don't know, and in the meantime we have to be prepared for anything.

The crying need today is for young men. The largest pool of such men is on the country's farms. Those farms have 600,000 men under 26, and of these 400,000 are under 22. The Army wants to get these men, but thus far General Hershey—who, by the way, is not under the Army's authority, but gets his orders direct from the President—has not desired to tangle with the Senate farm bloc, and has left them alone.

Patterson argues that Hershey could get these men tomorrow if he would. There is no law preventing it. But thus far he has been combing industry, on the theory that when he has got all there is out of industry the farm leaders will be shamed into allowing Selective Service to draft young farmers.

The Army, in this set-up, calls upon Selective Service to furnish men in certain numbers, as does the Navy. But the trouble is that the Army has found that it cannot count upon getting the numbers for which it asks, which makes for a difficult situation. Despite this, the Army got up to its planned strength in April, but is worried about the replacement situation when the big fighting starts.

Tying in with this is Judge Patterson's flat statement that we now have an enormous food surplus, except in some few commodities. The Army, the Navy and Lend-Lease have got the food they need, and there is still a tremendous amount left over. And if War Food's plans for this summer pan out, there will be an even bigger surplus next year.

Patterson believes that we are out of the woods on food, barring a disastrous drought—which, he points out, could hardly be ameliorated even by putting the entire Army on the farms to work. In other words, his position is that our food situation is such that it is no longer necessary as a war move to keep the young men on the farm. Therefore, they should be drafted, leaving the older people to keep the farms going.

Patterson believes farm people are as patriotic as anyone else, and is inclined to blame the farm bloc in Congress for the difficulty in getting young farmers into the armed services.

The Judge would also like to see some direction of activities of 4-F boys, but doubts there will be any National Service Act this year, anyway. As to war labor, it has been his experience that in such plants as Boeing, making the B-29, and other industries in which the workers have good conditions, and where they are producing tangible weapons that can be used against the enemy, there is no shortage. But labor is hard to get for such hard and dirty jobs as foundry work, casting, etc.

Reverting to youth for the Army, Patterson says the young men are fast being weeded out of home service units and being sent overseas, their places being taken by older men. The average age of the Army, he said, is 25, as against 23 for the Navy and 22 for the Marines. This is in considerable part due to the fact that in 1942 Draft Boards began sending along large numbers of older men. The Army was finally compelled to put a stop on men over 37. Patterson himself wanted 35 as the top limit, Selective Service wanted 40, and they split the difference. Men over 37 aren't useful. They can't, as a general rule, stand up to the work.

Negro Troops. Patterson admitted frankly that Negroes are sore about the treatment colored troops have been getting. That is, Negroes feel they should be given an opportunity to show that they are good in combat. We have recently started one Negro division on its way to the Pacific. In time of peace there are two Negro cavalry and two infantry regiments, and they are excellent. But they haven't been used yet for combat.

The truth is that area commanders in the normal course of things get the troops they want. They take the position that they cannot shoulder responsibility if they can't have them. And they don't seem to want colored troops. At least, they don't ask for them. Patterson's attitude seemed to be that it was a tough situation, but that it had to stand as it was. It was remarked to him that there was considerable hard feeling among Negroes on the point. He answered simply, "Yes, I suppose there is."

B-29. Patterson refers to this as our decisive aerial weapon. It will be used in the Pacific only, its great range not being needed in Europe. It has an unloaded range of 6,000 miles, and a range of 3,300 miles with ten tons of bombs. Last October the B-29 was in arrears, and General William Knudsen was put on the job. He was ordered to get 200 planes by 1 March. He got 205, and Patterson commented that no other man in America could have done it. Apparently the engines were the difficulty. Already 100 of the planes have gone overseas. They apparently have to fly the Atlantic in order to get to the Pacific area where they can be used. Supply is the problem.

The fact is that we are still confronted with a shortage of tankers, and when you consider the amount of fuel a B-29 will burn you see that this presents difficulties. It is not to be expected that the B-29 will get into combat for some weeks yet.

While on the subject of supply, Patterson figures our need for tonnage will increase rather than decrease after the invasion starts.

Neutrals. Patterson favors putting real pressure on Sweden and Switzerland, especially the former. He points out that Germany gets more help from Sweden than she ever got from Spain. Through no desire of their own, but through German force, both Sweden and Switzerland must be regarded as part of the German war effort, Patterson says. Sweden sends high grade iron ore, timber, ball bearings and machinery to Germany. Switzerland sends fuses and precision instruments. It is pretty tough for us when our planes knock out German production and then see the Nazis turn to the bomb-proof (because neutral) plants of neighboring countries. The Swedes, he says, know we won't attack them if they refuse to do as we say. They fear the Germans will. So they naturally play ball with the latter and not with us.

Patterson says we are sending four basic rations to Sweden: petroleum (120,000 tons a quarter), hides and leather, textiles, food. These goods are carried in Swedish ships and are inspected by the Germans. The State Department says the Swedes get all the stuff we send. Patterson is convinced that as a practical matter the Germans grab some of it. He thinks we should cut off these supplies, since whether they go directly to Sweden or not, they still help the German war effort.

Toward the close of the evening, the discussion was directed toward Army Public Relations, which are seldom Army in the sense of experienced military contacts, frequently not public, and sometimes hardly even relations. The greatest loss the press here has suffered was when Col. Fitzgerald was sent overseas. He was always available, and always knew the answers. He was, in consequence, invaluable. Al Warner, who replaced him, is a nice guy and an able newsman. He wants to be helpful, but he simply hasn't the military background. Fitz was so good that generals used to come to him to find out what was going on.

It was suggested to Patterson that a general, no less, be detailed to the sole duty of acting as press liaison the way Fitz was. Patterson didn't commit himself, but we are hopeful that he will do something about it. Swope appeared convinced.

There is also the possibility that once the invasion starts, King and Marshall will make joint statements weekly on the progress of affairs. That would be helpful, but not as much so as a press contact who knows his stuff, will talk if he trusts you, and is always available.

I find more and more feeling in the War Department that it is not going to be so easy to tell when the real invasion actually starts. Phelps and I are trying to work things out.

And that's all of Patterson. For your information, I get from other sources the news that Marshall and Arnold are either in London or en route there. I am quite sure they will return here before the big blow-off in Europe.

Also that the Navy has a remarkable new bomb that is detonated by some sort of emanation from the target if the target is metallic. It is supposed to be a never-miss proposition, that's all I know about it.

Regards

PROPOSED DEPARTMENT OF NATIONAL DEFENSE—RUSSIA AIMS FOR WORLD PEACE AND COLLABORATION

CONFIDENTIAL

Friday
12 May 1944

Dear Bart,

I have got a great deal of material for you. This is going to be a long memorandum, and every word of it is hot.

First, as to Mr. Forrestal. The Thursday Evening Supper and Study Club were guests aboard his yacht, YHB9, on Wednesday night, just after his nomination [as Secretary of the Navy] was sent in. We steamed down the river as far as Mount Vernon, had a buffet supper and some interesting talk. Present were Paul Leach, *Chicago Daily News*; Bill Murphy, *Philadelphia Inquirer*; Pete Brandt, *St. Louis Post-Dispatch*; Roscoe Drummond, *Christian Science Monitor*; Jim Wright, *Buffal Evening News*; Paul Wooton, *New Orleans Times-Picayune*; Dewey Fleming, *Baltimore Sun*; Ted Alford, *Kansas City Star*; Vice Admiral Horne; Rear Admiral Radford (naval aviation), Commander Mumma, Forrestal's aide; Forrestal, myself.

Conversation ranged over a variety of subjects, but centered mostly on the proposed formation of a Department of National Defense. The Navy does not favor it, especially at this time. Here are the reasons educed last night:

1) Efficiency and cooperation derive from individual personalities that can work together, and not from any particularly set-up. The Army and the Navy are, on the whole, cooperating very well in this war. The reason is that the top officers, as well as the top civilians, work smoothly together. A Department of National Defense would not necessarily eliminate Army-Navy friction. Men can be at odds within an organization quite as well as in different organizations. Thus the proposed department might or might not meet this test, depending on the men involved. Further, it might work smoothly under one administration and badly under another.

2) The Department of National Defense would presumably—since economy is one of the main reasons for it—have a common Division of Supply. This has been tried in France and Great Britain. Both times the results have been that the Supply Service has forced on the military the weapons it thinks they ought to have, rather than the other way about.

Whether this happened in the United States or not, the common supply service would certainly end the present keen competition between the services in the development of weapons. Competition is obviously essential to progress, and while the Franklin Field relationship has its disadvantages, civilized competition between the services has proved a most valuable asset for the United States.

Example: the Army went for water-cooled plane motors. The Navy stuck with air-cooled. Had it not done so, we might have been in real trouble when war came. A unified Division of Ordnance would presumably choose one or the other, and the element of competition would be lost. Further example: the Navy developed the Norden bomb sight and then turned it over to the Army when it proved better suited than anything that service had for use against fixed ground objects. Would there have been such a development with Supply or Ordnance Service? Nobody can say, but there is a reasonable doubt.

3) Size does not connote efficiency. On the contrary, it usually means sluggishness. The Department of National Defense would be so huge and unwieldy that it might bog down into a futile organization. Business history shows that the smaller and more alive organizations are the ones that

develop new products and processes most of the time. United States Steel didn't bring out the stainless alloy steels that have been so valuable in the war. They were developed by smaller companies which forced them on the big ones. Size too often means red tape, and inefficiency.

4) The Navy frankly concedes that economies can be effected through common purchases in some instances. Food and cloth are purchased jointly right now, and the Navy sees no reason why this should not continue without unification. On the other hand, there are many fields in which no gains could be effected. Example: an 8-inch gun for the Army and an 8-inch gun for the Navy are completely different animals. The same is true of anti-aircraft guns. Due to constricted space, the Navy mounts four barrels in a group. The Army mounts one. Of course, small arms munitions and such stuff can be and are purchased jointly.

5) The Navy is determined to keep control of its own air force, and suspects most of the pressure for unification comes from the Air Force, which wants those Navy planes. The British Fleet Air Arm was at its inception part of the RAF, and was kind of a Devil's Island to which unsatisfactory pilots were banished. It received such antiquated equipment that the raid on Taranto that hurt the Italian fleet so badly had to be carried out with ten-year old planes that carried only one torpedo apiece.

On this point, you will recall that Judge Patterson told us the Army didn't want the Navy's carrier-based planes, and believed they should remain in the Navy.

6) The Navy feels that the Army will, after the war, lapse quite a lot from its present strength, whereas the navy will continue at more or less its present pitch. They believe the Army knows this, and is trying to ride the Navy's coat-tails when it comes to appropriations. Also Admiral Horne asserted—with complete lack of accuracy, in my judgment—that Army officers are slick politicians while the Navy officers are naive country boys, with the result that the Army would city-slick the hell out of them.

I feel that it will be most unfortunate all around if this last reason dominates Navy thinking, for that kind of service jealousy is the thing the unificationists are in large measure shooting at. As for the other reasons, I am quite sympathetic to them, and the Navy has got a real case if it would only stick to it.

So much for unification. Let's turn to the Pacific. Our Navy people are convinced that the Japanese Navy has suffered very severe losses in carriers, cruisers and destroyers. They are supposed to have left just two modern carriers, although more are presumably being built. On the other hand, the signs are multiplying that the Japanese high command doesn't intend to use its fleet until it can operate in constricted waters with land-based air. This will do much to offset the losses in the various categories, especially since the Japs will be fighting near home, while we shall be working at the ends of very long supply lines.

Still, our fleet travels with a very complete train, even including a floating drydock. It can operate efficiently at great distances, which is one advantage we have over the British Navy. The latter is tied to land bases, and is restricted to something like a thousand miles from those bases. We can go five times as far.

I forgot to say that Artemis Gates, Assistant Secretary of the Navy for Air, was also aboard. He said that while Japanese pilot personnel has gone downhill in quality, there is some reason to believe that a backlog of first class pilots is still available, being held on Jap carriers for any showdown fight that might occur.

Japan's big disadvantage in this war is an inferior industrial potential. The men with whom we spoke that night are sure the individual fighting man is very good. They think Japan took a long gamble in attacking a nation with our productive ability, but that it wasn't such a bad gamble from the enemy's point of view. The Japs figured the Germans would take Moscow and that Russia would be defeated. They figured that Britain was so tied up with Germany that she couldn't take on Japan too. They figured that we had gone soft so that even if we fought at all we wouldn't wage a tough war.

Events have showed how each of these calculations has gone sour, and it is easy to imagine just how badly the Jap high command feels about its war.

Forrestal spoke about Russia. He noted that people are coming increasingly to realize that our republican form of government is neither understood nor coveted in countries such as Russia, Yugoslavia, etc. If we are going to get along with them, we have got to have a realistic appreciation of this fact, and must accept the difficulties under which we will labor. Our form of government is expensive to the point of luxury, which is all right as long as it applies to this country alone, but will make it hard for us to compete, especially economically, in world markets with countries that have no labor standards or regard for the common man.

———————

Now for Stettinius, who saw the press off-the-record a few days ago. Here are some of the highlights:

The European Advisory Council has taken a new lease on life. It was developed to provide a continuous conference table so that the three major allies could deal jointly instead of trilaterally with European problems of mutual concern. It turned out to be a fearful flop. It was given little to do, and didn't do that. Talks were almost always Anglo-Russian or Anglo-American. But it is coming to life. Its role is to be enlarged, its responsibilities broadened, and its procedures more clearly worked out.

The formation of a United Nations Executive Council, in implementation of the Declaration of Moscow, is still in the informal discussion stage. It is possible that the framework of this organization will be brought into being before the war ends.

American, British and Russian representatives are making very satisfactory progress in plans for the occupation of Germany. There has been no serious disagreement, and all three nations will share in the task. Studies are also in progress for the treatment of Germany both in the armistice and post-war periods.

It seems generally accepted that this country shall retain and operate in the interests of the common peace the military bases taken from the Japanese in the Pacific, including the former mandated islands.

Stettinius' mission was in essence to strengthen the machinery of Anglo-American diplomacy. Except for Hull's brief stop on his way to Moscow, no high-ranking State Department official had been in London for two years. His mission was a success.

Finally, Averill Harriman [U.S. Ambassador to Russia] held an off-the-record press conference at the State Department yesterday. I made quite a few notes, and will run through what he said as he said it.

He began by noting that in general the Russian government is attached to world collaboration and security. There is genuine interest in working with us. He finds no reservations in the desire and the will to collaborate with us and Britain in world planning and security. This, he said, is both realistic and increasingly obvious. The Russians are interested in questions involving all parts of the world. There is no world problem abut which Moscow is not anxious for information.

The Russians, he said, are very close-mouthed until they have decided what they are going to do. Sometimes it takes them a long while. But when they have decided, they are very frank and forthright in speaking out. One of our difficulties is that there are some problems which we have studied for a long time, but which are new to the Russians. They are taking their time in studying them and making up their minds. He did not specify what problems. He added that there is a tremendous interest in all aspects of the United States throughout Russia.

He admitted frankly that there are real difficulties facing an understanding of Russia. Some of the Russian policies and statements make us suspicious of their revolutionary intent. This we have got to expect, he said. We have, he added, been somewhat over-enthusiastic about Russia following the Moscow Conference. Our feeling tended to be that a good relationship had been fully established, and that from then on we would walk together without difficulty. This, he pointed out, was simply not feasible in view of Russia's historic policy of isolation and the mutual suspicions that grew up after the Revolution. He believes there has to be a certain disillusionment to restore the balance, and he expressed gratification that it had come now, so it can be out of the way. Patience and understanding will be necessary on both sides to work matters out satisfactorily, he went on.

Then he turned to a report on the Russian attitude toward Poland. The break in relations came about a year ago, and Harriman says it was not an idle act. Russian views on the subject he finds have been consistent ever since. The Russians believe that General Sosnokowski and the military group dominate the Polish government in exile, and that Sosnokowski is going on the twin principles of a "strong" Poland and ultimate war with the Soviet Union.

The Red Army, Harriman commented, is not going to be used to put into power in Poland any regime with ideas like that. The real Russian worry, however, is that Germany may recover her strength and that the military spirit to turn it into another attempt at conquest will not die. Russia simply won't stand for neighbors who will flirt with Germany in view of that possibility.

Moscow, he said, is ready to deal with the democratic elements in the Polish government in exile if that government broke up so that the military caste could be kicked out. When the Red Army gets to Poland it does so under orders to be friendly to the Polish people in the belief that this will lead to friendly relations between Poland and Russia in general. He has seen no evidence of any attempt to communize Poland or to establish a puppet government. Moscow, he said, is not playing up the Polish Committee there. (I'm reporting, not commenting, you will note.)

He believes the Soviet pattern for dealing with neighbor states is to be found in the agreement with [President] Benes which manifests no interest in Czech affairs. Only time and events, he went on, can prove if things will work out as expected. He said he had no information, and volunteered that he doubted if anyone else had, as to how Poles in Poland feel about things today.

It is his guess that an acceptable solution to the Polish question will be found if the Polish people react favorably. The Russians, in their interest for world collaboration, are not eager to make Poland an issue between us. However, peace along the Russian borders Moscow regards as vital, and peace there will be. Harriman believes the Curzon Line, probably with some adjustments favorable to Poland, will ultimately be the basis for negotiations.

Harriman was asked how seriously he takes the dissolution of the Commintern. He takes it seriously. The Russian government, he said, is interested in peace and collaboration, and the Commintern was an interference with such an objective. However, Harriman discounts talk that Russia is moving rapidly toward capitalism. The revolutionary spirit is strong in Russia still, and you find considerable interest in all radical activities everywhere. But he believes this interest will not take the form of Russian leadership of world revolution.

Decentralization of the Foreign Affairs Commissariat, he said, makes for greater interest in such matters throughout the country, but decisions are still taken in Moscow.

Harriman sees no indication of an imperialistic attitude on the part of Russia beyond the limits of already stated demands. That is, Karelia from Finland, eastern Poland from Poland, the Baltic States. In this connection, he indicated that he did not take very seriously the Free Germany committee in Moscow. I gather he regards it as essentially a weapon in psychological warfare.

He finds in Russia violent hatred of Germany. He said he was satisfied that the stories of atrocities committed by the Germans are essentially correct. There is plenty of evidence. The indemnity demand on Finland he referred to as an indication of the way Russia might go after Germany. That indemnity, as you know, would be utterly beyond Finland's ability to pay.

The post-war Russian attitude toward Germany will be very tough. There will be both retribution and punishment, and these will be combined with an effort to break Germany's lust for conquest. Appeasement as a propaganda line for Germany has lessened. Probably the Russians think the Germans know darned well what they have done to Russia, and simply don't believe the Russians would be kind once the Wehrmacht is beaten. In this connection, the Red Army intends to destroy the German Army so it will never rise again.

The talk then turned to Russo-Jap relations. The less said about them the better, Harriman believes. Mention of that situation is not in the interests of the United States. He believes Russia will join us after Germany is beaten, especially since Russia regards itself as a world power with interests in both hemispheres, as it is, of course.

He was asked if this country was consulted by Moscow on the Polish and kindred problems. The answer was that our policy is not to become involved in boundary questions until peace has come. In a general way he said, however, that Russia has been very meticulous in consulting us, with the exception of the Italian move. In return they expect us to consult them.

As to Yugoslavia, Russia is supporting the people who are fighting, to wit, those of Marshal Tito. They regard Mikhailovitch as a German collaborator. Moscow has given no indication about its feelings as to a future Yugoslav government. (I'm still just reporting, pal.)

Moscow, he went on, hopes for a peaceful and friendly relationship with China, and hopes that the present difficulties between Chungking and the Communists in Northern China can be worked out.

As for Finland, Moscow regards the terms as fair, but it looks as though the Finns are too suspicious of Russia to trust them to keep the terms. Harriman believes Russia would observe them. He doesn't see that the Finns have anything to gain in the way of better terms.

Finally, the Russians regard the United States as anxious to cooperate. When the press is critical of Russia, Moscow expresses doubt that the American press reflects American opinion. The Russians, he concluded, are realists, and will work with any administration, but they tend to think in terms of Roosevelt, and they would like to see him reelected.

And that's all from Washington at this time.

Regards

Secretary of the Navy Knox died of a sudden heart attack on 14 April 1944, and the Assistant Secretary, James Forrestal, was sworn in as his successor on 19 May 1944. A day or so later his civilian aide, Eugene Duffield, telephoned me and asked if I would come to his office. I did, promptly, and the following lengthy conversation took place:

"Mr. Perry, Secretary Forrestal knows all about your King conferences. He has asked me to urge you to continue them just as you have been doing."

"We certainly intend to continue them. And thanks very much for giving me the word."

As I returned to the *Sun* office, I reflected that it had never occurred to me to think about whether the Skipper (which was what I had called King ever since I found myself quite unable to accede to his suggestion that the members of the Arlington County Commandos call him Ernie) had or had not cleared the whole idea with the Secretary of the Navy before agreeing to meet with us.

I wasn't too proud of myself for not realizing from the start that he would have done nothing of the sort without clearing it with the civilian brass, since he well knew that Cabinet members react badly when surprised by things like hitherto unheard-of-conferences by the Navy's top officer with a small group of newsmen, however distinguished and discreet. I am sure Secretary Knox's journalistic background made it much easier for him to grasp the possibilities of the idea.

PREDICTIONS OF LONG, DIFFICULT MOP-UP OPERATION IN GERMANY

CONFIDENTIAL

Undated, but probably in early September, 1944

Dear Bart,

Bill Murphy of the *Philadelphia Inquirer* gave an off-the-record dinner party Tuesday evening with Field Marshal Sir Henry Maitland Wilson, British member of the Combined Chiefs of Staff, as guest. I sat in for

Phelps. This is a brief outline of how he sketched the war. Of course it is understood to be completely confidential.

First, concerning the German situation: He started off by pointing out that Hitler went into the war with practically 300 crack, highly trained divisions, all imbued with the Hitler philosophy. The High Command estimates that Hitler now has under arms between 150 and 175 divisions made up from 25 to 50 percent of the veteran storm troopers and SS troops but filled in with raw recruits and youths ranging from 15 to 25 years of age. These latter are the most fanatical of all and the worst to handle. While Germany has been occupied in large part, the Hitler military force is still far from beaten.

Sir Henry pictures the war as a long drawn out conflict which will have to center on cleaning up pockets. The Ruhr, the first pocket, is fairly well taken care of now because that was not fortified for long defense as a separate unit. The Holland pocket, covering north Holland, Bremen and Hamburg is a bad situation. That is stocked with provisions and supplies for a long siege, and because of the water hazards is a difficult military operation.

Norway presents another terrific problem. Because of the terrain and the heavy fortifications, it will take months to blast the Germans out of Norway. He sees little chance for a long time of breaking through from the sea to Bremen and Hamburg and opening these ports for short-line communications.

Helgoland and the islands off northern Germany are tremendous fortresses where the Germans have laid in great supplies for a long siege, and the waters are so thoroughly mined and guarded by radar and small submarines that it is simply impossible for the Allies to get a ship through that area. The mining and the little submarine boats fill the estuaries all the way up to the debarkation ports. The Germans have practically given up their big submarine operations and are concentrating everything on the little submarines which can get into the shallow waters well up to the estuaries and along the coast near to shore, making the invasion of that section doubly difficult.

Sailors and seamen in large numbers are being withdrawn from all kinds of German shipping, put into uniform and sent into land fighting forces. Among those who have been captured far inland from Bremen, many prisoners have complained bitterly of their having been drafted, and there is the possibility of a revolt from that quarter, but the sailormen are pushed to the front with pistols at their heads and haven't much of a chance of saying anything about it.

On the Continent: With Germany cut in half following a union of the Allied and Russian forces, he estimates there will be an army of 25, 30 or even more divisions in the north section which will constitute a separate pocket and mean another long battle. The army in south Germany will be equally strong but less concentrated and fortified. The Germans are holding off everything they have as they move frantically to establish their national redoubt in the Alps and the southern section of Germany. He estimates that will cover an area of about 80 square miles. Between 150,000 to 200,000 troops, armed and provisioned for a six-month siege will be in that redoubt. They are already moving there in large numbers and have access to the area through eastern passages.

How to deal with the last surviving German Nazi Army after the other pockets are wiped out poses a problem which the Allies will have to meet. Can that army be treated as a national force, or as an outlaw gangster force? If the Allies determine to brand the redoubt army as outlaws, they can be gassed and eliminated, but it will take a combined action of the Allies to make that declaration since no single nation would care to take on such a responsibility. That's a tough one.

As to the situation in Italy: Our offensive there now is designed wholly to keep the Nazis engaged so they cannot withdraw troops to either battle front in Germany. Hitler recently tried to transfer one division from Italy to Vienna, and it took a month for what ordinarily would be a four-day trip. The troop trains were strafed and bombed. Half the division was destroyed and the other half was supposed to have gone into the redoubt.

Now the Germans appear to have given up hope of getting reinforcements from that area and are trying to hold with a view to harvesting the fall crops from the rich Po valley which, it is estimated, could be moved into the redoubt to supply an army of 150,000 for several months.

The Pacific Front: Sir Henry parried all queries regarding Britain's plan for transferring supplies as soon as possible to the Pacific. As you know, that is a sore spot with the Allies and our High Command is pretty angry about it. He said the fleet is already in the Pacific, based off Sydney and is being used as a task force to relieve our forces and engage in actual battle as it has been doing. The impression he gave was that Britain would not transfer infantry forces to the Pacific area, but he did indicate that Britain's plan might and probably would be to go through the Suez, drive through India and open a second front from that area. That, of course, obviously would be designed primarily to recapture the British possessions in the South Pacific.

He said that Franz Von Papen has surrendered on condition that he be given the first opportunity to go back into the Ruhr area, where he has large financial holdings. Von Papen thinks he has a chance of setting up a new government succeeding Hitler's, and becoming the new big boss of Germany.

The Allies estimate that there will be at least 25 to 30 million people in Germany, including soldiers, civilians who have lost their homes, and all the rest of a motley crew to be taken care of by the Allies in some way after the war. And that already is one of the major problems on the Allied agenda.

The Field Marshal is ponderous. He must weigh close to 300 pounds. He is more than 200 percent British and is very friendly and likeable. He speaks as deliberately as an elephant walks. The newspapermen talking about it afterwards said that he didn't measure up at all to King and Marshall and our other high commanders who run circles around him, but that in this particular situation he may have been rather cautious and restrained because he wasn't familiar with the American off-the-record system.

Regards

1945

Admiral King had a session with the Arlington County Commandos in Phelps Adams' house in Arlington, Virginia, in January of 1945. Several things had happened to bring this about. There had been a prolonged hiatus in background sessions coincident with the greatly stepped up military activity brought about by the Invasion and ensuing combat in France, the Low Countries, and, rather quickly, all things considered, in Germany. So far as military matters were concerned, all this made Washington a news backwater. The Kings and the Marshalls had little time for talking. And the big news was breaking thousands of miles away.

There was another factor. World wars are all very well, but it was clear that President Roosevelt was going to run for a fourth term and that he would be opposed by Governor Thomas E. Dewey of New York, who had unsuccessfully sought the Republican nomination four years earlier, setting up a real blood match. Alice Longworth had been quite wrong when she said you had to know the Governor well to dislike him. I managed it in one easy lesson and, I guess, so did the President.

As I said, world wars are all very well, but a national election is IMPORTANT for Americans, and so far as men whose primary occupation is politics are concerned, it is an over-riding mission. These two situations—the land war in Europe and the election campaign—explain, I am quite sure, the dearth of memoranda from June to December of 1944. There were, for example, two national conventions to be covered.

Also, on June 10, 1944, Nelie Bull died of a sudden heart attack while talking with his boss, Admiral Gatch, at the latter's desk. Phelps and I had alternated in attending the King sessions in Alexandria. The two of us had a conference with Comminch, and it was decided that the best solution would be to shift the meeting site to Phelps' lovely home across the road from the Washington Golf and Country Club in Arlington.

I suppose, as the originator of the meetings, that I might

have been the logical successor to Nelie as host, but the Perrys lived in a three-room apartment in the third alphabet Northwest, a place quite unsuitable for such occasions as these. And since the rule was that no paper could have more than one representative at any one session, this let me out, and the last one I covered was in the late spring of 1944.

Finally, it was in the summer of 1944 that Harold Brayman asked me to become Assistant Director of Du Pont's Public Relations Department. After thinking it over, and making a trip to Wilmington to meet with the Vice President-Adviser on public relations, I accepted the offer. A wise and worldly man once said that one should never give a reason for something he had done, because everyone else will come up with reasons and he can pick the one that was most satisfactory to him. In my case there were several. There was no longer any doubt as to who was going to win the war, which removed a chief reason for my declining a couple of offers from *Look* a year or so before. Financial considerations were important. I could see no way in which working for the *Sun* would enable me to make provision for the future of my family. And, as military and naval writer for the *Sun*, I no longer had much to do. Phelps covered both the Marshall and King Conferences, he was a member of the Overseas Writers and the Thursday Night Supper and Study Club. And finally, I wondered if, after the excitement of the war, the post-war period in Washington might not be a little flat. I began my new job on October 1, 1944, my 41st birthday.

Anyway, the January King session began dramatically when Admiral King stepped into the Adams living room and said, calmly, "Gentlemen, at this moment our forces are entering Linguyan Gulf."

The legendary Bart, to whom all but one or two of these memoranda were addressed, was a special guest at this meeting, so that there was no need for a memorandum to New York. Bart made a few notes when he got back to New York, and suggested a year or so ago that I see what I could make of them (he being 88 at the time he made the suggestion).

The following points were made in his notes:
- China's situation was improving. Stettinius and Hurley had made some progress toward a rapprochement with Chiang. Also, General Wedemeyer was getting

everything that Stilwell had asked for and been denied.

- As to our objectives opposite Japan, there was no mention of the destruction of the Empire. However, we intended to keep our flag in the Marianas, protect all roads to the Philippines, and keep Tokyo under control. There are 100,000 Japs in the East Indies who have the Dutch worried. It is their problem. Also it will be up to the British to restore their own possessions. There are 150,000 Japs who are NOT withering on the vine in New Guinea and New Britain. They are growing their own food and are self-supporting. This must be cleaned up.
- The Japanese withdrawal from Burma is messed up. Trucks try to get over the Hump piecemeal, and are piled up with no means of moving.
- Admiral King gave the impression that he preferred not to have the British fleet active in the Pacific after Germany was beaten, since he did not hold with multinational commands at sea.
- The Black Sea has been opened up, a possibility mentioned by him as desirable in an earlier memorandum, saving our shipping much time in getting munitions to Russia.
- Submarines are improving, and are increasingly hard to detect. It is not clear whether he meant theirs or ours, or both.
- It was King's idea that the French should undertake to provide food for the Italians, since they had a good harvest last year. He also sees France as the best source of manpower for cleaning out isolated German garrisons.
- Something new had been added to the conference, I gather. The presence of Senator Harry Byrd of Virginia and Eugene Meyer, publisher of the *Washington Post*, is mentioned.

By the time of this conference, maybe earlier, the *Sun*'s Washington Bureau seems to have fallen into super-awareness of the need for security. The more sensitive memoranda were mailed to Mr. Bartnett's home in New Rochelle. There was a proliferation of pseudonyms. Admiral King had long since vanished, to become The Thin Man. General Marshall was now, simply, The MAN. And in the memorandum that follows we have a man "hereinafter to be known as G," who could only have been, and in fact was, James F. Byrnes, Director of War Mobilization and generally regarded as Assistant President. He was also, at one time or another, Secretary of State, Justice of the United States Supreme Court, Governor of South Carolina. But for the opposition of organized labor, he would almost surely have been elected Vice President in 1944, and would have become President instead of Mr. Truman when Mr. Roosevelt died in 1945.

BYRNES REPORTS ON YALTA CONFERENCE

CONFIDENTIAL

Monday
21 February 1945

Dear Bart,

Our guest (hereinafter referred to as G) has just returned from the Yalta Conference in the Crimea, as you know, and the discussion, up to the last few moments, was devoted exclusively to this, no mention being made of domestic difficulties until he was on his feet and starting to walk out the door. The ensuing exchange yielded little of persuasive interest, and I won't bother with it.

Like everyone who has returned from Russia, he has been tremendously impressed by Joseph Stalin. I have yet to meet a man in Washington who has met and talked with Stalin who does not come back singing his praises. That guy must really have something.

G proved to be the best source of information we have yet found about these international conferences. Because of the President's increasing deafness, G took stenographic notes of the entire conversation for the President's protection. He made it clear that FDR himself missed much of what was said at the meetings. His left ear is virtually useless, and anything that was said on that side of the table was likely to be missed.

Therefore G felt that since he knew shorthand, he had better make a complete transcript. Churchill had a man doing the same, as did Stalin. G said he is going to put all his notes together some day "for his own pleasure," but if he follows the practice of other New Dealers, another book is about to be born. Looks like he may have competition from Winston this time, though.

The closeness with which he followed the discussions, however, enabled him to repeat whole speeches made by Stalin, and at many points he stressed the fact that he was using Stalin's exact words.

They got down to business quickly. Stalin was his charming and genial self throughout, except when the subject of Poland was broached. On that point he talked in deadly earnest, bluntly and passionately, without resort to any of the mordant humor that spiced his conversation on other occasions. Whenever he spoke, his own earnestness brought him to his feet before he had finished, despite the fact that no one else at the table rose when talking.

It looked bad at the start. (The Thin Man the other day told me that many of the sessions had been "very intense." G made the same thing clear without actually saying it.) FDR pointed out that our national honor was at stake in a large degree in the question of providing a truly Polish government for Poland. Stalin responded that he recognized this, but that his own national honor was equally involved. For a while it looked as though the three would come away with two of us recognizing the London Government and the third the Lublin Government. It was evident to all, however, that this must not be allowed to happen—that complete agreement must be reached.

G said that time after time Stalin proved his readiness to compromise; that throughout he proved to be tractable and to possess a malleable mind. He made concession after concession. When both he and the President had made the opening statements of their positions, he said, very earnestly: "I would not want to do anything that would embarrass the President of the United States." Then he offered to agree to an extension of the Lublin Government to embrace elements of other Polish political groups. He pointed out that he must have a friendly government behind his lines. Expressing it with characteristic simplicity, he said: "I cannot march on Berlin while I keep my eyes fixed on Warsaw."

He declared that 202 Russian soldiers had been assassinated by the Polish underground, not as a gesture of emnity toward the Soviet, but in order to obtain arms for use against other Poles.

Churchill challenged this statement, saying he had never heard of these assassinations before. It was suggested that Stalin produce at the conference the heads of the Lublin Government and the underground leaders so that the true facts of the matter might be ascertained. The suggestion came to nothing, and the Big Three slugged it out among themselves. Stalin finally agreed to a reorganization of the Lublin Government instead of a mere "extension" of it, and before the final decision was made he capitulated, agreeing to the creation of a "new" government to be made up in part of the Lublin group. G attached great importance to the technical triumph of winning this language from Stalin in the declaration. To me it seems more important politically than factually.

As to the boundaries of Poland there was never any great argument. Stalin put his case eloquently. He pointed out that the Curzon line was not drawn by a Russian, nor did the idea of it originate in Russia. The line, he said, was originally worked out by a Harvard professor, chiefly on ethnological and economic considerations. It was adopted by Clemenceau and fixed ultimately by Lord Curzon.

"Can I be less Russian than an American, a Frenchman and an Englishman?" Stalin demanded.

The Curzon line, he pointed out, was determined by the whole world at the end of the last war to be the rightful boundary of Poland. Taking advantage of Russia's weakness at that time, and her reluctance to fight, the Poles, acting as the aggressors, took Russian territory and pushed their borders eastward.

G says that Stalin is right about the Polish border, and that if the case were before him in the Supreme Court, he would have to decide it in Russia's favor.

In this connecton both G and the Thin Man cited to me this week the same example of Stalin's rather gruesome humor. The subject came up of what a tremendous task it will be to shift the German population within the new eastern and western boundaries of Poland, when they are fixed. About 9½ million people are involved. Stalin conceded that it would be quite a job, but added, smiling:

"It seems to me that the Red Army is already doing it rather successfully."

On the other items of the agenda, Stalin was even more agreeable. He seemed as anxious as FDR to end the "balance of power" alignments in Europe and to agree that the three great powers, acting together, should handle internal difficulties in the liberated nations.

He also accepted readily enough the compromise proposed by the President in regard to the voting procedure among the members of the Security Council under the Dumbarton Oaks peace machinery. G insists that Stalin has very little interest in the Dumbarton Oaks plan, and seemed not even to have read it. Stalin is pinning his faith wholly on the continued alliance of Britain, the United States and Russia. Together, he feels, these powers can maintain peace in the world. What the other nations do, he regards as unimportant.

"I am always interested in, but seldom influenced by, the actions of Albania," he put it. "I only want to know what you will do (pointing to Churchill) and what you will do (pointing to Roosevelt)."

G agrees with Stalin. He points out that Russia will come out of this war as the most powerful nation in the world. Stalin has definite plans in the Pacific, he reported, but apart from that wants only to rebuild Russia and to bring it to the standard of living that it ought to enjoy with its vast resources. He believes that once Stalin has settled with the Japs, we can trust him to keep the peace. But about Stalin's successor—whoever he may be—he feels no such assurance. Therefore he is extremely happy that the

Dumbarton Oaks agreement makes no provision for the limitation of armaments, although personally G ardently sponsored armament limitation after the last war.

The one reservation he has in connection with Russia—the one thing that leads to keeping suspicion and distrust alive—is Stalin's evident determination to use German slave labor in rebuilding Russia after the war, and there is every prospect of a sharp disagreement among the Big Three about the interpretation of that innocent phrase. To Russia's way of thinking, this undoubtedly includes Germany's human resources as well as her machines and tools and raw materials. To our way of thinking, it definitely does not. The question was never discussed—not even in whispers—at Yalta. But the British stand firmly with us, and G says that when the time comes we are really prepared to dig our heels in.

G left no shred of doubt that completed and detailed plans for Russia's participation in the war on Japan were agreed upon at the conference, but he was greatly perturbed by the stories which have appeared in the American press speculating chiefly on the peculiar coincidence between the date of the San Francisco conference and the provisions of the Russo-Japanese non-aggression pact which fix the same date as the last upon which either party may denounce the agreement. He says that if he had the power he would issue an order that would confine any newspapermen to jail if he wrote a story suggesting Russian participation. He says that Russia will have to transfer 50 divisions to the Japanese front after Germany is defeated, and that it will take from 60 to 90 days to do this. If Japan—who surely must be aware of Russia's intentions by now—attacks first, this will leave a terrible hole in the Russian lines on Germany's eastern front and cost untold American lives.

My understanding is that Russia already has a trained army—fully adequate for her defensive needs—on the Japanese border, and that this explains Japanese reluctance to take the initiative. Perhaps G doesn't know that. Then again, perhaps I don't, either.

Incidentally, De Gaulle is behaving badly as usual. Although he blames us for his absence from the Yalta meeting, Stalin certainly didn't want him there. Stalin doesn't get along with him at all, and doesn't want him around. It was Roosevelt who urged that De Gaulle be given a place on the Control Commission which will govern Germany after the war; nevertheless, De Gaulle is gumming up the Dumbarton Oaks works.

The text of the revised agreement as you know is being held up pending approval by the Chinese and the French so that they may join in extending the San Francisco invitation. China responded within 24 hours. De Gaulle has already held up matters for ten days, and has now sent to the State Department for further clarification of the provisions of the agreement.

Regards

IMPRESSIONS OF VICE PRESIDENT TRUMAN

Following Franklin Delano Roosevelt as President was about as frustrating for Harry Truman as trying to fill Babe Ruth's shoes was for George Selkirk. His first term was no barn-burning success, and it was taken for granted that Tom Dewey would walk all over him in November of 1948. He didn't, partly because Dewey himself figured his victory was so certain that he should abjure hard-hitting campaigning and try to have a united country behind him. But it wasn't until Truman left the White House that his administration was reevaluated and his reputation took off for the higher regions of public esteem. Shortly before Roosevelt died in April of 1945, several reporters dined with Truman and had a chance to take his measure.

CONFIDENTIAL

Monday
5 March 1945

Dear Bart,

The usual group of us had dinner with Vice President Truman last night. The session provided nothing of world-shaking importance or news value; but it did give me an opportunity to appraise to my own satisfaction at least this man who probably stands the best chance of inheriting the Presidency that any man has stood in recent years.

In spite of my preconceived notions, I liked him a lot as an individual, and was forced to the conclusion that the country would at least be safe in his hands—perhaps far safer than it is at present. I doubt that he has the mental capacity to be a Great President, but he has a natural facility in his human relationships that seems to guarantee that he would be far from the worst President we have ever had. I think he would get along well with Congress, and that government would work fairly smoothly.

His outstanding characteristic is plainness. He is an ordinary common garden variety of Middle Westerner, with a quiet but lively sense of humor that tempers the frankness of his speech. His next most distinctive characteristic is that he is a Democrat. His fellow Democrats, be they Wallace or Aubrey Williams, command his unfailing support. No matter what else they are, if they are Democrats he is for them. His stout insistence that Williams should be confirmed because he is a "good administrator" and his evident respect for Senator Harley M. Kilgore (a strong left winger) were to me the only two disturbing features of an otherwise pleasant evening.

Finally, in a world beset by a wide variety of "ists" preaching a confusing babel of "isms," Truman with his Midwestern drawl, is refreshingly a plain, old-fashioned American. He characterized himself as a "common-sense liberal."

"There's nothing I hate worse," he said, "than a professional liberal, unless, perhaps, it is a blind, unregenerate conservative."

Those who know him best here say that if he ever succeeds to the Presidency he will be far more conservative than Roosevelt and a great disappointment to the PAC (Political Action Committee). In this connection, I asked what he would do with John L. Lewis under the present circumstances were he President today.

"If I had been President these last four years," he said, "I would have stood him up against a wall and shot him."

Truman attended his first Cabinet meeting last week, at the conclusion of which Roosevelt asked him to act as liaison man between the White House and the Congress—just as Garner used to do when it pleased him. He says that he told the President he would be glad to as long as he was traveling a two-way street. The President, he says, made no reply to this and no commitment. He believes that the President will cooperate with him and with Congress quite satisfactorily, however, until the Dumbarton Oaks treaty has been ratified at least. After that it may be different. He says that as Governor of New York, Mr. Roosevelt always had to fight with a strongly opposition legislature, and that he has never gotten over the complex that the legislative body is the natural enemy of the executive.

He insists that he has no ambitions for 1948 and that he never did want his present job. He says he had carved out a nice little Congressional district for himself in Missouri and hoped to come to Congress from that district for the rest of his life. Then he got sent to the Senate, and he hoped to keep that job for the rest of his life. Now he's Vice President and he doesn't know how he's going to like it.

"I never wanted a job I got," he said "and I never wanted to give it up when I quit it."

He says he has only one ambition in life: to do whatever he can to bring about prompt ratification of the Dumbarton Oaks Treaty.

"After that, I'm through," he said.

His own private poll of the Senate, as of the moment, reveals that 12 Senators are firmly opposed to ratification, and he lists 13 others as doubtful. Total necessary to reject is 33 if all members vote. His list is as follows:

Against: Brooks, Ed Johnson, Hiram Johnson, Lafollette, McCarran, Moore, O'Daniel, Taft, Thomas of Idaho, Wheeler, Wiley, Willis.

Doubtful: Bushfield, Butler, Capehart, Gerry, Langer, Millikin, Revercomb, Robertson, Shipstead, Tydings, Vandenberg, Walsh, Wherry.

All the rest, he believes, strongly favor ratification. How good his poll is, of course, remains to be seen, but personally I would be inclined to put considerable credence in it. He is well liked by all the members of the Senate and gets along very well with the Republicans particularly.

Back of the Senate chamber proper is a room reserved for the Vice President—a good, large office with a desk and a toilet. It was here that Garner used to strike his traditional "blow for liberty" about midmorning, followed by frequent additional blows as the day progressed and as one crony after another would drop in for a snort or a leak or both.

Wallace, when he took over, had the toilet removed, and rigorously banned liquor from the premises. No member of the Senate ever ventured into the office without a specific invitation from him—and these were seldom forthcoming.

Since Truman took office, the toilet has been replaced. A metal cabinet, which looks like an electric refrigerator, is well stocked with Bourbon, Scotch, White Rock and Pepsi-Cola.

The military aide who was assigned to him and who was his former secretary before being wounded in the war, was mixing drinks one day last week when half a dozen of us went up to bend an elbow with Truman before lunch, and while we were there a constant procession of Senators dropped in for a quickie and a chat, as did the Governor of Rhode Island. No one is invited. It is just open house and all of them come, Republicans and Democrats alike.

Such influence as Truman exerts emanates chiefly from these little chats held in this room, and through them he manages to keep his finger on the pulse of Senate opinion. In these personal relations he is definitely a smart operator and a good politician, and it would surprise me if he did not prove fairly effective as the term goes on. He ranks himself squarely with Barkley in his attitude toward the Administration, but whereas Barkley, in his role as majority leader, has no truck with the Republicans, Truman, in his role of hail-fellow-well-met, can do a lot for the administration among them.

He says he gets to his office in the Senate Office Building about 8:30 every morning, and gets his mail out of the way by 10. Then he chins with everyone who wants to see him until about 10:30 when he goes over to the office in the Capitol that I have described above. There he sees all comers until the Senate convenes at noon. He is always in the chair to call the Senate to order, and unless someone wants to see him particularly he remains there until hunger overtakes him. Then he goes out to lunch, stops in again at his office, chins with whoever happens to come in, and goes back to his chair in the Senate chamber until the session ends.

"That's what they pay me for," he says, "and that's what I'm going to do."

One little interchange at the dinner amused me because it seemed to reveal a definite chink in the Truman sense of humor. He was asked to describe a Cabinet meeting, and he explained that the President sat in the middle of one side of the long rectangular Cabinet table, while he, Truman, sat in the middle on the opposite side. Ranging from the President right and left—strictly in order of rank and protocol—were the various members of the Cabinet followed by the heads of other agencies, with Byrnes, the last, sitting at Truman's left.

"Then," said an undiplomatic and unthinking reporter, "you sit at the foot of the table."

"Oh no," said Truman quite seriously and quite emphatically, "I sit in the middle of one of the long sides, right opposite the President. There isn't any foot of the table."

Yet—without having any evidence to back it up with—my guess is that wherever Truman sits is the foot of the table so far as the President is concerned. He was only a political expedient after all.

Regards

HURLEY EXPLAINS ATTEMPTS TO UNIFY CHIANG AND THE CHINESE COMMUNISTS

CONFIDENTIAL

Sunday
11 March 1945

Dear Bart,

Barnet Nover of the *Washington Post*—whom you met here in January—gave a small dinner Friday night for Pat Hurley, our Ambassador to China who got in last week and who is returning next week, via London. Including Pat and Mrs. Hurley, five couples were invited, and apart from Barney, only three newspapermen were present [Herbert] Elliston, editorial writer for the *Washington Post*, Dick Wilson and myself.

Pat is in fine shape, loves his new job, is obviously well pleased with his accomplishments, and even in casual conversation in that small group still speaks with all the oratorical flourishes that were the mode in the days of Andrew Jackson. Every phrase contributes to a tremendous rhetorical build-up, and the conclusion of every sentence is reached on a stirring patriotic note like the finale of a George M. Cohan show.

He spoke with amazing frankness, however, censoring his normally salty Oklahoma vocabulary in deference to the ladies, and restraining his customarily enthusiastic Republican tendencies in deference to the fact that Supreme Court Justice William O. Douglas was also present. Within these circumscribed conversational channels, however, he managed to pack the evening with considerably more information on Pacific Theatre plans than the Thin Man disgorged the Sunday previous.

He said he went to China to perform a three-point mission:

1. To prevent the collapse of China, that at the time was imminent.
2. To restore harmonious relations betwen Chiang and the military.
3. To uphold the government of Chiang Kai-shek.

He emphasized the fact that he was not given the task of unifying China and he clearly resents the stories that have been published since his return about his "failure" to bring the communists and the Kuomintang (Chiang's political party) together. He says that China has not been unified for 400 years, and the newspapers here should give him a little more than four months before describing his efforts as a failure.

As for the mission assigned him by President Roosevelt, he insists that it has been fulfilled successfully and to the letter. For the accomplishment of point number one—the saving of China on the brink of collapse—he gives General Wedemeyer full credit.

Wedemeyer, he says, saved China in one of the most brilliant—probably *the* most brilliant—strategic victories of the war to that date. At the time Wedemeyer replaced Stilwell the Chinese were in full retreat before Kunming, which is the great American base in China and the nerve center of the whole defense effort. The Chinese Army was ill-equipped and ill-trained and the psychology of defeat pervaded the entire nation.

In Chungking the Government officials were trying to console themselves with the argument that Kunming was not really important and that China could afford its loss. It was the old Chinese philosophy, apparently—when rape is inevitable, relax and enjoy it. Hurley dissented.

"If we permit Kunming to fall," he preached, "though all the angels of Heaven proclaim the rightness of our decision, history will hold us culpable of failure."

Wedemeyer was called in, and to the high disgust of Lord Louis Mountbatten, he took 16,000 American-trained and American-equipped Chinese troops out of Burma, flew them over the Hump and interposed them between the retreating Chinese Army and the advancing Japs. In his argument with Mountbatten he took the position that the Americans and the British had no right to hold those troops in Burma when China stood in such dire need of every trained Chinese that could be rushed into the breach.

Then Wedemeyer and Hurley persuaded Chiang to withdraw 6,000 of his crack troops from the North China Frontier, where they were being used to hold the communist armies in check, and these too were interposed, making a total of 22,000 really good troops to stand as a wall between the Japs and Kunming.

The result was that for the first time in eight years of China conquest, the Jap suddenly struck something solid. He was surprised and confused. It was not according to plan. And there were complicating psychological factors. . . .

By coincidence it was exactly at this moment that Nimitz was striking at Formosa, MacArthur was landing on Leyte, and 60 percent of the Japanese fleet was being disabled in the Battle of the Philippines. Never had Japan lost so much face so quickly, and the little sons of Heaven dared not risk an important land-army defeat at the hands of the Chinese. They were stopped before Kunming, and the turning point of the Chinese war had been reached very much as it was reached in the Russian war at Stalingrad.

It was at this time that Owen Brewster and Happy Chandler—returning from their peregrinations abroad—were telling the world that the collapse of China was inevitable and that only a miracle could save the day.

When this news reached China, Hurley in an off-the-record aside, told a press conference to tell Owen and Happy to keep their shirts on; that the miracle men were at work.

"Will Rogers once told me never to make a wise crack that I didn't get paid for," he grinned to us, "but I couldn't resist that one."

Point Number Two in Pat's mission was to improve relations between Chiang and the American military. This as you know was done through the removal of Stilwell. Pat didn't go into that picture as Nelson had done, saying only that it was evident that Chiang and Stilwell could not get along together and that a change would have to be made. It was.

Wedemeyer, he said, has changed everything but the weather, and there is a prospect that he may be able to do something about that. He likes Chiang, and vice versa. He is a diplomat, where Stilwell was not. When Chiang wants him to do something that he is perfectly willing to do, he handles it about like this:

"I am entirely at your orders, Generalissimo," he says. "If in your wisdom you believe that this is the proper course for us to take, I shall take it without question. It shall be done at once."

Then when Chiang wants him to do something he doesn't want to do, he says, "Generalissimo, you know that I have done everything you wanted me to do—that I hold myself in readiness at all times to fulfill your requirements, but this I cannot do."

He goes on from there to point out why the course in question would be disastrous, what the disadvantages are, and after tearing Chiang's plan to shreds, suggests a wholly different course—not as an alternative or a substitute, but as a "modification" of Chiang's idea—and by the time he is through, he has Chiang believing that he (Wedemeyer) regards the whole project as a mere improvement upon the basic plan which Chiang advanced. Chiang of course is too smart not to know that Wedemeyer has taken a course that may be exactly opposite to the one Chiang originally advocated, but as long as Wedemeyer appears to think it is a mere revision of Chiang's plan, the Generalissimo can save face.

Into the hands of a British officer whose name at the moment escapes me, Wedemeyer has put the job of organizing the Service of Supply that Hurley had promised to build for Chiang. So for the first time, the Chinese Army is getting an efficient and effective SOS, which is making a tremendous difference in supplying Chiang.

The whole suppy situation in China is improving tremendously. Nelson's work is beginning to pay off in the increased production of rifles, trenching tools, etc. by Chinese industry. Between 38,000 and 40,000 tons per month are being flown in over the Hump, and this will soon reach 50,000 tons. The Ledo Road is also working well, within limits. Because the stuff being trucked in over it must be largely gasoline if the trucks themselves are to return, they are left in China to be used by the SOS in supplying combat troops. (Nelson told us, you recall, that at present there is fewer than one truck to a division, so that supplies have to be carried almost exclusively by coolies.) One difficulty here is that there are so few Chinese who can drive a truck, and there is a definite manpower shortage in this particular field.

Besides all this, there is now a pipeline in operation which brings in about 16,000 tons a month (even gasoline is measured in tons out there) but even so it is estimated that a gallon of gasoline, laid down in Kunming, costs us approximately $100.

"Remember this always," Hurley warned us. "We will never be able to supply the Chinese Army effectively until we get a port on the coast of China, and a sea train operating constantly."

With what we *are* getting in, however, we can put the Chinese Army in shape to go on the offensive by August, he estimates, and we can use it in taking and holding a seacoast port and protecting a supply line from that port to China's interior.

By that time, he says, there will be 36 fully trained and equipped Chinese divisions. (He says there are 25 Jap divisions in the general seacoast area.) These Chinese divisions will have American "advisers" who will actually act as officers down to the level of battalion commander. Below that rank the officers will be Chinese. He regretted that it would take until August before the Chinese can actually attack.

I pointed out that, from what we heard here (see Thin Man memo) our sea forces would not be ready to go in and take a Chinese beachhead before that time. Pat said there was a nice, cosy spot on the coast where we could do it much earlier than that. I asked what we were going to do about the "west wall" defense or the "Maginot Line" that the Thin Man spoke about. He said that he believed that our superior air power and unchallenged naval supremacy could, between them, build an effective wall of fire around such a beachhead while we were building our air and supply bases on it.

One critical feature of our whole supply problem in China is oil—as it has been from the start. There is a great shortage of tankers, and it is a hell of a long haul from the United States. If the total potential Chinese production could be developed, we would still not get as much oil from China in a year as we produce at home in a single day.

We would like very much, therefore, to go into the Indies and get our oil back, but we can't do it. We can't turn our backs on Tokyo now and take time out to go campaigning elsewhere. We have built up tremendous momentum in our naval drive in the Pacific and we don't want to lose it. We have the little yellow men off balance and must keep them that way. We can't afford to give them a chance to get reorganized, to repair their damaged ships and to replace their lost planes.

I asked if this wouldn't be a damned good place to use the British fleet which seems so anxious to gather a crop of kudos in the Pacific. He said it certainly would be, but that there are reasons—many reasons—why we can't put pressure on the British now. They're sore enough as it is.

It seems that when Wedemeyer had finally saved Kunming—and China with it—Lord Louis wanted his 16,000 troops back. Mainly, however, Mountbatten wants a slew of Lend-Lease, *all* of which is going to China. Wedemeyer pointed out to him that with all the British, Dutch and French forces in the area the only nation that was actually fighting the Japanese was America, and that if Lord Louis could show him exactly where he was going to use the troops to beat Japan, he would gladly give them back. He pointed out also that when Japan falls, Britain will get Rangoon and Mandalay back anyway, and there's no use using the troops down there now, which is what the British want to do with them.

I gather that Hurley fully shares my own opinion that the record of the British under Lord Mountbatten, so far—while better than it was before Lord Louis took over—is one of the deplorable chapters in the history of a great Empire, and does much to support the Axis contention about the impotence of the decadent democracies. It is not Mountbatten's fault, of course.

Hurley says that our "cousins" protested bitterly that we were exerting undue influence upon Chiang and wanted to get tough about it.

"I told them I understood their views perfectly," he says. "I pointed out to them that I was thoroughly familiar with their 'divide and rule' policies; that I had seen them divide the Jews and the Arabs and rule Palestine, divide the Hindus and the Moslems and rule India, divide the Kuomintang and the communists and rule China, and that if we ever gave them the chance they would divide the Republicans and the Democrats and rule America."

Instructions finally came through to the British Embassy from London fully endorsing American policy in China and instructing the British officials to go along with it.

"We had no more trouble for at least two days," Pat chuckled. "These imperialists don't give up easily. They didn't get where they are by doing so—or by following orders from London that displease them."

So we can't seem to interest either the British or the Dutch in getting their oil back for themselves. They just sit around and wait for us to finish the job, knowing that when we do, they can just move back in and take over again.

Full recognition of this attitude on the part of our Allies, I gather, pervaded our whole military and naval strategy in the Pacific. I do not of course know how well-informed Hurley is about our actual battle plans, but he thinks, obviously, that he is thoroughly informed on the subject, and such revelations as he made (which I thought were considerable) did not seem to contradict at least anything that we have gotten from our other sources with which you are familiar.

Our strategy as he described it is this:

We do not seek to send land forces into China to meet and defeat the Japanese forces there. We shall supply the Chinese (apparently through a coastal port) and leave the rest to them and to the Russians. The Russians, he made it obvious, are determined to carve themselves little slices of China, which they intend to keep.

Barnet Nover, who is quite an authority on all matters historical, pointed out that several hunks of what is now China were taken from the Russians by acts of Chinese aggression. Pat confirmed this and said that Russia was about to get them back, and that if we were willing to go into China and do the fighting there, all the Russians would have to do would be to sit back like the British and the Dutch and wait for us to hand them to her on a platter. Therefore we are not going to do it.

We obviously expect Russia to take Manchuria, while we concentrate on the Japanese Archipeligo from the sea. Somewhere in the Ryukus (pronounced ree-YOU-kews, I understand) and in the Kuriles, the rest of the Japanese fleet is hidden, we believe.

Point Number 3 in Hurley's mission was to uphold the government of Chiang. This was accomplished by the successful fulfillment of the other two points—saving China and restoring harmony between the American military and the Kuomintang. Chiang's government now seems safe and strong.

Nevertheless, Pat wanted to unify China at least to the extent of bringing the communists into the fold, so he sought and won Roosevelt's permission to go out with Nelson via Russia, primarily to explore the Russian attitude toward the Chinese communists. Nelson, he said, did the talking. Pat just listened. Stalin told them:

1) He has no interest in the Chinese communists, and is not giving them any help or support.

2) He does not regard them as true communists.

3) He does not seek to establish communism in China at this time.

4) He wants a strong and unified China.

Chiang had to be convinced that this was true. He let Hurley go to North China, therefore, and start dickering.

Pat links the Chinese communists not to New Dealers as Nelson did, but to the Farmer-Labor party here. In other words, extremely leftist and composed chiefly of agriculturalists and laborers. He pointed out this essential difference, however: The "political parties" of China are really bands of armed insurrectionists, and unity in China will never be obtained until they have all surrendered their arms, or placed them at the disposal of a central government. Besides the communists, there are numbers of war lords, some of whom have as many as 200,000 armed men at their command. Then there are the Japanese puppets, who likewise command armed Chinese forces.

The communists are devoted to the principles of Sun Yat Sen and seek to establish them throughout China. As Pat explained it, Sun Yat Sen took Lincoln's immortal phrase and set it up as the foundation upon which a democratic China was to be built: Government of the people; government for the people; government by the people. He adopted our Constitution virtually in toto with special emphasis on our Bill of Rights.

He set up a plan for the democratization of China, dividing the process into three periods: The first, a period of dictatorship which would establish order in China; the second, a period of education which would prepare the people for self-government; the third, the calling of a constitutional convention, establishment of a constitutional government and the beginning of a full-functioning democracy.

The Japanese invasion of China occurred just as the second period—the period of education—had begun. And while the years have duly elapsed there has been no opportunity to put them to the educational purposes that had been contemplated. Therefore, in Hurley's opinion, the people are NOT ready for the democracy or for the third phase of the program.

So much for background. Now . . .

The communists submitted to Pat a five-point program, to which they asked Chiang's assent: The first three points were merely an expression of their political ideas and beliefs as described above. Point four was a demand that Chiang establish a coalition government representing all political parties in China as well as the Kuomintang and their own. Point 5 was a promise that, if Chiang accepted the other four, they would place their arms and their troops at the disposal of the central government.

I gathered that Hurley thought this was fair. Chiang, however, shied at the word "coalition" which, Pat says, seems to take on some monstrous connotation when translated into Chinese.

It seemed obvious too that Hurley understood and sympathized with Chiang's position, which was essentially that he had held China together, defended it and saved it; and now the communists wanted to set up a wholly new government to take over as the price of their cooperation.

Pat then persuaded Chiang to hold a committee meeting composed of men representing all shades of Chinese opinion. Communist leaders were brought down to Chungking under pledges of immunity and a promise that they would not be tailed by Chinese Secret Service men. This promotion in status from their former rank as outlaws (in Chiang's opinion) to conferees representing a Chinese political party gave them vast new confidence in themselves and was largely responsible, Pat feels, for the manner in which they kept raising the ante, as described in the Nelson memo.

Right in the midst of the conference, however, and responsible primarily for its failure, in Hurley's opinion, came the story that Chiang had sold out to the Japanese and that there were documents to prove it. Our State Department worried about it, but Hurley reassured them, explaining that such a deal was simply not in the cards. Chiang was strong again. And more than that, he was getting lend-lease—all of it, including what the British were trying desperately to get and couldn't. Clearly the report was foolish, and ultimately the "documents" were produced and proved to be an attempt started by one of the Chinese communists to amass some $20,000,000 of Kuomintang gold.

But the show busted up anyway.

Chiang, nevertheless, has called a constitutional convention for 5 May, for the purpose of establishing a Constitutional Democracy and an elected government in China. The communists are none too pleased. They point out that the Kuomintang still controls the governmental machinery, and it is obvious they fear that when the smoke all blows away, China's democracy will still be in the hands of the Kuomintang party.

Hurley likewise looks forward to the session with certain mental reservations. Believing as he does that China cannot be unified until the insurrectionist parties have laid down their arms and until the people have been educated sufficiently, he's looking for trouble ahead. But he does take great comfort from Chiang's own views and ambitions which are surprising indeed, coming as they do from a man who is undoubtedly a complete dictator. Chiang has expressed these views to Pat as follows:

"If I were to die a dictator," he says, "I will be forgotten within 48 hours. I will have achieved nothing. But if I succeed in unifying China and establishing here a real democracy for the Chinese people, then I will be immortal—the George Washington of China."

With two opposing factions as close together in their fundamental aims and desires as the communists and Chiang, Hurley says, the achievement of their common goal is only a matter of time.

Meanwhile there is a good prospect of an immediate rapprochement between the Kuomintang and the communists, arising out of the communist demand that they be permitted to send a delegation to the United Nations conference in San Francisco next month.

We of course have rejected that demand on the ground that we cannot permit individual political parties within the several nations, any more than we would permit the Republicans in our own country to have a separate delegation.

Nevertheless we have suggested to Chiang that he appoint at least one communist leader as a member of the Chinese delegation at Frisco, pointing out that our own delegation embraces both Democrats and Republicans. Chiang has not yet agreed to this, but Hurley seems to think he can persuade him when he returns. If he does so, he believes that this will really settle the fight and that the communist armies will join fully in the coordinated battle of China against the Japs.

There is only one more item of outstanding interest to report, although Pat regaled us at length with amusing descriptions of some of the leading Chinese personalities of the day.

I asked him about the reports that the Generalissimo and his wife (of whom Keats Speed already suspects that I am deeply enamored) are en route to a divorce. Hurley replied that he would tell me exactly what a leading Chinese official had told him.

Said the offical:

"The Gimo and Mm. Chiang have separated permanently. To my personal knowledge this is the fortieth time they have separated permanently in the twenty years of their marriage."

Hurley explained that while Mm. Chiang was in Chungking she was poisoned, and not easy to get along with. She came first to South America and then here to recover. Mrs. Roosevelt called to see her the other day, but was not admitted to her room because Mm. Chiang was too ill to receive her. Pat is going to try to see her before returning to China.

But withal there are signs that the romantic urge still burns in the Gimo's heart. Just before Pat left Chungking, Chiang took him out to the airport to see his new plane—a plane for the Generalissimo's personal use.

"Do you know what I'm going to call it?" Chiang asked.

"No. Do tell," said Pat, or words to that effect.

"I'm naming it Mei-ling!" said Chiang.

That's what Pat wants to tell her. He thinks the Gimo wants him to. Tell her he's naming his plane for her.

Incidentally, Washington as you know has been all agog for weeks over whether or not MacArthur is to be overall commander of our Asiatic operations, once we land somewhere. On his way back to the States, Pat stopped in the Philippines and found that the General has a grievance.

"He always has a grievance, ever since I've known him," Pat said, "but this time it's a real one. It seems he is to stop in the Philippines. He is all through when he has finished there."

Hurley seems to feel that this is unfair, in view of MacArthur's brilliant military record. I gather that he, like everyone else I have met who knows the General, doesn't really like him, but recognizes him as one of the outstanding military geniuses of our time.

All I want to tell you is that you're not going to get another word out of me this Sunday. I'm through for the day.

Regards

THE WAR IN EUROPE WINDS DOWN— REDEPLOYMENT OF TROOPS TO THE PACIFIC

CONFIDENTIAL

Friday
23 March 1945

Dear Bart,

The conference of which I spoke to you on the telephone today was apparently called quite hastily and was probably the most interesting I have attended to date. We arrived at THE MAN'S office to find that a circle of chairs had been arranged around two easels piled deep with enormous maps. Before one easel stood a general and in front of the other was a colonel, each armed with a pointer and thick packets of notes. THE MAN explained that he was going to show us the procedure through which he and his immediate associates went every morning in reviewing every aspect of the war in every section of the globe.

He told us that the easel at our right held maps fully disclosing our own operations during the past 24 hours. The easel at the left held corresponding maps on which were depicted all the information assembled by our Intelligence Forces about enemy activities and plans during the same period. On both sets of maps were shown by name and number the exact units of the Allied and German Armies that were participating in that particular sector.

It took almost two hours to finish this briefing, which covered everything from the weather over Europe to the most minute of gains made by the British in Burma. Every small island in the Philippines upon which any action of any kind had occurred was duly discussed in a detail that my mind, at least, could not absorb.

After this briefing was over the maps were removed from the room and THE MAN himself began a discourse that lasted an hour and a half. Here are the highlights so far as I can piece them together again.

The final big push in Europe that should be under way by the time you receive this is the crucial test of our war effort in that theatre. It is clear from our Intelligence report that the Germans know exactly where we plan to strike and have for the past 48 hours been building up heavily their defenses in that area. The area, of course, is the northern end of the line in the sector now held by the British and the Canadians.

I have already told you what D-Day is as planned, but that depends on the weather. Weather over this area yesterday was excellent with ceiling and visibility unlimited. The weather forecasts for today were the same, and as I write you the prospects are that everything will go off according to plan. We are disturbed, of course, by the fact that German Intelligence knows as much as it does of our plans and we must depend upon luck to some degree.

If the Germans happen to place their troops in exactly the right spots, it will be bad for us and the war will be greatly prolonged. If they do not, we expect to succeed and that the war will not last much longer in this theatre. Our tactical position is excellent. Although the Germans do not know it, our combat forces are now completely deployed. All the combat divisions we have are now trained and in the field ready for action.

We still have individual replacements training and some specialized units such as supply units in this country, but otherwise everything we have is in the battle. When Patton and Patch drove through to the Rhine and wiped out the bulge that was formed by our line in that sector, we shortened our lines materially. The result is that we were able last week to take 44 divisions out of our lines, send them back to the rear for rest and re-equipment and ready them for the big push. Thirty-three of these divisions were still out of the line yesterday, and our line in the northern sector where the advance is scheduled to take place was held merely by some cavalry reconnaissance divisions.

Our supply situation is likewise greatly improved. In December just before the bulge, we were getting up to our front lines only about 40,000 dry tons daily and 15,000 wet tons (gasoline, etc.).

Now we are getting between 70 and 80 thousand dry tons a day and 40,000 wet tons. At the time of Patton's spectacular drive across France, we were stopped by the failure of our gasoline supply. Had it not been so, we could have reached the Rhine at that time without difficulty as the Germans had nothing to stop us. As it was, the delay gave them the opportunity to reform their lines and it cost us heavily in time, lives and military treasure.

We are determined that should not happen again. The drive that is beginning now represents a final all-out sustained effort which we believe can be maintained without relaxation until the war is finished. Within three weeks the spring thaws, rains and mud will set in—weather conditions that heretofore have always blocked military operations. We plan to go slogging along as we did through the monsoons in Burma.

The enemy's tactical position is not good. The bridgehead at Remagen is a dangerous threat to him. We can either burst to the north or to the south, or go straight ahead through the rugged and difficult country that lies immediately to the east of it. The Intelligence maps show that the enemy—

fully conscious of this—has concentrated large numbers of his troops around this bridgehead.

Similarly, to the south, Patton's huge force constitutes another such threat which is tying down large numbers of the enemy's troops. If he weakens his defenses in either of these places to get reinforcements for the battle to the northward, we can break through below and trap him. Furthermore, his communications are badly shattered by our air attacks. On Wednesday of this week we sent out 1,400 heavy bombers from England, along with 750 fighters. The RAF sent out half that many. The Tactical Air Force in France sent everything it had in the way of fighter-bombers and medium bombers into the air, and it was the same with our forces based on Italy.

THE MAN told us that during the past 20 days we have dropped an average of 5.8 tons of bombs on Germany every minute of the day. We have also bombed Yugoslavia and Northern Italy and some strategic points in Greece quite liberally during the period. Our Intelligence tells us that a German division which was ordered to leave Italy 20 days ago has not yet reached the Brenner Pass, so completely have we devastated communications in that area.

Meanwhile—and also unbeknownst to the enemy—we have removed from the Italian front some of our best divisions and transported them to France for the big push. The Germans believe that some of the British divisions have left the Italian line, but this is incorrect. Our Italian line is now held on the west by two Negro divisions, in the center by some Canadian, British and Polish divisions, on the east by a Jewish division that just showed up on the line two days ago and which, apparently, came out of Palestine, and on the extreme east by an Italian division which is no good but which is pitted against a Turkish division recruited by the Germans experimentally which is a complete flop.

That's about the way it stacks up in advance of the big show. The Russians will start their great drive approximately simultaneously. THE MAN said that he has gone to great pains NOT to find out exactly when or where the Russians would move.

There are signs that the German war effort is falling off. On Wednesday only six V-1 bombs were directed at London, and four of these were shot down by anti-aircraft before they struck. Two struck in the target area causing 88 casualties and some property damage. Two V-2 bombs fell outside the target area. In Antwerp, the only other V-bomb target, only one V-1 landed in the target area and that was far from the port which is the only vulnerable spot. This represents a great lessening of V bomb activity in recent days and is provocative of thought.

Among the highly confidential things THE MAN revealed was a map of the city of London, superimposed upon which was a cellophane sheet showing where every V-bomb had dropped. According to him, London has been all but wiped out. One out of every two houses has been rendered uninhabitable and 70,000 civilian casualties have been suffered in the past six months. He said this knowledge might help us to understand the somewhat impatient attitude which the British display editorially and otherwise in controversies with our own people.

We have a very good V-bomb of our own now—you may have seen it in the newsreels—but we are not using it in quantity. We could manufacture this bomb at the rate of several thousand a day, but it would cost us about 40 percent of our artillery producton and Eisenhower had no hesitancy when queried in saying he wanted the artillery shells and to hell with the bomb. Therefore, only a small quantity of these bombs is being manufactured.

Our most devastating weapon apparently is the proximity fuse which we have devised for our bombs and artillery shells, and of which the Thin Man spoke, as I recall it, more than a year ago. Until recently we had to use this only over Allied territory because we didn't want the Germans to find any fragment or dud which could disclose our effort.

At the time of von Runstedt's Ardennes drive at the Bulge, however, a group of distinguished American scientists called to study this fuse reported that even if the Germans got hold of a dud it would take them nearly a year to put the thing into production, and we felt the war would be over before they could accomplish this. Therefore we began using it freely and THE MAN says that this fuse more than any other single thing was responsible for von Rundstedt's defeat. The fuse can be set so that the shell or bomb will explode when it gets within a given number of feet of an object—50 feet or 500 feet, whatever you wish.

Shells loaded with shrapnel and set for 60 feet were fired over the on-rushing German troops, and when they came within 60 feet they exploded and wiped out whole divisions to the last man. The Germans thought we had a new secret weapon, as indeed we had. It is shells equipped with these fuses that are now proving so effective in destroying the V-1 bombs. Of course they can't touch the V-2s.

THE MAN was obviously deeply disturbed by the tank controversy. He points out that General Patton and General Devers—the two men who have had most experience in tank warfare on our side—have stressed mobility and speed as the prime requisites for our tanks. The German Tigers are much heavier and much slower and adapted primarily for defense purposes. The Germans dig them in and they become forts. We, being on the attack rather than on the defensive, have no use for forts. Therefore our tank—for our purpose—is far better than theirs.

We now have a new tank. It is a 40-ton job with a low silhouette, a 90 mm gun and heavy armored protection on the front. The most important thing about it is that it is just as fast and mobile as the General Sherman. We have had this tank since October, but not until February would we put any into action in Europe, for this reason: the German tanks are only 100 to 200 miles from their factories at worst. Ours are several thousand. If bugs develop in a new Geman tank they can be corrected and replacement parts put in quickly. If bugs develop in ours—as they do in all newly designed products—they become junk. Therefore, we had to wait until the last bugs were out. We now have 200 of these tanks in action in Europe and are turning them out at the rate of 300 to 400 a month here at home.

Meanwhile, we have a new shell that will go clear through a Tiger tank, armor and all. This is undoubtedly the shell that Luman Long telephoned me about and is one of our most closely guarded military secrets. It is doing a swell job.

As of Wednesday, our Intelligence reports charted 55 German submarines in the Atlantic. This is about half the number that were charted, as I recall it, about a year ago according to reports received at one of the Thin Man's conferences. Highly confidential reports reveal that we have been sinking U-boats at the rate of some 12 to 16 per month for the last five months and that we have lost about twice that number of ships—some of them very small. As it works out, therefore, one German sub during its lifetime now gets two Allied ships. There are about 16 German subs ringing the British Isles today.

Apart from his natural concern about the big push, the thing which most disturbs THE MAN is the problem of redeployment—the transfer of our boys from Europe to the Pacific as soon as the European war is over. He points out how costly it was for us to let the Germans reorganize themselves west of the Rhine last fall when we had them on the run, and is determined that we shall not make that same mistake in the Pacific now, as we have the Japs completely off balance there.

As he describes the war, our whole effort has been to overcome one bottleneck after another and without going through the long succession of bottlenecks we have broken, suffice it to say that today our critical shortage is of ships and supply troops. He is particularly worried, therefore, by the fact that those men in our European armed forces who are to be discharged following the German collapse, will be isolated there for many months while every available ship is being used to transport combat and service troops to the Pacific. In order to prevent rumors from spreading, and to kill political pressures back home, he has taken two steps, as follows:

1) A film has been prepared (it was made eight months ago) and has been distributed under seal in every theatre of the war throughout the world. This film explains exactly what the problems are of transferring our men to the Pacific, what forces will be needed there, the speed with which they must be gotten there, and the basis upon which they will be selected for future combat instead of being discharged. Within eight hours after the German collapse, therefore, every soldier in our armed forces will know whether or not he is to be discharged and if so, will understand why he cannot be sent home immediately.

2) An elaborate educational program has been fully set up for those men who will be marooned in Europe for a time after the war there. Textbooks on all kinds of subjects from grade school to fairly advanced college courses have been printed and are now assembled in Paris awaiting distribution. Leases have been signed on school properties. Teachers have been recruited.

The courses are so devised that each will embrace only 20 sessions—that is, if the course is taken five days a week, it will be completed in four weeks. Thus if a man is transferred he can take up the next 20-session course in his new post. All men will be required to take such of these courses as they choose, to keep them occupied during their period of waiting and to prevent a collapse of morale. Personally, I think this is damned good planning.

As for the men who are going to the Pacific, that problem is even more difficult. The regrouping process will be accomplished in Europe and the new divisions formed there from the remnants of the old. The problem of retraining and supply is much more difficult and apparently can be accomplished best in the United States. THE MAN is trying to arrange it so that troops for the Pacific can be brought back to New York, have a ten day leave with their families, proceed to the West Coast, be re-equipped there and embark for the Orient. Here again the shipping shortage raises its ugly head. Obviously, it would be much simpler to take the ship from Europe directly through the Panama Canal and on out to the Pacific, shortening the turn-around time by many days and speeding the entire process. The stop in New York and the reembarkation in Frisco will require the use of more ships. Perhaps it cannot be done. It is necessary, however, to get our Air Force, its ground forces and some 275,000 supply units out to the Pacific immediately. For these men there will be no 10-day leaves at home and even so it will take, it is estimated, from four to five months to do the job.

These are the high spots, but only the high spots. However, they're all I have time for now. I've got a date with Senator Wagner.

Regards

ADVANCE NEWS OF SECOND ATOMIC BOMB DROP

Some idea of the confidence the American military and naval leaders had come to have in the ablest of the Washington correspondents with whom they met periodically during the war is demonstrated by the fact that on August 7 General Marshall gave this startling information to a group of us:

"Another atomic bomb will be dropped on Japan tomorrow night."

It might be argued that no harm could be done by such an announcement even if it did leak, for the Japanese had no defense against this new and terrible weapon. But the military mind does not work that way. No one could be sure that a leak might not cause things to go awry, and one of the guiding rules of running a war is never to take a chance unnecessarily—and never to hesitate to take one when it is necessary.

No, I think General Marshall was speaking in absolute confidence that what he said would be held completely secret by the correspondents meeting with him, as well as confidence that their papers, alerted by the off-the-record bulletin, would sit on any leaks sent by news services or anyone else.

After I had gone with Du Pont, it fell to my lot to write the release covering the Du Pont Company's critical role in the development of the atomic bomb, and writing it was an emotional experience. We knew by then that it had worked, and that something new, with infinite potentialities for good or evil, had been brought into the world—fortunately for the Free World by the Allied side.

It was clear that our possession of this weapon meant that the war would end in a few days, and that no one would ever know if Allied plans for conquering Japan would have been as difficult and costly as the Combined Chiefs feared. Could we have won the Pacific war by taking a port on the China coast and letting the land forces of China and Russia take on the Japanese Army on the Chinese mainland? It is certain that those concerned were just as pleased that they didn't have to find out. I was happy about that, too. I was proud that the company for which I worked had written a bold page of American history. I was proud that Du Pont had agreed to do this work only under government acceptance of two stipulations: that Du Pont receive a fee of $1 (less tax) over the life of the project, and that any patents developed in the course of it become government property. I was proud of my country.

It had never occurred to me, although perhaps it should have, that well meaning people would surface who would have preferred to see as many as a million young Americans dead on the battlefields of Japan rather than to admit that, like it or not, this new force was here to stay and that it must be tamed by human beings with heads and hearts in good working order.

I remember reading once that a famous English novelist had led a movement to abolish the steam locomotive because it was a threat to civilization. Fortunately for civilizaton, few took him or his cause or his followers seriously. I await confidently the day when some important scientific group discovers that water—pure, cold, uncontaminated aqua pura—is a carcinogen, thus compelling the Food and Drug Administration to ban its use, either by itself or mixed with any other substance.

But atomic energy was energy whose time had come. If we had not discovered ways to put it to use, Germany might well have done so and those of us still alive would be heiling some Nazi fuhrer, on pain of the gas chamber. It was not a question of if atomic energy should be used, but of who would be the first to use it.

Anyway, it is fitting, I think, that this memorandum, among the last of the war-time messages sent to New York by the *Sun*'s Washington Bureau, should have to do with this force that may—let's face it with courage and determination to prevent it if we can—destroy this world and turn it into another moon—sterile, lifeless, gray—but that, on the other hand, may end energy crises for all time, and make for a richer and a better life for more people than the world has ever known.

CONFIDENTIAL

7 August 1945

Dear Bart,

Here is the highly confidential memorandum containing the high spots of today's secret conference about which I spoke to you on the phone.

Another atom bomb will be dropped on Japan tomorrow night. Apparently it is our plan to drop a few of these at intervals at carefully planned sites where the greatest possible number of Japanese can see and learn of their effects.

The bomb which was tested in New Mexico had thirteen and a half pounds of atomic explosive in it. It was exploded, as you know, a half hour before dawn, and lighted up the surrounding countryside with daylight brilliance for a distance of 289 miles.

The bomb that was dropped on Hiroshima Sunday contained 25 pounds of explosive. We had no idea what it would do because there was no place in the United States where it was safe to explode a test bomb of that size.

We would like to have dropped a bomb over Japan by night because the effects of it would have been so much more devastating on the minds of so many people, but we did not dare do this because of the necessity for pin-point accuracy. The bomb tomorrow will be dropped by daylight also, for the same reason.

We selected Hiroshima as the target as a kind of second choice. We wanted a place which had a large number of military installations and where the least possible number of civilians would be killed, while at the same time the largest possible number of civilians would see the thing. Our first choice was on the northern end of Kyushu, Shimonoseki. The installations on the Kyushu side of the straits are wholly military, but the heavy population on the other side of the Straits, while being reasonably safe, would have seen and felt the blast. Unfortunately, the Japanese have located a prisoner of war camp in that area. They have also located prisoner of war camps near every other city they thought we might bomb. We did not KNOW if they had a prisoner of war camp at Hiroshima, which is why we chose it.

We did not believe the bomb would begin to do as much damage as it apparently has done. Our intelligence officers now believe that the Japanese themselves have been unable to ascertain the results of the blast because all communicaton facilities in the area apparently have been wiped out. We expected to destroy everything at Hiroshima with the explosion, but it seems probable now that we destroyed all the communications at Kure, the great Japanese naval base, twenty miles away.

The Japs have announced that this was a parachute bomb. It was not. The bomb exploded at 2,000 feet above the ground, it being the best scientific consensus that the explosive would do the greatest amount of damage at that altitude. While the charge itself weighed only 25 pounds, the detonating mechanism is extremely large and unwieldy, and one of these bombs is a full load for a B-29. Had that explosion occurred at night, it would have lighted the skies over the entire archipeligo with the brilliance of ten suns.

The plane that dropped the bomb was unhurt. Its crew had been especially trained for four months and had volunteered for the job. The pilot is about to get a medal. [I assume the crew was also decorated.] It was done by a matter of split-second timing. Scientists had determined that if the missile were dropped from a height of 30,000 feet, as it was, it would take 56 seconds for it to reach the 2,000 foot altitude at which it would explode, and 32 seconds more for the force of the explosion to get back to 30,000 feet. This gave the plane 88 seconds to get out of range, and as no one knew what the range was, it was a highly hazardous undertaking.

A very secret feature of this bomb, about which nothing thus far had been known except to a few scientists, is the fact that for an interval after the explosion a field of radio activity is set up that melts or virtually vaporizes steel and other radio-susceptible metals. This interval lasts for "part of a day." This was known at the time the test bomb was fired in New Mexico, and all automobiles and other essential metal objects were covered with a protective coating of lead in order to prevent their destruction.

The manufacturing program is so complex, and requires such specialized machinery that even if the Japanese—or the people of any other nation— were in possession of all our blueprints and formulae, it would take them from two to three years to manufacture the first small quantity of this explosive. Our informant said that we did not know on 16 July whether the mechanism for detonating the test bomb would work or not. We did know, however, that the mechanism on Sunday's bomb would work beyond a peradventure of a doubt.

We also knew that no other nation in the world has made any substantial progress with the atomic bomb. You may recall that the Thin Man once told us of a raid—two or three years ago—made by our air force on Peenemünde, on the Baltic Sea, where our sole objective was a laboratory in which we knew some of the greatest scientists in Germany were then congregated and working. We believed they were working on the atomic bomb. It was the knowledge of this project, and recognition of what would happen if Germany got there first, that drove the United States to go all out on our own efforts.

Actually, we have since discovered they had made very little progress with the atomic explosive, and were working on the rocket bomb, the advent of which we delayed by many months as a result of the Peenemünde raid. Highly confidential is the fact that we now know exactly how far the Germans had got with atomic power—and more important, how much further they had to go.

Most of today's conference other than the above was devoted to the question of the size of the Army. I found I couldn't get much interested in it. If you, however, are deeply interested, let me know directly, and I will try to reconstitute my atomically-shattered recollections.

Regards

What might be taken as a definitive validation of the importance of the King conferences did not come my way for many years. Not, in fact, until October of 1968, at the dinner given me by public relations friends and associates from all parts of the country. It was held in the DuBarry Room of the Hotel du Pont in Wilmington, Delaware, to mark my retirement as Director of Public Relations for the Du Pont Company.

One of the speakers was Arthur Newmyer, beyond all

question the ablest public relations practitioner in Washington or, come to think of it, most any other place you might mention. In addition, he was one of the greatest guys I ever knew. In the course of his remarks he said, addressing obliquely C. B. McCoy, then Du Pont's president, and directly all those present:

"I would like to tell a story tonight, but frankly I'm a bit hesitant to do so in front of Mr. McCoy, because I understand that Glen is still on the Du Pont payroll. I assume there is still time for management to request early retirement.

"Please don't do anything about it, Mr. McCoy, but the truth is that the best public relations job Glen Perry ever did was when he was still a Washington correspondent—before he joined your company. I know because I was an indirect beneficiary of Glen's inherent public relations talent.

"The time was late 1942 or early 1943. The recipient of Glen's advice—in the parlance of our trade, Glen's 'pro bono' client—was none other than Admiral Ernest J. King, Chief of U.S. Naval Operations in World War II, later to be Fleet Admiral King.

"Admiral King had been called to Washington and made the boss after the disaster at Pearl Harbor. He was tough as nails—maybe tougher. He was absolutely determined to chew up the Japanese fleet. Meanwhile, we were getting the hell beat out of us. So Admiral King used to keep in practice by chewing up junior U.S. naval officers. And he had absolutely no use—in fact, utter disdain—for anyone associated with the communications media.

"At that time I was masquerading in a naval uniform, and had been assigned to the Press Section of the Navy Department. My rank was all of Lieutenant (Junior Grade). My job was to get Admiral King to tolerate, if not love, the press—and the press to simply adore the Admiral. As I said, the war was going miserably. You can imagine how successful I was.

"Glen Perry showed me how to do it. Through a mutual friend, Glen persuaded Admiral King to dine one evening—informally and off-the-record—with a selected group of Washington correspondents, including, of course, Glen.

"At the start, the Admiral was highly skeptical—frosty as usual. But these private sessions continued. Under

Glen's tutelage, Admiral King became convinced that, properly briefed, journalists could be both trustworthy and responsible—and, more importantly, that the results could be highly beneficial to the Navy and the nation.

"As I said, to my mind, converting Admiral Ernest J. King has to be Glen's greatest public relations achievement."

My gratitude to Arthur Newmyer was and is beyond imagining, especially as he greatly exaggerated my contribution. As it was and is to the Navy Department, when Secretary Forrestal and Information Chief Rear Admiral "Min" Miller signed official commendations, one for Phelps Adams and one for me, "for outstanding service and performance to the United States at war, as an accredited Navy War Correspondent."

KING CRITICIZES MANY
FOR PEARL HARBOR DEBACLE

CONFIDENTIAL

Thursday
19 August 1945

Dear Bart,

We had another session with the Thin Man Sunday evening, which lasted until midnight. The discussion was general, a review of the war activities to date, and a disclosure of some of the contemplated operations which were, perforce, terminated by the Japanese surrender.

The Japanese surrender efforts were undertaken prior to 1 July, when Admiral Sato of Japan approached the Russians with a peace proposition which included giving Russia generous slices of various islands and mainland areas in Asia. Russia flatly refused this offer, which was continued aggressively by the Japanese up to the time of the Potsdam conference, and did not cease until Molotov handed Sato the Russian declaration of war on Japan, six days before the Nipponese surrender. [When the other Allies also refused this offer at Potsdam and presented an ultimatum of unconditional surrender to which Japan did not reply, the United States dropped the atomic bomb.]

The surrender details will be completed, and signatures affixed, on the battleship *Missouri* some time this week, probably near the end of the week if present plans follow through without a hitch. General MacArthur is

Supreme Commander *for* the Allied Nations. He is not Supreme Com-mander *of* the Allied Nations, a differentiation demanded by the State Department which meets the approval of the Navy, since it means that Ad-miral Nimitz will sign the surrender documents for the United States Government. Admiral Fraser will sign for the British. Russia and China will have representatives to sign the document as well. It has not been determined whether Australia, France, Holland, New Zealand and other interested par-ties in the Pacific will be co-signers or observers.

The invasion of Japan was scheduled for 1 November, and would have been on the southern coast of Kyushu. Upon consolidation of this opera-tion, a landing on 1 April next would have been made on the Tokyo plains. The interval between the Okinawa campaign and the Kyushu operations has troubled the Combined Chiefs of Staff considerably, and they sought almost desperately, it seems, for target areas which would not lessen the strength required for the Kyushu attacks. They contemplated several land-ings on the Chinese coast, but the pressing need for service troops in the Pacific made it impractical for them to divert any troops from the Kyushu venture.

Tactically, the landing was to have been made by three Army corps com-posed of three divisions each. A reserve and main strength of approximately 12 divisions would have followed consolidation of the beachhead. Kyushu was a likely target for the operation because it contains fifteen air fields which are either serviceable or could have been made serviceable in short order. There was, and is, according to the Thin Man, a tremendous short-age of troops in the Pacific, and this is likely to delay the return home of some people out there, since the occupation of Japan will be almost at the same strength planned as if it had been an actual invasion.

Our speaker certainly has a feeling of deep distrust for the Japanese and the possible attitude that they have on surrender generally. He said that en-voys at MacArthur's headquarters now would have with them charts of channel routes through the Japanese mine fields, which Admiral Nimitz will use in bringing the fleet into Tokyo waters. It is the Thin Man's fond hope and desire that the Admiral will still send his mine sweepers ahead of the convoys and escort vessels. He looks for considerable difficulty throughout the occupation.

The atomic bomb was discoursed upon, and our source admitted that the scientists have most of the information still in their heads concerning future use of the new weapon. He admitted frankly that he did not know how it would affect future naval warfare, but said that the Navy certainly was not ignoring the fact that it was likely to make "a hell of a lot of difference."

On Potsdam he talked at great length on the ability of President Truman to stand on his own feet and of the difficulty there of making it clear to the Russians that Great Britain and the United States were not constantly thinking alike or desiring to act as partners in every respect. He feels that they made it clear to Russia that the United States was looking out for American interests all the way, and not the interests of the United States and Great Britain together, as opposed to the interests of Russia. He spoke highly of the British system of interlocking secretariats which, he said, kept the British delegates informed of almost every decision of importance. He was highly critical of our State Department and its policy of keeping vital information to itself. He feels that Secretary Byrnes has been made sufficiently aware of the need for some system similar to the British in this respect.

He cited the example in which the Joint Chiefs of Staff presented five questions to the Russians concerning their entry into the war [against Japan]. The Russians answered the questions in a satisfactory way in every respect. They handed their translated answers to President Truman, who apparently gave them to the State Department. The State Department, for reasons best known to the clerks who were functioning for it, failed to notify the Chiefs of Staff that the answers had been received. The American military men were dumbfounded to learn from the Russians at a meeting held for the purpose of coordinating the Russian and American drives on Japan, that they were expected to have examined the Russian replies by the time of the meeting.

In connection with this, our speaker reiterated his previous assertion that if there were to be an aggressor in the future, Russia was the most likely candidate. He also had the feeling that Stalin, as he put it, was less potent as a leader than he apparently had been at Teheran and Yalta. This indicated to him that the military and the political had "caught up with him" by this time. He said Stalin would consult his military and political advisers frequently, where in the past his decisions were apparently his own.

The request of the peacetime Navy calls for 640,000 officers and men. Present plans call for retaining a large number of reserve officers who will be sent to a professional Navy school for one year after the end of the war, after which they will be assigned to the fleet on an equal basis with Academy graduates.

The opinion of our guest was that the people of the United States must guard against assuming that a Navy of quantity was equal to one of quality. He said there had been official indications already that the number of ships was impressing the important individuals, when in reality the retention of many of the old battleships and all the old cruisers built during the period of the Navy 5-5-3 ratio was useless, and they should be given the "deep six," which is Navy for "Sink them." He feels strongly about giving the reserve officers every opportunity to make their own way in the Navy, and said that if he had anything to do with it they would be given every possible break.

Later in the evening, the discussion turned to the personal future of the man who had been leading the evening's discussion. He said that within the next six months, if present plans were carried out, or at least underway, there would be little need for his staying on in the Department. He said that he is ready to step aside now that the war has been won. He said that unofficially he had been informed that he would retain his rank and in addition his full pay and allowances, which, he said, he sure hoped was true.

The probable clearing of the air concerning Pearl Harbor was brought up, and our guest had considerable to say about it. He feels that Admiral Kimmel will confirm his request for a general court martial, if and when the Secretary of the Navy asks him to confirm it. This action is not necessary, but apparently is expected in the near future, and will be the motivation for getting the trial underway. He hopes the Army will do the same thing at the same time for General Short. He expressed himself as being strongly in favor of a public court martial, feeling that nothing could be accomplished in the way of informing the public if the court martial were secret. He did not say so directly, but indicated to us clearly that in his mind Admiral Kimmel was guilty of neglect of duty. This is the way he put it:

There was, and is today, a definite danger area of approach which the enemy did and probably would use in the future for an attack on the Hawaiian Islands. Admiral Kimmel, he said, had the means of patrolling this area, and also could have interested the Army in the same proposition, and in the event that the patrol had been carried out, it is unlikely that the Japanese fleet could have approached undetected.

He did say, however, that the feeling of tension in Washington at the time of Pearl Harbor had not been communicated to the Hawaiian command. This, he indicated, was the fault neither of the Army nor the Navy, but was the fault of "someone" in Washington. He did not say who. He believes that if there is a court martial about the only finding will be, on the basis of the evidence, neglect of duty. He is not too happy about the Army's part in the Pearl Harbor affair, and said it was "something the Navy would never forget."

On the question of major strategical errors in the war, he said that insofar as he knew, the Italian campaign was the only one they wished they'd never gotten into. He added, however, that it did have some merit, as it served to quiet Churchill's insistence on going into the Balkans. He feels, generally, that the war was fought in an efficient way.

I think the general impression was that the Thin Man felt that the job was almost over, and that it had been done in a manner that should make us proud of being Americans. He reiterated his great faith in America, and his strong feeling that we were the "top dogs" in the world. He expressed his desired to have one more meeting, at which time we expect to make an appropriate presentation as a remembrance of his invaluable contributions and kindness throughout the war.

Best regards

ADMIRAL KING

What was Ernie King really like? What follows was written by Phelps Adams in the late 1970s in response to questions from Professor Lloyd J. Graybar, a member of the history faculty at Eastern Kentucky University, who was researching a book on the admiral. While it starts like an answer describing a specific meeting, it quickly becomes evident that it is conveying Phelps' observations on all the sessions held at his home after the death of Nelie Bull. I shall dispense with quotation marks.

He greeted the assembled correspondents, took his place in an overstuffed chair we had reserved for him, thanked me for the glass of beer I placed on the end table beside him, and began to review the entire war for us, on a global scale, as he always did on these occasions.

He spoke with great facility, without notes of any kind and, I might add, without expletives. It was the kind of report that he might have given to his colleagues in the Map Room at the Navy Department, reviewing the status of the war at the moment in every detail. As a member of the Joint Chiefs of Staff and also of the Combined Chiefs (Great Britain and the United States) he was intimately acquainted with all phases of the war—military, naval, air—in all theatres from Burma and India westward to the Middle East, the Russian front, Italy, Africa, the air war over Germany, England, the Atlantic anti-submarine effort, and on through all five areas of the Pacific back to Japan.

He told us what had happened, what was happening, and often, what was likely to happen next. He reported the bad news as fully as the good news, and in many cases explained what went wrong on the one hand, and what strategy, weapon, or combination of both had brought success on the other.

Throughout, he was completely at ease and always patient, welcoming the questions that frequently interrupted his narrative, and answering them frankly and easily. It was, in short, a conversational evening with group participation—not a monologue by a guest speaker. He was a friend among friends.

The thing that never failed to astonish me—and, I think, the others of our group—was the uninhibited disclosure of highly sensitive information which, if published by any one of us, might have seriously embarrassed the war effort and would certainly have ended King's naval career. There was never a moment's doubt that his words were gospel; nor was there the slightest suspicion that what he said might be shaded with bias in an attempt to place the Navy in a more favorable light than was justified by the events of the moment.

There were, of course, secret matters of which he did not speak to us—and of which, quite possibly, he could not have spoken to his colleagues in the aforementioned Map Room. For example, he never mentioned the atomic bomb or gave the slightest hint to us of its existence or impending existence until after Hiroshima.

But there was the dramatic night—in October 1944—when he came in, greeted us as usual, seated himself, looked at his watch and said, "Gentlemen, in 40 minutes we will be landing on the beach at Leyte and starting to retake the Philippines." It was some 49 hours later that news of the landing first came through to our papers. The editors of the *Sun* knew it, of course, from the confidential memo I had sent them, and had a leak somehow come through to them, prematurely, they would have killed the story instantly.

Nor were these confidences all blood and thunder. Admiral King had a delightful sense of humor, and despite the seriousness of the subject matter, the evenings had their share of amusement, too.

There was the evening following the Yalta conference when he was giving us the inside story of what happened there. It appeared that during a recess he found himself face to face with Stalin and, trying to think of something for a conversational opener, graciously complimented the Marshal on the heroism displayed so universally by Russian soldiers.

"Stalin," King told us, "permitted himself just the shadow of a smile, and replied, 'Admiral, it takes a VERY brave man to be a coward in the Russian Army.' "

And so it went, usually for three or four hours. During the first three, or three and a half, King would finish five glasses of beer, which had not the slightest apparent effect on him. Then he would rise, go upstairs to the "head" and return for one final glass before leaving. This gave us a chance to clear up the loose ends of the session. During the evening he would light, in a long holder, an occasional cigarette, consuming perhaps six or eight in an evening, I would guess. He smoked neither excessively nor compulsively.

He seemed to enjoy himself at these meetings. Perhaps they provided a release for him by giving him the opportunity to talk freely about these hush-hush things, sure they would never be used improperly. And perhaps—as he discussed with us the pros and cons of future plans of action that had not yet been resolved, it helped to clear his own thinking and sharpen his perspective. In any event, he always seemed genuinely pleased, and we who had shared the evening with him were completely fascinated.

As these conferences continued, it became apparent to us that Ernie King was—above all—a realist; that he did not indulge in wishful thinking or close his eyes to unpleasant problems in the hope that they would go away. It was probably this characteristic above all others that gave him the reputation of being an old curmudgeon with whom it was difficult to get along. When it came to decisions regarding the conduct of the war, or anything else affecting the armed forces in general and the Navy in particular, he spoke his mind forthrightly and argued unswervingly, whether his adversary of the moment was the President of the United States, the Secretary of the Navy, or the Prime Minister of England. The language of diplomacy was a tongue utterly foreign to him in disagreements of this nature, and he spoke to us freely about some of them.

Many of these were with the English, for it must be said in all charity that Ernie King was not exactly an Anglophile. His accounts of his frustrations at the actions of the Royal Navy, and the British High Command—including the redoubtable Mr. Churchill—ranged from the humorous to the distinctly irate.

When Mr. Roosevelt agreed that the British Fleet should aid our efforts in the Pacific, King's reaction was one of annoyance that had, he realized, its humorous side. But when Churchill—having committed himself to the cross-Channel invasion of France—"chickened out" and proposed an attack through the "soft underbelly" of Europe, which would have necessitated our fighting our way over the Alps to get at our enemy, King did not hesitate to stand against the Prime Minister and the entire British command. And in this, as in virtually all such matters, he and General Marshall stood shoulder to shoulder.

In 1945, when the Japanese had been pushed back to their own shores and our carrier-based planes were bombing Kyushu, while our battleships shelled shore installations with their 16-inch guns and our land-based bombers were attacking Honshu from Iwo Jima, King talked frequently and freely about the major problem confronting us in the Pacific: could we weaken the Japanese sufficiently with these air strikes while waiting for the Russians to join in the war against Japan and attack by land in Asia? Or should we "grasp the nettle firmly" (a favorite phrase of his), and make a landing on Kyushu or Honshu, knowing such a landing would cost 50,000 American lives?

At Yalta, it appears, the Navy had taken the position that the waiting game was the one to play, but in his conversation with us later we got the distinct impression that he was facing the situation more realistically. Russia, he told us, would come into the war "at five minutes to midnight" or, in other words, not until after the defeat of Japan was assured.

And in the end a bold frontal attack on the heart of Japan—despite its staggering initial cost—might claim fewer casualties than the prolongation of the conflict for many months and, possibly, a year or more. It was probably the toughest decision that King and his colleagues faced during the entire war in the Pacific. But the matter was decided by two monstrous explosions, at Hiroshima and Nagasaki, which made the whole question moot, and saved the lives of those 50,000 Americans who would have been lost gaining the beachhead, and the hundreds of thousands who would have died in the subsequent fighting.

Japan surrendered almost before Russia had time to declare war on her. [Actually, it was six days. Russia declared war on 8 August 1945, and Japan surrendered on 14 August 1945.] Later, in a conference held two days after V-J Day, King told us that the decision had been made to land on the beach of Kyushu on 1 November, with a landing on the Tokyo plains on 1 April of 1946.

And at the same session he expressed a wish for one more meeting with us—a wish that was, indeed, mutual. So, calling ourselves "The Surviving Veterans of the Battle of Virginia" all of us who had ever attended these conferences [there were only four absentees] formally invited Ernie to a dinner in a private dining room of the Statler Hotel, where we presented him with an illuminated scroll, the text of which is recorded on page 652 of his biography, "Fleet Admiral King."

It was a sentimental evening, and it left us in no doubt that the Admiral, too, had his sentimental side, for he was quite touched by the scroll and the presentation displaying the warmth and esteem in which all of us held him. To others he may have been a "sundowner"—a rigid disciplinarian, of himself as well as of others—an armor clad, crusty "old salt" and—as he once described himself—"a son of a bitch." But to the Surviving Veterans of the Battle of Virginia he was, beyond all that, an intensely human being, capable of great warmth and deep friendships, and a delightful companion on any occasion.

Late in the year, at the first post-war Gridiron Dinner, Glen Perry, whose guest he was, brought him to the after-dinner party in the hotel suite I always shared with my friend Harold Brayman, to join our other guests and their wives. Numerous other guests from the dinner dropped in for a drink and pleasant conversation. In all there were, I suppose, sixty or seventy people, including Congressmen, Senators, Governors, business leaders and other notables. But on this occasion Admiral King was outstandingly the center of attraction. Seated on the sofa, he had half a dozen or more of the wives in a semi-circle at his feet, listening enraptured to some of the untold tales of the war, while Ruth Adams—as hostess—kept his glass brimming with Scotch.

And when the party finally began to break up, about 3 o'clock in the morning, he said his goodnights, wrapped his scarf jauntily about his neck, donned his cap at exactly the prescribed angle and—with shoulders squared, his back ramrod straight, and his step firm—navigated down the hotel corridor to the elevator, under his own steam, with all the precision of a man who has taken aboard a considerable cargo and is determined nevertheless to bring his ship into port smartly and safely.

MORAL

While Admiral King was a major contributor to our understanding of World War II, along with General Marshall, what Phelps Adams wrote when he invited The Thin Man to that farewell dinner was true of every individual who sat down with the members of the Washington press corps during the war to keep them informed. Adams wrote, "It helped us; it helped our papers; and I sincerely believe it helped America."

There is a moral and a lesson to be gained from the history presented in this volume. Americans must realize and never forget that World War II was the last life and death struggle in which the United States could count on its allies to give them time to build and train a winning air-land-sea machine after hostilities had broken out.

Bibliography

Abercrombie, L. A. *My Life to the Destroyers*. New York: Henry Holt, 1945.

Armstrong, Warren. *Battle of the Oceans*. New York: Liveright, 1944.

Ayling, Keith. *Combat Aviation*. Harrisburg, Penn.: Military Service, 1943.

Bartimeus. *East of Malta and West of Suez*. Boston: Little, Brown, 1944.

Beach, Edward L. *Submarine!* New York: Henry Holt, 1952.

Belden, Jack. *Retreat with Stilwell*. New York: Knopf, 1943.

Berry, Bob. *Gunners Get Glory*. Indianapolis, Ind.: Bobbs Merrill, 1943.

Blunt, V.E.B. *The Use of Air Power*. Harrisburg, Penn.: Military Service, 1943.

Brodie, Bernard. *A Guide to Naval Strategy*. Princeton, N.J.: Princeton University Press, 1944.

Buell, Thomas B. *The Quiet Warrior* (Spruance). Boston: Little Brown, 1974.

_____. *Master of the Seas (King)*. Boston: Little Brown, 1980.

Burns, Eugene. *Then There Was One*. New York: Harcourt Brace, 1944.

Burr, John G. *The Framework of Battle*. Philadelphia: Lippincott, 1943.

Bryan, Joseph III. *Mission Beyond Darkness*. New York: Duell Sloane & Pearce, 1945.

Cant, Gilbert. *The War at Sea*. New York: John Day, 1942.

_____. *America's Navy in World War II*. New York: John Day, 1946.

_____. *The Great Pacific Victory*. New York: John Day, 1946.

Carmer, Carl. *The Jesse James of the Java Sea*. New York: Farrar & Rinehart, 1945.

Casey, Robert J. *Torpedo Junction*. Indianapolis, Ind.: Bobbs Merrill, 1942.

_____. *The Battle Below*. Indianapolis, Ind.: Bobbs Merrill, 1945.

Cassidy, Henry C. *Moscow Dateline*. Boston: Houghton Mifflin, 1943.

Cave, Hugh B. *We Build, We Fight*. New York: Harpers, 1944.

Churchill, Winston. *The Second World War*. 6 vols. Boston: Houghton Mifflin, 1948-1953.

Collins, Larry. *Is Paris Burning?* New York: Simon & Schuster, 1965.

Commager, Henry Steele. *The Story of the Second World War*. Boston: Little Brown, 1945.

Cope, Harley. *Battle Submerged*. New York: Norton, 1945.

Creasy, Sir Edward. *15 Decisive Battles of the World*. Harrisburg, Pa.: Military Service, 1943.

Custer, Joe James. *Through the Perilous Night*. New York: MacMillan, 1944.

Detzer, Carl. *The Army Reader*. Indianapolis, Ind.: Bobbs Merrill, 1943.

Driscoll, Joseph. *Pacific Victory 1945*. Philadelphia: Lippincott, 1944.

Elliott, W. Y. *The British Commonwealth at War*. New York: Knopf, 1943.

Ellsberg, Edward. *Under the Red Sea Sun*. New York: Dodd Mead, 1946.

Erfurth, Waldermar. *Surprise!* Harrisburg, Penn. Military Service, 1943.

Exton, William Jr. *He's in the Destroyers Now*. New York: McBride, 1944.

Fahey, James C. *The Ships & Aircraft of the U.S. Fleet*. New York: Ships & Aircraft, 1944.

Field, James A. Jr. *The Japanese at Leyte Gulf*. Princeton, N.J.: Princeton University Press, 1947.

Forester, C. S. *The Last 9 Days of the Bismarck*. Boston: Little Brown, 1959.

Fuchida, Matsuo. *Midway, Battle that Doomed Japan*. U.S. Naval Institute, 1955.

Fuller, J.F.C. *Armored Warfare*. Harrisburg: Military Service, 1943.

Gallery, Daniel V. *Clear the Decks*. New York: Morrow, 1951.

Giles, Lionel. *The Art of War*. Harrisburg: Military Service, 1910.

Griffin, Alexander. *A Ship to Remember*. New York: Howell Soskin, 1943.

Hailey, Foster. *Pacific Battle Line*. New York: Macmillan, 1944.

Halsey, William F. (with J. Bryan III). *Admiral Halsey's Story*. New York: McGraw Hill, 1947.

Horan, J. D. *Action Tonight*. New York: Putnam, 1945.

Hough, Richard. *Dreadnought*. New York: Bonanza, 1979.

Huie, William Bradford. *Can Do!* New York: Dutton, 1944.

_____. *From Omaha to Okinawa*. New York: Dutton, 1945.

_____. *The Case Against the Admirals*. New York: Dutton, 1946.

Ingersoll, Ralph. *The Battle is the Payoff.* New York: Harcourt Brace, 1943.

Ingraham, Ralph. *First Fleet*. Indianapolis: Bobbs Merrill, 1944.

Isely, Jeter A. *The U.S. Marines and Amphibious War*. Princeton, N.J.: Princeton University Press, 1951.

Johnson, Stanley. *Queen of the Flattops*. New York: Dutton, 1942.

Jensen, Oliver. *Carrier War*. New York: Simon & Schuster, 1943.

Karig, Walter. *Battle Report*. 5 vols. New York: Simon & Schuster, 1946-1952.

Kato, Matsuo. *The Lost War*. New York: Knopf, 1946.

Keegan, John. *Who Was Who in World War II*. Philadelphia: Crowell, 1978.

Kimmel, Husband E. *Admiral Kimmel's Story*. Chicago: Regner, 1955.

King, Ernest J. (with W. M. Whitehead). *Fleet Admiral King*. New York: Norton, 1952.

Lanza, Conrad H. *Napoleon and Modern War*. Harrisburg: Military Service, 1943.

Leahy, William F. *I Was There*. New York: Whittlesey, 1950.

Leeming, Joseph. *Brave Ships of World War II*. Nashville, Tenn.: Nelson, 1944.

Lockwood, C. A. *Sink 'em All*. New York: Dutton, 1951.

Lord, Walter. *Midway! Incredible Victory*. New York: Harper & Row, 1967.

MacKenzie, Colin. *Sailors of Fortune*. New York: Dutton, 1944.

Maguire, William A. *The Captain Wears a Cross*. New York: Macmillan, 1943.

Markey, Morris. *Well Done!* New York: Appleton Century, 1945.

Marsden, Lawrence. *Attack Transport*. Minneapolis: Minnesota University Press, 1946.

Mears, Frederick. *Carrier Combat*. New York: Doubleday Doran, 1944.

Miller, Max. *Daybreak for Our Carrier*. New York: Whittlesey, 1944.

_____. *It's Tomorrow Out There*. New York: Whittlesey, 1944.

Mitchell, William A. *Outline of the World's Military History*. Harrisburg: Military Service, 1931.

Morison, Samuel Eliot. *History of U.S. Naval Operations in World War II*. 14 vols. Boston: Little Brown, 1948-1960.

Norton-Taylor, Duncan. *With My Heart in My Mouth*. New York: Coward McCann, 1944.

Oeschner, Frederick. *This Is the Enemy*. Boston: Little, Brown, 1942.

Perry, George Sessons. *Where Away?* New York: Whittlesey, 1944.

Pratt, Fletcher. *Fleet Against Japan*. New York: Harpers, 1946.

_____. *The Marines' War*. New York: Sloane, 1948.

_____. *The Navy, A History*. Garden City, N.Y.: Doubleday, 1938.

_____. *The Navy's War*. New York: Sloane, 1948.

_____. *Night Work*. New York: Henry Holt, 1946.

_____. *Sea Power and Today's War*. Hilton: Harrison, 1940.

Puleston, W. D. *The Influence of Sea Power on World War II*. New Haven, Ct.: Yale University Press, 1947.

Rimington, Critchell. *Fighting Fleets*. New York: Dodd Mead, 1944.

_____. *This Is the Navy*. New York: Dodd Mead, 1945.

Roscoe, Theodore. *U.S. Submarine Operations in World War II*. Baltimore: U.S. Naval Institute, 1949.

Roskill, W. J. *U.S. Destroyer Operations in World War II*. Baltimore: U.S. Naval Institute, 1947.

Rutter, Owen. *The British Navy's Air Arm*. New York: Penguin, 1944.

Shafter, Richard A. *Destroyers in Action* Centreville, Md.: Cornell Maritime, 1945.

Shalett, Sidney. *Old Nameless*. New York: Appleton Century, 1943.

Shane, Ted. *Heroes of the Pacific*. New York: Messner, 1943.

Sherman, Frederick C. *Combat Command*. New York: Dutton, 1950.

Sherrod, Robert. *Tarawa*. New York: Duell Sloane & Pearce, 1944.

_____. *On to Westward*. New York: Duell Sloane & Pearce, 1945.

Sikorski, W. *Modern Warfare*. New York: Roy, 1943.

Simmons, Walter. *Joe Foss, Flying Marine*. New York: Dutton, 1943.

Smith, Holland M. *Coral and Brass*. New York: Scribners, 1949.

Stern, Michael. *Into the Jaws of Death*. New York: McBride, 1944.

Stettinius, Edward R., Jr. *Lend-Lease, Weapon for Victory*. New York: MacMillan, 1944.

Stirling, Yates. *Why Sea Power Will Win the War*. New York: Fell, 1944.

Taussig, W. K. *Our Navy, A Fighting Team*. New York: Whittlesey, 1943.

Theobald, Robert D. *The Final Secret of Pearl Harbor*. Old Greenwich, Ct.: Devin Adair, 1954.

Thompson, Lawrance. *The Navy Hunts CGR 3070*. New York: Doubleday Doran, 1944.

Tolischus, Otto D. *Tokyo*. New York: Reynal Hitchcock, 1943.

Tregaskis, Richard. *Guadalcanal Diary*. Toronto: Blue Ribbon, 1943.

Trumbull, Robert. *Silversides*. New York: Henry Holt, 1945.

Vilfroy, Daniel. *War in the West*. Harrisburg: Military Service, 1942.

von Clausewitz, C. *Principles of War*. Harrisburg: Military Service, 1942.

von Leeb, Ritter. *Defense*. Harrisburg: Military Service, 1943.

White, William L. *They Were Expendable*. New York: Harcourt Brace, 1942.

Wolfert, Ira. *American Guerrilla in the Philippines*. New York: Simon & Schuster, 1945.

_____. *Battle for the Solomons*. New York: Simon & Schuster, 1943.

Woodward, C. Vann. *The Battle for Leyte Gulf*. New York: MacMillan, 1947.

Zacharias, Ellis M. *Behind Closed Doors*. New York: Putnam, 1950.

Index

About the Author

GLEN PERRY was Assistant Chief in the *New York Sun*'s Washington Bureau from 1937 to late 1944, when he resigned to become first Assistant Director and then Director of Public Relations for the Dupont Company. He is the author of *Watchmen of the Sea,* and of the numerous articles which appeared in such popular magazines as *The Saturday Evening Post, Look, The New Yorker, Esquire,* and *McLean's.*

Date D